MEANING, MIND, AND
SELF-TRANSFORMATION

D1600476

MEANING, MIND, AND SELF-TRANSFORMATION
Psychoanalytic Interpretation and the Interpretation of Psychoanalysis

Victor L. Schermer

KARNAC

First published in 2014 by
Karnac Books Ltd
118 Finchley Road
London NW3 5HT

British Library Cataloguing in Publication Data

A C.I.P. for this book is available from the British Library

ISBN-13: 978-1-78049-112-7

Typeset by V Publishing Solutions Pvt Ltd., Chennai, India

www.karnacbooks.com

CONTENTS

ABOUT THE AUTHOR   ix

FOREWORD   xi
by James S. Grotstein

PREFACE AND ACKNOWLEDGMENTS   xix

AN INTRODUCTORY NOTE   1

CHAPTER ONE
Psychoanalysis at a crossroads: between science and
   humanism—a path to understanding   5

PART I: INTERPRETING INTERPRETATION:
PSYCHOANALYSIS AND HERMENEUTICS

CHAPTER TWO
Freud's *The Interpretation of Dreams*, ancient and modern
   thought, and the hermeneutics of Greek antiquity
   and Judaic sources   29

CHAPTER THREE
Romantic era hermeneutics   57

CHAPTER FOUR
Twentieth-century Continental philosophy: Husserl,
    Heidegger, Derrida   75

PART II: HERMENEUTICS IN PSYCHOANALYTIC
PSYCHOTHERAPY

CHAPTER FIVE
The psychoanalytic situation: scientific "laboratory" or
    interpretive process?   103

CHAPTER SIX
Dimensions and dualities: the architecture of psychoanalytic
    interpretation   113

CHAPTER SEVEN
Hermeneutics in the unfolding process   135

CHAPTER EIGHT
Interpretation and self-transformation   159

PART III: PARADIGMS OF CONTEMPORARY
PSYCHOANALYTIC UNDERSTANDING

CHAPTER NINE
Melanie Klein: the phenomenology of the unconscious   187

CHAPTER TEN
Donald Winnicott: the infant's being-in-the-world   201

CHAPTER ELEVEN
Self psychology, intersubjectivity, and relational psychoanalysis:
    "American originals"   213

CHAPTER TWELVE
Bion's psychoanalytic work: from positivism and Kant
  to psychospirituality and beyond   239

CHAPTER THIRTEEN
Psychoanalysis and neuroscience: an uneasy marriage   257

REFERENCES   282

INDEX   298

To my patients, who have graced and entrusted me with their inner lives—their meanings, minds, and self-transformations

And in loving memory of my friends and mentors, Gunther Abraham, Bertram Cohen, and John Sonne

ABOUT THE AUTHOR

Victor L. Schermer, MA, LFAGPA is a psychoanalytic psychotherapist in Philadelphia, PA. He received a master's degree in psychology from the University of Pennsylvania and certification with honors in psychoanalytic psychotherapy from the Institute for Psychoanalytic Psychotherapies where he later served as a faculty member. He is a Life Fellow of the American Group Psychotherapy Association.

Schermer has published seven previous books and over forty journal articles and reviews about psychoanalysis, group psychotherapy, object relations theory, self psychology, psycho-spirituality, and the psychoanalytic interpretation of poetry and cinema. He is on the editorial board of the *International Journal of Group Psychotherapy* and has served as guest editor of special journal editions on countertranference, organizational dynamics, and other subjects.

Schermer is a frequent presenter at professional conferences and clinical and training facilities worldwide. In 2006, he gave the 30th Annual S. H. Foulkes Lecture on "Spirituality and Group Analysis" for the Group Analytic Society, London. In 2002, he was co-recipient of the Alonso Award for scholarship in the field of dynamic group psychotherapy awarded by the Group Psychotherapy Foundation of the American Group Psychotherapy Association.

When not working, Schermer enjoys listening to classical and jazz music and has contributed reviews and interviews to the All About Jazz and Broad Street Review websites. For recreation, he takes special pleasure in conversation, reading, cinema, dining, long walks, meditation, and travel.

Schermer enjoys corresponding with readers and can be reached via email at VLScher@comcast.net.

FOREWORD

*James S. Grotstein**

The author's endeavor

This laudable and fascinating contribution shows not only the results of the author's diligence in researching the foundations of psychoanalysis. It also reveals his subtle, profound, erudite, meaningful, and comprehensive grasp of "fault lines" within the psychoanalytic corpus. He uniquely centers his discussion on highlighting (really, interpreting) "interpretation" itself, emphasizing its hidden complexity, diversity, nature, purpose, and effect on the analysand, its multiple cultural origins, and its differing conceptualizations, that is, *science* as contrasted with, *inter alia*, human meaning (hermeneutics), literature, and philosophy. As the reader will discover, the author's horizon of inquiry is vast; his intent is to establish *bridges* between the conceptual sources for psychoanalytic interpretations rather than impose *integration* upon them, in which case the value and uniqueness of differences might become diluted or even lost, as, for instance, the author's

*Clinical Professor of Psychiatry at the David Geffen School of Medicine UCLA
Training and supervising analyst at the New Center for Psychoanalysis and the Psychoanalytic Center of California, Los Angeles.

xi

understanding of the fate of the concept of *projective identification*. Klein's (1946, 1955) version, we recall, was that of a primitive uncconscious phantasy involving part-objects, and was considered in the main to constitute an unconscious intrapsychic pathological defense mechanism, and considered to be unilateral even when countertransference occurred. Bion's (1967) version originally constituted an extension of Klein's but with far-reaching implications. For example, he conceived of it as the necessary force that instituted thinking in the infant as well as the conduit for normal communication between the infant and his/her mother, and enshrined it within the all-encompassing, intersubjective embrace of *container* ↔ *contained* (Bion, 1963) as well as the foundation of the transference ↔ countertransference situation. In other words, it may be preferable at times to employ a stereoscopic approach in studying ideas—and individuals—so as to get closer to Truth "in parallax."

The author's aim, as I have stated, is the examination of a number of major contemporary psychoanalytic schools and an in-depth study of their individual characteristic background contexts (premises, preconceptions, that is, natural science, humanism, literature, linguistics, etc.). His purpose is to designate the sources of the individual psychoanalytic schools, their paradigms, assumptions, preconceptions, "camera angles," and "ground language" so as to understand the perspectives which constitute the hidden order of interpretations in order to comprehend the rationale for the nature, structure, content, and timing of the interpretations which issue from them. I would like now to consider such understanding from the particular vantage point of Bion's penetrating views of psychoanalysis, which Schermer discusses at length in Chapter Twelve of this book.

Binocular vision

As we take a cursory look back at the history of psychoanalysis, we see first a unitary theory and technique, followed by divisive dissensions, some of which failed to succeed as worthy rivals—and then we saw the development of rival schools that remained within the embrace of, originally, "orthodox," then later, "classical analysis." Eventually, the proliferation of the "heresy schools" within the fold seemed to devolve into a dyad of schools, specifically the bifurcation between the relational/intersubjective perspectives (Brown, 2011) versus the conservative schools centered upon classical analysis, much like the Democratic and

Republican parties did politically. I shall not develop this theme further since it would take us far a field of the focus of this contribution.

In order to explicate his theme the author has chosen "two streams of thought … Anglo-American psychoanalysis and Continental European philosophical hermeneutics …"—in other words a contrast between an emphasis on language, meaning, and dialogue (hermeneutics) and the natural and social sciences (Anglo-American psychoanalysis). Finally, the author appoints Bion as his example extraordinaire to be representative of what one may call "the journey toward ever expanding, always elusive *wisdom*" (even transcending *knowledge*)—by displaying for us his "pilgrim's progress" through the thickets of epistemology, ontology, phenomenology, philosophy, mathematics, poetry, mysticism, religion, history, astronomy; inter alia, to find the "Holy Grail" of how we *evolve* and continue *becoming* our ever destined and ever changing selves (entelechy, "Memoirs of the Future," "O").

Put another way, an important difference between (a) individual transference/countertransference and (b) the analytic field (Baranger & Baranger, 1961–1962; Ferro & Basile, 2009) is that, despite the fact that the former indicates an unconscious emotional interaction between the analysand and the analyst, its context is, nevertheless, that of two alternating or even simultaneously interacting individuals. The context of the latter represents the indivisibility of the two participants, a theory made possible by the application of Bion's (1961) theory of groups to individual analytic understanding and technique. This change might be expressed thus: (a) one-person analysis, as in the classical Freudian school, Kleinian school, object relations school, interpersonal school, self psychology school; (b) two-person analysis, as in the work of Bion, the Barangers, the post-Kleinian school, the American intersubjective school, and relationism.

Binocular vision is achieved by the analyst (a) suspending his sensory-based faculties of symbolization and representation (substitution, memory, desire, understanding, preconception) of the patient as object; (b) allowing him/herself to submit to having his/her own emotional repertoire (countertransference, reverie) becoming *activated* by the analysand's transference; and (c) being aware of the many *vertices* (Bion's term which approximates to "perception," "point-of view," or "camera angle"). I suggest that we can include hermeneutics, science, and all the schools of psychoanalysis in addition to the collective wisdom of all other learned disciplines as potentially worthy vertices.

Vertices and contexts: the backgrounds for interpretations

Bion (1967) uses the term "vertex," which he borrowed from plane geometry, to substitute for "perspective" or "point of view" because the latter two terms carry with them inescapable signs of their sense-derived origins. "Context" refers to the surrounding background of the (analytic) text. It is inclusive of Freud's (1900a) "day residue." I mention the term "vertex" because of its democratizing inclusiveness (as the author has noted) in regard to differing and otherwise competing theories. For example, when an analyst wishes to interpret his/her analysand's envy, (s)he may wish to interpret envy outright, for example. "You seem to have become angry with me after learning I was being honored by ... . I wonder if your envy may reflect my getting more well-known, 'bigger' in little girl terms, and that you automatically become 'smaller' as well as more dependent and helpless—at your expense."

From another vertex I might add: "I think you may feel endangered by this turn of events—that I shall forget you, give myself over to more appealing patients and abandon you. I can understand why you feel the need to hate me and attack me as well as minimize my worth to you. You may be trying to take back all the goodness and worth you had invested in me—so as to protect yourself."

The first interpretation corresponds to (my understanding of) the traditional Kleinian vertex (which assumes that envy is the mental manifestation of the death instinct), but it also touches on the "here-and-now," which is characteristic of the post-Kleinian vertex. The second interpretation continues from the first but adds yet another vertex to interpret from. It reflects Hartmann's (1939) concept of "adaptation" and issues from a Darwinian (1871) *context* of "survival of the fittest." From the vertex and context of my suggestion the ideal analyst would be sufficiently knowledgeable, as well as respectful, of many psychoanalytic (as well as many other) disciplines.

The languages of achievement and substitution and memory and desire

I alluded earlier to the close relationship between Truth and parallax (i.e., binocular thinking). (This association may be confusing. Parallax actually designates the confused unclear picture that emerges when attempts to achieve clear binocular vision fail.) Some of the more salient of Bion's technical considerations in regard to interpretation hint at this bipolarity. Consider the following.

Bion believes that the analyst must listen to the analysand with his mind emptied of memory, desire, preconceptions, and understanding, all of which are derived from the "language of substitution" (of sense-derived images, icons, language, representations, and symbols). Thus, for Bion, when sensory images and the like are "substituted" for psychic reality as such, the analyst remains distant and critically inexact in regard to conveying the immediacy of emotions, feelings, and interaction convincingly (language of substitution contrasted with the language of achievement).

He must suspend memory and desire, etc., so that the analyst can allow himself to be meditatively (passively) focused on the "here-and-now" of the session, that is, can be experienced in continuous, living time.

He must *listen to himself listening to the analysand's emotions* (spoken and unspoken), not just listen to him/her directly. Truth ultimately emerges from within oneself, with one's own native emotional version of an experience. Bion also gave the same advice to the analysand.

He must in his reverie be able to resonate with the analysand's feelings and emotional experience. His trained and human "global position satellite," reverie, *and* countertransference must be ever keenly receptive to his own experience of O, the analysand's experience of O, and of the O experience of the charged emotional atmospherics (O) hovering between the three participants, (a) the analysand, (b) the analyst, and (c) both the analysand *and* the analyst as an indivisible couple. Thus, according to Bion, individual analysis additionally and inescapably becomes group therapy—and vice versa.

He must *observe* the text (*"digitally"*) of the analysand's behavior and free associations and *"analogously,"* or *intuitively*, via his own reverie ("third ear").

He must not (attempt) to repeat an interpretation because it cannot be repeated owing to the constancy of change (flux, catastrophic change, O). For the same reason the analyst cannot give the analysand a make-up session: a missed session cannot be made up ("The moving finger writes, and having writ, moves on ...").

One of the most notable theoretical changes in Bion's endeavors is his radical alteration of our conception of the Unconscious and the resultant "catastrophic change" this imposes on psychoanalytic theory and interpretations. I should like to develop the background of this assertion. When Bion presented the idea of alpha-function (giving mental content to beta elements or things-in-themselves), he conceived of it as consisting of both divisible *and* indivisible primary *and* secondary processes. One may think of this idea by invoking Lévi-Strauss's (1958) model of the structure and function of "binary opposition" (like the thumb versus the forefinger). Another more fateful application was that of O, which he also conceived of as binary. Put succinctly, he conceived of two connected oppositional functions for O: (a) O as the Absolute Truth and ultimate unknowable and uncertain reality (similar in many ways to the id, as the author has noted), and (b) the "hereditary treasure trove" of the unconscious: Plato's Ideal Forms and Kant's primary and secondary categories, noumena, things-in-themselves.

What I have listed above is only a tiny, but, I hope, representative sample of Bion's recommendations for clinical technique. I listed them to reveal some hidden order behind them: (a) that of the unknowability of Truth, especially when it is gleaned from the senses; and (b) the need for "binocular vision," which amounts to what Bion (1967) associates with a parallel function, "common sense" (Bion, 1963).

Transformations in K versus transformations in O

I should now like to turn to the author's citation from Conze, the Indian mystic, which so keenly expresses my sense of Bion:

> "... Is perfect wisdom beyond thinking? ... and why is perfect wisdom beyond thinking? It is because all its points of reference cannot be thought about but can be apprehended ... ."

Bion, I believe, would concur. Thinking is a transformative function that emerges consciously, more often than not originating in the unconscious. Wisdom emerges as the resultant summary of all the possible mental inputs from within (intuition through reverie; transformations in O) and without (sensory apparatus; transformations in K)—with unconscious editorial selection and always existing in flux. Ideally, but not obligatorily, these two types of transformations occur in a "binary-opposition structure" (Lévi-Strauss, 1958).

The "Tower of Babel" and the "confusion of tongues"

As does Schermer, I have found the myth of the "Tower of Babel" to be a useful metaphor for the subject being discussed. Briefly, the people of Babel wished to acquire God's wisdom and omniscience, and to accomplish this desire, they sought to build a tower to Heaven. Learning of this planned plunder, God became angry and destroyed the tower but also attacked their unity of language, thereby destroying their ability to communicate ("confusion of tongues"). I believe that this myth captures the author's theme about the diversity of analytic tongues. It also deals with the stage (and stages generally) of *weaning*—from the universal pre-lexical emotional and intuitive language of at-one-ment between infant and mother—to the specific, differentiated "mother tongue" of newfound verbal mastery.

Epilogue

Perhaps all that I have written above might be epitomized by the model of *holography* in which each of the individual components of an entity can have two existences: (a) being independent of one another and (b) being indivisible as a composite unit at the same time. Analogously, holography relates to the question of whether the "United States" is a single or multiple noun—or, ambiguously, both. The same can be said of psychoanalysis. One last word must be said: psychoanalysis, like Bion's O, is ineffable, owned by no one, and may be a Platonic Ideal Form or Kantian Category. Put another way, psychoanalysis alone is the rightful owner of its own mystery. The analysand envies the analyst because (s)he believes that the analyst knows his/her mind, which is consciously unknown to him or her. The analyst may be envious of the analysand, who has the information that is important for the analyst to know but will not reveal it because of resistance. Unbeknown to each participant, they each are really envious all along of the analysand's unconscious, the only one that does know.

PREFACE AND ACKNOWLEDGMENTS

The ideas for this volume developed over several years during which I periodically thought about two related concerns that have haunted psychoanalysis since its inception. If, as Freud asserted, psychoanalysis is a deterministic science, why are there so many competing theories and ideologies with little or no hope of deciding which of them is the most valid? Further, if psychoanalysis is an introspective and subjective mode of treatment, what gives it any semblance of objectivity, explanation, and understanding? These questions became highlighted during a time when "evidence-based" requirements for treatment are emphasized in clinical psychology, social work, psychiatry, and insurance coverage for mental health care.

In search of answers, I found myself asking a more pointed question: What is the fundamental activity and operational basis of psychoanalysis? The answer I arrived at is: *interpretation*. Whatever else the analyst does or presumes to do, he invariably assigns a set of meanings to what the patient experiences, expresses, and understands. Interpretation crosses the divide between subjectivity and objectivity, truth and imagination, scientific and humanistic criteria of care. That awareness led me toward philosophy and more specifically, hermeneutics, both of which explore in depth and breadth the sorts of questions I had been thinking about.

My interest in philosophy goes back to the early 1960s, when, as a student at Brooklyn College, I had courses with Professors John Hospers, an empiricist and logical positivist, and Walter Cerf, a phenomenologist as well as an interpreter of Kant and metaphysics. Both courses were fascinating, and issues of epistemology (philosophy of knowledge) and ontology (philosophy of being) continued to accompany me in my subsequent journey as a psychologist.

My philosophical interests were rekindled when, at the beginning of the new millennium, with long experience as a psychoanalytic psychotherapist, I participated in an email listserv called "Bion 97" which focused on Wilfred Bion's psychoanalytic theories. One of the other contributors to the list was the late Corbett Williams, a brilliant thinker who had worked in the field of artificial intelligence, became disillusioned with the corporate world, and then independently pursued interests in neuroscience, group dynamics, psychoanalysis, and philosophy. I became especially interested in what he wrote to "the list" about philosophy, and then we engaged in our own discussions of Kant and more deeply of Heidegger. Corbett was a true Socratic teacher who sent me material to read and responded to my thoughts with questions rather than answers. It was an enriching and fulfilling experience, and when I visited San Francisco, where he resided, I met him, and we spent the afternoon near the Art Museum in view of the Golden Gate Bridge, and talked through the evening at his favorite coffee shop. Corbett taught me to think about psychoanalysis "out of the box," to integrate it with other modes of thought rather than stay within its own confines.

My interest in hermeneutics was stimulated by another colleague from the West Coast. Robin Gayle is a professor of psychology at Dominican University and a psychotherapist in Marin County. I read an advance copy of an article she wrote on hermeneutics and group psychotherapy (Gayle, 2009) and was so impressed by it that I contacted her, and we began an extended discussion on how meanings are co-created in relationships, dialogue, and community.

I then went my own way, trying to mesh these new ideas with psychoanalysis. Soon, I gave a talk at York University in Toronto on "The subjectivity/objectivity/hermeneutical triad: The epistemological foundations of psychoanalysis and their relevance to contemporary pluralism" (Schermer, 2010). I asserted that psychoanalysis incorporated seemingly contradictory paradigms of knowledge: objective science, subjective introspection, and interpretive discourse. This presentation led to an expanded published version (Schermer, 2011) in which I viewed psychoanalytic interpretation from the perspectives of Aristotle's objectivity and representation, Husserl's phenomenology, Heidegger's existential analytic, and Bion's references to mystical experience. It became clear to me then that the discipline which linked these viewpoints together was philosophical hermeneutics. I felt that a larger work needed to be written about the implications of hermeneutics for psychoanalysis, and that work is this book.

Up to then, my scholarly and therapeutic interests were limited to psychoanalytic theory and practice as such. I had focused on object relations theory and self psychology, thinking and writing about them clinically, conceptually, and with applications to group therapy as well as individual therapy, spirituality, film, and poetry. Before that (1975–1980), I trained at the Institute for Psychoanalytic Psychotherapies in Philadelphia and Bryn Mawr, PA, a highly respected institute for non-medical practitioners, where I received certification as a psychoanalytically oriented psychotherapist. (For several years afterwards, I served on their faculty.) My training emphasized Freudian analysis, ego psychology, self psychology, and object relations theory, and at the same time, I was exposed to the emerging interest in borderline and narcissistic personality disorders. The Institute stressed the distinction between psychoanalysis and psychotherapy, with the paradigm of classical "couch" analysis serving as the gold standard for psychotherapy.

Such training is one reason why in this book I alternately refer to the practitioner as "analyst" and "therapist". I use "analyst" to refer to the generic listener/thinker and "therapist" for the actual provider of treatment. Although the book is about psychoanalysis as such, I believe it is relevant to all approaches that utilize psychodynamic understanding. I also believe that a distinction should be made between how analysts conceptualize their work, and how they behave in the consulting room, where they function as therapists. What analysts do in "the rooms" is often a far cry from standard technique.

Another detail concerns the case examples. It is important, for reasons of patient privacy and confidentiality, that the clinical illustrations are disguised and altered. In some instances, also for this purpose, I have combined cases into a single vignette. Thus, the vignettes do not constitute proof or evidence for my arguments. Rather, they are illustrative, aimed at giving a "feel" for my ideas. In any event, my overall intent is not so much to justify a position or theory, but rather to stimulate thinking, dialogue, and difference.

I also want to note that the literature on both psychoanalysis and hermeneutics is so extensive, and the ideas cover such a wide spectrum, that it was necessary to be very selective in choosing topics and thinkers for exploration. The same ideas could have been developed in very different ways using different resources. I found that the subject matter kept opening up into new pathways. It is not the sort of material that narrows itself down as you go along; rather it keeps revealing new possibilities and connections. I think that such openness derives from the nature of interpretation itself, which is a multifaceted rather than a conclusive process.

To list all who stirred and influenced my thinking with regard to this volume would be overwhelming. First, I would like to thank my patients who have participated with me in the process of introspective self-exploration. I believe it takes curiosity, courage, and trust to open oneself in this way, and I am grateful for what they have given me. Of course, Corbett Williams and Robin Gayle directly impacted the project. I have also been honored to have been mentored and inspired by distinguished psychoanalysts and psychotherapists such as Gunther Abraham, Yvonne Agazarian, Harold Bernard, Christopher Bollas, Bertram Cohen, Patrick DeMare, James Grotstein, Earl Hopper, Howard Kibel, Robert Klein, Marty and Louisa Livingston, Malcolm Pines, John Sonne, and Vamik Volkan. Michael Graves, a poet by profession, is profoundly interested in psychoanalysis and frequently offered me his invaluable insights. Lewis Krieg, a seasoned therapist and wide-ranging intellect, read parts of the manuscript and made numerous helpful comments and criticisms. Jeffrey Kauffman, a revered bereavement therapist, has made searching studies of philosophy and offered me his insights about the work of Derrida and Levinas in particular. Joseph Berke, psychiatrist, psychoanalyst, and Judaic scholar, shared with me important insights into Talmudic exegesis.

It is also important that Karnac's staff members played a key role in bringing this book to fruition. In addition to their assigned tasks they served as muse, friend, and counselor. The staff at Karnac, especially publisher and managing director Oliver Rathbone, as well as Rod Tweedy and Kate Pearce in its London office, were supportive, insightful, and empathic, sustaining me through all the phases of preparation and writing.

While writing this book required considerable solitude and an individual perspective, I was always aware that it resulted from countless therapy sessions, conversations, readings, long walks, meditations, and sudden impressions that come from known and unknown sources. Moreover, I know that readers will add ideas and connotations which become an important part of a book's legacy of understanding. In that sense a book is a collective endeavor, in some sense "written" by many individuals who thought, wrote, or said something that eventually found its way to expression through the writer. I hope I have "channeled" something of value and meaning from that collective. I am fully responsible for what I have written, but I am indebted to what I have received from the communal "other" that made it possible.

Philadelphia, PA

Everything has been thought of before, but the problem is to think of it again.

—*Johann Wolfgang von Goethe*

Psychic Life is something unfathomable. Whoever is concerned with the human sciences simply must, at some point, have strained to plumb this inexhaustible source.

—*Wilhelm Dilthey*

AN INTRODUCTORY NOTE

This book explores the intrinsic nature of psychoanalytic interpretation as method, process, and experience. For that purpose, two streams of thought are brought into dialogue with one another: Anglo-American psychoanalysis and continental European philosophical hermeneutics, the study of meaning and interpretation. Until recently, they have been separated not only geographically and by different languages, but also by the two cultures of which C. P. Snow wrote, those of the sciences and the humanities. Psychoanalysis in England and the United States has been dominated by the natural and social sciences. Psychoanalysis in Europe, and France in particular, has largely been associated with the humanities, literature, and history, with influences of anthropology and linguistics.

Philosophical hermeneutics, the study of meaning and interpretation, flowered in Europe during the Romantic, modern, and postmodern periods of the nineteenth and twentieth centuries, spurred on by philosophers such as Johann Gottfried von Herder, Friedrich Schleiermacher, Wilhelm Dilthey, Edmund Husserl, and Martin Heidegger, each of whom assigned central importance to language, meaning, dialogue, and emotion, as distinct from the Enlightenment emphasis on the natural sciences, causality, sense data, and metaphysics.

1

Hans Georg Gadamer, Maurice Merleau-Ponty, and Emmanuel Levinas were among those who, following Husserl and Heidegger, carried forward the agendas of hermeneutics into mid- to late twentieth-century discourse. At the same time, Jacques Derrida brought hermeneutics into the postmodern *avant garde*. Their views profoundly impacted psychoanalysis in Europe. Psychoanalysts and analytically oriented scholars such as Jacques Lacan, Luce Irigiray, Janine Chasseguet-Smirgel, André Green, Julia Kristeva, and others were influenced by hermeneutics and shaped some of their ideas around it.

Meanwhile, Anglo-American psychoanalysis, rooted in science and pragmatism, maintained the biosocial emphasis which Freud, based upon his neurological education and the psychiatric bias of his time, strongly advanced. For them, meanings and interpretation were of importance but beholden to scientific proof and causal explanation. As a result, Freudian, ego psychological, and object relations theories were cast in terms of natural and social science. Ideologically at least, and despite their differences, they adhered to the framework of the empirical sciences. Even Donald Winnicott and Ronald Fairbairn, whose concepts addressed existential concerns, held to a biosocial base.

In the 1970s and 1980s, with the advent of self psychology, intersubjectivity, relational psychoanalysis, mother–infant research, the British independent tradition, and Wilfred Bion's skepticism about metapsychology, the Anglo-American paradigm began to admit a measure of philosophy, religion, and humanism into its formulations. Self psychology and the intersubjective perspective emphasized self experience and phenomenology in their understanding of the interpretive process and the nature of transference and countertransference. Bion, in his reflections on the listening process, acknowledged parallels to the religious mystics. Anna-Marie Rizzuto, William Meissner, Nina Coltart, and Michael Eigen incorporated religious themes and ideas into their work. Relational psychoanalysts such as Stephen Mitchell and Lewis Aron echoed Heidegger and Gadamer in their emphasis on authentic dialogue in the consulting room. Finally, in the first decade of the new millennium, intersubjective analysts like Robert Stolorow, George Atwood, and Donna Orange began to write explicitly about philosophical hermeneutics. Quietly, modestly, and slowly, a dialogue between Anglo-American psychoanalysis and Continental philosophical hermeneutics has begun.

For the purposes of this volume, a very important distinction must be made between hermeneutics as the interpretation of texts, a noble preoccupation of biblical and literary scholars, and *philosophical* hermeneutics, the study of the foundations of human understanding. It is the latter which is of primary interest here. The word hermeneutics has acquired an esoteric connotation of decoding textual elements in mysterious ways. Hermeneutics, as used here, refers rather to philosophical and psychological understanding of human enterprises and the human condition in which interpretive processes play a significant role.

The current volume makes explicit and loudly trumpets the value of interchanges between the natural science paradigm and philosophical hermeneutics. Interpretation was defined by Freud as the main intervention of psychoanalysis, but his hope was that it would maintain a foundation in the natural sciences. At the same time, Freud was steeped in the humanities and held strong views about the human condition. Although bringing together science and hermeneutics has not been popular, indeed derided in some circles, such a synthesis was in fact the basis of Freud's magnum opus, *The Interpretation of Dreams*, and shades of such a merger are cropping up everywhere today. For example, the Nobel Prize winning neuroscientist Eric Kandel (2012) has written an extensive volume, *The Age of Insight*, seeking connections between the neuroscience of memory and cognition, artistic creativity, and the unconscious. Interpretation is the *sine qua non* of psychoanalysis. Now is the time to begin serious discourse about the implications of interpretation and how it shows up in theories and in the consulting room. That is the purpose of this volume.

The book is divided into three sections, preceded by a consideration of the relationship between psychoanalysis, hermeneutics, and the sciences—and the importance of that relationship to the socioeconomic, methodological, and conceptual considerations that govern theory and practice. Part I then begins with a consideration of Freud's methodology in *The Interpretation of Dreams*, moving to a review of ancient, Romantic, and modern theories of interpretation as they relate specifically to psychoanalytic method and treatment. Part II, which is largely intended for clinicians, provides a hermeneutical view of the psychoanalytic situation, the dimensions and polarities of treatment, the components of the unfolding process, and a discussion of self-transformation and personality change. Part III, which may be read as a series of independent essays, offers reflections on selected Anglo-American schools of psychoanalysis from the standpoint of hermeneutical philosophy. Included are considerations of the work of Klein; Winnicott; intersubjective, self, and relational psychoanalysis; Bion; and neuroscience.

The spirit of hermeneutics is openness to experience and the ongoing search for understanding. The author hopes this book will be read in that spirit. It is meant to be an adventure in thought, not so much a coherent theory as an exploration of possibilities. If the psychoanalyst or psychotherapist appreciates some of the ideas put forth, he or she should let it inform his own work and orientation. If scholars from other disciplines read it, hopefully they will find that psychoanalysis continues to have rich potential to provide multidisciplinary knowledge that goes well beyond a theory of personality and a method of treatment. If patients and lay persons read the book, it may help them understand some of the conundrums that analysts face in their work.

The main thing about psychoanalysis is that it encourages us to think deeply about what we are doing in life, love, and work. As an unusually insightful Chinese fortune cookie, opened after a satisfying meal, said, "All men should try to learn before they die what they are running from, and to, and why." Freud himself might have said the same.

CHAPTER ONE

Psychoanalysis at a crossroads: between science and humanism—a path to understanding

WOYZECK: You see, Doctor, sometimes a person has that sort of
character, that sort of structure.—But nature's different,
you see with nature [*he clicks his fingers*] that's something,
how can I say, for example—

DOCTOR: Woyzeck, you are philosophizing again.

—Georg Buchner (1963; orig. pub. 1879): *Woyzeck*

The following brief vignette will serve to introduce a much larger subject:

"A young woman (Ava) early in treatment spoke of her discomfort disclosing her inner life to her therapist. Subsequently, reviewing her history of self-abnegation vis-à-vis an intrusive mother and her efforts to protect herself from her mother's invasive control, Ava recalled a time in her childhood when she took the "little book" she was reading for her own enjoyment and hid it from her approaching mother inside the "big book" her mother insisted she "should" be reading. As therapy progressed, it became clear to both patient and therapist that this image had provided an apt metaphor to convey the patient's felt need to be cautious in what she disclosed about herself in her dealings with the therapist". (Cohen & Schermer, 2004, p. 580)

The little book concealed under the big book is also an apt metaphor for psychoanalysis itself, which at its roots seeks to uncover the hidden story beneath the patient's free associations and transactions with the therapist. Psychoanalysis attributes causal and explanatory significance to what is undisclosed. If, among what has been called the plurality (Wallerstein, 2005) of analytic concepts and approaches, there is a common thread, it is the belief in the "hidden dimension" (Wurmser, 1978). The meaning and theoretical account attributed to the concealed phenomenon, whether understood as a wish, an archetype, a primitive phantasy, a self-state, an attachment pattern, an intersubjective co-creation, a relational matrix, or an ineffable realm of transformation, depends on the orientation of the particular analyst. But what distinguishes psychoanalysis from cognitive-behavioral and other forms of therapy, as well as the empirical and rationalist understandings that dominate modern psychology, is the belief in the power of the undisclosed, unknown, and unknowable and their importance both for mental illness and, conversely, self-transformation and the alleviation of symptoms.

The centrality of interpretation in psychoanalysis and life

The hidden dimension constitutes the underlying meaning of what is known, experienced, and understood. Interpretation is the process of uncovering and elucidating meanings. It is the chief intervention of psychoanalysis. The manifest content for psychoanalytic interpretation, or what Bion (1962a, p. 72) called "selected facts," includes dreams, slips of the tongue, fantasies, and memories. These appear on the "radar screen" of the analyst's evenly suspended attention, and he interprets what is implicit or concealed within them.

Interpretation is more than psychoanalytic technique, however. It is a human experience necessitated by the depth, complexity, and concealment inherent in the personality and human affairs. While interpretation has often been discussed by analysts from a technical standpoint, it is not the exclusive province of psychoanalysis. Rather, it is a ubiquitous aspect of human life. Interpretation takes on special significance in psychoanalysis as a means of "making the unconscious conscious." Yet, despite its central place in technique, psychoanalysts themselves have said relatively little about interpretation as a generic human experience and a force for change.

Even within the treatment process, interpretation is more than an explanatory comment of the analyst at a particular point in time. It is the evolving cumulative understanding of the patient's inner life and complexes. But beyond the consulting room, interpretation includes all human acts of inferring implicit meanings of behaviors and self-expression. This process is invoked at every moment of life, as when a person smiles, says "Hello," lifts a cup to his mouth, or dreams a dream. Every human act is by its nature interpreted and understood by self and other as having a purpose, intent, and context. Psychoanalysis is not, as it is sometimes portrayed, an esoteric practice known only to initiates. It is an extension and elaboration of what occurs spontaneously in everyday life. Interpretation is necessitated by the fact that every human action embodies an intention that most often is implied but not stated. One has to "read" the intent.

Often, an interpretation contains or resolves uncertainty and ambiguity. Is the smile a sign of affection, happiness, doubt, or even hostility? Is the cup lifted to the mouth intended to supply sustenance or stimulation? The meaning and intention of an act or expression may be elusive. While many interpretations are obvious and unspoken, providing the simple understanding that allows people to relate to one another, in other cases, the accuracy of interpretations is far more challenging, requiring introspection and sometimes considerable expertise.

In psychoanalysis, interpretation deepens towards that which is concealed and inaccessible, the other. It aims towards that which is barred from the conscious mind: "the *un*-conscious." Thus, hidden even from the "little book" of childhood recollections, there is yet another book of impulses, repressed memories and fantasies, neurobiological events, social forces, and genetic archetypes that play a powerful role in human life but are concealed from ordinary view, a very big book that contains the ultimate sources of mentation and behavior.

Interpretations differ from statements of fact or logic in that they leave ambiguity and emotion in their wake. Like poetic metaphors, they have a center of meaning, but they carry a penumbra of suggestive implications that enrich their meaning and leave room for differences. The unconscious, like life itself, has many faces. Shakespeare wrote,

"All the world's a stage;" many dramas could be enacted on this stage. An analyst might tell a patient that he is harboring sexual or hostile wishes, but, by making that interpretation, he also wants to stimulate the patient to express the unique way these wishes specifically play out in his own past and present. Interpretations open up possibilities and scenarios as much as they seek accuracy and closure.

The analytic emphasis on the unconscious implies that some meanings are implicit and are only known by their effects. Unconscious meanings require a theory that accounts for and explains what cannot be experienced directly. Theories that form the basis of interpretations are, in principle, subject to modification and change. Yet unfortunately they are sometimes experienced as absolute and concrete. Thus, despite their ambiguity and uncertainty, psychoanalytic theories are all too often taken literally and dogmatically, and as such, they become talismans that can have great consequences for the lives of those affected by them, whether patients or analysts. Psychoanalytic theories and interpretations carry great weight, which sometimes brings them into collision with socio-economic and ideological realities. They become controversial and impactful in the lifeworlds of persons and ideas.

Interpretation at the center of the storm: lives, economics, and a crisis of confidence

The psychoanalyst's emphasis on unconscious sources of thought and action can have fateful consequences. For example, careers and treatment outcomes have hung in the balance depending on interpretive bias and conviction. Freud's troubles with the psychiatric profession (Jones, 1953, v. 1, pp. 249–251), Jung's and others' breaks with Freud (Jones, 1953, v. 2, pp. 107–151), and John Bowlby's alienation from Anna Freud and other analysts (Karen, 1994, pp. 113–115) were epochal and life changing events in the history of psychoanalysis propelled by the ways in which these analysts interpreted hidden meanings. In the history of psychoanalysis, ideology has too often triumphed over tolerance, leading to schisms and excommunications more typical of religious doctrines than scientific investigation.

Patients themselves have suffered significantly from misinterpretations of their dynamics. One instance of such a distressing treatment outcome was Freud's analysis of "Dora," which Deutsch (1957) discovered to have had a disastrous result. While psychoanalytic interpretation is a resilient method, allowing for clarification, qualification, and amendment, it can sometimes become a high stakes game. In the case of Dora, Freud ignored her distress as he pressed her to disclose her fantasy life and prove his theories. These missteps happened at a very vulnerable point of her life when Dora's sense of self and identity were fragile, so the misunderstandings did considerable harm, if we are to believe Deutsch, who had contact with "Dora" (real name, Ida Bauer) when she was an adult.

The impact of "managed care" on contemporary training and practice

If meaning and interpretation have precipitated difficulties within psychoanalytic circles and in treatment outcomes, the recent medical emphasis on so-called evidence-based treatment, which often dismisses interpretive modalities as wave-of-the-hand "magic" (McClendon & Burlingame, 2011) doubts the entire enterprise of psychoanalysis. Depth interpretation is not considered a "medical necessity" and therefore not paid for by insurance companies or by those patients who seek quicker solutions such as medication and cognitive-behavioral interventions. For such reasons—practical, economic, and political—managed care and psychoanalysis have come into conflicts that adversely affect practice and training (Pyle, 2003).

These contingencies constitute a threat to the very survival of psychoanalysis. Psychoanalysis is now in crisis and requires a thorough rethinking of what it is about. The current emphasis on quick treatment reflects a serious misunderstanding of interpretive modes of treatment that need to unfold in their own time. A full grasp of the nature and use of the interpretive process is essential in order to properly place psychoanalysis as method (*praxis*) and science (*gnosis*) in the contemporary world. Psychoanalysis may not offer rapid alleviation of symptoms, but it is a milestone within a profound heritage of interpretive care and understanding that has great value for suffering individuals and for the betterment of humanity. Capitulation to financial pressures and formulaic treatment protocols is not the solution. Only a re-examination of fundamentals can rejuvenate and revitalize psychoanalysis as a unified effort to understand the human mind and its care.

A theoretical Tower of Babel

In these ways and others, psychoanalysis is in a time of "trying to find its way." In any endeavor, when persistent difficulties or impasses arise, it is wise to consider anew the foundations of a discipline. Even within this time of crisis, psychoanalysis is a lively art and science, and its therapeutic method continues to benefit many suffering individuals. Yet its viability is complicated by an intrinsic problem. Today, we witness within the profession a veritable Tower of Babel with varied pursuits and explorations each going its own way with its own language and assumptions, with little consideration of how each relates to the whole. Among the plethora of psychoanalytic theories that claim curative and truth value are classical Freudian theory; Jungian psychology; object relations theory (itself divided into Kleinian and independent schools); ego psychology; self psychology; intersubjectivity; relational psychoanalysis; attachment theory; developmental theories of attunement, separation-individuation, self-regulation, and mentalization; diverse applications of neuroscience, Lacanian linguistics-based theory, and Bion's theory of thinking competing with his own quasi-mystical understanding! Moreover, each approach claims to be on the cutting edge of theory and practice. Each contains its own explanations and interpretations of dynamics and development, and while there is some overlap among them, there is little consistency and equivalence between them that could sustain a unity of theory and practice. "Plurality" is a polite term that hardly describes the chaos implicit in psychoanalytic thought today.

This fragmented state emerged from an initially positive development. It was salutary that the impositions of a few dominant ideologies (e.g., Freudian, Jungian, Kleinian) loosened up, so that newer ideas could be considered on their own merit in what Blass (2011) views as a welcome "diversity" of approaches. Since then, a democratic atmosphere has prevailed, and many streams of thought have come into play from other disciplines: neuroscience, spirituality, attachment research, trauma studies, cognitive psychology, social psychology, philosophy, religion, and linguistics. Nowadays, trainees are thankfully less often indoctrinated with "cook book" solutions for conducting an analysis and more frequently exposed to a variety of approaches and concepts, even encouraged to find their own creative syntheses of what they have learned. Such an ecumenical approach surely benefits patients, therapists, scholars, and researchers.

The need for a common grounding of diverse theories

The problem is that, with the enthusiasm for new ideas, there has been little consistent effort to relate the partial views to the whole. Contradictions and oppositions abound without ever being acknowledged. For example, the types of understanding and experience utilized in various explanatory constructs and their data bases may differ to the point where it is difficult to ascertain how they relate. Attachment dynamics and developmental processes like mother–infant attunement and mentalization are rooted in observational research, while intersubjective perspectives emphasize introspective empathic experiences as their data base. Neuroscience investigates the physico-chemical world of synapses and neural networks. These variations in empirical data are further highlighted by the additional distinction between the "reconstructed" infant inferred from adult treatments versus the infant known through direct observation. Since the infant has no words, it is not a moot point as to which perspective provides the most accurate picture of neonatal inner development.

These explanations and understandings, each with its own research criteria and epistemology, are naïvely assumed to dovetail with and account for one another. Bion, for one, utilized ideas from group psychology, object relations theory, logical positivist and neo-Kantian philosophy, and Christian, Judaic, and Hindu mysticism, perspectives that are very difficult to reconcile with one another (see Chapter Twelve, this volume). More recently, Siegel (2012) has attempted syntheses of psychoanalytic, neuropsychological, Buddhist, and child developmental perspectives. Self psychologists, intersubjectivists, relational analysts, and mother–infant researchers, each starting out as independent groups, now talk amongst each other and cite each other's work as if they belong together in the same discourse. But are they all speaking the same language?

It is true that even the natural sciences use multiple and complex data bases, but considerable effort is made to reconcile them and seek internal consistency. Unfortunately, in psychoanalysis, the problem of dovetailing and translating among the diverse observational and conceptual foundations is often bypassed. The only common element that unites them is a belief in the process of interpretation and the underlying "little book" of underlying meanings that it discloses. But is everybody reading the same "little book?" A broader understanding of interpretation-as-process, including its historical and philosophical implications, especially with respect to the relationship between interpretation and empirical research, could help sort out and resolve such difficulties and inconsistencies. To place interpretation at the center of psychoanalytic discourse is to relate interpretation as method and technique to the broader context of interpretation as an evolving life form, as part of what makes us human.

The ubiquity of meaning and interpretation

To understand psychoanalytic interpretation requires an exploration of a much wider subject than psychoanalysis as such, namely, the psychology and philosophy of meaning and interpretation, the study of which is called hermeneutics. As central as interpretation is to analysis, it is nearly always addressed from a technical standpoint as an intervention rather than as a human experience. While Freud's (1900a) iconic *The Interpretation of Dreams* explored the history, depth and breadth of the interpretive process, most of the subsequent literature on psychoanalytic interpretation has focused on *technical recommendations* and/or *content* rather than the *nature of interpretation as a living process*. Although taken seriously by major figures within continental European philosophy (for example, Husserl, Heidegger, Gadamer, Ricoeur, Merleau-Ponty, Derrida, Levinas), little attention has been paid within English-speaking psychoanalytic circles to hermeneutics, the study of interpretation as a way to knowledge and understanding.

The word hermeneutics derives from Hermes, the Greek messenger of the gods. The reference to a messenger implies an intermediary between what is given and how it is understood. How then does interpretation fit in to human life and understanding as such? This question cuts to the foundations and roots of psychoanalysis.

Interpretation is an ever-present human activity. Everything understood about self and world is interpretive. All living systems are interpretive in the sense that they metabolize material, energy, information, and experience into new forms relevant to their survival, adaptation, and growth. Although an analyst's interpretations are based on criteria appropriate to the consulting room, they occur within a matrix of interpretive activity that begins shortly after birth, when mother and infant relate to one another on the basis of the meaning of each other's responses. The mother infers whether baby's cry means that he is hungry or wants to be held. The infant discriminates between imminent emotional gratification versus frustration depending on mother's behavior. Such a process of mutual cueing and interpreting occurs throughout the life cycle. Raw experience has to be translated and metabolized into meaningful form in order to be assimilated and used.

Two primary differences between psychoanalytic and everyday interpretations are a) that the former entails a strategy and technique, while the latter arises spontaneously as part of the "unthought known" (Bollas, 1987, pp. 277–283); and b) the psychoanalyst tries to elucidate deeply concealed elements for the purpose of healing, while in daily life interpretations serve the function of orienting the person in a practical way to his world.

The dream as both interpreter and interpreted

Nevertheless, there is a neglected and critically important connection between the carefully framed treatment-driven interpretations of the analyst and the patient's everyday "interpretive world," the way he spontaneously perceives his ongoing life and transactions.

> For example, a patient, Marco, shared a dream about being in an empty, half-constructed building with his ever-consoling pet dog from adolescence. The therapist interpreted the dream as an expression of the patient's feelings of being abandoned by his family, who had in his youth sent him to live with a relative against his objections. In making this interpretation, the therapist intended to elucidate historical and developmental aspects of the dream, the affective layers of abandonment and compensatory self-soothing (the pet), and their current manifestation in the "half-constructed" building of the analytic treatment itself. The patient agreed with this understanding, and went on to recall how his dog was a comforting mate to him and almost seemed capable of reading his mind, alluding perhaps to his relationship to the therapist.

While the therapist made a timely and useful interpretation of the dream, it could be said that the dream itself already contained that interpretation *in statu nascendi*. That is, the dream constituted in "primary process" form the very interpretation given by the analyst. What the therapist did was translate a private experience into verbal discourse. In the dream, the patient is in an empty, half-finished space, alone, living a "dog's life." Such imagery taken as metaphor already contained a significant part of the analyst's understanding. The patient-as-dreamer was already doing interpretive work (what Freud called dream work), albeit via imagery rather than words.

If we allow that interpretation can occur on an implicit non-verbal level, humans are ever and always fathoming meanings in their inner selves and their world, even during sleep. The analyst intervenes when there is a problem in this understanding that persistently haunts or discomfits the individual. The seeds of the interpretation are already there before the analyst speaks the words. They are part of an ongoing life process. In this case, the analyst's interpretation served to bring the patient's private, inner struggles with abandonment into the interpersonal dialogical context of the therapy process. The patient was no longer alone and isolated with the problem. It could now be understood and explored with another.

The therapist in this example simultaneously utilized two different paradigms, science and humanism, when thinking about the patient and the dream. He was thinking scientifically about ego development, family dynamics, trauma, separation, and loss. At the same time, he was aware humanistically of an evolving dream, story, and narrative as a sort of non-fiction novel in the process of being written by himself and the patient. And he was empathic towards the existential condition of the patient in the session and in the historical context of his adolescence. In this case, the analyst perceived himself partly as scientist doing research about the mind, and partly as encountering another person in an intersubjective dialogue. The scientific and humanistic paradigms of knowledge interweave in complex ways in the psychoanalytic process. How then, can we reconcile interpretation as scientific explanation with interpretation as humanistic experience?

Interpretation in psychoanalysis, science, and humanism

The distinction between interpretation as a consciously applied methodology in psychoanalysis, versus its spontaneous occurrence in nature and life, rekindles the heated debate about whether psychoanalysis is a science. Can interpretation, a phenomenon of human discourse, be refined and operationally defined to meet the rigors of scientific method, with its hypothetico-deductive methods of careful observation, experimentation, classification of facts, and validation? This is the question raised at the beginning of this chapter by Buchner's troubled character, Woyzeck. Human beings are complex and elusive, having "that sort of character, that sort of structure," while nature becomes apparent through manipulation and control, at the click of a finger. Psychoanalysis begins at a critical crossroads between science and humanism.

While Freud and many psychoanalysts then and now have regarded psychoanalysis as a science, others in various disciplines do not agree. The scientific status of psychoanalysis has been debated from day one, and came to a head in the 1980s with philosopher Adolph Grunbaum's (1984) critique of Freud's claim that psychoanalytic interpretations are validated by the therapeutic gains they produce, the so-called "tally argument," namely that a theory, hypothesis, or interpretation is true when its application produces a positive result. The ensuing discussion of Grunbaum's critique by analysts, psychologists, and philosophers (cf. Levy, 1988) led to little resolution because the nature of science itself is complex. Whether psychoanalysis is considered science depends on how one conceives the nature of science and in particular, the role of interpretation within the sciences. It also depends on the type of research used as well as the way in which theories are interpreted and applied. We take up this matter in a preliminary way now because its clarification will place further discussion of interpretation in the context of a problem which haunts psychoanalysis, especially in an "evidence based" medical culture, namely its claim to science while at the same time embodying humanistic and existential concerns. Indeed, it is precisely at this interface that the goals of analytic treatment, emotional insight, and self-transformation reside.

What distinguishes science from other human endeavors has been of philosophical interest ever since the ancient Greeks defined science as one of the major fields of understanding. Aristotle, in particular, propounded a theory of knowledge and a scientific methodology based on perception, classification, and inference. During the seventeenth and eighteenth centuries' Age of Enlightenment, philosophers like Hume, Locke, and Kant took up the problems of causality and the nature of knowledge (epistemology) in an intellectual climate in which the natural sciences possessed unparalleled elegance, sweep, and potential. In the idealized and mechanistic thought of that era, it appeared as if the entire universe could be elegantly encompassed in a set of mathematical equations such as Newton's laws of motion. Although biblical scholars and philosophers such as Schleiermacher strove, if vainly, for an interpretive rigor that rivaled the sciences in its precision, later developments in hermeneutics such as those of Herder and Dilthey in the nineteenth century and Gadamer in the twentieth, placed interpretation squarely in the context of their relational and personal dimensions, emphasizing the role of language, history, biography, and culture. This shift from scientific explanation to human understanding has contributed to the sharp divide between the hard sciences and the humanities that has subsequently haunted psychoanalysis and the social sciences.

This is not the place to scrutinize this dilemma, but merely to make a beginning inquiry about how and in what way psychoanalytic interpretation is or is not a scientific method. Some discussion here is important if only because many psychoanalysts and their patients are greatly invested in pursuing a science-based, as opposed in particular to religious or existential modes of treatment. It also bears on the relationship between psychoanalysis and medical care. Moreover, from a purely conceptual vantage point, one cannot ignore controversies about the nature of the knowledge acquired in psychoanalysis and the type of proof required.

Freud's legacy

When Freud founded psychoanalysis, he expressed his hope that its findings would acquire respectability in modern medicine and psychiatry. He anticipated challenges to its scientific status from the medical community. So he carefully framed his ideas in scientific language. However, his thinking took a radical turn as he shifted from the behavioral and diagnostic classification of symptoms, as had been the case in studies of hypnosis and trauma, to introspective phenomena such as the dreams and free associations reported by patients (cf. Jones, 1953; Ellenberger, 1979). The latter were not part of the biomedical universe of matter and energy as such, but disclosures of subjective states whose introspective sources were less reliable.

Yet Freud continued to hold that his findings would acquire the status of scientific truths consistent with the neurology that was his main interest prior to becoming a psychiatrist (Amacher, 1965). He thus developed a vocabulary and a way of elucidating clinical cases and human phenomena that fused scientific and humanistic world views. His use of the terms "psychic energy," "cathexis," and "drive," for example, implied bio-physical entities with properties of attraction-repulsion. Yet they also referred to desires and motives subjectively experienced in daily life. Subjective versus biophysical phenomena are as different from each other as the color "red" is to the particular wavelength of light and the electrical nerve impulses that produce it. Yet many terms in the Freudian vocabulary treat them as if they are interchangeable.

In fairness to Freud, others of his time such as Gustav Fechner (Heidelberger, 2004) sought a direct relationship between stimulus and sensation, physics and perception, initiating a field called "psychophysics," which remains today an important subdivision of experimental psychology. Freud, in "A Project for a Scientific Psychology" (1950a), was searching in earnest for a psychophysical model of the mind, but had serious doubts about his success, and the work was not published until after his death. Even today, the mind and the material world seem to be two different substances, but there is hope that their relationship may some day be clarified.

Nature and human nature: the experimentum crucis, disconfirmability, and the ambiguities of interpretation

Freud's struggle between mind and matter, subjectivity and objectivity in science was not new. During the Renaissance, Reformation, and Enlightenment eras, the defining observational kernel of natural science shifted from perception and intuition to classification of facts, and finally to the *experimentum crucis*. This is a process of objectification which takes an intuited subjective experience, attributes to it a particular form or "thingness," and subjects the object of scrutiny to a "crucial" either/or test. A classical example was Galileo's famous Leaning Tower of Pisa experiment. Galileo questioned the intuitive idea that objects fall at different rates under the influence of gravity, where, for example, on casual observation, a feather falls to earth more slowly than a stone. Legend has it that he dropped two balls of different mass from the tower and validated the counterintuitive hypothesis that they would reach the ground at the same time, explaining the difference between a feather and a stone on the basis of air friction.

The validity of subjective experience also fell to the ground with Galileo's stones. Rather than rely on intuition and classification, Galileo and others used the experimental method which since that time has become the ideal towards which science strives. Similarly, in the early twentieth century, scientists withheld judgment about Einstein's theory of relativity until the universe provided a large scale "experiment" where light was deflected as it passed near the sun as his theory predicted. The elegance of Einstein's "interpretation" of nature was not nearly as convincing to physicists as one single precise measurement. The value of the experimental method has proved inestimable in that it has markedly increased the ability of theories to predict the course of events on a reliable basis. We marvel at the natural sciences because of their efficacy in forecasting events and exposing new events and correlations to our view, which then have marvelous applications that enhance and ease our lives. Would that the human sciences could claim the same victories!

Disconfirmability

The *experimentum crucis* makes it possible to prove a theory false in one fatal blow. The philosopher Karl Popper (1959) contended that what makes experimental methodology effective is the principle of disconfirmability, whereby a scientific hypothesis can be shown by information and logic to be "falsifiable," negated, proven untrue. Some room, of course, must be given to the uncertainty of all knowledge, but for Popper disconfirmability based on observation makes scientific investigation a distinctly fruitful enterprise. The parallel to disconfirmability in psychology is the procedure called "rejection of the null hypothesis" whereby the proposed hypothesis is true if and only if the probability of it being untrue is small. The null hypothesis provides the margin of error of the outcome. The overall point of Popper is that science requires hypotheses that are falsifiable, specific enough to avoid ambiguity about their meaning and consequences.

Unfortunately, as Popper correctly pointed out, psychoanalytic interpretations are incapable of being proven false in this sense. Interpretations, while sometimes presented to the patient as "trial interpretations" (Lemma, 2008, p. 165), that test the patient's ability to assimilate them, differ in this respect from scientific hypotheses. In fact, the value of an interpretation lies partly in its ambiguity, which opens up possibilities, paradoxes, and differences at the same time that it points the patient in a particular direction. In psychoanalysis as in art, a useful interpretation enriches experience rather than affords final closure. Art and human experience are "polysemous." They have multiple meanings. Good interpretations are not always scientifically provable or falsifiable. Rather, the criteria for their validity are internal consistency and evocative power.

Ambiguity and paradox in psychoanalytic interpretation

Freud (1910e) pointed out that in the unconscious opposites attract and coexist. Matte Blanco (1975) enlarged this understanding by defining the unconscious as "infinite sets" with "both-and" symmetry of meanings rather than true-false opposition. Similarly, Grotstein (1997) called the unconscious "the infinite geometer," a generator of manifold possibilities. As meanings approach the unconscious level, they become ambiguous and paradoxical, until ultimately they dissolve into infinity, darkness, and otherness which Bion (1970, p. 26) called "O," the cipher, the other, the no-thing. The complexity and ambiguity of the unconscious is quite the opposite of the decisive disconfirmability of scientific experimentation. But, in fairness to psychoanalysis, the outcomes of scientific experiments and research contain their own uncertainties and ambiguities that require scientific interpretation and debate. Popper's disconfirmability principle is not always applicable even in the most rigorous scientific discourse. Indeed, scientific advances are as valued for the mysteries and ambiguities they open up as for their indisputable conclusiveness. The universe itself may be an "infinite geometer."

Nevertheless, there is an elusive difference between science and the process of psychoanalysis. Although collection and classification of facts, as well as some quasi-experimental cause and effect tests of hypotheses do occur in an analysis, such as when an analyst notes how a patient responds to an intervention, the interpretations that drive an analysis do the opposite. They deconstruct certainty by opening up vulnerability, emotionality, depth, and uncertainty in the patient, albeit with episodic moments of insight, resolution, and self-transformation. In this way, they further the introspective process and undo objectification as such. Bion (1970, p. 124) conceptualized the movement between ambiguity and clarity with his formula PS <-> D, an oscillating movement between cognitive-emotional uncertainty and clarity, with the initials derived from Melaine Klein's paranoid-schizoid and depressive positions, from splitting to wholeness.

Winnicott (1976) understood interpretation as a form of mutual play within the transitional space. He compared it to the "squiggle game" he improvised with his child patients, where they would trade off marks made on a piece of drawing paper until together they created a sketch in the transitional space between them. This creative process may help structure the child's ego as much as, say, Melanie Klein's direct interpretation of the child's play in terms of the latter's unconscious fantasies. The two methods—interpersonal play *vs.* direct interpretation—are very different procedures, yet both may facilitate growth and development. Interpretation has many faces, and sometimes, as in the squiggle game, interpretation occurs tacitly, without words.

What makes an interpretation "true" is not its objective correctness as such (although one hopes it would be reasonably consistent with the "facts"), but rather its value in fulfilling the aims and goals of an analysis. (That is one reason why Freud used the "tally argument," namely, that clinical gains are evidence of theoretical validity (Grunbaum, 1984, p. 128). Like any doctor, Freud was interested in successful outcomes.) An interpretation is "true" in the sense that a projectile is true to its course and not deflected. True and virtuous are synonymous in this respect. "Wild" interpretation has no place in psychoanalysis. However, we do not "tame" our interpretations with Popper's disconfirmability principle, but rather by attunement, authenticity, purpose, patience, and containment.

The "Wolf Man" case illustrates how Freud himself confused these two (scientific and therapeutic) notions of interpretation. Freud (1918b) insisted how his interpretations led the Wolf Man to the presumed source of his symptoms in a memory, that of his parents' coitus "a tergo" (vaginal intercourse from the rear), presumably witnessed during his infancy. Freud never doubted the dynamic importance of this memory in the patient's symptom formation. He wrote as if it he were taking the patient through a reconstructive progression whose logic was absolutely convincing. However, subsequent reflections by the Wolf Man himself (cf. Gardiner, 1971) suggest that the reconstructions as such did not necessarily constitute the cure. This does not cast doubt on Freud's theory of neuroses or on infantile sexuality in general, but it does suggest that Freud's view of interpretation as leading to a verifiable cause of a neurosis may not get to the heart of the matter. Even if the Wolf Man truly recalled a preverbal infantile experience (rather than unconsciously creating a story to please Freud), the case does not in any way demonstrate that the repressed memory retrieved in the analysis was the source of the Wolf Man's symptoms. Indeed, there were many other "selected facts" in the case, such as the Wolf Man's experiences with his governess and the fragmentation of his cultural world in Russia, which also could have been causative agents. Freud himself often emphasized that symptoms were overdetermined and had multiple causes.

Grunbaum and Popper, while differing in their arguments, are thus correct in holding that psychoanalytic interpretation is not a rigorous method for establishing the truth or falsity of a theory of neurosis. And it is equally fair to say that contemporary psychoanalysts are far less troubled by this shortcoming than their predecessors. In today's discussions, there is much less emphasis than before on whether a particular dynamic understanding is universally demonstrable and more of a focus on the process and its consequences. There is also a corresponding trend to regard interpretations as reflections of the inner lives of both therapist and patient, not just the latter. But most analysts, including those, such as Bion and Eigen, who in some of their writings invoke mystical understanding, believe in the scientific value of clinical experience in the consulting room. How can that be?

A broader view of science

The answer rests on a broader understanding of the natural sciences than that implied by the centrality of the experimental method and its logico-mathematical rigor. As Thomas Kuhn (1962) suggested, the theories and paradigms of the natural sciences are affected by social, intellectual, and other factors that influence their acceptability in the scientific community. Quantum theory, for example, could not have emerged in the Enlightenment vision of the universe as a perfect clockwork mechanism conceived in the mind of God. It took a modern sensibility, disillusioned with certainty, to make the quantum "uncertainty principle" plausible. From the perspective of a working chemist, economist, and philosopher, Michael Polanyi (1974) argued that science has elements of faith and intuition. Moreover, scientists like physicist Richard Feynman (2005), have placed great emphasis on accident, creativity, ambiguity, and play in generating theories and applications. In the current quantum physics and string theory understanding of subatomic phenomena, alternative "interpretations" of rigorous mathematical formulations form an important part of discussions, and an aesthetic notion of "beauty" becomes an important criterion for deciding between competing theories (Zee, 2007). Moreover, the operation of chance and chaos/complexity in the universe is today the basis of much scientific thought (Waldrop, 1992). Even the notions of objectivity and determinism, so much an essential aspect of "classical" science, are cast in doubt by the quantum notion of the inseparability of observer and observed. In light of contemporary physics, psychoanalysis does not need to feel badly about its interpretive method and the difficulty of objectifying subjective experience.

However, such tolerance does not free psychoanalysis from the need to struggle with the problem of how it retains scientific validity. The scientific posture of psychoanalysis is not only questioned with some cogency by empiricists and logical positivists such as Popper and Grunbaum, it is also doubted by their sworn enemies: Continental European thinkers with hermeneutical and existential orientations. They argue that the natural sciences are incapable of providing a meaningful approach to human understanding. The empiricist-positivists and the humanist-existentialists, from opposing perspectives, both relegate psychoanalysis to the fate of phrenology (readings of bumps on the head) and the ether (ethereal matter that fills empty space, which by the way is now coming back into vogue in the guise of "dark matter"). The scientific claims of psychoanalysis have always been held suspect.

This book, with deference to the profound thinkers in both positivist and existential-humanist camps, proposes that a middle-of-the road position on the matter is useful and desirable. A closer look at psychoanalysis and its interpretive mode of discourse vis-à-vis scientific understanding can make such a middle course profitable and worth considering.

Consilience

The argument is as follows. While psychoanalysis, like the humanities, is introspective, intersubjective, and interpretive, it is *consilient* with the natural sciences, in the sense that E. O. Wilson (1999) used that term, as a "jumping together" of diverse disciplines. First and foremost, the constant aim of psychoanalysis is to contribute to an understanding of human experience that is an integral part of a scientific world view. Whatever regions of the mind it pursues, including literary, existential, mystical, and, for some like Jung, supernatural realms, psychoanalysis keeps returning to nature as the bedrock. For example, the objective study of child development is a foundation on which both psychoanalysis and the study of human behavior rests and which forms a nexus between them. Moreover, as it is now doing in major ways, psychoanalysis often taps neuroscience and psychopharmacology for insights that might link it to biology.

Psychoanalytic interpretations, while they do not themselves meet the criteria for scientific proof, both incorporate and supplement the "story" of human nature and evolution as understood by the sciences. The simple distinction, for example, between reality and fantasy is the direct outgrowth of the scientific world view. Moreover, the rich interplay of reality and fantasy occupies a place in quantum physics and string theory, where multiple outcomes and realities are possible and the observer influences that which is observed. Psychoanalysis remains closely linked to physics and biology in its world view, and it could even be argued that the most advanced theories of physics bear a resemblance to the vagaries of mental phenomena explored by psychoanalysis.

For example, the physicist David Bohm (1980) proposed a hidden dimension to physical reality somewhat analogous to the unconscious with respect to the mind. He employed relativity and quantum theory to develop his concept of "implicate order." Bohm held that there is a deeper order in the universe than the ones currently envisioned by physics, an order that is enfolded within the universe as we understand it. This notion offers an interesting way to understand psychoanalytic interpretation, as inferring levels of organization that are enfolded in consciousness and the ego but which embody an "implicate order," in other words, deep unconscious structure. Bohm's work gives the implicate order an almost revelatory significance in the natural world, and is not unlike the psychoanalyst's use of interpretation to discern the unthought known (Bollas, 1987) within the "quantum" stream of consciousness). Bohm has in fact speculated on parallels between physics, neuroscience, and subjectivity. Bohm, in an effort to further world peace and dialogue, and with the inspiration of British psychiatrist and group analyst Patrick DeMare, developed a method of interpersonal communication related to the "implicate order" (Bohm, 1996).

Thus, as Kuhn and others have said, science itself does not strictly follow the model of "normal science" taught in school. The hypothetico-deductive method of establishing and testing hypotheses is only one feature of what takes place in "real life" scientific laboratories and discussions. Just as there are diverse interpretations that can be made of a patient's dreams and free associations, there are large ambiguities in science that are subject to interpretation. The foundations of relativity theory and quantum mechanics are in fact subject to multiple complex understandings that may never be resolved. Scientific endeavor is far more of an interpretive, hermeneutical matter than the view of science presented to the public as a finished, elegant product. Darwin's theory of natural selection, so much an integral part of psychoanalytic thought, today is variously interpreted by scientists in terms of the genetic mechanisms involved, the role of inter- and intra-species cooperation, and the global ecological consequences of the mechanisms of survival.

Indeed, despite the search for the Holy Grail of what makes a theory incontrovertibly true, science itself is an all-too-human enterprise that is subject to interpretation in a manner not unlike the analyst's interpretation of a dream. In modern physics, the universe, with its big bang, dark holes, and quantum leaps and paradoxes, resembles a demonic dream that is different for different observers/dreamers. The gap between the inner world of psychoanalysis and the outer world of physics seems to be closing. As the artist Marc Chagall said, "Our whole inner world is reality, perhaps even more real than the apparent world. To call everything that seems to be illogical a fantasy or fairy tale is to admit that one does not understand nature" (Harshav, 2003).

That being said, it remains problematical that the psychoanalytic method in and of itself does not follow the "rules" of scientific investigation as such. There is no way to arrive at conclusive findings about human nature from the data of the consulting room alone. Psychoanalysis is a deeply personal, subjective, unrepeatable, and interactive experience, not a controlled experiment yielding immutable truths (see Chapter Five). However, it also provides an extraordinary probing of the psyche, and the insights gained can be subject to scientific scrutiny in other situations.

Conversely, the psychoanalytic experience has been informed by rigorous research, especially in child development. Examples include Mahler's (Mahler, Pine, & Bergman, 1975) research on how children respond to separations from mother, Ainsworth's (Ainsworth, Blehar, Waters, & Wall, 1978) "strange situation" attachment studies, and Stern's (1985) videotape analysis of mother–infant interactions. There are many experimental and observational paradigms in psychology, anthropology, and the other social sciences that have been generated and applied in the crucible of psychoanalysis.

Moreover, it is possible to use research methodology directly within psychoanalytic treatment by finding correlations among variables in the psychoanalytic frame and the matching of patients and analysts.

The Luborskys' (2006) lifetime research on therapeutic process and outcomes led to protocols for conducting psychoanalytic sessions. A small but accumulating number of empirical studies of psychoanalytic treatments take the sessions themselves as the phenomena of observationally controlled investigation.

In conclusion, psychoanalysis should be modest in its claims to scientific validation, and psychoanalytic treatment should always be considered first and foremost an experiential and interpretive endeavor. But psychoanalysis does occupy an important place in the human sciences in terms of its time-tested generative capacity to enrich the understanding of motivation and the underlying causes of our thoughts and actions. To maintain and enhance this consilience with the natural and social sciences will require a degree of humility by both analysts and non-analytic members of the professional and scholarly community. But the result can be salutary for all, especially perhaps our patients, who deserve optimal care that is scientifically based but rooted in a deeper understanding of the human condition.

Therapeutic hermeneutics

Psychoanalysis has two basic purposes: epistemological—to further knowledge of the mind—and ontological—to facilitate changes in persons that resolve inner trauma, turbulence, and conflict. One could say with Freud that psychoanalysis cures through the transference, through the relationship. While that is certainly the case, such an explanation obscures the problem of how interpretations themselves can act as agents of change. Meaning and understanding all too often become mere words that have little or no impact on the mind or behavior. Yet, they are capable of promoting inner development, not only in psychoanalysis, but through rhetoric, religion, and the arts, as well as in impactful personal encounters throughout life. To grasp how that can happen, above and beyond social influence and persuasion, requires the in-depth study of the nature of interpretation, the study of hermeneutics. In addition, psychoanalytic interpretation is itself subject to interpretation. These "meta-interpretations," if you will, underlie the diversity of models and theories in contemporary psychoanalytic thought and practice. Hermeneutical philosophy provides one avenue to reconcile the multiple languages in the Tower of Babel and provide a better grounding for psychoanalytic theory. That, in turn, can increase the consilience of psychoanalysis and science. For that purpose, we must shift our focus from science to hermeneutics, from fact and proof to meaning and understanding.

Hermeneutics, the study of interpretation, is a discipline which had a great bearing on the thought of the late nineteenth and early twentieth centuries when psychoanalysis was conceived. Freud's *The Interpretation of Dreams* was itself a venture into hermeneutics, a discipline that originated in ancient times. The ongoing legacy of hermeneutics offers insights into the subtleties of meaning making. However, it has received relatively little attention in American and British psychoanalysis. The following three chapters offer a bird's-eye view of hermeneutics in historical perspective, with a selective emphasis on its relevance to psychoanalysis. The hope is that hermeneutical understanding will establish a richer palette of the interpretive process than can be achieved by an examination of technique as such. There is no greater instance of the importance of hermeneutics for psychoanalysis than Freud's *The Interpretation of Dreams*. It is there that we begin our journey through the historical development of hermeneutics as a discipline and a rich source of understanding for psychoanalysis.

PART I

INTERPRETING INTERPRETATION: PSYCHOANALYSIS AND HERMENEUTICS

Freud's *The Interpretation of Dreams,* ancient and modern thought, and the hermeneutics of Greek antiquity and Judaic sources

Hermeneutics is what psychoanalysis is all about. One of the greatest masterpieces of interpretive analysis, Freud's *The Interpretation of Dreams*, is unique in the history of ideas. It was a tour de force of exegetical understanding that brilliantly brought together the natural sciences and interpretive method. Equally remarkable was that it was written by a physician who saw the relevance of dream interpretation to treating mental illness.

At the very moment a patient enters a psychoanalyst's office, everything becomes grist for the mill of deciphering meanings of the mind. Patients have an innate curiosity about how their minds function and what their feelings and thoughts mean. Even the most naïve individuals are curious about the meanings of their dreams. In a revolutionary way, but using insights of the ages, Freud concluded that dreams unmask what is hidden in human nature. Psychoanalysis was conceived in a primal scene in which dreams and their interpretation were the cohabitants.

Early in her therapy, a patient, Jeri, dreamt that she was a newborn baby in a maternity ward, and her parents were watching her through an observation window. Jeri's own interpretation was that the glass partition conveyed feelings of deprivation from an emotional connection with her parents and with the therapist. The therapist noted to himself the possible dynamics of voyeurism as well as allusions to the patient's feelings of helplessness, her difficulty putting feelings into words, and her search for oral gratification. He wondered whether the dream could be an actual sense memory. He further guessed that it may have represented a temporally reversed screen memory or fantasy, standing paradoxically for something later, such as parental intercourse she might have witnessed at a subsequent point in childhood. However, Jeri's own reflections were the most useful at the moment, and the therapist simply encouraged her to further examine her difficulties with attachment and intimacy.

The dream could also be understood as a commentary on Jeri's self and fate. We might wonder as the patient did, what would become of this baby? Would she remain the "little angel" her parents wished for, or become the "ugly duckling" the patient felt she was inside? Would therapy transform her into the untarnished, freely spontaneous eternal child that she sought vainly to be in her sex life? What would therapy make of her?

In some ways, Jeri's dream seems to go beyond Jeri herself to more universal concerns. It is as if its imagery and story sheds light on the nature of the mind which could conceive it. Like the previous chapter's "big book/little book" memory, Jeri's dream provides a felicitous metaphor for psychoanalysis, and perhaps for Western culture in general. Like the analytic couch, the window separates, yet allows for a degree of intimacy, a way of "peering into" the other. How does one know another's mind (and heart) in the first place? Is it close and empathically felt by the observer, whether parent or analyst (or for that matter lover or novelist), as the loving parents welcome their baby, as if the knowledge is intuitive and we are the other? Or is there an "observation window" which both connects and separates us? Are we predestined to be alone, separate, and apart from one another? So much so that we cannot even hear the other's cry? Sometimes dreams speak to the human condition itself.

Jeri's dream also conveys the inequality of the parents and the baby, the subject and object, the analyst and patient. How does that difference influence what we know? Can analyst and patient, researcher and subject of research, thinker and thought, exist in an equal, mutual partnership? What sort of new understanding would come from removing the barriers of privilege and authority? Is it even possible to do so?

Then there is the dream phenomenon and context, a dream within the larger co-transference "dream" of the patient's therapy. Are dreams coherent? Do they form a whole, or are they mere fragments? Is there a metaphysical "dream in itself" beyond the recalled telling of the dream? Who is the dreamer who dreams the dream? Is it Jeri herself or a ghost, another self that takes possession of her in the night? Can we give the dreamer a name or gender? Is there a self-organizing force, a unity of the mind that regulates the dream? Or is the mind eternally divided against itself, or even a yawning hole of nothingness?

Finally, Jeri's dream raises the question of psychological birth, of transformation and change. What will emerge from the infant and her relationship with her parents? Can what one knows through the window of interpretation alter how one is in the world? Do these transformations amount to sea changes of almost mythic proportions or small adjustments of psychic energy? In the film, *A Dangerous Method* (Cronenberg, 2011), about Jung, Freud, and Jung's love affair with his patient Sabina Spielrein, Jung sees the goal of analysis as the transformation of human potential, while Freud regards it as a modest alteration in the balance of emotional forces. (The movie asks, "At what cost?") The question of what transformations of self are possible, indeed desirable, is central to both psychoanalytic therapy and to a world befuddled by human irrationality and self-destruction.

Interpretation and philosophy

The problem of interpretation of another's mind is inherent in many of the dilemmas underpinning Western thought in the modern and postmodern eras of the nineteenth and twentieth centuries: the problems of ontology (the nature of being and beings), epistemology (the nature of knowledge and specifically knowledge of man and the mind), and ethics (the nature and origins of the moral sense and values). Psychoanalysis emerged in the midst of these controversies, influencing and influenced by them. During the same time period, hermeneutics—the study of texts and meaning—came to play an increasing role in philosophical discourse. The interpretation of being, knowledge, story, history, persons, and ideas intertwined with one another. Within that conjunction, psychoanalysis became more than a psychiatric treatment modality. It came to represent the cutting edge exploration of meaning, mind, and human nature, the therapeutic apotheosis of science, philosophy, and literature in a time of crisis and change. Such significance can only be fully understood in the context of history and culture. In particular, hermeneutical philosophy provides a lens and a context through which to see how history and culture impacted psychoanalysis and the meaning of interpretation within it.

Prolegomena: Freud, philosophy, and hermeneutics

In *The Interpretation of Dreams* (Freud, 1900a), published at the turn of the twentieth century, Freud, up to then known as a neurological researcher and budding psychiatric clinician, entered the arena of hermeneutics. In a manner unparalleled in the history of science, Freud brought together two hitherto unrelated disciplines: medicine and dream interpretation, the latter until then a matter of folk psychology, prophesy, and occasional scientific observation. He drew upon earlier understandings of dream interpretation, including those of ancient times and everyday life. He reviewed scientific and other writings on dreams, noting their relationship to waking life and to sensory stimulation while asleep. He accepted some of these ideas, while rejecting others, concluding that dream interpretation should properly focus on the inner mental associations of the dreamer rather than external reality. For explanatory purposes, he utilized notions of poetic metaphor and metonymy in his dynamic concepts of condensation and displacement. And he formulated understandings of the unconscious, wish fulfillment, and repression, which became the hallmarks of his own theory of the mind.

Historical and contemporary influences vis-à-vis freud

Psychoanalysis was conceived when psychology had only recently become a separate discipline from theology and philosophy. Consequently, Freud's entire corpus of work drew richly from diverse streams of Western thought, for example, the ancient Greeks, Helmholtz's understanding of experimental science (Amacher, 1965), and the philosophies of Kant and Schopenhauer, among others. Some (Bakan, 1958; Berke & Schneider, 2008; Handelman, 1982, pp. 129–152) have held that Freud was also exposed to Talmudic and Kabbalistic teachings which despite his tendency to minimize their significance, may have influenced his understanding of exegesis (interpretive methodology), ethics (superego), and the mystical and uncanny.

There were also contemporary trends which as part of the *zeitgeist*, the spirit of the time, influenced Freud. For example, the roles of imagery and intentionality in psychology were frequently discussed then. The phenomenology of Edmund Husserl, with its emphasis on imagery and perception had commonalities with Freud's notion of primary process, an imagistic mode of thought. Both Husserl (Rollinger, 1999) and Freud (Jones, 1953, v. 1, pp. 37, 56) attended lectures of the philosopher-psychologist Franz Brentano, whose concept of intentionality had a broad influence on both philosophy and psychology. Husserl's phenomenology and Freud's psychoanalysis had a common basis in Brentano's so-called "act psychology" in which every mental phenomenon, perception, and psychological action has an intended object. For Freud, intentionality meant that every motivation or drive had an aim and object, while for Husserl, it meant that the subject, intention, and object are inseparable in experience. While Freud, unlike Brentano and Husserl, was not a phenomenologist, phenomenology later came to play a key role in self psychology (Kohut, 1971, 1977) and the intersubjective perspective (Stolorow, Atwood, & Brandschaft, 1994).

Conversely, Freud's work profoundly influenced trends in European thought. The works of existentially based thinkers like Sartre, Derrida, Foucault, Levinas, and Habermas are direct descendants of Freud's ideas, even in the breach. There are echoes of Freud in Heidegger out of which existential therapies developed. The surrealist movement in art drew directly from Freud. The list goes on and on. The point is that all of these mutual influences revolve around how one makes meanings and interprets them, and whether and how meanings can be concealed or revealed. So, in understanding how interpretation operates in psychoanalysis, these mutually impacting ideas from psychoanalysis, philosophy, and the arts come into play. Moreover, these trends and influences were themselves stimulated by teachings going back to antiquity, the Middle Ages, the Renaissance, the Protestant Reformation, and the Enlightenment and Romantic eras.

Hermeneutics is the link in the chain that brings all these diverse influences together. What follows in this and the next two chapters is a condensed and selective exploration of the evolution of hermeneutics within philosophy, exegesis, and related disciplines. It speaks to how the interpretation of texts intersected with concepts of mind, eventuating in psychoanalysis as one of several focal points for viewing meaning, mind, and self-transformation. Here, we can only give an impressionistic overview with the purpose of elucidating ideas that inform psychoanalytic interpretation as such. Nearly every point could be nuanced in ways that would take a lifetime of study. The conclusions reached would also vary in responses to the nuances. If the reader gains the insight that psychoanalytic interpretive methodology is not merely a strategy and technique but a complex historically evolved process, this overview will have made its point. Hermeneutics explodes interpretation into a complex, manifold picture of human understanding. But first, we go back to Freud.

Freud's transformation of ancient dream interpretation

Freud did not invent dream interpretation anew, but made use of the legacy of the ages. As Einstien and Infeld (1938) wrote regarding the revolution in physics, "Creating a new theory is not like destroying an old barn and erecting a skyscraper in its place. It is rather like climbing a mountain, gaining new and wider views, discovering unexpected connections between our starting point and its rich environment." Freud's revolution of the mind followed a similar path.

Freud's interest in dreams was informed by his lifelong fascination with ancient Mediterranean cultures, where they had prophetic implications. Early on, dreams were taken as "signs." They were interpreted prophetically and believed to contain familial and tribal implications. The dreams contained within epic legends of antiquity involved strivings for leadership and power.

For example, Gilgamesh's dream of an encounter with an axe prophesied his future as a struggling leader. According to the legend (Kovacs, 1998), Gilgamesh had several dreams that he told to his mother. One was about an axe that he found at the gate of his marital chamber. Gilgamesh's mother interpreted the dream to him, saying, "The axe that you saw is a man" (did she perceive the phallic symbolism?) prophesying that the dream would lead him to a valued friend and adviser (and curiously pointing out the resemblance of the adviser to a "wife" and to herself, pointing up the bisexual, familial, and tribal origins of the dream, with perhaps his own mother as interpreter foreshadowing the notion of "the analyst-as-maternal-entity.") A parallel to Gilgamesh's mother exists in the Sphinx who poses the riddle to Oedipus. The

Sphinx has a woman's face. Interpretation as a human process is very early linked to femininity, child-bearing, and bloodlines.

In these early interpretations of dreams, self and world were not strongly differentiated, and dream interpretations consisted largely of references to the outer world. The inner life was understood as connected with external reality, especially as inner experience provided signs and omens that foretold future events. In everyday life, and in patients' own interpretations of their dreams, this concatenation of inner and outer reality is still common. Psychoanalysis educates the patient in a new way of thinking about him or herself as a self-contained mind with its own introspective set of explanations and understandings, a modern way of relating to self that Feldman (1974) called "a psychoanalytic addition to human nature."

Freud provisionally accepted some of the insights contained in ancient and traditional dream and interpretation, but transformed them in three ways. First, as mentioned, he contended that *dreams are primarily the reflections of the inner life*, the associative connections among thoughts and images. Second, he *reversed the temporal factor to reflect causation rather than prophesy*, explaining dreams not in terms of future events, but as related to memories and reminiscences. Third, he proposed *a domain of thought that is repressed and unconscious*, of which the dreamer is unaware due to *censorship*.

With these three transformations of the interpretive matrix, Freud engaged modern thought in ways that mirrored developments in science, art, and literature, and at the same time presented challenges to the modern sensibility that subsequent thinkers would take up in earnest. (But as we shall see, the seeds of these insights were planted in Western soil before Freud.)

The mind–body connection

By making the inner life of the mind a distinct domain of investigation, Freud engaged in the new discipline of psychology with the likes of William James, Havelock Ellis, and Gustav Fechner. He dwelt on the philosophical investigations of Descartes and Kant regarding the "problem of mind" and its relationship to the body (soma) and the physical world. Well before Freud, the mind–body dualism had attained holy status in Descartes's vision of the mind (an idealized version of the mind connected to God) as immaterial perceiver peering out of the pineal gland in the brain. However, with the nineteenth-century rise of experimental neurology and psychiatry the notion of the pineal gland as the center of thought and, more important, the Cartesian dualism were shaken. Hysterical symptoms such as paralyses and blindness of psychological origin suggested the intimate connection between psyche and soma. Vast regions of the brain, not just a single location, were shown to be implicated in changes in sensation, perception, speech, and consciousness. As Freud's ideas about dream interpretation were germinating, he wrote a paper entitled "A Project for a Scientific Psychology" (1950a: draft written in 1895), in which he sought the Holy Grail of the mind–brain connection, only to file the paper away in a desk drawer because he concluded it was scientifically premature. Thus, while he turned his attention to interpretive psychology, he remained at heart a neuropsychiatrist. Psychoanalytic interpretation is impregnated with psychosomatic implications. Freud played a major role in breaking down the mind–body split.

More broadly, as Freud worked and wrote, thinkers like Husserl and Heidegger began to challenge the metaphysics of the idealists and empiricists, the heritage of Plato and Aristotle. Millennia before Descartes, Plato's and Aristotle's philosophy demarcated two separate worlds: 1) the physical world including the human body, and 2) the mental world of sensations, perceptions, and ideas. Freud, although steeped in Greek philosophy, began to look for connections between these two worlds. Indeed, he posited that the largest part of the mind, the id, was intimately related to the body. In this respect, although he never considered himself such, Freud was to some degree a phenomenologist like Husserl and an existentialist like Heidegger. That is, like Husserl, he sought to describe embodied experience prior to intellect and censorship. And like Heidegger, he held that much of our being is "already there" (Heidegger's phrase; Freud called it "latent content") prior to conscious thought about it. Thus, psychoanalytic interpretation aims to elucidate direct, unmediated experience and its bodily components, phenomena which ultimately link to biophysical and existential realms.

Given his scientific bent and interest in neuroscience, it is paradoxical and indicative of his genius that Freud also contributed vastly to the notion that the mental life could be interpreted in a manner analogous to scripture, literature, or art, linking the parts to each other and the whole, seeking out discrepancies in the text, and pursuing ideas to their historical roots. However, because he wanted to retain the natural science paradigm of his own medical profession, his work is peppered with contradictions which have provided ample stimulation to those who followed him. For example, like Descartes (and also Plato and other philosophers who believed in disembodied ideas), he presented the inner life as self-contained, but then, he discovered profound interactions of the mind with both the body and the social world. At the same time, he proposed a law of "psychic determinism" which links thoughts exclusively to other thoughts, but then they are also linked to interpersonal relationships and the body. The mind, for Freud, was a (Cartesian) closed (instinctual, observing, thinking, emotional) system—but it was also an open (biosocial) system!

Time, space, and intentionality

Furthermore, during Freud's era, the notions of time and space were transformed by scientists and philosophers alike. In 1905, only five years after the publication of *The Interpretation of Dreams*, Einstein (Einstein & Infeld, 1938) altered forever the cherished belief that physical time and space were absolute, the same for all observers. In Einstein's theory of relativity, time and space acquired flexible properties similar to subjective time. Real time could shrink and expand the way a subjective moment seems like a flash or a lifetime, and so on. Freud showed that dreams and the unconscious contained the same paradoxes and displacements that scientists would find in the universe.

On another level, philosophers like Husserl, Heidegger, and Bergson gave temporality and intentionality a central place in human experience, questioning the Platonic notion of "timeless" eternal forms as the basis of thinking. Indeed, Heidegger would argue that time sets limits on all human experience and mortality defines the human condition, not unlike Freud's later positing of the death instinct.

Until Freud, the mind was a conscious rational decision-maker, the master of its fate. Freud showed that volition was partly an illusion, that "free choice" was largely conditioned by remote past events which the mind distorted and to which it added imaginative features.

The system unconscious

Perhaps the greatest contribution and yet the most controversial idea that Freud initiated in his writing on dreams was his notion of the "system unconscious." In proposing the "*ucs*" (his frequently used abbreviation) as a distinct topological component of the mind, he drew upon the insights of many thinkers before him, from Plato to Schopenhauer and Nietzsche, that much of who and what we are remains hidden from our view, that we are ignorant of our deeper motives and layers of experience. That "awareness of unawareness" provided a ground for the understanding of what makes us human rather than divine (that word having the dual meaning of god-like and perceptive). However "enlightened" we are, we nevertheless live in the "dark night of the soul," as above, so below. To the extent that Freud transposed that insight into psychological understanding, he was on the firm ground of age-old wisdom and supported by many brilliant thinkers.

However, he took an additional step by giving a specific neuropsychological connotation to unconscious mental processes. That is, he proposed scientifically that a thought, a memory, an idea could persist in an unconscious, latent state and still influence the thinker, the ego. He thus established the paradox of thoughts that were not thought about by a thinker and still had the influence of thoughts on thoughts. In philosophical terms, he employed the notion of meaning without understanding, a limbo state that Enlightenment philosophers such as Bishop Berkeley and John Locke had found impossible to accept. For them, a thought had to have a conscious mind or perceiver to think it. Many modern day psychologists have also rejected the notion of unconscious thought. For them, thoughts and consciousness are inseparable. "Unconscious thoughts," while intuitively possible, make for crazy science!

On the other hand, philosophers, artists, and writers have lined up to explore the significance and implications of the Freudian unconscious. Thus, in proposing a system unconscious, a functioning mind outside of conscious experience, Freud entered the science-humanism divide. For scientists, the notion of a mind without a conscious thinker sounds too much like a ghost or a god or a hallucination, while for many in the humanities, there is something appealing about its paradoxical nature.

To sum up, in *The Interpretation of Dreams*, the theory of the unconscious, and the treatment approach of psychoanalysis, Freud drew upon many ideas already present in Western thought and transformed the mix into a new understanding that fell right at the cusp of modernity in philosophy, literature, and the arts. His unique concatenation of science and the art of interpretation, of mind and body, of fantasy and reality, solved many problems and created many others. As a result, psychoanalysis calls for interpretation of itself, what amounts to a philosophical hermeneutics of psychoanalysis.

To provide a backdrop for discussing such efforts to understand psychoanalysis at its most fundamental level, we now embark on a "bird's-eye view" tour of the history of hermeneutical ideas that led up to Freud, and then turn to those that emerged during Freud's lifetime and afterwards, all with the purpose of establishing a ground for the exploration of psychoanalytic interpretation and the interpretation of psychoanalysis. To begin that journey, we go back to Plato and Aristotle, whose influence on the Western mind is monumental, and with whose ideas Freud was familiar through his academic education.

The pervasive influence of Plato and Aristotle— and some modern critiques

Nearly every idea in Western philosophy harks back to Plato and Aristotle, whether in agreement or disagreement. This influence includes Freud, whose interest in antiquity is well documented. He studied Aristotle with Brentano (Jones, 1953, v. 1, p. 37). His choice of Oedipus to represent the fundamental dilemma of the child, as well as his famed collection of Greek and other artifacts and his travels in the Mediterranean area, reflect his lifelong identification with those cultures. Several key ideas from Aristotle such as catharsis, representation, and deductive/inductive reasoning bear directly on Freud's understanding of interpretation.

Neither Plato nor Aristotle elaborated upon hermeneutics as such, although Plato used the term in a number of dialogues, contrasting hermeneutical knowledge to that of *sophia*, wisdom (Ramberg, 2003). Plato's relegation of hermeneutics to a lower status than wisdom, taken to be true knowledge, has persisted even to this day. The marginalization of Freud's thinking in medicine and science is partly due to this abiding skepticism about interpretive methods. Plato and Aristotle laid the groundwork for such doubt, although, in all fairness, Aristotle had much to say about poetry, theater, and rhetoric as interpretive forms, and Heidegger's student, Gadamer, was an Aristotelean scholar.

Although profoundly interested in the irrational and the uncanny as well as myth and story, Freud, like Plato and Aristotle, was a rationalist and empiricist. Most notably in *The Future of an Illusion*, Freud (1927c) asserted his allegiance to the forces of reason, scientific method, and ethical values that come down to him from Plato and Aristotle. So it is natural to look for parallels between their thinking and psychoanalysis.

The "talking cure" itself embodies elements of the Socratic method of dialogue invoked by Plato. The analyst is the Socratic explorer of the ideas, wishes, and fantasies the patient brings to the consulting room. Every interpretation poses a question, namely, "What you say might mean something else; consider this possibility." Like Socrates, the analyst rarely contradicts the patient directly. Instead, he invites him to consider possible ways of looking at things.

Reality and psychoanalytic interpretation

Freud's "reality principle" is the psychological embodiment of an objective world that is learned about through experience. The "reality" which we take so much for granted in Western culture is in fact part of the legacy of Plato and Aristotle. The reality principle is the basis of therapeutic alliance. It places every interpretation in the context of a shared reality that, by contrast, reveals the patient's inner world to be that of illusion or drama, which the patient eventually compares with "reality" in resolving the transference. "Reality" presumes a particular Platonic world view that divides experience between veridical and imaginary. The presumed reality co-owned by patient and analyst is not universal to all cultures. It is a "Eurocentric" concept that was originally defined and described in many respects by Plato and Aristotle. They anticipated Freud and catalogued many of the patient's "distortions" and defense mechanisms in the form of philosophical errors of logic and judgment.

So who defines reality? To a great extent Plato and Aristotle did! But in clinical practice, as in hermeneutics, reality itself is subject to interpretation. For example, a patient, Lucas, whose therapy helped him to recover well from a major depressive episode, was stunned when the therapist told him that an end had come to his treatment. He fought off this possibility vigorously and argued that he could keep benefitting from therapy indefinitely. Lucas had fallen in love with therapy. He spent much of his treatment trying to make the therapist into a friend, and resisted to the last minute the idea that his helper was a professional clinician who served a more limited consultative purpose. The therapist said to Lucas that he was in denial of both the reality of the therapeutic contract and the time-limited nature of all human relationships.

But where does this reality come from? Perhaps it is the other way around. Maybe the "reality" of the therapeutic contract only serves to put the therapist in control of the situation, while in actuality relationships never end—after all, we have relationships with Plato and Aristotle! So who defines reality? Lucas was a man who dwelled in the arts, history, and literature. Those worlds were "real" to him, and they live on in perpetuity. So why should it not be the same with his relationship to the therapist? Who sets the calipers that define what is real and what is transference?

Nevertheless, interpretation in the psychoanalytic tradition carries the meta-message of a shared and often frustrating reality surrounding the inner world of desire, fantasy, memory, and defense in which wishes are always granted and nothing ever ends. In fact, when the patient cannot access what the analyst considers reality it is considered a possible sign of psychosis. By analogy, it would not be too much of an exaggeration to suggest that Plato and Aristotle were metaphorically treating a collective "psychosis" in Greece, namely a world of illusion that in their view was populated by impulse-driven gods and goddesses, disordered thinking, and delusional beliefs.

The Platonic vision of an underlying reality came to be called metaphysics. In broad strokes, this view of a reality that is independent of immediate personal experience prevailed in Western thought through the eighteenth-century Enlightenment. In the nineteenth century, it began breaking down with the new emphasis on individuality and personal autonomy, with the individual forming his or her own sense of reality rather than being ruled by an agreed upon version of it. The new view in which each man creates his world was most forcefully articulated by Nietzsche. While Freud utilized some of Nietzsche's ideas about individuality, power, and authority, he clung tenaciously to the conventional notion of a shared external world which he incorporated in his notion of the "reality principle."

The Freudian notion that interpretation uncovers falsehood and delusion, especially in the form of transference distortions, derives from Plato in particular, and eventuated in what modern philosopher Paul Ricoeur (1970, p. 10) called "the hermeneutics of suspicion," a tendency to doubt the surface of experience, and especially the fault lines in the ego's vanity. Such hermeneutics that doubted everything the patient said dominated psychoanalysis until Harold Searles (1979) and Irwin Hoffman (1983) argued that the patient's transference contained important and relevant veridical perceptions of the analyst's character. Much earlier, Ferenczi (1932) had made the same point, but his ideas were discounted.

Psychotic patients, presumably out of touch with reality, nevertheless acutely and accurately perceive the concealed aspects of the analyst's mental life. I once participated in a seminar where Herbert Rosenfeld supervised a case of a schizophrenic woman and demonstrated repeatedly to the supervisee how the patient's bizarre imagery was an indirect communication of her correct perception of his negative judgmental attitude towards her. Hoffman's paper had a direct influence on the development of relational psychoanalysis which emphasizes the mutuality and the egalitarian nature of the analytic relationship. Thus, contrary to the hermeneutics of suspicion, interpretations could recognize the *truth* in the patient's perceptions. For relational psychoanalysts, interpretation is no longer a purely objective commentary by the analyst, but consists in negotiated transactions with the patient's subjective experience as a container of truth. "Reality" becomes a negotiated product of dialogue, not a metaphysical absolute.

Aristotle's "representation" as a cornerstone of psychoanalysis

Closely related to but different from the idea of an underlying reality is the concept of representation advanced by Aristotle and frequently utilized by Freud. For Aristotle, all human thought utilizes representations in which a word, a concept, a symbol, a story signifies an idea or object in various combinations and permutations. Representations can be manipulated by logic and intuition in a host of ways that objects as such cannot, and thus make rational thought and inference possible. The basic human vehicle of representation is language, although it is likely that there are ways that prelinguistic infants, for example, create wordless representations of their inner and outer worlds. And we all use images to represent experiences for which we cannot quite find the words. Artists do that sort of representation especially well.

A simple example of a language representation in psychoanalysis is the word "mother." When a person speaks of his "mother," it is natural to assume that he is referring to a conventional, generic female caregiver. Not so in psychoanalysis. A dream or memory may suggest that "mother" is linked to an idiosyncratic private image, a voice, a face, a movement, a color, a body part. The "mother imago" is full of ownership and intentionality: it is the patient's own personal maternal entity, and he creates and relates to it on many levels. In order to think and talk about it, he needs to represent it in words or pictures. Freud called the word mother a "word presentation" while referring to the personalized image as an "object representation."

From such a perspective, an interpretation restores and elaborates the connection between words (language), object representations, and their emotional significance. Lacan (1977, pp. 126–129), applying the structural linguistics of Ferdinand Saussure, referred to language and what it represents as signifier and signified respectively, and credited Freud with showing that the signified can "slide" beneath the signifier, taking on unconscious meanings and associations not encountered in everyday speech. In other words, language itself does not define meaning. That is the very reason interpretation is necessary. An interpretation discloses the shifts in signified meaning brought about by desire and defense. Like Aristotle, Lacan was a structuralist. Because we are steeped in the Aristotelean thought that permeates Western civilization, such connections between language, imagery, and representational meaning seem undeniable. What Freud accomplished beyond Aristotle was to expose some of the "secrets" and fault lines in the representational process. Lacan made explicit how those fault lines are embedded in language.

Modern critiques of the concept of representation

Particular trends in modern philosophy have pointed to significant shortcomings in the notion of representation, sometimes utilizing psychoanalysis itself to upend its own use of that term. This critique has come from philosophers as diverse as Ludwig Wittgenstein, a logical positivist; Derrida, the father of deconstructionism and postmodern thought; and Richard Rorty, an American pragmatist. Their ideas are complex and nuanced. The purpose here is to offer a simplified understanding that bears on psychoanalytic interpretation as such.

Wittgenstein's (1953) critique of representation comes from a consideration of how words relate to other words and to objects in the world and in the mind. He compared the elements of a language to the streets of a city. These streets are defined and located by their positional relationship to other streets. Similarly, the elements of a language: sounds, words, sentences, and so on, are defined by their relationship to all the other elements in the language. By contrast, their usage as representations of things in the real world is arbitrary. They have nothing to do with language as such. Language is a game, an activity, and the words and meanings are like pieces on a chess board. For Wittgenstein, there is nothing inherent in language to link it to what it represents, any more than the bishop in a chess game relates to the Catholic Church. Therefore, language does not "represent" anything. It is an invented structure that we use for our own purposes. For Wittgenstein, language in itself does not embody meaning. From a psychoanalytic perspective, that is one reason that the ego can use language to conceal motivations rather than disclose them. If language were attached to motives as true representations of them, the ego would not be able to lie.

Rorty (1979), from the point of view of an American pragmatist, suggested that language is fundamentally a practical means of conversation and dialogue. For that purpose, a common set of meanings and expressions is arranged by the parties to the conversation. Those conventions dissolve as soon as the conversation ends, to be resurrected later if the dialogue continues. Nothing in discourse means or represents anything except insofar as a given community agrees to it for the sake of a conversation having certain goals and objectives. Rorty would argue that the notion of representations residing permanently in the mind is fictional. He would probably critique all of the psychoanalytic metapsychology in the same way. He would be interested in the nature of the conversation taking place in the analyst's office and what sort of conventions the two participants have agreed upon to talk with one another.

From a philosophical stance radically different from either Wittgenstein or Rorty, Derrida (1978), utilizing Freud's neuropsychological notions of "trace" and "difference" (see Chapters Four and Thirteen) held that, ultimately, all that remain of text and discourse are memory traces and differences left in the dust that immediately follows any experience. Meanings consist of traces and differences that are disseminated throughout a "text," whether that text is a novel or a psychoanalytic session. The "reality" of what we think is "represented" in the text can be "deconstructed" by rigorous examination, exposing its inconsistencies and alternative understandings. Similarly, an analyst's interpretations deconstruct the conscious assumptions and beliefs of the patient's ego. And the analyst's interpretations can themselves be deconstructed. In this way, Derrida deconstructed the idea of representation, which assumes a permanence of the object and its representation.

Such critiques of representation imply that psychoanalytic interpretations are conversation pieces, aspects of a particular text or language, not disclosures of a pre-given emotional reality. That is, the patient and analyst co-create systems of meaning as they go along. If we agree with these modern and postmodern critiques, if we hold that all meanings are games that can be deconstructed and/or revealed to be conventional or pragmatic in origin, then psychoanalytic interpretation becomes, in effect, not a search for objective truth, but a scaffolding that is erected for the purpose of having a series of sessions! In a way, there is something obvious about this. When the patient goes home, he re-enters the world of everyday meanings of traffic jams, meals, bills, marriage, and so on. He is then released from the temporary world of "representations" conjured by the psychoanalytic *magus*.

To summarize, psychoanalytic interpretation was conceived within the framework of objectivity and representationalism first articulated by Plato and Aristotle and carried forward into Enlightenment thought. From this perspective, interpretations uncover and disclose the preconscious and unconscious systems that underlie what the patient represents in the form of language, gesture, imagery, and free association. Thus, the unconscious is a psychological reality, and, just like physical reality, we may never "see" it directly, but we can open its door and glimpse some of its effects and patterns. Interpretation takes us into this realm of thought. However, the modern challenges to metaphysics and representationalism suggest that the more we pursue a so-called unconscious psychic "reality," the more it evades us, and we come to realize that all human experience is ephemeral, time-bound, and in certain respects arbitrary. From that perspective, interpretation, like the Zen master, does nothing other than to expose this troubling condition. Of course, the debate about such matters continues, and variations on these perspectives abound.

Thought as rhetoric, symptoms as dramaturgy, hysteria as mimesis

One additional aspect of the Aristotelean legacy is worth pursuing at this point. While Plato was skeptical about the value of art, poetry, rhetoric, and drama, Aristotle held that there was an important place for them in our lives and in philosophy. (See the good (1984) translation of Aristotle's *Rhetoric and Poetics* by Roberts, Bywater, and Corbett.) He believed that such means of expression revealed emotional truths that evade pure logic, and his writings on poetry, rhetoric, and drama remain vital to this day for the creative and performing arts. Breuer and Freud (1895d, pp. 253–306) similarly stressed the importance of catharsis in psychotherapy. Moreover, Freud's understanding of character types is based to a large degree on Aristotle and other classical thinkers, as well as Shakespeare, Dostoevsky, and others, although Freud notably added the aspect of libidinal development (oral, anal, and phallic character types).

Along with his understanding of drama and emotions, Aristotle's ideas on rhetoric are definitional even today. The psychoanalyst is a rhetorician, a purveyor of ideas and influence in the form of speech, and Aristotle wrote about the importance of the poetic and rhetorical forms of metaphor and metonymy. Metaphor makes a link between one idea and another, and at the same time opens up additional implications and associations. Shakespeare's metaphor "All the world's a stage" adds many dimensions to our understanding of human relations. Metonymy substitutes part for whole, as in the use of the phrase "the White House" to refer to the executive branch of government, or the use of "on the couch" to refer to analysis. Freud's idea of condensation is related to that of metaphor in that both contain multiple meanings, and metonymy is one form of displacement, namely from the whole to the part. In its use of metaphor and metonymy, the unconscious itself is a rhetorician, seeking to attain its desires through forms of thought and speech. The analyst's interpretations offer a hopefully persuasive rhetoric that aims to convince the unconscious to modify its goals. In this process, patient and analyst exchange metaphors which in turn help them to adjust their thinking to one another (Cohen & Schermer, 2004).

Finally, Aristotle viewed art, poetry, and especially theater as forms of mimesis or imitation, representing life itself in illuminating ways. Similarly, Freud (1913j) viewed hysterical symptoms as "pantomime." In this sense, symptoms and behaviors are theater, a psychodramatic interplay of Eros and Thanatos.

The psychoanalytic situation itself is a stage or scene of drama, specifically of the transference. In this respect, the analyst at various times represents the Greek chorus, an oracle, or a prophet commentating on the hubris and inevitable downfall of the prideful patient as protagonist. Of course, it is the patient's ego that is the tragic hero. By inviting the patient to "free associate," the analyst is making a suggestion that he let his guard down and reduce conscious censorship, thereby giving freer play to illusion and desire. The patient then produces a story or narrative (Schafer, 1994) with the analyst serving as the other characters in the drama. The patient's symptoms and character structure gradually reveal themselves as elements in the drama. The analysis of the transference provides a plot summary and interpretation of the play, ultimately exposing and disclosing aspects previously unknown to the protagonist, just as Teiresias reveals to Oedipus his history of incest and parricide. The "cure" consists in the abreaction and working through of the emotional components of the new awareness. The patient moves from being the prideful protagonist in the play (in the transference and the consulting room) to becoming a humble member of the community, and as Breuer and Freud (1895d, p. 305) said, "transforming ... hysterical misery into common unhappiness".

Enter the mysteries into the psychoanalytic drama

Interpretation as a disclosure of psychic reality and its representations and as an aspect of mimesis and theater can thus be traced back to Aristotle and the Greeks. However, there is an aspect of the psychoanalytic tradition beginning with Freud that does not reflect Platonist and Aristotelean thought and appears as a ghostly presence. It is the realm of the mysterious, the numinous, the esoteric truths which reside in the unconscious along with the instincts. Well before the Socratics, the Eleusinian Mysteries (Eliade, 1981) provided cult-like rituals that took the initiates of pre-classical Greece into these darker realms. Indeed, it is possible that the rationalism of Plato and Aristotle were reactions to such practices and beliefs concerning the "underworld." In some ways, psychoanalysis constitutes such a journey into a nether world unfamiliar and shrouded in darkness. It is perhaps through immersion in this world that deep personality change comes about through Bion's "transformations in O," the mysterious "Other", the presence of which is known only in a trance-like state, in the "absence of memory, desire, and understanding."

Freud himself was not very familiar with pre-Socratic Greece or with other mystical traditions such as the contemplative Christian thought of the Middle Ages. He knew little about Hindu and Buddhist forms of meditation that lead to equally mysterious realms. However, it has been suggested that Freud did acquire some awareness of mysticism through the Judaic traditions of the Kabbalah and Talmudic exegesis, and that because of his cultural background and deep Jewish roots, these sources influenced him more than he himself knew or would admit. In any case, regardless of the degree of historical convergence, the parallels between Jewish exegesis and mysticism and psychoanalysis are important in understanding the full scope and implications of the interpretive process.

Talmudic exegesis and Kabbalah

Freud was a well-read individual, and his passion for the written word was partly the legacy of his Jewish upbringing. (As we shall see, the emphasis on writing also plays a major role in Derrida's understanding of psychoanalysis. Like Freud, Derrida was Jewish in an anti-Semitic social environment, and some scholars, such as Handelman (1982) have emphasized the important subterranean influence of Jewish teachings on both Freud and Derrida.)

It has been said that Judaism is a "book religion." The object of worship in the altar of a synagogue is an anomaly among religions. The revered Being is not personified in an icon, but rather represented by a book, a text: the Torah. Bakan (1958, pp. 246–252) suggests that in some circles, the Torah was considered the embodiment of the living messiah. Many other religions have sacred texts, and some of these writings are believed to be direct revelations of the divine, but *in Judaism the text itself is divine*. The truth revealed in that text is to be found not only in its manifest stories, laws, and principles. It is a living, growing, organic being, with infinite connections and possibilities, like a person, a language, a nervous system, a living God.

Free association, Talmudic exegesis, and "hypertext"

Freud's interest in the unexpected connections among thoughts, affects, and other components of mentation bears a relationship to Talmudic exegesis. In psychoanalysis, linkages among elements of the mind are revealed which are ordinarily selected out of awareness for reasons either of attention to a task, grammatical coherence, and/or censorship.

Through the suspension of such everyday filters of communication (free association), other previously concealed relationships and meanings within the patient's stream of consciousness reveal themselves to the discerning ear of the analyst. In modern computer webpage parlance, these implicit meanings are analogous to "hypertext," an invisible symbol system which includes both instructions for "formatting" the visible pages (grammar, consciousness) as well as links to additional content (derivatives, reconstructions). In computer science, hypertext has its own "markup" language, and similarly various authors have referred to the unconscious as a "forgotten language" (Fromm, 1957), an archaic and archetypal symbolic idiom of its own, the "language of the self" (Lacan, 1981). Talmudic exegesis is a towering and age-old example of hypertextual linking and searching. Similarly, psychoanalysis seeks hypertextual links in patients and their symptoms.

A comparison between Talmudic exegesis and psychoanalytic interpretations of free association is thus inevitable. In a certain way, Talmudic scholars anticipated the modern "stream of consciousness" technique. It was as if they were seeking to decipher the flow of thought of higher and lower powers hidden within a human-authored text. James Joyce, the exemplar of the stream of consciousness technique in literature, was profoundly interested in Jewish culture, and of course one of the two protagonists of *Ulysses*, Leopold Bloom, is a Jew. Basso (1982) suggested that Joyce, in his second and almost indecipherable *magnum opus*, *Finnegan's Wake*, combined modern literary experimentation with Talmudic and Kabbalistic influences. Both Joyce and Freud were modernists who recognized the profound value and significance of puns, word associations, allusions, and remote connections and references which some Talmudic scholars had endlessly pursued in the centuries before them.

As Bakan (1958) has pointed out, the evidence of Freud's familiarity with Jewish teachings is largely circumstantial, but it at least suggests that if he did not actively study the Torah and Kabbalah, he may have readily absorbed some of their ways of understanding. Freud grew up in Galicia, an area of Eastern Europe (then Austria, now part of the Ukraine), where both Talmud and Jewish mysticism were deeply ingrained in the culture. His father studied Talmudic teachings and, when Freud was already a successful physician, gave him a gift of his own Jewish bible (Kleinberg, 2010). There is no proof that Freud read this book or directly applied an understanding of Talmudic exegesis to his theory of unconscious meanings. However, regardless of the extent of Freud's direct familiarity with and use of it, certain aspects of Judaic exegesis bear such a resemblance to the psychoanalytic interpretive method that they deserve attention here.

Talmudic texts and the Freudian mind
as living, organic systems

Most interpretations of scriptures, at least in Western culture, focus on manifest content. Their purpose is to discern what is intended by a statement or story within the Bible, which until the Enlightenment period was held to have been of divine authorship. The functions of Christian biblical interpretation were to decide which lessons were to be learned and what God really meant the reader to understand. The texts were taken literally, and their precise meanings and implications were sorted out. In some ways, this approach parallels the way we commonly appreciate a poem or a painting as well as the everyday psychology that most of us use to grasp each others' intentions and purposes.

Talmudic interpretation includes such discussions of story and lessons, but in addition it regards the text as an organic whole in which all elements and features, no matter how incidental or remote in the writing itself, are interconnected. Above and beyond narrative and teachings, such seemingly incidental features as the placement of a word within a sentence, spaces and pauses in the text, the recurrence of particular letters and numbers, or the appearance of images, allegories, or personages at points in time in the narrative, are considered potentially of great significance. All the linguisitic and imagistic elements used in its construction—not just the narrative—are considered meaningful. It is as if the Divine Being is playing with the text in all sorts of ways that might not be immediately apparent, and the devout had better leave no stone unturned. In Judaism, the word G-d is hyphenated because to write or say His name compromises its holiness. To take the Torah as merely a linear, sequential narrative is to compromise its deeper meanings and resonances with the Almighty.

If one substitutes "Unconscious" for "G-d", the detective work involved in psychoanalytic interpretation is almost identical with Talmudic exegesis. The analyst listens with suspended attention to the patient's flow of associations, and certain deviations and anomalies within the conscious narrative register as significant. Everything is "grist for the mill:" a stutter, an unexpected pause, the rise or fall of an emotion, a word pun, a mispronunciation, an image, a random recollection, and so on. To paraphrase Hamlet, "The text is the thing wherein I'll catch the conscience of the king." The conscious subject or ego fades into the background as a larger and truer world of living experience discloses itself through the details, fabric, and flow of embodied speech.

Talmudic exegesis is the prototype of the interpretive strategy found in the use of free association accompanied by the analyst's commentary. There, meanings are not merely explicated and elaborated; they are decoded by searching for various forms of order within apparently random occurrences. Other, implicit meanings are discovered and uncovered through this process of decoding. Some of them take on significance and truth value such that they themselves become part of the therapy, the teachings, and the tradition. On an individual level, they constitute the patient's dynamics. On a generic level, they constitute psychoanalytic theory itself.

A closer analogy than Talmudic exegesis to the *in situ* development of analytic insight would be hard to find. If we were to screen out the various theoretical formulations that psychoanalysts use to explain events—what Freud called the metapsychological "scaffolding," implying that it is a useful structure that can be dismantled—what we would observe in sessions are a series of "commentaries" by the analyst of the patient's productions, on the basis of which the patient modifies his "text" through reflective understanding, eventually leading to a new version of the "text" (balance of forces in the patient's psyche) which patient and analyst agree is more truthful and adaptive than the original one. The seemingly "free" associations of the patient turn out to have their own determinism of a primitive psychosomatic nature. It is the occurrence of insight that allows for the true freedom that is given by emotional maturity. This emphasis on maturity emerging from investigation matches well with what Bakan (1958, pp. 246–252) calls "man as Torah."

Depth psychology, Talmud, and Kabbalah

Another feature of Talmudic exegesis is the notion of depth. The full history of depth psychology has yet to be written, and the conventional wisdom is that it began with Freud's probing of hidden aspects of the mind. Some ascribe the origins of depth psychology and the concept of the unconscious to thinkers such as Schelling and Fichte a few decades earlier than Freud (cf. Bowie, 2010). Yet mankind has always had an intuitive notion of inner depth since ancient times, appearing in various studies of human character, from those discussed within the Old Testament to the writings of Thucydides on up to Shakespeare, Cervantes, and Dostoevsky. Human character, will, and choice reveal themselves in layers, and each layer comes closer to a core that governs the nature and actions of an individual. There have been allusions to such a layering of the mind and personality in philosophy, religious teachings, and in the science of psychology that commenced in the nineteenth century. What Freud added was a specific method and set of working principles for uncovering and studying the layers, for making depth soundings into the "deep sea" realm of the unconscious.

Ages ago, however, interpreters of the Talmud had worked out such a set of principles for understanding the layers contained in the Torah and related teachings. Although notions of psychological and/ or spiritual depth can be found in other religious traditions, such as *The Yoga-Sutra of Patanjali* in the Hindu tradition, as well as in alchemy, witchcraft, and other esoteric practices, few traditions of understanding are as systematic and complex as that of Talmudic exegesis.

The Talmudic approach to layers of depth is summarized in a formulaic way by the acronym PaRDeS, suggesting that the deepest, most sought after layer is "paradise" (compare to Freud's "wish fulfillment" and "desire.") (See Rotenberg, 1991, for a depiction of PaRDes and its potential use in psychotherapy.) The acronym stands for the following four levels of understanding:

PESHAT: the "plain" ("simple") or direct meaning, that is, a literal understanding of the text taken at face value.

REMEZ: suggestions of deep allegorical hidden or symbolic meaning beyond the literal sense.

DERASH: from the Hebrew darash, to inquire or seek, the comparative meaning, as given through similar occurrences.
and

SOD: the "secret" mysterious or mystical meaning, as given through inspiration or revelation.

The first, *Peshat* is comparable to the "manifest content," the patient's explicit narrative. Even at that level, there can be diverse interpretations of the same narrative, depending on how one understands particular words as well as inflections, gestures, and other paralinguistic features. This is the level of the ego, and many analysts work with their patients at this manifest level for extended periods of time, fleshing out the subtleties of ego functioning and defense.

The remaining three levels together constitute the equivalent of "latent content" at increasingly deep and concealed levels. *Remez*— allegorical or symbolic meaning—seeks implications of metaphorical significance. In the dream at the beginning of this chapter, the patient used the observation window as a metaphor for the disconnection between herself and her parents. This insight, her own, helped her pay more attention to the significance of interpersonal relations as they related to her feelings of anxiety and insecurity.

Derash is the equivalent of the analyst's discovery of unconscious meanings through discernment of connections and details of free associations, dreams, and reminiscences. Regarding Oedipus, it was Freud who delivered the then astonishing revelation that parricidal and incestuous wishes occur regularly in the minds of children. This level, in both the Talmud and psychoanalysis, is somewhat esoteric and reaches into the extremes of the demoniacal and the divine. *Derash* is the level of the repressed unconscious and must be inferred through a painful process of self-examination.

Finally, the deepest level of *Sod*, the mystical dimension, was of great interest to Jung and has more recently come into object relations theory through the work of Bion, Eigen, and others. In some Jewish traditions, this level includes supernatural occurrences, as it also did for Jung and of course the Christian believer's literal understanding of the Resurrection. However, in Bion, Eigen, postmodern thought, and some meditation practices, this level can refer to transformative experiences without the supernatural implications.

In the Oedipus story, such a depth of meaning characteristic of *Sod* arises in the encounter with the Sphinx, as well as in the various prophesies given to Oedipus. Something other-worldly, puzzling, futuristic, or "not present" is taking place. Then there is Oedipus's self-transformation, his absolute shame and humiliation at discovering his heinous crimes, his reduction to nothingness and alienation from society, his ultimate acceptance of his limited self, and his forgiveness by the kings and the gods. Oedipus's shame on learning of his incest and parricide is so traumatic as to be beyond words and understanding. It is the mystery of the incomprehensible and intolerable. Similarly, the mystery of *Sod* is about the "beyond," the "wordless, formless infinite," the inexpressible, the wholly Other, and nothingness. Bion, as well as Eigen (1998), posited this level as the root of the unconscious, while others regard it as pure fiction. As it does among theologians, the acceptance or rejection of the mysterious, *Sod*, as either supernatural (outside or beyond the order of nature) or transformational (transcendent, ineffable, existential) marks a divide among analysts that no amount of logic or case material can reconcile. It marks the difference between rational and mystical world views.

Naturphilosophie: *the hermeneutical turn in German romanticism*

To summarize, Freud's *The Interpretation of Dreams* and his early forays into psychaoanalytic treatment utilized insights from ancient times to develop his method of interpretation of the mind, the self, and the unconscious. The heritages of Plato and Aristotle and of Talmudic exegesis provided a legacy of antiquity that presaged psychoanalytic interpretive methodology. The former is concerned with the nature of reality, desire, representation, and values, and the latter with living, organic connections among elements of a text and their arrangement in layers of increasing depth.

The seventeeth- to eighteenth-century Age of Enlightenment drew upon Plato and Aristotle to advance a rational-empirical scientific view of the world. During that time, interpretive methods were dismissed as literary speculations, in contrast to the analysis of fact and reason, from which all truth would become evident. In a sense, Freud was a stepchild of the Enlightenment, seeking to conquer the mind as a scientist conquers nature. However, Freud was also born into the intellectual world of German romanticism, which revived a humanist and literary understanding of life and nature (also, not incidentally having precedents in Greek antiquity), questioning the relevance of cold scientific abstraction to pulsating life and individuality and proposing a new perspective, *Naturphilosophie*, where the humanities and sciences flowed together. In this new intellectual climate, hermeneutics became a valued endeavor working in tandem with the disciplines of philosophy, philology (the study of language), literature, and history to explain and understand the lived life, *Erlebnis*. Some of those ideas were anticipated a century earlier, in another country, Italy, by Giambattista Vico, a multidisciplinary thinker who questioned many aspects of the Enlightenment.

German romanticism played a major role in the development of psychoanalysis and modern thought. It is to that era of the flowering of hermeneutics that we now turn attention.

CHAPTER THREE

Romantic era hermeneutics

In addition to the Greek and Talmudic influences on Freud's interpretive method, a "third stream" of influence emerged in Europe during the nineteenth century: hermeneutical philosophy as an organized scholarly discipline. During that time, means were sought to explain and understand human experience that were different from the methods of the natural sciences. While natural phenomena could be conceptualized as cause and effect relationships among events and objects in the universe, the Romantics believed that human life called for its own methods of interpreting experience and expression manifest in language, the arts, individual biographies, religion, and sociopolitical institutions. Human relationships and creative productions are based on shared meanings, and it became imperative to develop principles of meanings and intentions as distinct from the cause and effect "bodies in motion" of the natural sciences. The Romantic search for human universals became the art and science of philosophical hermeneutics.

Philosophical hermeneutics as a discipline congealed from other areas of study such as theology, law, history, literature, and philology, the study of language. Until then, each of these disciplines had its own interpretive principles and rules. For instance, biblical interpretation was mostly based on the *telos* of the advent of Christ as the criterion for understanding and resolving problematics within Old and New Testament texts. Interpretation of secular law has always maintained an evolving set of rules applying to legislation, judicial decisions, and precedent. Literary criticism utilized notions of dramatic action, character development, and plot going back to Aristotle. Interpretations of political and historical events were based on understandings of power, conflict, commerce, and the necessities of life. Even today, each of these fields maintains its own principles for making sense of its subject matter and resolving differences among scholars.

Psychoanalysis as a specific discipline and a general interpretive discourse

Similarly, psychoanalysis formulated its own interpretive principles and strategies as a specialty within psychiatry, formulating unique concepts, for example, regarding the analysis of transference (cf. Gill, 1983; Greenson, 1967). These technical procedures specific to psychoanalysis, however, are in themselves insufficient to explain the phenomena of the consulting room. I am reminded of a remark attributed to Phyllis Greenacre when she was asked to define transference. She responded, "If you put two people in a room for a long enough time, something will happen between them." The development of transference is a complex interpersonal process that defies formulaic explanation. It is left to the listening process, the life experience and cultural background of both analyst and patient, and other individual and situational factors to decide what dynamics are of greatest importance and that highlight a particular analytic inquiry. There is considerable room within psychoanalytic strategy and technique for the cross-disciplinary interpretive understanding of German romanticism which in fact reached a peak of interest during Freud's lifetime.

Freud was not schooled in German hermeneutics as such. However, his general knowledge of philosophers such as Schopenhauer, Kant, and Nietzsche, as well as his lifelong interest in history, literature, and the life sciences, would have led him to assimilate some of its ideas. Freud's frame of reference was empirical science. Nevertheless, the Romantic era hermeneuticists and their views are so directly relevant to psychoanalysis that they deserve more attention. Indeed, a hypothetical "compleat" manual of psychoanalytic interpretation would be rich with citations and references to these works. One function of this book is hopefully to integrate psychoanalytic theory and practice with the wider legacy of European philosophical hermeneutics, the attempt to discover the "first principles" that link interpretive method to human understanding as ontology (the study of being and becoming), epistemology (the foundations of knowledge), and ethics. We will shortly begin a tour of the interpretive studies and philosophical hermeneutics of the Romantic era, again with emphasis on its relevance to psychoanalysis. However, before we do that, it is worth calling attention to the Neopolitan lawyer, historian, and philosopher Giovanni Battista (Giambattista) Vico (1668–1774), an early critic of Descartes and Enlightenment philosophy.

Vico's "verum ipsum factum"

The milestones in the history and development of Western hermeneutics are difficult to pinpoint, in part because it emerged as a counterposition to the dominant natural sciences which regarded interpretation and exegesis as occult arts. To this day, hermeneutics lacks departmental status within universities (although it sometimes merits a position as a section within such departments as literature, religion, and philosophy). So it is difficult to say exactly who initiated such studies. It is possible to argue, however, that the "forefather" of modern hermeneutics was the Neopolitan political philosopher, rhetorician, historian, and jurist Giovanni Battista Vico. His *verum ipsum factum* principle questioned the prevailing idea of Descartes that truth and reality are discerned by the mind through reason. Vico contended that the mind itself was a product of human existence. He offered an approach to the truth of human experience that was guided by interpretive methodology that included the non-rational and affective sides of life so important to Freud.

Vico's *verum ipsum factum* principle, first formulated in 1710 as part of his *De Italorum Sapientia* (Vico, 1710) controversially stated that truth is not, as Descartes held, discerned through rigorous observation and logic. Rather, truth is created and invented in the context of human civilization. Said Vico, *"The criterion and rule of the true is to have made it.* Accordingly, our clear and distinct idea of the mind cannot be a criterion of the mind itself, still less of other truths. *For while the mind perceives itself, it does not make itself"* (Costelloe, 2012; italics added). This cryptic statement requires explanation. It was Vico's way of affirming, as did Freud, two centuries later, the importance of the irrational and paradoxical in human life. It also anticipated modern existential philosophy, offering a glimmer of Heidegger's *Dasein* or "being-in-the-world" as a precondition for thought, and Sartre's dictum, "existence precedes essence."

Mind as reason vs. mind as human invention

For Vico, mind and truth are "made" in a manner analogous to a work of architecture in the process of creating the accoutrements of civilization, a decidedly modern view that has much later echoes in Marxism, Erich Fromm's socially-based psychoanalysis, existentialism, and social constructivism.

As conceived by Descartes, the mind or "cogito" ("I think; therefore I am") arrives at knowledge through reason. For Descartes, mind is the "I," the self, the "eye" that perceives and understands truth and pursues a logico-mathematical ideal out of which human existence ("I am") develops. So mind and reason are the basis of human endeavor. But, for Vico, it is the reverse: the mind itself is the product of social, economic, and political developments that are co-created in dialogue, customs, history, and institutions. The powerful social and historical forces that affect human life and thought are pre-logical, yet they inform all knowledge and awareness. Thus, an interpretive understanding of the totality of human phenomena is necessary to arrive at truth "as made." In his major work, *The First New Science*, Vico (1725) outlined a science of human affairs, institutions, and history which aimed at understanding truth through the historical development of language, customs, and the social order.

Vico thus anticipated a number of Romantic and modern developments which would emphasize language, myth, and literature as major components of anthropology, biography, religious texts, and other humanist studies. He thus took knowledge to the social, historical, and institutional levels, a focus which later resurfaced in late Romantic philosopher Wilhelm Dilthey's concept of *Erlebnis* (Makkreel, 2011), the experience of events of the world and community through which an individual's life becomes meaningful. Still later, Heidegger, drawing on Dilthey's work, deepened *Erlebnis* into *Dasein*, being-in-the-world.

Such ideas were articulated in nascent form by Vico. In psychoanalysis, Freud's view that the unconscious has its own internal logic and mode of thinking echoes Vico's notion that thoughts are "made" to include non-rational elements (fantasy). Freud's use of archaeology as a metaphor for the unconscious resonates with Vico's ideas about civilizations building upon the past. Jung's "collective unconscious" is consistent with Vico's thesis that the mind is co-created over time by a process of cultural evolution.

Because they represented a countercultural development to the dominant "Age of Reason," Vico's theories were unpopular in the years that followed his death, but nevertheless they were disseminated among some philosophers, writers, and literary scholars. For example, the poet Coleridge, who was transitional between Enlightenment and Romantic sentiments, became interested in and disseminated Vico's ideas (Costelloe, 2012). Importantly for our discourse, Vico's ideas migrated north to influence some of the key figures in German romanticism such as Goethe, Schelling, and Herder (Berlin, 1976). In turn, German romanticism, culminating in Dilthey's and Nietzsche's thrusts into the modern era, had a strong impact on Freud and psychoanalysis. Herder's interpretive principles in particular are so clearly enumerated that they could easily be adapted as a handbook on interpretation for aspiring psychoanalysts.

Romantic era hermeneutics

Hermeneutics achieved the status of an academic discipline during the late Enlightenment era and the onset of romanticism. For the Enlightenment, science was the source and prototype of all truth and progress. For the Romantics, science, by reducing everything to a set of classifications, machines, and equations, diluted the rich complexity of both human experience and the natural world, which they vowed could and should thrive in a harmonious relationship with one another (think of modern ecology). The new outlook emphasizing individuality, wisdom, and emotionality took increasing hold in Europe, most notably in the world view of German romanticism called *Naturphilosophie* (Richards, 2004). As anticipated by Herder and propounded by Schelling and Goethe, *Naturphilosophie* sought to reconcile human consciousness, intention, emotionality, and free will with the deterministic struggle among the blind forces of nature. Freud was born into such a Romantic world view, and it is likely that his felicitous movement between science and humanism was a product of this legacy, which also laid the basis for many of the intellectual developments of twentieth-century modernism.

There are so many Romantic era thinkers associated with these developments that it would be impossible to consider all of them. I will focus here on two thinkers who steadfastly took up the problems of interpretive methodology: Johann Gottfried von Herder (1744–1803) and Friedrich Schleiermacher (1768–1834). Again, many of their contemporaries presented similar formulations, and scholars debate who initially conceived them. Importantly, the romanticists Schelling and Fichte anticipated some of Freud's thinking about the unconscious, but it was Herder and Schleiermacher who developed specific formulations about the interpretive process itself. We can look to them for some concepts and principles that bear a significant relationship to psychoanalytic interpretation.

Herder

Herder, a stepchild of the Enlightenment who was especially influenced by Kant, appreciated the importance of facts combined with logic (Kant's "synthetic a priori" things in themselves, of which Bion made great use; see Chapter Twelve), but felt that Kant's theory of knowledge was inadequate to grasp human expression in language, art, literature, and culture. Moreover, taking seriously the Enlightenment emphasis on democracy, Herder sought a philosophy which was relevant and useful not just for philosophers but for the people in general, a universalist sentiment that later informs Gadamer's hermeneutics viewed as practical understanding (Aristotle's "*phronesis*"). Herder's thinking was subtle and sophisticated, in some ways anticipating Freud. Both of them struggled in different ways with the problem of knowing another person. By considering how a representative of one culture (context, situation, and life history) could understand and interpret the mind and experience of another, Herder laid an important grounding for the social sciences.

To the extent that psychoanalysis consists of the mature part of one individual comprehending the primitive inner world of another, it encounters the same anthropological concerns that Herder articulated, even when the two parties have similar cultural backgrounds. For example, a child's "understanding" of parental intercourse (the primal scene) is so markedly different from an adult's concept of sex that it must at first be regarded as a kind of foreign artifact. For a child, "sex" may mean a concatenation of noise and struggle that threatens his inner security, rather than a playful intimacy that culminates in ecstasy. For Herder, a humanist who was yet steeped in science, such differences and details were of great import.

Herder considered language the basis of all understanding, and so he felt that by penetrating another's language usage, one could in some sense come to "know" him from the "inside," as it were. This view is consistent with the emphasis in psychoanalysis on the flow of verbal associations and its value in the exploration of the inner life. In addition, both Herder's and Freud's understanding of language included preverbal aspects of sensation, perception, and the body.

The problems that Herder took up were graphically illustrated in analytic treatment by a patient who spoke excellent English but who dreamt in the language of his childhood. An additional layer of interpretation had to be added, namely the connotations of the words of the patient's dreams, which could only be approximated in a treatment conducted in English in a way that paralleled translations of literary works. The patient offered the translations, and the therapist asked questions about the nuances of meaning. In exactly that manner, Herder wanted to see how one could grasp the meaning of texts in a way that reflected not only the literal definitions of words but also the inner emotional world of the text's author in a manner that was not contaminated by the assumptive world of the interpreter as it was embedded in his own language and history.

Herder challenged the "folk psychology" belief that people understand one another "naturally" through their common humanity. Freud also questioned this naïve assumption by looking for meanings beyond the awareness of the conscious ego. Herder believed that the necessity to explore and interpret deeper meanings stemmed from the fact that the interpreter and object of interpretation (literary work, cultural artifact, or another person) were *radically different* from one another. Resonance or empathy between individuals or cultures was, for him, an entrance-way to understanding, but it was important to look at the context as well as its details. This issue became crucial in psychoanalysis when Kohut (1977, pp. 252–261) proposed that empathy rather than "experience distant" interpretation was the way to understand the patient's self, in effect a reversal of Herder that we will take up in greater detail in Chapter Eleven. Indeed, the expanding psychoanalytic literature on attunement, mentalization, and other intersubjective processes harks back to issues first raised by Herder.

For Herder, a disciplined inquiry into the "radical difference" between observer and observed was required for true understanding of the subject. Herder would, for example, reject any idea that the mother understands her child or the analyst his patient through a natural affinity or intuition. Rather, he would argue that true understanding comes through a process of careful introspection, questioning, and dialogue. For example, the mother does not intuitively recognize what her child wants, but arrives at the correct assessment of his or her needs through multiple encounters with the child until a common "vocabulary" of gesture and facial expressions develops between them. Attunement, in this view, is more of a readiness to attend to details of the child's communications than an immediate grasp of the child's need states. Similarly, the analyst's awareness of the patient's inner world is not simply an empathetic response of one person to another's experience. Rather, empathy serves only to bring out certain features and initiate a further inquiry into the meaning of the patient's discourse and the gradual construction by the analyst of a "working model" of the patient's inner world.

> Thus, a patient was speaking in a nonchalant intellectualized way about the conflicts in her family during childhood when suddenly her body became frozen and tears welled up in her eyes. The analyst, via empathy, correctly intuited that she was experiencing grief. However, further inquiry suggested that what was grief for the patient was not the simple sorrow that the analyst felt via empathy in the moment. Through subsequent investigation, it became clear that the patient's grief was laden with anxiety, confusion, and hatred. Her grief was saturated with ambivalence, while the analyst's empathy was not. Herder was one of the first thinkers to point to such complexities of human understanding. His impact on psychoanalysis can be seen in Freud's searching inquiries into meanings, always examining the details.

Interpretation as a process of "feeling one's way in"

Herder called such a disciplined investigation *Einfühlung*, "feeling one's way in," a complex process of reaching the core meanings inherent in the text and its authorship (Frei, 1980, pp. 184–192). The word

Einfühlung means empathy, but for Herder it was the sort of empathy that develops through extensive inquiry and immersion, not simply affective resonance.

Under the rubric of *Einfühlung* Herder discussed five components of discovering or "feeling one's way into" meanings (Forster, 2007). His guidelines and cautionary notes bear directly upon psychoanalytic interpretation.

Radical differences

First, as noted above, for Herder, there is a radical difference between what is "in" the mentality of the interpreter versus that which is inherent in the "mind" of the subject being investigated. The difference is "radical" in the sense that the subject's meaning is understandable only within a context different from that of the interpreter. For example, language usage and historical context might differ between the two. This radical difference is what makes interpretation necessary in the first place. The relationship of radical difference between the interpreter and the original subject or text has formed a major preoccupation of modern hermeneutics. Here, Herder anticipated ideas of Levinas about alterity (cf. Chapter Four), the impenetrability of the other.

Achieving a full, imaginative reproduction of the subject's experience

Second, from such considerations, an additional principle emerges: in order to "feel one's way into" the subject, the details of the latter's communications as well as the historical and social context must be carefully examined.

Third, the interpreter must achieve within himself an imaginative reproduction of his (perceptual and affective) sensations. It is not sufficient to have an intellectual grasp of the experience. The interpreter (in our case, the analyst) must understand it as if he had undergone it himself, from the inside, as it were. Patients are the first to tell the analyst when he lacks such an understanding. The value of an interpretation stems not only from its surface accuracy, but from the analyst's recognition of the connotations and nuances of the experience. Without it, the analyst can make serious errors in responsiveness, and patients know this. Imaginative reproduction of another's experience is an intuitive process to which both analyst and patient have access.

Awareness of emotional bias

Fourth, according to Herder, hostility or other emotional bias or reactivity towards or overidentification with the subject of understanding can result in a distorted interpretation, a response which in psychoanalysis is called countertransference. Herder anticipated what would make psychoanalysis a "dangerous method," namely, the analyst's own personal complexes.

Internalizing the experience of the subject

The fifth and culminating stage of Herder's method is *Einfühlung* or "feeling one's way in." He urged that the interpreter strive to develop his grasp of the various details to the point where it achieves within himself something akin to the immediacy and reflexivity that it has taken on for the subject, so that the understanding takes the form of a personal experience and acquires the status of phenomenological awareness. This is an extension of the third principle of imaginative reproduction. For Herder, understanding is not a mere intellectual exercise. Rather, the interpreter must experience on an emotional and personal level what it is to live in the world of that which he is trying to grasp. (Think of the Stanislavski method of acting, which requires total immersion in the character.) When this is achieved, what is called empathy takes on a much deeper significance, amounting to enduring the experience on an existential level. (This summary of Herder's method is derived from Forster, 2007.)

Few psychoanalysts achieve the level of immersion and mutuality required to "feel one's way into" the other by Herder's standards. Beyond attending to complex details, the analyst must listen directly over many hours to a suffering human being. This places a great emotional strain on the analyst which Herder as a philosopher and scientist did not have to face. In addition, under such conditions, it is very difficult to separate authentic engagement from countertransference. To suffer with the patient's severe trauma, for example, may be an act of moral courage and heartfelt care, but it may also reflect the therapist's inability to maintain healthy boundaries and differences, creating only confusion in the treatment. For instance, a patient, Mel, had witnessed the injuries and deaths of members of his combat unit. His descriptions were graphic and painful. The therapist genuinely suffered as he tried to "feel his way into" these excruciating experiences. His efforts to reproduce the patient's experience within himself were appreciated by Mel and helped him feel supported and understood. But the therapist had to be careful not to undergo the disorientation and fragmentation that had also been Mel's experience. Mel appreciated the therapist's containment more than he might have had the therapist broken down in the session. Herder's fifth principle is that of total immersion in the subject. However, it is balanced by his caution about overidentification. In addition, Herder was considering interpretation of subjects of biographies, texts, speech, and artifacts for which he did not have medical and moral responsibility.

One can see from this brief exposition that, in his five stages of interpretation, culminating in "feeling one's way in," Herder ventured far beyond conventional interpretive methods that relied on facts and figures, historical events, and consistencies of discourse. These were important to him, but he sought a deeper level of psychological and biographical understanding of human phenomena. His methodology of *Einfühlung* possesses many of the features inherent in the psychoanalysis of character and personality disorders. Although he did not quite offer a "theory of personality" as did Freud, he explored such aspects of psychology as sensation, perception, language, and the relationship between language and cognition. Moreover, like Freud, Herder did not regard science and humanism as opposing positions. Rather, seeking a bridge between natural science and human understanding, Herder held that ideas (cognitions, images) are attached to physical energy and force (Forster, 2007), a notion that anticipated Freud's ideas of psychic energy and cathexis. Modern thought in general owes a great deal to Herder's pioneering efforts to understand experience and dialogue from the "inside" and from the standpoint of existence as deriving its meaning from struggle and social context.

Schleiermacher

Schleiermacher's life and work emerged soon after Herder's at the height of German romanticism, of which he is considered a central figure. He made a great contribution to intellectual history when, as a theologian, he challenged established authority and held that biblical and scriptural texts were best understood in terms of their human authorship and therefore subject to the same interpretive vicissitudes as any literary work. His view of religion and scripture as human experience set the stage for the psychological understanding of religious experience of William James (1902), Freud, and Jung. Arguably, Freud's *The Future of an Illusion* (1927c) could not have been written without Schleiermacher's earlier understanding of religion as a human process.

Schleiermacher's hermeneutics overlaps considerably with Herder's, although there are significant differences between them. For example, Schleiermacher held that thought could not occur without language, while Herder had advanced the more resilient view that language is a mode of thought, but cognition is possible without language. Here, we will focus on a specific contribution of Schleiermacher's which had a lasting impact on hermeneutics as well as on Freud's approach to interpretation: the holistic understanding of meaning and its correlative idea, the "hermeneutic circle."

Interpretation as a holistic activity means that "Any given piece of text needs to be interpreted in light of the whole text to which it belongs, and both need to be interpreted in light of the broader language in which they are written, their larger historical context, a broader pre-existing genre, the author's whole corpus, and the author's overall psychology" (Forster, 2002). Modern biographical and historical studies are so indebted to this principle that it is difficult to believe that before Schleiermacher, scriptures, lives, and literary works were scrutinized in a linear fashion, often in chronological sequence, with little attention to context, a practice which today would seem dull and boring. Schleiermacher also freed the interpretive method from disciplinary compartmentalization. In doing so, he expanded the scope of interpretation to include widening circles of understanding from the here-and-now to the historical, from the individual to the group and society, and from the immediate details to the contextual frame of reference.

The hermeneutic circle

In this way, Schleiermacher formulated the notion of the "hermeneutic circle" (Forster, 2002) which has influenced many further advances in philosophy and interpretive theory, notably those of Dilthey and Heidegger. (The origin of the phrase "hermeneutic circle" has been variously attributed to all three of them.) Interpretation requires a circular loop from the particular to the general and back again until an interpretation consistent with both the parts and the whole is found. Thus, for example, in studying the life and work of Freud himself, a biographer might suggest that Freud's ideas on the death instinct in *Beyond the Pleasure Principle* (1920g) were partly a function of his own recent experiences with mortality and death. Biographical evidence could include the recent death of Freud's daughter Sophie, the ravages of World War I, and his growing old himself. The hermeneutic circle is then completed by going back to Freud's writing itself to see if it is consistent with the text. There, Freud refers to his grandson's spool game, suggesting thoughts about being a grandfather and the importance of family. He mentions war neuroses. He acknowledges contradicting his youthful theory about the primacy of the pleasure principle. The circular loop between the text and the biographical data is repeated until a coherent picture develops. (Curiously, in *Beyond the Pleasure Principle*, the circularity between Freud the person and Freud the scientist is so enmeshed that its "true" meaning still eludes us and is frequently subject to reinterpretation. The incompleteness and elusiveness of interpretive understanding is a matter we will take up in the discussion of Derrida, Chapter Four.)

At his best, Freud himself proceeded in the way of the hermeneutic circle, carefully examining the minutest details of a case, and then considering the broader situation and context, and vice versa. His analysis of his own dream of "Irma's injection" (Freud, 1900a, pp. 106–121) illustrates how he first focused on a detail in the dream, namely that in treating "Irma" he feared he had made a medical error. He then related it to a real event, namely his colleague Fliess's actual misdiagnosis of a patient. Finally, he invoked his theory that dreams represent the fulfillment of a wish, to interpret the dream as a wishful denial of his own guilt feelings, displacing them onto Fliess. By going in a circular loop from the dream detail to the associated memories to theoretical concepts, and then back to the details, Freud sought to avoid both the Scylla of formulaic symbolic meanings of the "dream book" and the Charybdis of "wild analysis." Of course, the reader must decide whether in this and other instances Freud provided strong evidence for his interpretation, or whether he "injected" it into the discourse as a fulfillment of his wish to prove his theory! In a nutshell, this is the central limitation of the interpretive method. It is not a method of proof but of understanding.

Ideally, psychoanalysts in practice proceed in a similar circular manner between the particular, the contextual, and back again.

For example, in work with a patient, Marla, who suffered from compulsive overeating and obesity, the therapist, following Marla's free associations, shifted his focus from the specifics of her current eating patterns to feelings of shame about her body, and then to ever-widening current and historical contexts such as her early experiences of gratification and deprivation with her mother, her tendency to please the analyst, and the norms of her culture of origin which stereotyped women as impulsive and hedonistic. Then the role of Marla's father became increasingly clear as a man who made his daughter into his self-satisfying indulgent mistress. In time, a consistent dynamic picture emerged of an Elektra complex of incestuous enmeshment reinforced by cultural norms and mother's submissiveness. The therapist's reflective inquiry between the diverse specific and wider dimensions had the ego-strengthening benefit of helping Marla to grasp the relationship between historical circumstances in which she was an unwilling victim versus current opportunities where she could make healthy choices, thereby giving her greater freedom of movement in her life. The interpretive cycle of parts and whole, text and context, is the legacy of Schleiermacher, and psychoanalysis is part of that heritage.

Circle or Spiral?

The hermeneutic circle begs the fundamental question—raised by modern philosophers—of whether the circle is self-limiting or ever-expanding, whether we are eternally caught up in a tautological, recurrent cycle of understanding that cannot transcend itself, or whether we develop ever-widening circles of understanding that lead to growth and transformation. To accommodate the latter, Strasser (1985) preferred the phrase "hermeneutic spiral," an evolving cycle of experience, expression, and understanding that overcomes solipsism and tautology and leads towards greater understanding through ongoing dialogue. Schleiermacher, despite his use of the circle, very likely intended such an implication of growth and development, whereas Nietzsche's concept of "eternal recurrence" (1882, sections 285, 341) implied a repetitive loop of eternal rebirth. The repetition-compulsion also can be likened to a Nietzschian circularity from which escape or change is difficult or impossible, except that such repetition is typically regarded as a symptom not an inevitable part of life and understanding.

Thus, Herder, Schleiermacher, and their contemporaries guided hermeneutics beyond disciplinary formulas into a resilient but rigorous human understanding of literature, history, art, and religion as phenomena embedded in language and thought, distinct but not entirely apart from explanations and theories of causation in the natural world. They also considered that hermeneutics could address philosophical problems such as the nature of knowledge. And they gave a thrust to interpretive investigations of personality, biographical narratives, and psychological phenomena. For them, hermeneutics afforded a cross-disciplinary view of an investigative process leading to more rigorous understanding of human experience.

It is likely that psychoanalysis in part owes its existence to German Romantic hermeneutics, which provided the zeitgeist in which Freud conceived and wrote *The Interpretation of Dreams* (1900a) and which helped him to think of dreams and the mind in an interpretive, biographical, and developmental manner. As Freud wrote this groundbreaking work, a major shift in the tectonics of hermeneutical understanding was about to happen. With the emergence of Husserl, Heidegger, and other twentieth-century thinkers, life itself came to be regarded as hermeneutical, that is, embedded in meaning. Hermeneutics would no longer be just the scholarly, disciplined study of meaning, but the very process by which human existence unfolds. This change was presaged and fostered by the philosopher Wilhelm Dilthey (1833–1911), a pivotal figure who negotiated the transition between the old and the new.

Dilthey

Dilthey was a historian, psychologist, sociologist, and philosopher who held Hegel's chair in philosophy at the University of Berlin. His life spanned much of the nineteenth and the beginning of the twentieth century, so he was positioned historically to facilitate the transition between Romantic and modern hermeneutics. He was steeped in and yet critical of the work of Schleiermacher as well as knowledgeable about Kant and Hegel. Dilthey's own thinking evolved over time, and his later ideas doubted his own prior thinking that is still attributed to him. Therefore, although he had a major impact and influence, it is difficult to assign a specific philosophical "school" to him. His thinking, however, initiated an important evolution from hermeneutics as a scholarly discipline to a broader perspective of meaning as definitive of human existence.

It is this development which is of utmost importance to European continental philosophy. Both Husserl and Heidegger acknowledged a debt to Dilthey, although with a critical eye as well. Freud knew little if anything about him, even though Dilthey, like Freud, grappled with the problems of depth psychology and human understanding (Tauber, 2010, p. 93).

Explanation vs. understanding

Steeped in both Enlightenment and Romantic thinking, Dilthey strove to synthesize the ideas of Herder and Schleiermacher with the very different Enlightenment views of Kant into a comprehensive scientific-humanistic view of knowledge. In order to accomplish this objective, he highlighted the already present dichotomy between a) causality in the natural sciences, and b) the interpretive exploration of historical and social intentionality and intersubjectivity in the humanities and social sciences. He framed this difference as that between *explanation* of causal relationships and *understanding* of historical, linguistic, and contextual experiences. (Again, psychoanalytic interpretations veer between these two poles of scientific explanation and intersubjective interpretive understanding, and this duality is the very problem and promise that has followed psychoanalysis since its inception.) Dilthey drew a very sharp line between the two, but at the same time claimed, as did Herder, a scientific status for the methods of the humanities, but quite unlike Herder, making the surprising assertion that the knowledge of human experience was more certain and direct than that of the natural world. Most of us feel that self-knowledge and interpersonal relations are far more confusing and complicated than navigating the physical world about us! Dilthey's assertion appears at first to violate common sense and scientific sensibility: a ball rolling down a hill is surely easier to understand than a person falling in love! However, by "certain and direct" Dilthey meant "immediacy to experience," which makes perfect sense. We all "know" what it is to fall in love, while the gravitational calculus requires a great deal of study. As a modern exemplification of Dilthey's emphasis on the immediacy of human experience, Merleau-Ponty's (1976) embodied phenomenology of perception has a similar emphasis on subjective experience as the natural starting point for understanding (see Chapter Eight).

Detachment vs. immersion

Dilthey's unusual formulation of the equal truth value of natural science and human understanding, which was radical at the time, proved to be philosophically conservative in the long run, as it advanced the formalized notion of the interpretive method as "research" akin to science. He attempted with only moderate success to integrate the material world of science and the spiritual nature of human experience, placing interpretive work on a methodical par with scientific investigation, which was also Freud's intention. In this respect, Dilthey maintained that interpretive work, like scientific method, took place on a transcendent plane detached from the concrete phenomena under study. Twentieth-century thinkers would question such detachment about the human condition. Yet, paradoxically, Dilthey developed a progressive understanding of truth and being that fostered the development of phenomenology and existentialism.

Facticity and Erlebnis

In this respect, Dilthey said that interpretation of human experience is made possible and necessary by its "facticity." That is, the human world, as distinct from the "blind forces" of the physico-chemical universe, is already and always impregnated with meaning and intentionality. The human world is not abstract, but is one of lived experience, *Elrlebnis*. Human life is lived historically in the context of time (Moran, 2000, p. 276). Husserl, with some critical adjustments, later used the phrase "life world" for the phenomenologically inherent nature of time/place/ intention in which all human subjectivity is embedded. Heidegger, again with critical qualifications, credited Dilthey with "an existential analytic of concrete human existence" (ibid., p. 235). On account of human immersion in a world of lived experience, interpretive understanding of that experience requires more than abstract, explanatory thought. Dilthey powerfully stated that "We explain through purely intellectual processes, but we understand through the cooperation of all the powers of the mind activated by apprehension" (Makkreel, 2011, p. 18). Human understanding involves not only cognition, but intuition, emotion, and intention as well. Importantly for psychoanalysis, interpretation is for Dilthey a socially committed immersion in the human condition. It is not a theoretical abstraction.

As it was for Dilthey, a central concern of psychoanalysis is whether a) its universe of discourse is primarily that of a physico-chemical world of cause and effect transposed into the realm of mentation and emotion, a branch, as it were, of physiological psychology; or whether b) psychoanalysis is a study (understanding) of concealed, suppressed, or repressed aspects of *Erlebnis*, the world of lived, meaning-laden experience in which we all are embedded. It could be said that Freud navigated both worlds. For example both "realities" can be found in his concept of instinct, which can alternately be understood as drive (a physiological construct) or desire (an experience of want, need, or attraction always seeking contact with the personal world of another).

Such nuances in the understanding of mind were explored and systematized by Dilthey and expanded upon in great depth and detail by modern philosophers such as Husserl and Heidegger, with Dilthey's concept of *Erlebnis* playing a central role in modern continental philosophy through the writings of Merleau-Ponty, Ricoeur, Gadamer, Derrida, Levinas, and others. It is to the twentieth-century turn in philosophy and hermeneutics that we now direct our attention.

CHAPTER FOUR

Twentieth-century Continental philosophy: Husserl, Heidegger, Derrida

According to Sellars (1962), "The aim of philosophy is to understand how things in the broadest sense of the term hang together in the broadest sense of the term." Romantic era hermeneutics culminating in Dilthey established an emphasis on inter-subjective, historical, biographical, and cultural understanding of the life experience of individuals, events, and societies, pursuits well beyond the earlier emphasis on internal consistency of texts and narratives. This paradigmatic change culminated in Dilthey's concept of *Erlebnis*—the lived experience as distinct from abstract knowledge. Such a focus on being-in-the-world, as differentiated from both scriptural consistency and scientific explanations of cause and effect, would occupy modern philosophy and hermeneutics when, during the twentieth century in which psychoanalysis was born and developed, continental European thought underwent radical changes, in some part inspired by Freud, but which also left psychoanalysis struggling to close the gap with the new ideas that emerged. In particular, the viewpoint that interpretation is not simply a superimposed technique or method, but occupies a central place in all human understanding and indeed life itself, has yet to be given full scrutiny by psychoanalysis.

This change in hermeneutical understanding meant that much of it became assimilated into philosophy, addressing the fundamental questions of epistemology and ontology. While the Romantics were multidisciplinary thinkers, twentieth-century philosophers were primarily concerned with age-old concerns of, to quote Sellars (see above), "… how things in the broadest sense of the term hang together in the broadest sense of the term." They were not so much preoccupied with interpretive procedure as such as with the nature of being and knowing. Hermeneutics, which began as interpretation of texts, ultimately proved useful in addressing these fundamental questions.

The critique of empiricism and metaphysics

While Continental philosophers questioned empiricism and metaphysics, Freud's metapsychology, which still prevails in variant form in American and British quarters, was built primarily on those two foundations of scientific knowledge. Empiricism places sense data, controlled research, and logic at the center of knowing and is currently represented philosophically in logical positivism and philosophical analysis. Metaphysics, often contrasted with empiricism, but sharing some key assumptions, holds that beneath appearances, there is an underlying reality, a substance, a structure of the world which is invisible and inferred through the consistency and order that emerges in the laws of nature. This metaphysical stance, which runs through Plato, Descartes, Berkeley, and Kant is maintained in modern philosophy by the neo-Kantian thinkers who influenced Bion in particular (See Chapter Twelve). It should be said, however, that, contrary to popular belief, Kant was no lover of metaphysics. Even so, he strove for its modification rather than abandoning it (Grondin, 2012, pp. 131–152). Nietzsche launched a more severe critique of metaphysics, but left it with a nostalgic glow harking back to the Greeks. It was Heidegger who dealt metaphysics the decisive blow.

Most of the American and British schools of psychoanalysis, whether classical analysis, ego psychology, Kleinian object relations theory, Bion's theory of thinking, attachment theory, and affect regulation perspectives, are expressed in metaphysical terms, or at least with empiricist underpinnings. For empiricists, scientific observations consist of sense data, or in the case of psychoanalysis, introspective reports. In metaphysics, the mental life has form and substance, follows certain laws and necessities, and exhibits a reliable, objective order that is independent of the observer. Anglo-American psychoanalysts for the most part claim to arrive at underlying laws that govern all human motivation and psychodynamics. Recent developments such as Kohut's self psychology and Stolorow's intersubjective approach represent departures from these premises and have roots in Continental philosophy, especially phenomenology (see Chapter Eleven). For them, the self is inherently subjective and the mental life is inseparable from the interubjective context in which it manifests itself. Partly for these ideological reasons, Kohut was criticized by mainstream analysts in America when he shifted from an empirical ego psychological frame of reference to an "experience-near" empathic understanding of the self (Kohut, 1977).

The ontological "turn"

During the first half of the twentieth century, with Germany and France as epicenters, European philosophy took a radical turn away from empiricism and metaphysics towards intersubjective and existential thought. Indeed, this turn could be considered one of the great revolutions in intellectual history, although some who are committed to science and logical analysis as the ultimate deciders of truth would consider it an involution! In the new perspective, meaningful understanding of the world, of life, of experience, claims primacy over explanations derived from pure reason, controlled experiments, and methods of classification. The term "existentialism," often invoked to depict the new emphasis, hardly does justice to the complexities, twists, and turns that occurred in European thought. The entire foundation of truth was shaken up as human experience, meaning, and values challenged the supremacy of abstraction and inference from formalized observation and hypothetico-deductive reasoning. This radical shift owed something to psychoanalysis, and in turn, led to new versions of it, but in large measure, the theoretical pillars of American and British psychoanalysis itself were impervious to those changes, standing firmly on the bedrock of Freud, the strictly disciplined scientist of the mind.

What was so easily forgotten by the faithful was that Freud himself, in his own way, was a free thinker who utilized ideas and concepts that were valuable to him regardless of whether they matched his metapsychology. Freud knew intuitively that his explorations of human life could not be assimilated into the exclusively scientific discourse which he hoped to achieve. Psychoanalysis, as Laplanche (1976) maintained, is not an internally consistent theory but subsumes multiple theories as well as complex interpretations of those theories. Psychodynamics is not reducible to a consistent hypothetico-deductive system, and psychoanalysis is enriched by the connotations and paradoxes contained in Freud's and others' thinking.

In this chapter, we take up some of the major developments in twentieth-century thought that derive from and/or bear upon hermeneutics and on psychoanalytic interpretation in particular. Of necessity, such an exploration must be highly selective, with a focus upon only a few ideas that are of particular relevance to psychoanalytic interpretation. Again, there are controversies and nuances in each point of view to which great study has been devoted, and there are a host of additional thinkers whose significant work cannot be taken up here. I will focus in a highly condensed way on those Continental philosophers whose work brings out certain aspects of interpretation and hermeneutics that are pertinent to my discourse. And of course, my views are themselves interpretations (is there no way to get out of the hermeneutic circle?) but hopefully will capture something useful to the reader.

The three giants whose work stimulated, exemplified, and elaborated the trends I am considering are, in chronological order, Edmund Husserl, Martin Heidegger, and Jacques Derrida. In important ways, each derived many of their ideas from their predecessors, and then diverged, developing a new point of view. I will take up their work, with some attention as well to others whose contributions grew out of or in proximity to them, specifically Hans Georg Gadamer, and Immanuel Levinas. In subsequent chapters, I will discuss Maurice Merleau-Ponty, whose ideas on embodiment grew out of Husserl's work (Chapter Eight) and Paul Ricoeur, indebted to both Husserl and Heidegger (Chapter Eleven) as well. My intention is to show that there is a thread of hermeneutics that runs through their thought, one which places interpretation at the very center of human life. Hermeneutics is no longer only a discipline for investigating man and nature. Rather it defines the main ingredient of all existence. In that respect, *interpretation is not only the method, but in fact the subject matter, of psychoanalysis.*

Husserl and phenomenology

Edmund Husserl (1859–1938) challenged the cherished assumptions of Enlightenment philosophy at the same time as he revered them. He was a pivotal figure in modern thought, but yet a conservative who irked some of his students, notably Heidegger, by both his minute attention to details and his practice of critiquing beliefs and then adhering to them! Husserl covered many areas of philosophy, from logic, mathematics, and perception to metaphysics and the philosophy of science. He had a major impact on psychology and the social sciences, although he objected to such use because he felt they depended upon assumptions that did not fit with his thinking. In addition, he wanted to address fundamental problems of philosophy, as distinct from the more specific function and content of human behavior. Knowing that Husserl might have strenuously objected to my forays into psychology, and respecting him for that, I nevertheless want here to focus on aspects of his work that bear upon hermeneutics and psychoanalytic interpretation.

Phenomenology as a practical necessity for psychoanalysts

A psychologist or psychoanalyst who is not familiar with Husserl is like an airline pilot flying without a map and instruments. He might successfully fly and land the plane, but he is taking an awful chance in doing so. Husserl's philosophy stemmed from his keen awareness of the slippage and errors that can occur when we take for granted our interpretation of what we are experiencing in ourselves and the world around us. He taught the importance of carefully describing and mapping out experience in order to avoid errors in thinking that had escaped even the greatest philosophers before him, much less psychologists. Husserl's (1900–1901, p. 168) famous maxim "Back to the things themselves" meant grasping the phenomena, the experiences that form the basis of knowledge, prior to the assumptions that are so readily projected onto them. While, as his students and critics have pointed out, the "bracketing" (*epoché*) of unmediated experience from ideas about it can never be totally achieved, it can be tried resolutely. Husserl recognized the basis of philosophy to be careful description of experience prior to what we "know" about it, which already projects certain beliefs into the experience, and psychoanalysts know all about projection, how it distorts "reality." But *Husserl held that so-called "reality" itself is a projection and distortion.* He was seeking to describe the "things themselves," the directly apprehended experiences that could then legitimately form the basis of a theory or system instead of being contaminated by it. He was not, as some have contended, opposed to theories; rather he wanted to avoid the fallacies attendant upon superimposing theories upon experiences, coloring, twisting, and distorting them.

To give a basic example from psychoanalysis, when a female patient says she is "attracted" to a male therapist, the word "attraction" itself may suggest a set of dynamics, namely, that the so-called attraction is sexual or in the nature of an infantile attachment, that there is a transference displacement of a parental figure onto the analyst, and further that by her romantic inclinations the patient is avoiding the task of insight. What may be disregarded in such a process of theorizing is the richness of experiential phenomena to which the patient is merely alluding when she uses the word "attraction." In her phenomenological world, she might have noticed the low level of lighting in the room, a slight distancing of self, the blueness of the analyst's eyes, a glazing of her own eyes, and/or an interruption in the analyst's attention to her. Were the analyst to obtain a more detailed description of the patient's flow of experience, he might conclude that the patient, far from being attracted to him, is describing an experience more akin to a disruption of her state of awareness. This could take the analysis in an entirely different direction of exploring perturbation rather than attraction, absence rather than presence. If the analyst had been a student of Husserl, he might have "bracketed" his assumptions and encouraged the patient to further describe the subtle details of her experience.

A conclusion that can be drawn from Husserl's emphasis on the primacy of experiential phenomena is that the patient's flow of verbal associations needs always to be supplemented with an inquiry into the nuances of the associative elements. Stolorow, Atwood, and Brandschaft (1994, p. 44) incorporated such a method into their intersubjective perspective, calling it "sustained empathic inquiry." The empathic aspect involves the analyst forming an image of the patient's experience within himself, as in Herder's concept of *Einfühlung*, "feeling one's way in." What Husserl added to empathic inquiry was his absolute insistence on grasping the phenomena as freely as possible from the assumptive worlds of the participants. Bion alluded to such a process when he stated that the analyst's understanding of the patient ought to remain "unsaturated with preconceptions" (Bion, 1962a, p. 3).

The intersubjective unity of self, intention, and world

Husserl, however, was a philosopher, not a psychologist, a point he himself frequently reiterated on the grounds that empirical psychology is based on assumptions that he wished to avoid. His interest was not in psychological judgments as such, but in the most fundamental questions of knowledge. Carrying out with his students detailed descriptive studies of experiences from colors to relationships, he concluded that all consciousness, all human experience involves a self intending towards an object. Importantly, for Husserl, *the object of an experience is inseparable from the self and its intentionality.* The experience comes into being, not as an independent entity such as sense data, but is constituted by the self for itself. This seminal idea represented Husserl's critique of Descartes's "cogito," the detached self that observes a separate reality. A similar critique could be launched on Freud's distinctly Cartesian concept of the ego as a kind of I = "eye" on which sensations and instincts impinge. For Husserl, self and world, ego and object, are interdependent, and rather than being stable structures, they constitute one another in the moment of awareness.

In addition to his critique of the subject-object dichotomy, Husserl also questioned the metaphysics of substance, which assumes a material or ideational entity "behind" the experience, or as Kant put it, the noumena beneath appearances. In psychoanalysis, the noumena are the instincts and other unconscious "forces" out of which conscious experience arises. Husserl placed the emphasis on the experienced phenomena, not the noumena, as the basis of knowledge. However, criticized for his allegedly subjective, solipsistic position, Husserl tried to avoid a relativistic notion of truth by his advocacy of disciplined "transcendental reduction," a state of the self which could in principle know and describe intentional experience in an uncontaminated way. Husserl's "transcendental ego" parallels the analyst's so-called neutrality and observing ego as objective, detached positions for working with the material presented by the patient. The questioning of the analyst's neutrality and transcendent objectivity is what led to the intersubjective and relational perspectives (see Chapter Eleven). Heidegger's (1927) *Being and Time* was also based on a critique of the "transcendental ego" as unattainable. The problem haunts both philosophy and psychoanalysis. We try to be objective and universal in our assertions while the material that presents itself is subjective, personal, and embedded in context. We are scientists pursuing phantoms and intimations.

Overall, Husserl believed that philosophy and understanding should be derived first from transcendental descriptions of the phenomena of experience. In such descriptions, ghosts, apparitions, and hallucinations are just as "real" phenomena as are chairs and tables. The only question is how they fit into the self's experience and world. Atwood, Orange, and Stolorow (2002) offered phenomenological accounts of psychotic states that are especially rich and poignant because they avoid judgments about their realism. Rather than doubt the psychotic's world as imaginary or delusional, Atwood et al. fully explore the experiential component and only then delve into the developmental and traumatic historical roots of these experiences. The patients do not "give up" their hallucinations and delusions. Rather, their inner world and intentions gradually become more adaptive and interpersonally fulfilling. Relationship rather than reality testing becomes the criterion of cure. Whose world—the analyst's or the patient's—is more "real" seldom comes up in such dialogues with patients. (Of course, therapists can only approximate such conditions—we are always attached to our own reality.)

Husserl's concept of Lebenswelt, the "lifeworld"

At first approach, Husserl's phenomenology would appear to be the polar opposite of hermeneutics or for that matter of psychoanalysis. It is as if he is saying that experience is independent of understanding, meaning, and interpretation. The so-called "phenomenological reduction" or *epoché* eschews interpretation, which comes later, upon recollection and reflection. However, his premise that experience includes a self and its intention entails a primordial meaningfulness to all experience. Intention implies a use or apprehension of the object of experience. All experience involves the self's intentional relation to its world, and the nature of this relationship is its meaning, its interpretation.

Husserl came increasingly to the position that raw experience is impregnated with meaning that goes well beyond the individual perceiving self to the intersubjective and collective context in which all experience is embedded. In 1936, shortly before his death, and in somewhat abstruse language, Husserl introduced the concept of the lifeworld or *Lebenswelt*:

> In whatever way we may be conscious of the world as universal horizon, as coherent universe of existing objects, we, each "I-the-man" and all of us together, belong to the world as living with one another in the world; and the world is our world, valid for our consciousness as existing precisely through this 'living together.' We, as living in wakeful world-consciousness, are constantly active on the

basis of our passive having of the world ... Obviously this is true not
only for me, the individual ego; rather we, in living together, have
the world pre-given in this together, belong, the world as world for
all, pre-given with this ontic meaning ... The we-subjectivity ... [is]
constantly functioning. (pp. 108–109)

In other words, Husserl, probably under the influence of his former
student, Heidegger, ultimately concluded that primordial experience
(phenomena) cannot be separated from intersubjective meaning and
understanding. His concept of the "lifeworld" (*Lebenswelt*) was derived
partly from Dilthey's notion of lived experience (*Erlebnis*) and contains
elements similar to it.

Husserl's phenomenology suggests a different understanding of
psychoanalytic theory and interpretation from the "standard edition"
of them (reference to the decidedly Anglicized translation of Freud by
Strachey of "The Complete Psychological Works" is intended). The
"standard" understanding of psychoanalysis is empirical and metaphysical. In this mode of thought, the psyche is "built" from elements
of sensation, drive, and inhibition that form increasingly complex layers of imagery and cognition. In turn, these constitute "objects" which
become what Melanie Klein called "positions," constellations of primitive reactions and ideas in relation to the body (soma) and the external
interpersonal world of the infant. The function of psychoanalytic interpretation is to revive or reconstruct the original infantile object relations
(sensations and drives).

For Husserl, primordial or infantile experience, rather than being a
concatenation of instincts and sensations that cumulatively form internal "objects," is already *meaningfully and intersubjectively organized*—in
terms of the infant's own lifeworld, which is of course different from
that of the adult. In some way, the infant may experience some portion
of his world as concretized particles, projectiles, or objects, which is the
impression we get from play therapy with children, but they are part of
the child's meaningfully constituted lifeworld, not isolated sense data.
(Klein used the term "object" in both phenomenological and theoretical
senses, which gives her writing a paradoxical feeling of being abstract
and obtuse while at the same time uncannily capturing an inner world
that we all know from a time remembered; see Chapter Nine).

In   the   "standard   edition,"   psychoanalytic   interpretation
"reconstructs" the root causes of the patient's neurosis in the sensations,

images, instincts, and objects out of which development is constructed. By contrast, for Husserl, the purpose and function of psychoanalytic interpretation would be to investigate the self-experience and lifeworld of the patient as they emerge in the intersubjective context of the analytic situation. Interpretation does not consist of ferreting out causes and explanations. Rather, it elucidates the meanings already implicit in the patient's own experience in the present moment. Since history is part of the lifeworld, early development comes into play as part of the here-and-now experience of the adult patient.

Meaning and experience emerge and converge in ways that are uniquely constituted in each personal encounter such as an analytic treatment. In the process, additional meanings and experiences are discerned in the "horizon" of the patient's lifeworld: emotions, memories, desires. Since the lifeworld is inherently historical, in some ways constituting an "autobiography," it has aspects that echo infancy and childhood. The analyst does not so much "reconstruct" the childhood experience as he invokes it with his words and analytic attitude. Together, analyst and patient constitute their lifeworlds as they work together.

Winnicott used an apt phrase for this relived experience of infancy. He called it "regression to dependence." His analysand, Margaret I. Little (1990), herself an analyst, recalled her own regression to dependence experience during her treatment with Winnicott. She described it essentially as a lived re-entry into the lifeworld of her infancy rather than an objective historical reconstruction. The experience was so vivid and anxiety-provoking for her that she needed the safe environment of a hospital to protect her during the depth of her regression. While for good reason we ordinarily do not permit the regression to reach such risky levels, it is safe to say that in many analyses, the patient gets a genuine "taste" of infancy that is far more than a recollection in tranquillity about it. Without that "taste" (phenomenology), the analysis is not transformative, but an intellectual exercise.

Heidegger: interpretation as pre-reflective "being-in-the-world"

In sum, Husserl brought philosophy back to the "things themselves," the phenomena, and analysts can accomplish something similar with regard to introspective self-experience through careful empathic inquiry. Husserl, partly under the influence of his student, Heidegger, also came to see that phenomenology is embedded in an interpretive lifeworld that informs our existence. Heidegger, however, took the revolutionary step of transitioning philosophy from phenomena to existence, holding that subjectivity is itself embedded in *being*, the nature and ground of human existence which, in his view, must be "already there" in order that conscious thought and subjectivity (phenomena) can occur at all. He questioned both traditional metaphysics and Husserl's "transcendental ego," maintaining that experience is inseparable from "being-in-the-world," temporal, historical being, which he called *Dasein*.

There is some qualified resemblance between Heidegger's notion of being-in-the-world and Freud's unconscious. Both refer to that which is outside but is a precondition for awareness. Heidegger's *Being and Time* was published in 1927, a decade after Freud published his major papers on narcissism, mourning and melancholia, and metapsychology. However, each phrased his ideas in such different terms that it is difficult to know what sort of connection can legitimately be made between the two. These difficulties will become apparent as we explore how Heidegger took both phenomenology and hermeneutics to the "next level."

Heidegger's tarnished life and influence

The legacy of Martin Heidegger (1889–1976) is bound up with three events which unfortunately have diminished our collective valuation of him, perhaps obscuring the brilliance of his insights. The most shattering occurrence was his egregious association with the Nazis. Even though he became disillusioned with National Socialism, he did irremediable injury to some of those within his academic circle (Safranski, 1999). It is difficult to comprehend how such an essentially humanistic thinker, whose lover Hannah Arendt became an avowed critic of Nazism, could reconcile himself to authoritarianism and butchery. It speaks to the power of dissociation, splitting, and repression in character development that they can make a man's public and academic life so horrifically deviant from his intellect.

A second eventuality was French existentialism. When Jean-Paul Sartre recognized parallels between Heidegger's thought and his own, he absorbed Heidegger's views on "being" into his own views of the absurdity and meaninglessness of existence. Although parallels can and have been drawn, Heidegger's philosophy stands on its own and resists the popularization and generalities of existentialism as a literary and social movement. Heidegger's writings in no way imply that life is absurd or dispensable. Indeed, he conveys the sense that life is made precious by its finality and elusiveness.

The third development consisted of applications of Heidegger to psychiatry and psychotherapy. Although Heidegger was favorable to such work and gave a series of lectures for psychiatrists (the Zollicon Seminars, 1959–1969) at the Switzerland home of Medard Boss, the notion of "existential psychotherapy" has implications that only partly reflect the scope of Heidegger's philosophy. Nevertheless, the connection to existential therapy has led many psychoanalysts to distance themselves from Heidegger. This is unfortunate because his philosophy, properly understood, has a direct bearing on mainstream psychoanalytic theory and practice.

All three of these eventualities obscured Heidegger's most important philosophical intentions in a manner not unlike the way in which he himself said that "everyday existence" conceals authentic human being-in-the-world. Thus, in the American and British psychoanalytic community and elsewhere there persist misunderstandings of Heidegger that dilute his profound insights about interpretation and the hidden dimension that could be of great use to psychoanalysis. Let us now try to examine some of them.

Being-in-the world

The foundation of Heidegger's thought is the proposition, which formed the basis of his groundbreaking opus, *Being and Time* (originally published 1927), that beings (objects of thought and discourse) and Being (the fact and basis of the existence of beings) were confounded with each other in Western philosophy since Plato and Aristotle. Simply put, the noun "beings" and the verb "to be" carry different philosophical significance, a difference which was sidestepped and substituted with the notion that an idea or representation can be (exist) in a particular form or substance. In metaphysics, beings "exist" by virtue of their permanent realization in a medium or world. For example, if one points to things in the world that look like circles (beings), Heidegger questioned the long-held assumption that circles have permanent "being" in the world.

Beginning with Plato, being (the verb "to be") was portrayed by philosophers as permanence and an ideal, rather than in its *urgency and immediacy as it presents itself to us* (here Heidegger not only took a swift turn away from Plato but also from Husserl by shifting the focus from "I see and know" to "I exist," in other words, from epistemology to ontology. Being, he held, always presents itself to us through its urgent temporality: the immanence of mortality. Thus, for Heidegger, being is not permanence, but paradoxically discloses itself as an anxiety-provoking abyss. Western thought, and especially metaphysics, represented a turning away from this abyssal experience. Freud made a similar point when, in *Civilization and Its Discontents* (1930a) he held that society is the product of repression, of forgetting, although for Freud, like Nietzsche, the repressed aspect was desire (for Nietzsche the Dionysian), while for Heidegger, it is authentic temporal existence itself that is "concealed"—and feared.

Along with his change of the meaning of being from permanence to temporal existence, Heidegger, again like Freud, diminished the importance of the perceiving subject, of consciousness, the centrality of which Husserl had tried to resurrect. Heidegger's so-called *Dasein* analysis took a very different turn from Husserl's phenomenology and also from Freud's portrayal of the unconscious as rooted in biology. Heidegger stated that most of who we are—our Being—is *un*-thought, not because it is repressed but because it is "at hand," that is the basis of everything we think and do as a "ground" for them. He used the analogy of a hammer. We do not think about the nature of the hammer—we pick it up and use it as part of our care (the German word is *Sorge*) for the lifeworld we inhabit. Thought emerges when matter matters, that is, it arises when a difficulty arises with our being-in-the-world, which we otherwise take for granted in our everyday existence. Heidegger's use of the hammer analogy also resembles the neurological concepts of implicit and procedural memory, but he took it in a very different direction from neuroscience. (See Chapter Thirteen for further discussion.)

From this idea of being as an anxiety-producing temporal ground for human existence, Heidegger developed the crucial notion of *Dasein*, our individual and collective being-there or being-in-the-world. *Dasein* is characterized by *Sorge*, care for its being. That idea sounds initially like "self-consciousness." However, it is not about subjectivity but about what is already present in how we live. In this emphasis on care for time-bound existence rather than thought as such, Heidegger challenged nearly every eminent philosopher before him, from Plato to Descartes to Kant to Hegel. He also gave a new turn to hermeneutics.

Heidegger and interpretation

Based upon the above line of thought, Heidegger held that *human existence and "care" is "already there," that is, it is laden with language and meaning, so that most of what we call interpretation (or understanding) is pre-reflective: it is inherent in the way we relate to our world.* Meaning is given to us by our being-in-the-world (*Dasein*) and needs to be "unconcealed" and disclosed to us by the authentic relationship we bear towards our existence and towards other *Daseins.* Our world (including our inner world) is meaningful because it is "our" world. It reveals itself through our existence in it. This creates a living environment of meaning which I would like to call the "interpretive matrix" that each of us carries with us. For example, we look up at the stars and are filled with awe and a sense of humility at our smallness and insignificance. We do not learn this from books. We breathe it in. Its meaning comes from a source outside of our conscious self, and, in Heidegger's terms, it is our own being that is "unconcealed" in this moment of awe. One thinks here of Jung's archetypes as templates of racial inheritance and Freud's "primal unconscious." However, Heidegger's "already there" is more of a process and activity than a pre-defined content or ideation. For Heidegger, we are defined by the temporality of existence, not by preconceptions, archetypes, or representations.

Heidegger himself illustrated the concept of interpretation as "already there" in an essay entitled "The Origin of the Work of Art" (1929, pp. 139–212), where he discussed van Gogh's famous painting, "A Pair of Shoes" (pp. 158–162).

Here he reflected on how the artist uses the material of the world (earth, paint, a canvas) to create another world of beings (shoes, or more precisely shoes-painted-on-a-canvas). But it is neither what is on the canvas nor the shoes that are important. Rather, it is the way that they unconceal what is already there, our *Dasein*, our human being-in-the world. The meaning of the work is unspoken; it reveals itself and then recedes. In the van Gogh painting, the shoes, which are laden with the struggles and weariness of the wearer, are surrounded with darkness, the abyss of authentic being. The meaning is "already there" in the

Figure 1. Vincent van Gogh: "A Pair of Shoes".

material and content of the painting by virtue of what it evokes in the person who engages with it.

Hans Georg Gadamer's dialogical heremeneutics

Heidegger's student, Gadamer, made explicit and developed the implications of his teacher's work for hermeneutics—meaning and interpretation—as such (Gadamer, 1960), He held that meaning appears at the "fusion of horizons" (of two human beings, historical epochs, or art work and critic), the edge of understanding of each that reaches out towards the other. It is neither the one nor the other which establishes the interpretation, but the conjunction of the two at the horizons of their awareness. For Gadamer, meaning results from contact between the linguistic-historical-social contexts of the interpreter and the object of interpretation, between self and other. Again, the meaning or interpretation is "already there" to be unconcealed in the meeting of horizons of the two parties to the interpretive discourse. Gadamer thus extended Heidegger's *Dasein* (being there "at hand") to interpretive dialogue, so that, for him, much of interpretation is non-personal and non-subjective. For Gadamer, interpretation arises or is disclosed in the process of being-in-the-world-with-others. It is not superimposed by a scholarly method.

Gadamer's hermeneutics is implicit in contemporary relational psychoanalysis. For relational analysts, as for Gadamer, interpretation is far from a methodological dissection or microscopic observation of the patient's free associations and mind. Rather, it consists of a freshly created set of meanings that emerge in a mutually impactful dialogue. Interpretations emerge as the patient and analyst reach out to each other in the horizons of mutual uncertainty within their discourse. Interpretations are co-created within the context of the relationship. (However, Gadamer did not imply that such co-creations are arbitrarily constructed. He held that interpretations derive truth and universality from the living historical and language contexts in which they are embedded. The analyst, for example, uses his skill, heritage, and knowledge with great discipline to formulate his interpretations. But, for Gadamer, they are not "provable" by any method.)

Truth as "alatheia"

What Heidegger and Gadamer challenged was the dominance of metaphysics as the foundation of understanding. For them, as for Husserl, rational dissection and analysis of objects and things does not lead to truth, but obscures it. They do not deny the practical utility of reasoning from facts as occurs in the natural sciences, but assert that science masks the deeper truth of our mode of being-in-the-world, our lived existence. For the latter truth, Heidegger used the Greek word, *alatheia*, which means unconcealment or disclosure. Thus, what is unconcealed in the scientific mode of being-in-the-world is the appropriation and manipulation of nature for specific ends. Challenging science as the ultimate form of knowledge, Heidegger said that there are other truths which transcend the sciences and are disclosed, not by manipulation of sense data and objects of nature, but by "letting beings be," a more authentic kind of care. Heidegger and others have argued that the human sciences should reflect such authentic care rather than be governed by agendas of control. Ultimately, science must be understood and respected as a powerful mode for "penetrating" and manipulating nature. However, whatever its merits, science also represents an anxious avoidance of our humanity, our death, our time-bound being-in-the-world.

From this standpoint, what is important in psychoanalytic cure is not so much the patient's conscious awareness of his motivations and desires as his capacity to face his life as it is given to him, the unconcealment of his being-in-the-world. *Alatheia* implies a radical shift in the way we understand "insight" as a curative agent. Beyond cognitive understanding, *alatheia* implies a lived experience as much as an idea, an "undergoing" over time, and an "opening up," a clearing of a path.

Heidegger, for such reasons, indeed took a strong stand against advanced technology as a dehumanizing force, and many of his followers have been critical of the so-called "hard sciences," but, in my opinion, his philosophy is not hostile to science as such, but calls for a humble recognition of its limitations and proper place in human thought and action. Heidegger, like Husserl, offered a serious critique of science as the conceptual model for philosophy. One of the functions of this book is to try to place a particular science, psychoanalysis, within the broader context of hermeneutics and philosophy, recognizing its place and position within human life and thought, rather than taking its tenets and theories as final explanations of human nature and manipulating the patient through social control.

So-called "existential psychotherapy" is based upon the Heideggerian value of authenticity and its relationship to confronting the anxious abyss of being. I think this development is of considerable importance, and has influenced contemporary relational psychoanalysis in its stress on mutuality and authenticity in the analytic dyad (Aron, 1996). However, here I wish to bring out a broader perspective on psychoanalytic interpretation implied by Heidegger's work.

The "standard edition" view of psychoanalytic interpretation is that it consists of statements offered to the patient that are based upon an application of dynamic theory to the specific patient. Such interpretations are science-based explanations, pointing for instance to a particular defense mechanism, wish-fulfilling fantasy, or pattern of attachment. These insights then build gradually to an in-depth look at the patient's unconscious motivation and character, not unlike the way a CT-scan image is composed of multiple views from a revolving X-ray camera (compare to the hermeneutic circle). There is nothing wrong with such an approach—and sometimes we find that it is quite on target and to the point. But to suggest that interpretation is based on a composite view of the personality is nothing more or less than a convenient intellectualized myth that works under certain circumstances and unfortunately not in others.

The analogy to the CT-scan breaks down as soon as we realize that we do not interpret the results of a scan to a kidney or a lung but to a human being! As soon as we "tell" our interpretations to another human being, namely the patient, we are no longer in the realm of scientific explanation and causation. Rather, we have entered Gadamer's dialogical world of narrative, story, and meaning which is the basis of all human thought and intercourse. We have moved from the objective "beings" of science to the "being" (*Dasein*) of the patient, whose primary interest is in being personally understood, not explained mechanistically.

What is neglected (Heidegger would say "concealed") when we apply a theory (Gadamer would say "method;" Bion would say "preconception") in psychoanalysis is that the patient can only "hear" the interpretation in terms of his own "already there" interpretive matrix that is "at hand" (preconscious, partly unconscious, or better yet, non-conscious). No matter how much a theory is utilized—and there are sound reasons to utilize theories—what transpires between analyst and patient is Gadamer's meeting of interpretive horizons (think of the horizon as the growing tip of awareness and knowing in the present moment) that may or may not lead to mutual understanding. (The same could be said developmentally of the relationship between a parent and child.) Such meeting of horizons often occurs through mutually perceived objects (beings) which serve as metaphors that analyst and patient can utilize to develop meanings. These then become transitional objects (Winnicott, 1953) that mediate between the two individuals, with hopefully an emphasis on care (*Sorge*) for the patient, as transitional objects provide a certain care for the child.

> For example, a patient, Rochelle, well into her analysis finally began to address her hitherto repressed affectionate feelings about her mother for whom she bore great resentment. (She had earlier dealt with current life displacements of maternal care issues onto her sister and her female supervisors at work without recognizing they had to do with her mother.) The repressed affection towards mother first showed up in the transference-countertransference. At a certain point in a session, the therapist noticed his gaze drawn to a locket that hung like a pendulum between the patient's breasts. He noticed erotic feelings stirring within him and entered a mood of sleepy, dream-like comfort and self-absorption. Realizing that

he was under the sway of his countertransference, he let himself free associate to the locket, and remembered that his grandmother, an especially comforting person to him in his childhood, wore a similar piece of jewelry. When he asked Rochelle what came to her mind about the locket, she said it had been given to her by her mother. The gift of the locket then became in treatment a "selected fact" that served as the entrance way to Rochelle's analysis of her relationship with her mother, which, over time, yielded significant therapeutic benefits. (Cohen & Schermer, 2004, pp. 594–595)

In this instance the analysis proceeded not from a theory but from an object, namely the locket, that had meaning that was "already there" in the worlds of both the analyst and patient. Theory (science, method) subsequently could be placed on top of that, as it were, but the crucial exchange consisted of a conjunction of meanings already present in both parties, meanings which were "unconcealed" though a mediating object that served as a metaphor for maternal care. Not incidentally, the therapist's inquiry about the locket was experienced by Rochelle as "authentic" (rather than seductive) in the sense that it increased her trust in the therapist and her willingness to probe more deeply into her feelings, memories, and anxieties.

Heideggerian *alatheia* as unconcealment (as distinct from truth arrived at by reasoned argument) is very important for understanding the "facticity" or "ground" of what goes on in an analysis, above, below, and beyond our theory about it. The exchange between analyst and patient is mediated by the "at hand" interpretive matrix of each, and more specifically that which is unconcealed in the moment of relating with care. Importantly, insight, transformation, and change cannot occur unless the patient's own interpretive world is reached and touched. This makes successful analysis an intimate process, pointing still further to the need for care as distinct from penetration and appropriation through scientific explanations as such.

Encountering the abyss: the "strangeness of care"

Among its values and purposes, the authenticity of the therapeutic relationship serves a special dynamic function, namely to help the patient tolerate an encounter with the abyss, what Winnicott (1974) called annihilation anxiety. Encountering the abyss, with its threat of extinction, will appear to some like an invitation to psychotic transference, but a different understanding of such an encounter comes from Alan Bass in his excellent book, *Interpretation and Difference: The Strangeness of Care* (2006), where he takes up the relevance of Nietzsche, Heidegger, and Derrida for psychoanalysis and specifically the therapeutic function of interpretation. Regarding all three philosophers, and especially Heidegger, Bass points to the psychic pain induced by an interpretation, the pain of tolerating the frustrating effect of differences between the patient's wishes and the analyst's interpretations. He holds that the psychic pain of depth understanding is the result of the death instinct coming *in service of* rather than in collision with the life instinct. An interpretation, like some other events in life, including orgasm, is a "little death," an ecstatic dying, a mourning, which allows the person to go on living in a deeper, more authentic way than before. In a certain respect, this ecstatic dying into life is implied in Heidegger's hermeneutics. Experiencing the unconcealed truth (*alatheia*) about himself, the patient has an encounter with temporality (abyss, death). For Bass, such an encounter is survivable and promotes growth. That is on account of the care value of interpretation, which is what makes a proper psychoanalytic treatment effective and non-destructive. But— and this is what brings Heidegger into relevance for psychoanalysis— such an encounter does not come from scientific reasoning, but from *Dasein*, the already-there-at-hand meanings of patient and analyst that emerge in their mutual horizons through authenticity and care.

Beyond Heidegger to deconstructionism and postmodern thought

It is difficult to think of a more radical critique of the Enlightenment philosophy of reason than that of Heidegger, but in fact there are those who felt that he did not go far enough in "deconstructing" the epochal "errors" of metaphysics and science (not to mention psychoanalysis, history, and religion as well). The progenitor of deconstructionism was the French philosopher Jacques Derrida (1930–2004), whose work played a key role in the broader postmodern European movement that attacked privilege and subjugation of man by man at its intellectual core of the metaphysics of presence and privilege. In the process of developing his ideas, Derrida immersed himself in Freud's writing and used it as a basis for critiquing not only Heidegger, but hermeneutics and the entire process of interpretation itself.

Jacques Derrida: interpretation and deconstruction

Jacques Derrida was one of the most controversial thinkers of the twentieth century. His avowedly rebellious nature and his dense and often obtuse way of expressing himself in his writing made him so. But if he did not have something profound to say, Derrida would have remained a mere gadfly. Instead, he had a major impact on many disciplines from philosophy and hermeneutics to literature, the arts, and the social sciences. His main point was deceptively simple: doubt all dichotomies and hierarchies. The task of the philosopher is to question-mark or strike-through all texts, positions, understandings, theories, authorities, points of view! That is essentially what is meant by the Derridean postmodern term: "deconstructionism." Derrida was like the child in the Hans Christian Andersen story "The Emperor's New Clothes" who is the only one with the courage to say that the king is naked. He sought to expose deceptions that he felt ran through all Western thought and expression. He considered himself a rebel, but he also turned to the great thinkers for inspiration and ideas. It is no accident that among his primary influences were the groundbreakers Husserl, Heidegger, and Freud.

Hundreds of books and legions of articles have been written along with numerous media events and films about Derrida and his work. While Derrida was profoundly influenced by Freud, only at one point did he write about psychoanalytic method (1998), and then only to reflect on theory. He rarely if ever wrote explicitly on psychoanalytic practice as such. Nevertheless, I will surmise what he might have said about psychoanalytic interpretation, first summarizing some of his ideas that are relevant to that purpose.

In a major essay, "Freud and the Scene of Writing" published in the collection *Writing and Difference* (1978), Derrida enjoined psychoanalysis as an ally to his arguments about deconstruction. He utilized two concepts stated by Freud (1950a) in his "A Project for a Scientific Psychology:" trace and difference. Speculating on the functioning of systems of neurons as a basis for his psychology, Freud held that neurons transmit and organize sensory and somatic input in two ways: a trace of the stimulus is left in the system, and a difference is registered in two ways: 1) a distinction and 2) a deferring or delay. Derrida, taking these terms out of their neurological context, combined these two senses in the neologism *différance*, with an "a" instead of an "e."

(He also used the change in spelling to point out that something might appear in writing that would not be heard in speech of his native language, French. Derrida argued that speech and writing were different modes of discourse. He viewed psychoanalysis from the perspective of "writing and difference.")

Freud said that the unconscious consists of traces of memories, thoughts, emotions registered with difference and delay. They vanish from awareness. This is consistent with his view that in primary process, opposites occur together and ultimately dissolve into what Matte Blanco (1975) called symmetry, where both opposites have equal weight, retaining only traces of differences. Derrida extrapolated this idea into the hermeneutical realm: the unconscious is the destroyer of opposites, of meaning, the ultimate deconstructionist! It reduces all input (meanings) to *différance* and holds only traces of them. Derrida proposed to do the same with the major texts of Western thought!

Derrida used this foundation, along with explorations of Heidegger in particular to develop the idea of deconstruction, that the only meaning that can be given to any text—whether a philosophical approach, a novel, or a patient's free associations is how it appears within all related texts, that is, its "dissemination" in language, thought, art, etc. All other meaning is superimposed ideology and can be deconstructed. We must seek traces (echoes, specters, ghosts) in other texts, to which the traces are deferred. The rest is deception.

The application of deconstruction to psychoanalytic interpretation occurs when the analyst takes understanding and meaning to its limit, where it surprisingly discloses its emptiness or lack of meaning. As a deconstructionist, the analyst is not looking for the golden egg of insight but for the place—the deepest unconscious—where the associative trail reveals itself to be "all there is," a platform of trace and *différance* that has deconstructed itself. In effect, psychoanalysis denudes the ego of pretense, deception, and privilege. But for Derrida, the patient is not going to find solace in an all-embracing understanding of his symptoms and complexes. For Derrida, there is no structure of the mind and therefore no system of meanings that can be assigned to it. Metapsychology and metaphysics begone!

Derrida had a pervasive influence upon the social sciences and literary thought in terms of what could be called the "deconstruction of privilege," the challenge to the hegemony of dominant and dominating views related to gender, sexuality, religion, race, and power. What Bion

(1970, pp. 112, 116) called the psychoanalytic Establishment, the powers that be, can surely be held accountable for its decidedly male, atheist (or at least agnostic), bourgeois, and Euro-Caucasian biases.

Derrida went still further, questioning all hallowed texts and beliefs, holding that they contain contradictory statements that are then covered over with unfounded assertions. For example, Freud's notion of penis envy implies that women's psychology is based upon a lack or absence. Yet the notion of the *vagina dentata* suggests that the vagina can also be experienced as a place of power (with "teeth"), and Melanie Klein further put forth the notions of breast and womb envy in the same vein. Thus, ideas about "lack" in women's psychology are asserted, and then contradicted in psychoanalysis. Derrida tried to show that all texts deconstruct themselves by manifesting their opposite within themselves.

The extent to which psychoanalysis, despite its revolutionary implications, has absorbed privileged beliefs of Western culture and put them forth as universal characteristics was clearly one of Derrida's targets. In a fascinating exchange with Lacan over the latter's essay on Poe's "The Purloined Letter," (Norris, 1988, p. 116), Derrida claimed that Lacan was writing about himself and not about Poe's narrative! One form of deconstruction is thus to suggest that all psychological theory discloses the biases and distortions of the (male, aristocratic) thinker more than it discloses human nature. This argument is difficult to dispel, although at its extreme, deconstruction can become a solipsistic and self-centered activity. Deconstructionism ultimately deconstructs itself.

The deconstruction of "presence"

Freud posited the unconscious as a structure that is present in the mind as a series of forces and influences impinging on the ego. For Freud, the unconscious is not a mere hypothesis—it is there, it exists, and it makes itself manifest. In modern Contintental philosophy, real existence is called "presence." For Derrida, presence obscures the truth that everything vanishes as a trace. Indeed, Derrida's work was part of a European trend that questioned the notion of presence in Western thought. Derrida faulted even Heidegger in this regard. He contended that Heidegger erroneously asserted the "presence" ("already *there*") of being even while he challenged the metaphysics of an underlying reality. Heidegger clearly places a high value on authentic being-in-the-world, and the unconcealment of being implies there is a presence to be revealed. Being can reveal its presence even if not categorizable. For Derrida, presence itself is an illusion that derives from Western texts, whether metaphysical writings or novels or speech. We unenlightened humans have for millennia navigated our world with the implicit assumption that it is all there before us, and it is very "real." Before Derrida, Western philosophers agreed with this naïve belief. By contrast, some Hindu philosophers say that it is all *maya*, illusion. Similarly, for Derrida, presence is an illusion, a ghost.

Psychoanalysis, despite its revelation of the illusions of the conscious ego, holds onto presence as a quality of the mind. Analysts regard the patient himself as a presence to be probed and understood, as if we could find out what is "inside him"—his dynamics. Derrida's French contemporary, Immanuel Levinas, deconstructed the "presence" of the human being in a radical way which leads to his conclusion that the belief we can "know" another person is actually an ethical violation, a disrespect for the other who comes before us. He used the term "alterity" for the absolute, almost sacred inaccessibility and unknowabilty of the other.

Levinas: presence as identity vs. alterity as otherness

Levinas held that presence disrespects the alterity of persons by assimilating them into one's own illusion of social identity. Alterity calls into question the psychoanalytic concept of identification, which implies that the other person is present as some "thing," a thing who could be equated with oneself. Levinas gave a poignant example of alterity from his own incarceration in a WWII German prisoner of war camp. He said that the dog in the camp was the only one who joyfully greeted the prisoners! The dog was the only being who did not know their identity!

For Levinas (1970), as for Martin Buber, a human being is not a known quantity, an identity or an object of thought. To a degree, psychoanalysis recognizes alterity since it questions the patient's own presentation of self, but by supposing there is an entity "behind" the person-as-presence, a doppelganger, an alter ego, a characterological tendency, psychoanalysis denies the alterity of the patient. An analyst who fully respects alterity would need to qualify his interpretations as questions rather than statements of truth or presence. Only then might a true dialogue of two separate individuals (alterities) proceed in all fairness.

Following Derrida and Levinas, the psychoanalyst is in the fateful position of all humans in producing speech and writing that "blows in the wind." Levinas (ibid.) held that we not only are unknowable to one another, but that in addition, we are subjugated to one another by the implicit demand for response and care. The psychoanalytic claim to intimate knowledge of the patient is thus blown away by alterity. Perhaps the wind is all that is needed to conduct an analysis: two individuals who exhale words towards one another, each submissively stating his own position, leaving only its trace. If the patient and analyst could genuinely reach this place of honest subjugation to one another, the treatment might be quite successful, because the patient's symptoms, which, after all, are only traces, would yield to their humbled status. But the danger is that the patient himself might also dissolve, becoming helpless and vulnerable, a mere echo of himself. In any case, Levinas leads us to a place where we have to question the foundations of any human encounter, and, for him, such questioning becomes an ethical responsibility to protect one another from our judgments and falsehoods. Such an ethical imperative challenges the psychoanalyst in every moment of his work.

From hermeneutics to psychotherapy practice

As already mentioned, the above overview is but a highly selective sampling of twentieth-century Continental philosophy. Lawlor (2012) gives a much fuller account of the richness and broad scope of those discussions and writings than is possible here. My purpose has been to bring out several key points that relate to psychoanalytic interpretation as such. First of all, interpretation goes beyond a method of understanding the patient. It becomes an integral part of human nature and nurture, of who we are and what we can become. Psychoanalytic interpretations are part of an underlying interpretive matrix, or being-in-the-world brought into treatment by patient, analyst, and the contexts of their lives and histories. To think of what an analyst says as an abstract statement about facts and dynamics denudes it of its power and implications for the patient's existence. Second, interpretations are as much statements of what is unknown or ambiguous as they are statements of truth and presence. The recognition of the alterity of the patient, his ultimate concealment and inaccessibility, the undisclosed nature of his being-in-the-world, gives interpretation a humble quality. We give our interpretations as a stranger on the road directs a traveler to a place he is seeking, but what he finds there will be his own unique experience (Schermer, 1999). Thus, Continental philosophy places interpretive understanding at the center of human existence and at the same time offers cautionary tales about the dangers and limits of understanding.

In Part I, I have offered a selective overview of the evolution of philosophical hermeneutics from antiquity to modern and postmodern developments with respect to their relevance for Freud, psychoanalysis, and psychotherapy. Practitioners may have found themselves asking how these understandings are useful within the cauldron of the treatment process in their day-to-day therapy sessions. Are there methods and techniques that can be developed to apply hermeneutics in various situations that arise? Modern hermeneutics itself cautions us to be wary of method, emphasizing the spontaneous nature of meanings and their tendency to reveal and then conceal and deconstruct themselves! A systematic approach to treatment or even a set of recommendations does not easily emerge from a study of the nature of meaning-making.

Rather, what I have tried to do in the next four chapters, Part II, is to articulate in a coherent way how hermeneutical philosophy can be utilized by therapists to achieve greater understanding of their dialogues with their patients. First, I consider what Leo Stone (1961) called "the psychoanalytic situation" and try to show why and how it is primarily a situation of meaning-making as opposed to a controlled environment for scientific observation. Then, I develop a way of thinking about hermeneutical dualities and dimensions of events transpiring in sessions. Next, I look at these dualities and meanings as they evolve over time during key events in psychotherapy. Finally, I explore the ultimate treatment objective, transformation of the self, in terms of the ways in which meaning promotes growth and change in the patient. In Part III, I examine several important Anglo-American perspectives from the standpoint of their philosophical and hermeneutical underpinnings. I invite you to join me in these explorations, and hope they will stimulate your own independent thinking in these matters.

PART II

HERMENEUTICS IN PSYCHOANALYTIC
PSYCHOTHERAPY

CHAPTER FIVE

The psychoanalytic situation: scientific "laboratory" or interpretive process?

Hermeneutics can illuminate psychoanalytic practice in many ways. Particular insights depend on where one starts theoretically and philosophically. Psychoanalysis today is a multifaceted discipline having many varieties of approach. It is important to know philosophically and operationally what they have in common and where they diverge. From the current vantage point, interpretation is the unifying core of psychoanalysis. An additional defining feature is the "psychoanalytic situation"—the framework and setting for practice. The structuring of that situation is the hub of psychoanalytic knowledge and treatment. Theory, research, and other avenues of understanding feed into and come out of the dyadic process conducted under a particular set of principles, protocols, and expectations established by Freud and maintained in their essential components to this day. In order to justify the ideas put forth in this book, it is important to look at this "staging area," and to make a cogent argument that it is essentially a setting for the study of meanings, a perspective that is different from and broader in scope than (although it can be integrated with and informed by) the traditional view that the consulting room is a place for a scientific type of investigation and therapy of the mind.

The concept of *The Psychoanalytic Situation* was highlighted by Leo Stone (1961) in a groundbreaking book by that title in which he advocated the analyst's spontaneity, warmth, and even a degree of transparency at a time when an almost monastic detachment and opacity was expected of the analyst. At the time, Kurt Eissler (1953), revered by the New York psychoanalytic Establishment, had recommended the most rigorous conditions to assure that interpretations accurately reflected the patient's dynamics and transference, with exceptions for patients with flawed ego development who he felt required special "parameters" to accommodate them. Eissler represented the school of thought which regarded the psychoanalytic situation as a controlled "laboratory" set-up akin to scientific research.

On the contrary, as I shall suggest, the hermeneutical perspective, far from requiring an almost "surgical" attitude, is facilitated by the openness and humanity of the analyst, so long as he maintains rigor and consistency in the attitude and understanding he offers to the patient. The discipline involves not so much neutrality and distance as it does mindfulness to the listening process, care and compassion, a degree of vulnerability, and willingness to risk one's self in the service of the patient, and a creative yet measured approach to the use of ideas, words, non-verbal expression, and gestures. The care that is exercised by the analyst involves a capacity for concern, not the detachment of the scientist.

To pursue this line of thought, it is important to elaborate specifically on why the psychoanalytic situation is not a controlled research setting, while allowing that a scientific "thread" is enabled through research efforts consilient with the sciences. Then, I will state why I feel that psychoanalytic treatment is first and foremost a process of exploring and elucidating meanings, hence a hermeneutical endeavor.

Contra Freud: the psychoanalytic situation is not a rigorous scientific research setting

There are many expectations surrounding psychoanalytic process. As discussed in Chapter One, Freud laid the groundwork for many of them, insisting that psychoanalysis is rigorous science. On that basis a belief has been maintained by the analytic Establishment that adherence to its method and technique provides a testing ground for scientific hypotheses. Many psychoanalysts claim that their theories are demonstrably true, and they draw their conclusions from their observations in the consulting room.

Their argument is that the structure and rules of the psychoanalytic situation provide an uncontaminated environment that minimizes the effects of suggestion and social influence, allowing the causes (etiology) of the patient's character and symptoms to be precisely discerned, as in a laboratory of the mind. The fixed time period of the fifty minute hour, the analyst's neutrality and non-disclosure, the abstinence rule limiting acting out, and the technical rules for analyzing transference and resistance purportedly provide a laboratory environment in which accurate observations and conclusions can be made.

Thus, for example, Glover's (1931) emphasis on "exact" interpretation implied that interpretation is science. Fenichel's classic work, *The Psychoanalytic Theory of the Neuroses* (1945) presented a compendium of symptoms and disorders as medical facts verified by findings of the consulting room. Langs's (1976) work on the bipersonal field called for a sorting out of mutual projective identifications between analyst and patient to assure that interpretations could be decontaminated and therefore correctly attributed to the patient's dynamics. In the examples in his book, Langs confronted supervisees about the impact of their countertransference on their patients' free associations, as if he as supervisor could identify a cause and effect relationship between them. He ignored the fact that the only way to identify a causal relationship is to change conditions and see what happens. As an astute clinician and supervisor, Langs might have correctly identified correlations between the therapist's countertransference and the patient's communications, but without active intervention he would have no way of knowing which caused the other to occur.

Langs (1992) subsequently proposed a dynamic systems view of psychoanalysis as an "Aristotelian science" which reads virtually as a counterposition to modern hermeneutics. In general, the idea of objectivity in science began with Aristotle and formed the basis of Freud's particular way of understanding the unconscious (Schermer, 2011, pp. 840–842). Analysts like Eissler, Glover, Fenichel, and Langs, who embraced this objective stance have been among the most powerful in the profession, setting standards of training and practice, so their views must be taken seriously.

With all due respect to these iconic figures, and while maintaining a strong allegiance to psychoanalysis, I do not believe that the psychoanalytic situation offers the types of controls that characterize scientific research. While, as in all human relations, cause and effect are sometimes discernible in a session, as when an interpretation is followed by an intense emotional response, or the analyst's vacation leads to an episode of depression, the psychoanalytic situation has no particular claim to being a controlled observational environment. In fact, in some respects, it is quite the opposite. I would go further and say, in support of psychoanalysis, that it is not at all necessary for it to be so. The scientific method can be applied more fruitfully outside the consulting room. The theories generated in practice can be and often are subject to more careful research elsewhere through multidisciplinary cooperation.

Contrary to the paradigm expressed by Freud, the rules of psychoanalytic practice do not, except in the most superficial sense, lead to accurate assessment of causal relationships, but rather fulfill a contract that hopefully protects the patient and to some extent the analyst as they undertake the difficult and risky task of probing the psyche. For one thing, the openness of the situation to free association and a multitude of unpredictable shifts in atmosphere and spontaneous responses, all of which distinguish analysis from forms of treatment that carefully structure the patient's responses, is diametrically opposed to controlled scientific study in which variables are highly specified in order to assure that the outcomes result from one or several factors of interest. For example, the use of the couch, and the invisibility, neutrality, and opacity of the analyst are no guarantee that the dynamics are exclusively the patient's or reliably inferred. The analyst cannot help but emit verbal and non-verbal cues that affect the patient and what he or she says and does. The patient may be supine and unable to see the analyst, but he or she gets to know the analyst quite well from how he speaks as well as how he responds at the beginning and end of the session when they are face to face. Moreover, since the visual cues are minimized, the patient often becomes acutely sensitive to other minute details about the analyst's deportment. It is common knowledge that patients produce dreams and fantasies that conform to the analyst's theoretical orientation. Social communication occurs at preconscious levels between them and could in principle only be controlled by so-called "double blind" experimental conditions in which neither subject nor observer is aware of the factors being investigated. Such an experimental protocol is not even closely approximated in the consulting room.

Thus, the rules and contract of psychoanalytic treatment, even under the most rigorous conditions, do not produce a causally deterministic situation. Indeed, the purpose of the rules and rituals is not to control the variables, but quite the opposite, to allow the patient maximum freedom of verbal expression. Given that freedom, the rules of the session serve to be evocative rather than limiting, reducing the external structuring of thought imposed on the patient. In addition, at least to some degree, the rules assure the patient that the situation is ethical, safe, and dependable, and specifically that he may express himself fully without negative consequences from his own actions or from the analyst's judgments.

Second, unlike the privacy of psychoanalytic sessions, scientific empirical observations are available for scrutiny and replication by the community of scientists. Data is objectified and made public so that it can be scrutinized and replicated by others. By contrast, the psychoanalytic situation is one of the most confidential, intimate, unrepeatable, subjective, and carefully guarded interpersonal exchanges ever conceived. Transcribed protocols and one-way mirror observations are exceptional occurrences. Very few sessions ever see such scrutiny. Moreover, in most case studies, even when countertransference is acknowledged, the analyst's mental processes are rarely if ever disclosed to the same extent as the patient's, so that a significant component of what transpires in the dyad is never reported. (A research study that omitted half the relevant data would be laughed out of a scientific journal or meeting!) In addition, each psychoanalytic session is unique and unrepeatable. Respect for the individuality, freedom, and spontaneity of the patient is the *sine qua non* of analysis. By contrast, a scientific experiment requires manipulation and repeatability.

Nevertheless, the picture is not all that dismal. Psychoanalytic insights from the consulting room are not pure mythology. There is room in psychoanalytic treatment to check theories to see if they are borne out in particular instances, and it is possible to make carefully controlled studies of some sessions, even to the point of measuring physiological variables such as heart rate, blood pressure, sugar and hormone levels, and brain activity. In addition, conclusions reached by analysts are frequently cross-checked with observations made on children, mother–infant pairs, and groups. In this respect, psychoanalysis provides an opportunity to develop hypotheses in an environment in which the richness of the material far exceeds almost any other human encounter. For this reason, if for no other, psychoanalysis occupies a very important place in the human sciences.

It is almost tragically problematical that Freud straitjacketed his remarkable observations and insights within the language of objective science. Most other analysts have followed him in this respect. Thus, it is difficult to separate oneself and one's understanding from the insistence on scientific provability and control. In fact, the point in briefly reintroducing here the perhaps tiresome question of whether psychoanalysis is science is only to make room for another, more encompassing view of the psychoanalytic situation as hermeneutical, an optimal situation for inquiry into meanings and understandings implicit in human thought and behavior. It is the interpretive endeavor that drives the analysis and makes it operative on various levels. The less clouded it is by presuppositions about scientific objectivity and predictability the better. (And, to repeat, such openness does not prevent psychoanalysis from having value in the sciences.)

Why the psychoanalytic situation is essentially interpretive

The transactions that occur in psychoanalytic therapy have been conceptualized in specific ways that characterize particular schools of thought. Thus, there are a number of current perspectives on psychoanalysis that define themselves in terms of what they regard as the essential nature of the psychoanalytic situation. A popular view today is that it is basically an interpersonal relationship. This viewpoint is incorporated into Sullivanian analysis, the British independent tradition of object relations, relational and intersubjective psychology, and attachment theory. Another vantage point emphasizes the study of human subjectivity. The Institute for the Psychoanalytic Study of Subjectivity in New York offers such an orientation. Still another orientation consists of a psychospiritual understanding. The Psychotherapy & Spirituality Institute, also in New York, includes psychodynamically oriented courses and teachers. Of course, there is the "mainstream" view that psychoanalysis is the objective study of the individual psyche as a bio-social process and structure. Many psychoanalytic training institutes around the world emphasize this model from classical Freudian, object relations, and ego psychological perspectives.

Hermeneutics incorporates all these orientations—the interpersonal, the subjective, the spiritual, and the scientific—as modalities of human understanding. The chief point of this book is that the common feature of psychoanalysis which subsumes all these modes is that it is a treatment modality based on hermeneutics. From this perspective, the method, strategies, and techniques of the psychoanalytic situation serve the ultimate purpose of "unconcealing" meanings in all their clarity and ambiguity, meanings that are pertinent to human life and personality and which have the potential to heal and alleviate unnecessary psychological suffering, meanings that include the unconscious as the unthought known within.

The reader's immediate response to such a hermeneutical stance may be that it is too broad a base to define psychoanalysis as such. Is it not the case that all human enterprises driven by sound values include studies of meanings with the hope of helping people? Indeed, but that question also points to the fact that psychoanalysis is not an esoteric practice but, on the contrary, has elements in common with many other human activities, whether art, parenting, even sports and law. However, *what makes the psychoanalytic situation decidedly hermeneutical is that it is optimally designed to increase and enhance the access to complex meanings and intentions pertaining to the lived lives of individuals who experience conflict, troubles, and psychological symptoms.* In essence, it is what Breuer's and Freud's patients first perceived it to be, namely, "the talking cure."

There are several reasons why the psychoanalytic situation is fundamentally hermeneutical and highly attuned to meanings:

1. The primary tool of treatment is interpretation, to be distinguished from argument, suggestion, behavioral reinforcement, cognitive restructuring, and other intervention strategies used by non-analytic modes of psychotherapy. Psychoanalytic interpretation imparts meaning whose primary purpose is to deepen and elucidate other meanings in dialogue. It "brackets off" other concrete goals and objectives which other therapies emphasize, striving for a rare openness to mutual experience.

2. For this reason, psychoanalysis is structured as an exceptionally ambiguous situation that allows a wider range of meanings and understandings to emerge than almost any other endeavor. The encouragement to "say whatever comes to mind," the hopefully non-judgmental and receptive listening by the analyst, the assurance of confidentiality, and the entire tradition of the "talking cure," all facilitate explorations of meaning that go well beyond that which

is sanctioned in most other therapies and life situations. The most important legacy of a century or more of psychoanalytic studies is the remarkable increase in the scope of human thought and understanding it has revealed. This legacy began with the then radical theory of infantile sexuality but now includes a virtually encyclopedic understanding of what goes on within the rooms of people's minds, the subtleties of their attachments to and interactions with others, and the cultural, historical, and developmental factors contributing to mind and identity.

3. The contract between patient and analyst is unique, namely to continue on an ongoing basis to explore these meanings in an atmosphere of mutual trust with the expressed purpose of deepening self-understanding that leads to transformations in the way one thinks, feels, and lives, with the least amount of premature conclusions, judgments, and biases (which of course hermeneutics itself contends can never be fully attained).

Thus, what fundamentally characterizes psychoanalysis and unifies its diverse approaches is the persistent and uncensored exploration of meaning. For this reason, hermeneutics can provide a framework for theory and practice with rich and useful insights into its process and structure. Again, this does not preclude science, but places the scientific aspect within the larger context of human experience involving dialogue, language, and history.

Freud was intent on giving a scientific cast to psychoanalysis. Yet the two events that led to the birth of psychoanalysis were interpretive: his book on dream interpretation and his substitution of a dialogical relationship with the patient in place of hypnotic suggestion. The first utilized methods of exegesis that had Talmudic and Aristotelean sources, among others. The second reflected his effort to arrive at deep understanding of another's experience and world. These are essentially hermeneutical endeavors.

Towards an "applied hermeneutics" for
psychoanalytic psychotherapy

The purpose of the foregoing arguments, some of which may labor the point, has been to anticipate a difficult further question. "OK," thinks the practical reader. "If we agree that meaning-making is the driving force of psychoanalytic therapy, then how can we utilize hermeneutical understanding in the actual treatment process? Since we can't call upon scientific method or even a favored theory to guide us, how do we formulate our work with patients?" We seem to be left in a sea of meaning and understanding without a compass or a rudder.

I make no pretense to providing an easy or convenient answer to this dilemma. The problem is fundamental to hermeneutics: how to bring the interpretive process into a particular discipline, whether law, literature, or, in our case, psychoanalysis. Freud accomplished this task by using medical practice—psychiatry and neurology—as his model. Medicine proved too confining, even to him. I am advocating a much broader base for our work. I am suggesting that we serve as "readers of meanings." Meanings of what? Meanings of experiences that cause people pain, suffering, and conflict. Meanings which are identified with some aspect of their selfhood, as distinct from a purely external source. Meanings that have hidden elements that we may never fully grasp, but which we can perceive as "through a glass, darkly."

To be "readers," we need a common language. To alleviate pain, suffering, and conflict, we need an awareness of how people change and transform in healing ways. In the next chapter, I propose a vocabulary of hermeneutical understanding that consists of basic dimensions or dualities that emerge from hermeneutical philosophy. For a sense of a plot, I then look for patterns of events that occur over time in the course of treatment. Finally, I explore the relationship between meaning and self-transformation, how meaning-making becomes a vehicle for healing at deeper levels of personality and existence. I begin with the "architecture" of the process, the dualities and dimensions of hermeneutical understanding as they occur in the consulting room.

CHAPTER SIX

Dimensions and dualities: the architecture of psychoanalytic interpretation

"I call architecture frozen music."

—*Goethe* (diary entry of March 23, 1829 (Moorhead, 1998))

D
elving into the rich and challenging ideas in hermeneutics hopefully stimulates thinking and creativity regarding the nature of interpretation as both a human and a psychothera-peutic process. Some practitioners will also be thinking about their own work and their patients and how to open up new possibilities and nuances for intervention and care. They may wonder whether there is a way to systemize hermeneutics in a convenient form that can be used to think about cases, situations, and dynamics. Because of the multiplicity and complexity of ideas contained in philosophical hermeneutics, this is indeed a difficult task. To some extent, the choice of emphasis is an individual matter that depends on the therapist's unique way of acquir-ing meaning and understanding. A technical manual or "cookbook" approach would go against the grain of hermeneutical understanding as an in-the-moment personal and intuitive experience.

Nevertheless, hermeneutics does stress several components and dimensions of interpretations that are important in psychoanalytic psychotherapy. Such a classification might suggest what to look for and think about in sessions from an overarching philosophical perspective, a type of meta-psychoanalysis or meta-therapy. They could be thought of as the "architecture" of psychoanalytic interpretation, from which the "music" to which Goethe refers above unfolds in time during the course of therapy, which is the subject of the next chapter. Of course, each building has its own architecture, and this one is of my own construction! Hermeneutics permits various architectures of understanding, and I invite the reader to create his own if this one does not suit for a good home.

With such a purpose in mind, I will now utilize the ideas developed in the historical survey of hermeneutics covered in Part I to provide a set of "building blocks:" six dimensions, polarities, or dialogical opposites deriving from philosophical hermeneutics with a discussion of how they manifest in psychoanalytic therapy. I will describe how they can be used by a clinician to listen to and think about patients and case material. Then, in the next chapter, I will consider the implications of particular events and dynamic components that occur in the treatment process, the "music" as it unfolds in time. Lastly, in the final chapter of Part II, I will discuss how interpretation serves as a vehicle for the self-transformation of the patient.

Hermeneutical oppositions and dualities

Derrida (1981) emphasized the oppositions present in all texts. Critical of the privileging which values one side over the other, he held that both poles of any duality are always to be found even if one of them is dominant. Certainly this is true of psychoanalytic theories, which are multilayered and multifaceted. In any theory, the opposite pole always appears as a qualification or addendum. A good example of a theory that makes room for its opposite as a qualification or exception can be found in Stolorow's and his cohorts' position that psychoanalytic inquiry is intersubjective, the result of the combined subjective experience of patient and analyst. The two participants form a system, and understanding only occurs within that interaction. Nevertheless, intersubjectivists also hold that each person manifests an internal pre-existing "structure" determined by his or her individual history (Stolorow, Atwood, & Brandschaft, 1994, pp. 26–27). Stolorow's later writings on trauma (Stolorow, 2007) likewise suggest that trauma is internalized and made permanent in the individual. The dominant intersubjective position here is that understanding results from the here-and-now relationship, but room is then made for the individual's personal history, disposition, cognition, and affect.

There are many other examples where psychoanalysts advance a theory, and then incorporate the opposite pole into that theory. This is because no concept or theory can contain the whole of any phenomenon. (Derrida used this point to deconstruct texts.) My revered teacher, the late Gunther Abraham, the nephew of Karl Abraham, who trained at the Berlin Psychoanalytic Institute and then with Anna Freud and Donald Winnicott, often said that psychoanalysis is a dualistic psychology that develops differences and oppositions, as distinct from perspectives which emphasize wholeness or a single track of development. We could say that Hegel's dialectic of thesis-antithesis-synthesis (Taylor, 1977) applies to psychoanalytic discourse, with the caveat that some modern philosophers reject Hegel's idealism and metaphysics. It is also a matter of current philosophical debate whether human polarities evolve, as Hegel contended, in an upward progression towards an ideal goal. The same question could be asked about the course of an analysis: does it evolve towards a goal of healing, or does it constitute a process without a "final cause," while the patient extracts something useful along the way? Existential and postmodern thought are skeptical of progression and teleology, movement towards a goal.

Six dimensions of hermeneutical understanding

Such controversies notwithstanding, I propose six key oppositions or polarities that manifest within the psychoanalytic situation. As Derrida said, both sides of the opposition always manifest together, but one side is highlighted over the other in any given therapeutic situation and context. Derived from the discussions of Chapters Two to Four, they include the following, with thinkers who emphasize either side of the polarity mentioned in parentheses:

1) meanings "at hand" *vs.* meanings discerned (Heidegger *vs.* Husserl); 2) intra-text understanding *vs.* contextual understanding (traditional exegesis *vs.* Herder and Schleiermacher); 3) Dilthey's distinction between explanation and understanding: objectivity and detachment *vs.* personal experience; 4) empathy *vs.* radical difference and alterity (Merleau-Ponty *vs.* Levinas); 5) construction, structure, and presence *vs.* deconstruction, ambiguity, and absence (Lacan *vs.* Derrida); and 6) mystical wholeness *vs.* mechanistic reductionism (Jung *vs.* Freud).

I will now consider each of these dualities in terms of their relevance to psychoanalytic theory and practice. While I contrast them as opposites, the "*vs.*" might better be thought of as "vis-à-vis," since each dualism really forms a continuum of awareness. It cannot be overemphasized that the dualities are paradoxical: one includes the other. It is just that one side or the other becomes highlighted in particular situations. Figure 2 summarizes the six dimensions and gives a general suggestion of how they show up in psychoanalytic interpretations.

Figure 2. Six hermeneutical opposites and their corresponding interpretive components in psychotherapy.

Hermeneutical dimensions, dualities	*Dualities as focal points in interpretation*
Meanings "at hand" *vs.* meanings discerned	Nonverbal implicit behavior *vs.* explicit, verbal expression
Intra-text understanding *vs.* contextual understanding	"Here and now" in-session material *vs.* cultural and historical life narratives
Objective causality *vs.* intersubjective experience, expression, and understanding	Theoretical constructs *vs.* dialogue in a common language of experience
Empathy and attunement *vs.* radical difference and alterity	Mirroring *vs.* mutual masks or opaqueness
Construction, structure, and presence *vs.* deconstruction, ambiguity, and absence	Conclusion and closure *vs.* openness, ambiguity, and emptiness
Mystical wholeness *vs.* mechanistic reductionism (spirituality *vs.* science)	"I-Thou" encounter and transformation *vs.* dynamic interpretation of biosocial forces

Meanings "at hand" vs. meanings discerned

One of the "missing links" in discussions of psychoanalytic interpretation is its embeddedness in meanings that are as Heidegger said, implicit and "already there," in *Dasein*, being-in-the-world. Analysts present and portray their interpretations as if they consciously elevate repressed aspects of the self to the level of rational discourse. But interpretations are expressions of what is already "at hand." Like the iceberg metaphor of the unconscious, interpretations too are mostly "under water," that is, unexpressed. Everything spoken in a session, including the analyst's interpretations, is conditioned by and absorbed into "at hand" meanings that are usually unarticulated and remain so throughout treatment. An interpretation can never be abstracted from its context, and in that sense it is always imperfect and incomplete.

The psychoanalytic situation as an "at hand" factor in interpretation

The psychoanalytic situation conditions and contextualizes meanings that are implied but not stated in the process of interpreting the patient's dynamics. Orne (1962), with regard to hypnosis and experimental research (and by implication, therapy), used the phrase "demand characteristics" to refer to the implicit staging that affects the behavior of the subject, whether the laboratory setting itself, the experimenter's commanding presence, or the nuances in the experimenter's speech. The psychoanalytic situation has its own demand characteristics which result from the "technical manual" that the analyst follows, such as the use of the couch, social distance, neutrality and opaqueness, the abstinence rule (expressing in words, not actions), precise adherence to appointment times, and so on. Taken together, these practice rules and guidelines constitute their own hermeneutics or set demand characteristics (implied meanings). For instance, the structuring of the psychoanalytic situation gives most of the power and authority to the analyst. They constitute a kind of initiation rite into the analyst's world and convictions. Hopefully, in the resolution of the transference, some of the analyst's authority is placed on a more equitable basis. But early in treatment the rules and rituals reflect the analyst's expectations far more than the patient's choices. They may strike the patient either as arbitrary demands or, conversely, comforting structures.

If an analysis is to be complete, the underlying implications of the frame itself eventually must be made conscious and explored with the patient (Bleger, 1967). Some of those implications are psychosexual. Psychoanalytic rules vaguely resemble the "missionary position" in sex, with the analyst "on top," often reinforcing social conformity, male dominance (even if the analyst is female), and economic privilege (the analyst collects the fee). Patients, like lovers, often express frustration with such rules. Not everyone likes to be in a submissive position, whether in bed or on the couch. But these tacitly erotized experiences about "being analyzed" are rarely brought to the surface. The analytic frame somehow escapes interpretive scrutiny.

The analyst's specific, consciously formulated interpretations are colored with the set-up and trappings of the situation. It is often forgotten that in order for interpretations to "take hold" and be internalized by the patient, sometimes the rules must be modified to accommodate the patient's personality and cultural background. Thus, for example, in order to help a woman patient better utilize his interventions, a seasoned analyst found it helpful to modify his technique to convey an atmosphere of conviviality which was more consistent with the patient's idea of a good working relationship. He responded in a conversational tone when she showed him pictures of her child, asked appropriate questions, and engaged in friendly chatter. The patient was better able to think about and utilize interpretations when offered in an informal, conversational style. The atmosphere and expectations in the consulting room have an influence which conditions both the transference and the ways in which specific interpretations are experienced and understood.

Optimally, the "at hand" atmospherics of the frame and setting should tell the patient that "I will have an opportunity to experience, express, and understand many aspects of myself and my life without being judged, and I trust the analyst to help me know myself better and guide me through the emotional difficulties I may encounter." Unfortunately, the accoutrements of the situation and the analyst's comportment may communicate obedience to authority or conversely, a laissez-faire permissiveness. These implicit "messages" can unduly inhibit the patient or cause him to act out his impulses, and then later be misinterpreted as transference and resistance.

Hermeneutical understanding of the psychoanalytic situation thus suggests that the analyst be aware of the implicit meaning the patient gives to the analytic frame. The frame itself is internalized by the patient and, as such, becomes part of the analytic work. Whether to bend the frame or maintain it can be problematic and calls for sensitivity, intuition, and compassion on the part of the analyst.

Culture, history, and lifeworlds influence
interpretive understanding

Another implicit "at hand" aspect of treatment stems from the fact that patient and analyst each brings into sessions his own developmental history and assumptive world, much of which is implicit and never stated. Language idioms, gestures, and cultural background form part of the *Dasein* of each participant. Such factors play a role in how interpretations are formulated and how they are received and internalized by the patient.

> For example, a patient, Sam, came from an immigrant Jewish family of Eastern European descent. His family members spoke dramatically to one another, with vigorous hand gestures, Yiddish expressions, and emphatic speech. His analyst came from a reserved affluent Protestant background and spoke in the mildest of voices with minimal words and body movement. Despite the analyst's care and the validity of his interpretations, the patient had trouble bonding with him and found himself upset by even the most innocuous of the analyst's remarks. Although Sam was "in transference," playing out an attachment difficulty reflecting childhood abandonments and trauma, progress in the case was stymied until the unspoken cultural difference was articulated. When the analyst acknowledged the cultural factor, Sam was better able to reflect on his own dynamics. Much that occurs in sessions is never spoken and yet affects the way the patient feels understood or misunderstood, impacting the course and outcome of treatment. The words of an interpretation are always heard and assimilated culturally. In this instance, the family backgrounds of analyst and patient had a profound impact on how interpretations were delivered and understood.

Intra-text understanding vs. *contextual understanding*

In principle, one could conduct an analysis strictly in terms of what transpires in sessions, linking everything the patient says to the transference. Some have advocated analysis of the transference in that way, de-emphasizing the patient's history and daily life, focusing on the patient's in-session transference fantasies, resistances, and defenses. The transference is the "text" that is necessary and sufficient to elucidate all the dynamics of the patient (Joseph, 1985). The transference then becomes the primary basis of interpretation.

Such an approach parallels the traditional "linear" mode of biblical exegesis that prevailed until the Restoration and Romantic periods. The scriptural interpreter adhered to the text itself and used a set of established principles to ferret out the most accurate understanding consistent with features of the text. The interpreter minimally referred to factors extraneous to the text such as authorship and the historical context of the writing. The same could in principle be done with the material of a therapy session. Indeed, there are times when it is useful to "bracket" the sessions themselves and focus on the ongoing here-and-now relationship. Wolf (1988, pp. 110–118), from the standpoint of Kohut's self psychology, held that an essential component of treatment involves resolving the narcissistic slights and injuries the patient feels in response to the analyst's interventions. The emphasis is on "what happened between us and how you felt about it." Cognitive-behavioral and gestalt therapists also emphasize the "here-and-now."

At the other end of the polarity is an emphasis on the patient's history, biography, memories, dreams, coping mechanisms outside of sessions, and other factors that provide potential explanations of the patient's symptoms. The goal is to ascertain the patient's life narrative, discovering how he related to and was shaped by his lifeworld, and the transference is but one vehicle for reconstructing the life trajectory. Erik Erikson's psychohistorical studies of Martin Luther (1958) and Mahatma Gandhi (1993) exemplify such life narratives where the individual personality and its context are seen as interwoven.

Objective explanation vs. subjective experience, expression, and understanding

As previously discussed, this polarity has haunted psychoanalysis since its inception and reflects issues of metaphysics, consciousness, and the Cartesian mind–body dualism that is the heart and legacy of Western thought. As previously suggested, psychoanalysis began with Freud's empiricist/rationalist and biological underpinnings. Today, mainstream psychoanalysis had veered away from empiricism and reductionism, incorporating strains of phenomenology, humanism, existential thought, and mystical "non-understanding." More than ever, there is a polarity of psychoanalytic process and discourse that moves between objective, detached observation, on the one hand, and subjective states, dialogue, internal reality, and personal and social constructions on the other.

The objective/subjective polarity became highlighted in psychoanalysis when Kohut proposed the concept of "selfobject," the word itself suggesting a confabulation or synthesis of the subjective self and the "mirroring and idealizing" external object. Kohut said that the selfobject is the *subjectively perceived* caregiver. But in many developmental studies, the actual (not subjectively perceived) ministrations and failings of the parenting figure come into play. In Margaret Mahler's stages of symbiosis/separation-individuation (Mahler, Pine, & Bergman, 1975), the same dualism occurs. For example, early separation from the mother is both objective (the toddler, as opposed to the infant, is able to move further and tolerate longer absences from the real mother in field research studies) and subjective (the toddler begins to resolve internal splitting of the mother imago and gain an integrated constant image of her as a whole, independent person). In psychoanalytic discourse, shifts between subjective (phenomenological) and objective (empirically validated, realistic, veridical) descriptions of interpersonal relations occur often. So too, do we as clinicians casually take one for the other. This is unfair to the patient and creates theoretical muddles as well.

The subject-object duality can also implode. In Bion's (1962a, 1966, 1970) writings about "transformations in O," the subject-object distinction vanishes as the analyst listens "in the absence of memory, desire, and understanding," and modifications occur in unknown and unknowable dimensions (the unconscious). Bion, in effect, triangulated the subject-object duality into the Other, and Ogden's (2004) "analytic third" now hovers around the consulting room. Much of Bion's work points to the limits of dualistic thought (see Chapter Twelve). These limits to meaning and interpretation are as important as the interpretive process itself and call for humility on the analyst's part. "Brilliant" interpretations are of much less value in treatment than the steady presence and emotional availability of the analyst.

Subjective and objective aspects of psychological trauma

The subjective/objective distinction takes on critical importance in psychological trauma. Are traumatic events real or imagined? Famously, Freud found reasons to withdraw his original assertion that reminiscences of childhood sexual trauma were real events, and held that they were fantasies (Israels & Schatzman, 1993). The "false memory" syndrome, which took on serious implications in trials of alleged abusers (Pope, 1996), seemed to support the latter position. On the other hand, Herman and van der Kolk (1987) and others found a high incidence of real life trauma histories in the general psychiatric population and especially patients with borderline personality disorder. The actual situation is probably that there are large numbers of cases in both categories, and even when trauma is real and severe, it becomes elaborated and altered by fantasy and defense in the victim, thus becoming a highly charged subjective and personal experience of an objective event.

In the psychoanalytic situation itself (and clearly not all trauma patients belong in analysis), the emphasis on the subjective (experienced) versus objective (factual) side of the trauma is often a function of the particular patient at a particular point in the treatment. For example, a patient, Abigail recalled repeated sexual molestation by an older neighbor. That this was not her fantasy was confirmed by her mother and later admitted by the perpetrator, in addition to what the patient herself recalled in significant detail. In a previous ego-supportive treatment, Abigail's therapist validated her perceptions and recollections and helped the patient to resolve some of her confusion and doubts about what happened, thus alleviating a suicidal crisis. In her second round of psychoanalytic psychotherapy, the emphasis was placed on Abigail's subjectivity, on how the molestation manifested in her experience of the therapist and significant others. Dream material helped elucidate the inner world that had evolved in Abigail as a result of the abuse.

In the lifeworld, all experience contains elements that are at once objective, subjective, and "at hand" (implicit; non-conscious; procedural). Psychoanalytic interpretation emphasizes the subjective aspect, especially that which might elucidate unconscious derivatives. In that respect, objective reality is generally given less importance than psychological perception. Psychoanalysis is the study of the *inner* life. However, even schizophrenic patients have registered and recall real events in their lives, which they sometimes express in "coded" forms (hallucinations; bizarre objects; delusions) and need to be interpreted in terms of the real events to which they refer. One schizophrenic patient spoke about delusions of persecution and hallucinations of ghosts that haunted his home. When he finally managed to tell the therapist that as a child he was subject to literal torture by a cruel father, it became clear that he was not merely "crazy," but communicating about real past events. The only way he knew how to express himself about reality was through hallucination and delusion! Psychoanalytic interpretations, despite their emphasis on subjective experience, must include reference to real time- and space-bound events in the patient's life, or they will lack the total picture and may even encourage psychosis in the patient. One of the great challenges to all clinicians is to sort out the real from the subjective and imaginary in the patient's lifeworld.

Ultimately, subjective and objective are not absolute distinctions. Admixtures of both are contained in all our perceptions and memories. Such a shuffling and shuttling between objective and subjective is played out on a large screen when we fall in love. We accurately perceive some aspects of the lover that ordinarily go unnoticed, and at the same time our perceptions are colored and distorted. This altered state of "love consciousness" where both subjective and objective become heightened may have influenced Freud's emphasis on love and desire in his self-analysis and psychosexual theory of development. The economy of his own and others' desire brought together his interests in objective biology and the subjective phenomena of the self.

Empathy and attunement vs. radical difference and alterity

We have already shown how hermeneutics was enriched and expanded by Herder's emphasis on "radical difference" between the interpreter and the subject. "Difference" later became fundamental in the writings of Heidegger, Derrida, and Levinas. Herder questioned the intuitive folk psychology idea of a natural affinity between people, which in psychotherapy we call empathy. In its place, he offered a more rigorous and extensive process of "feeling one's way into" (*Einfühlung*) the ways and mind of another. But without a degree of empathy and mutual understanding to begin with, going deeper is difficult or impossible, like deciphering pulsations from outer space to see if they betoken intelligent life. All human communication involves a degree of commonality and empathy as well as an inquiry into that which is unique and different.

This duality of empathy vs. difference is evident in child development. Infant research shows that the baby comes into the world ready to engage with mother in a playful interchange of utterances, facial expressions, and gestures (Trevarthen, 1985). The mother is spontaneously drawn to the infant and meets the baby on his or her own expressive turf. Without that empathic interchange, further emotional and interpersonal development is stifled, as can be seen with some autistic children who have trouble reading facial expressions (Weigelt, Koldewyn, & Kanwisher, 2012).

With separation-individuation and the child's development of language, however, mother and child must go beyond empathy and attunedness to "feel their way into" each other's minds through complex exchanges of ideas, emotions, and information. This facilitates the process of "mentalization" in the child, the ability to understand the mental processes of self and other (Fonagy, Gergely, Jurist, & Target, 2002). The interchanges that facilitate mentalization are often difficult and conflicted, with a sometimes troubling separateness and alterity experienced by both parent and child. Paradoxically, the ability to recognize and understand another's subjectivity develops from radical difference.

The Kernberg vs. Kohut debate: empathy vs. objectivity in the treatment of narcissism

In psychoanalysis, both empathy and "feeling one's way into," recognition of commonality and difference, play significant roles. Kohut's self psychology emphasized the importance of "experience-near" empathic understanding to the development of the self. With some justification, Kohut (1959) felt that psychoanalysts too often interpreted material from a theory-driven "experience-distant" perspective, and should depend more on empathy to help the patient feel understood, especially in patients with narcissistic personality disorder who lack a cohesive self. By contrast, Otto Kernberg's (1975) approach to working with narcissistic patients was based on object relations theory. He advocated confronting and interpreting the defenses of splitting and projective identification, as well as the sadistic features which Kohut believed were secondary to narcissistic injury. There ensued a famous controversy about which of them had the correct theory and strategy for the narcissistic disorders. (I do not know whether Kohut and Kernberg themselves ever participated in this controversy; others took up the cudgels for them.) It may be that some patients and disorders benefit more from empathy and some require the boundaries of alterity and confrontation of defenses. Many or most patients probably require well-timed measures of both empathy and difference, just as do children with their parents.

Construction, structure, and presence vs. deconstruction, ambiguity, and absence

In hermeneutics, deconstruction was central to the postmodern turn initiated by Derrida, where serious challenges were posed to long-held Western concepts of structure and presence, that is, understandings that attribute existence, substance, and order to elements of a text, philosophical and scientific explanations, literary/artistic criticism, and by extension, to psychoanalytic theories and patients. A striking example of such deconstructive critique occurred when literary scholars influenced by Derrida, such as Cixous (1972), articulated inconsistencies and diversions within Freud's essay, "The 'Uncanny'" (1919h), suggesting that his "scientific" discourse on phenomena like *déjà vu* and unexplainable coincidences were in fact expressions of Freud's own discomfort with uncanny experiences (Bartnes, 2010). These scholars tried to deconstruct the "presence" in Freud of "the rigorous scientist" by betraying the subjective element of his own ghostly haunting that pervades the writing. In a way, they turned Freud on Freud. The same duality could be applied to all psychoanalysts, whose interpretations are based on both the professional role and personal subjectivity and history. Which aspect becomes highlighted depends on the flow of the treatment process, the patient's needs, and the analyst's countertransference.

Deconstruction of the patient's world view and self-image

A considerable proportion of psychoanalytic work consists in deconstructing the patient's ego, examining the patient's narratives (texts) for their slips, inconsistencies, ambiguities, and fallibilities. Sometimes, when it becomes a serious obstacle to progress in therapy, we have to deconstruct the patient's biographical narrative and expose it as a fantasy or myth.

> Thus for a long time, a patient, Ellen, recalled her childhood and adolescent experience and family life as "quite normal," with a loving and high-achieving father and a nurturing and responsive

mother. She remembered very little distress during her childhood, and presented that time period as if she had been a happy and content little girl. Indeed, Ellen was quite puzzled about her anxiety symptoms and her need for treatment. "I had a good childhood. Perhaps my anxiety is in my genes."

Ellen thus found it difficult to explain her adult difficulties with men and relationships, not to mention her episodes of depression and anxious disorganization, which she attributed to "PMS" (premenstrual syndrome) and other psychosomatic factors like foods and allergies. Over time, however, she began to mention facts inconsistent with her narrative of an idyllic childhood. "By the way," she said, "my mother had relatives who were Holocaust survivors." And "my [brilliant and successful] father never got over his reluctant involvement in an unethical and harmful business venture." The patient said she first noticed symptoms when, at age ten, she first went away to summer camp and "naturally" felt anxious and lonely, "the way any child would."

The therapist felt that Ellen's prolonged denial of her disruptive family life posed a serious obstacle to any further progress in treatment. To move the therapy forward, he felt he needed to deconstruct Ellen's family myth. Finally, after much concern that Ellen might be re-traumatized by his interpretation, he urgently impressed upon her that her parents were not as easy-going as she portrayed them, and that she may have felt truly abandoned by them. He presented her with what she had disclosed that proved his points.

Ellen came to her next session in a state of panic. She said she had a terrifying nightmare of being captive in a concentration camp and the one person who could have helped her escape (the therapist?) disappeared. From this starting point of dream-awareness of terror and what Apprey (1999) calls "transgenerational haunting," Ellen began to recognize the profound implications of the fact that, far from having had an idyllic childhood, she had grown up in a home besieged by survivor guilt regarding the Holocaust. She saw that her parents were highly invested in maintaining a pseudo-normal but pathological family image (Sonne, 1992) of a happy, "American dream" middle-class family as a form of denial of Holocaust trauma and readjustment to post-war life. The analyst's interpretations were deconstructions in that they exposed inconsistencies in the patient's story rather than offering an explanation that provided structure and content. They exposed an unhealed wound. But fortunately, new structures developed in the wake of the exposure of the fault lines in Ellen's self-image. She did not decompensate but instead showed emotional resilience.

Psychoanalysis can be viewed either as a study of enduring structures, development, and dynamics; or it can be seen to be a process of deconstructing assumptions and strategies of the conscious self and ego, exposing fault lines, inconsistencies, and absences within the personality. The difference could be compared to that between Judeo-Christian teachings, which try to show by faith or reason the *presence* of a unifying God, as opposed to Zen Buddhism, which shows the fallacies, paradoxes, and emptiness in all assumptions and beliefs. Zen paradoxes are deconstructive of dualities, and psychoanalytic interpretations can be paradoxical in that respect as well.

Psychoanalytic interpretations are both constructive and deconstructive. They provide the patient with a new understanding of him or herself, and at the same time reveal ambiguities and contradictions that lead the patient deeper into unknown territory and tolerance for absence and non-being. In this latter sense, intepretations subvert underlying meaning, leading the patient to confront the emptiness of non-understanding (Epstein, 1996).

A patient, Charles, had a dream about standing anxiously at the entrance to a bridge that crossed a wide river from the familiar city where he stood to a precipitous cliff on the other side, beyond which were vast unknown expanses of land. In treatment, Charles had worked hard to "bridge" the distance between himself and his wife, who had recently ended a steamy extramarital affair in order to repair her marriage. For many months, Charles could only think of divorce, but eventually considered reconciliation as a result of a period of analysis in which he became aware of his competitiveness with his father and his lifelong feeling of being misunderstood by his mother, who could not relate to his intelligence and creativity and therefore was unable to "give birth" to them. As he became conscious of the resentment he had displaced from his parents onto his wife, Charles achieved greater empathy for her, which helped them to reunite. The therapist interpreted that the bridge in the dream represented his reconnection with his wife as well as with repressed parts of himself, and that the city symbolized the work he had done in therapy. The bridge itself was a "construction" that helped the patient integrate parts of himself and his fragmented marital life.

Charles agreed with the therapist's interpretation, but then pointed out that he felt anxious in the dream as he still felt about his marriage, and that his anxiety had to do with both crossing the "bridge over troubled waters" and the unknown territory that he would encounter if he did so. In treatment, he had previously tended to be obsessive and conflict-avoidant. The therapist told Charles that the dream pointed to his increased potential to live with his anxieties and with the unknown aspects of himself and his life. There followed a series of sessions in which Charles, with alternating feelings of anxiety and joy, expressed his feelings about the challenging aspects of his marriage, his career, his adolescent daughter's development, and his sister's medical condition. He was becoming better able to live with existential angst, the complex, uncertain aspects of authentic living which he had long avoided. In this respect, the bridge led to awareness of his uncertain, time-bound "being-in-the-world." It deconstructed his obsessive defenses.

For optimal development, human beings require both poles of structure, belief, and presence as well as absence, doubt, deconstruction, and even destruction. (Destruction of the old often precedes creation of the new, and this is one reason we fear the unknown.) Interpretation includes both construction and destruction, presence and absence. Bass (2006) called the combination of construction and deconstruction contained in interpretation "the strangeness of care." Authentic emotional truth—*alatheia*—results from interpretive encounters with both the life and death instincts experienced as movement between belief and presence on the one hand, and their deconstruction or absence on the other.

Destruction as a developmental necessity

Winnicott (1969) wrote about the constructive role of destruction in the development of the child's ego. According to him, "… destruction plays its part in making the reality, placing the object outside the self ... *There is no anger* in the destruction of the object to which I am referring, though there could be said to be joy at the object's survival. From this moment, or arising out of this phase, the object is in fantasy always being destroyed. This quality of 'always being destroyed' makes the reality of the surviving object felt as such, strengthens the feeling-tone, and contributes to object-constancy. The object can now be used."

The infant's discovery that the caregiver can be destroyed in fantasy and yet survive in reality is what makes caregiving real and safe. Children enjoy their games and fantasies of eliminating their parents because they know the parents are still there. Similarly, deconstructive psychoanalytic interpretations that "destroy" a patient's beliefs and deconstruct his transference wishes, when given with the supportive "presence" implied by proper tact, timing, and care for the patient's ego, can help him establish an internalized object world (inner and outer reality combined in the transitional space) in which he or she can survive and thrive. (See Chapter Ten for a further discussion of Winnicott.)

The dualistic understanding of interpretive construction *vs.* de(con) struction suggests a reconsideration of the nature of resistance. The patient's resistances to the analyst's interpretations are typically viewed as denial or disavowal of emotional truth. However, resistances may also represent helpful deconstructions of the analyst's interpretations, unmasking the paradoxes they contain in order to better utilize them. Thus, a patient who found himself withdrawing from women when he most hoped to initiate a relationship with them objected strongly to an Oedipal interpretation that he wished for a sexual conquest but feared he might be rejected and lose his manhood. He said angrily to the analyst, "You're crazy! I just want to talk to women! I can't understand why they always put me off." The patient's history of unempathic parenting suggested that his own feeling that women really misunderstood him was just as valid as the therapist's explanation based on castration anxiety. The therapist, instead of furthering his own interpretation, told the patient he wanted to hear more about what it meant to him to "get friendly and close." The patient was then able to work with both his castration anxiety and his difficulties with attachment as such, leading him to overcome the inhibition that kept him from meeting and talking to women. Billow (2010), discussing group psychotherapy from a relational perspective, pointed out the emotional growth and therapeutic values inherent in "resistance, rebellion, and refusal." Such a view is consistent with deconstructive and postmodern thought.

Mystical, organic wholeness vs. rational reductionism

In the aftermath of the schism between Freud and Jung, Jung appropriated the spiritual, uncanny, and supernatural aspects of the psyche, while Freud and his camp tightened the reigns on their rationalist reductionist view, making the biological drives the determining factor. Jung also considered the psyche to be an organic whole proceeding from an initial oneness through differentiation, individuation, and reintegration. By contrast, Freudian, ego psychological, and most object relations theorists have always utilized a biosocial reductionist model, explaining the unconscious in terms of lower level building blocks such as drives, needs, and internalized object relations. The whole is accounted for in terms of its parts, which are emanations of the natural, not spiritual, world.

Vattimo's postmodern turn, spirituality, and psychoanalysis

This differentiation between naturalist-reductionist and spiritual understanding is partially reconciled in postmodern philosophy and hermeneutics. Philosopher Gianni Vattimo (2010, pp. 3–36) divided hermeneutics into modern and postmodern periods, interestingly dating these eras earlier than most scholars. The former, modernism (many would call this period the Enlightenment), which he backdates to Descartes, included both the natural sciences and what he calls a "strong" concept of God, the traditional Judeo-Christian understanding of God as a metaphysical entity, a reality behind appearances. The latter, which Vattimo calls postmodernism (which many would call modernity), acknowledges both science and religion as sources of understanding.

Vattimo says that Nietzsche's famous dictum "God is dead" initiated postmodern thought. There are two possible interpretations of the death of God. One is that God is nothing more than a comforting illusion, as Marx and Freud maintained. The other is what Vattimo calls a "weak" form of faith and belief, a use of theological and spiritual ideas in frameworks which do not take a position on God as either Being (existence) or a being (object), but allow for ideas that have at least the traces of earlier God-based systems of thought. By "weak," Vattimo does not imply devaluation but rather a lack or absence that might itself have positive value.

In the age of psychoanalytic pluralism, which itself could be considered a postmodern phenomenon in which all truth claims represent "differences" that merit legitimacy, it is of note that spirituality has found its way into the "mainstream" of post-Freudian thought by way of a "weak" form (in Vattimo's positive sense) of understanding the unconscious as a psychospiritual preformative mind, a primal source that has god-like properties without the implications of deities, demons, and the supernatural. This development was foreshadowed and perhaps spurred on in part by Marion Milner's (1969) groundbreaking case study of a schizophrenic woman, *The Hands of the Living God: An Account of a Psychoanalytic Treatment*. While Milner did not offer a psychospiritual perspective as such, she did bring attention to the rich multilayered aspects of God in the psyche and in psychopathology.

But the breakthrough book that gave a mystico-spiritual aspect of the mind respectability and cache in some quarters of mainstream psychoanalysis was Bion's (1970) essay, *Attention and Interpretation*. Here, Bion discussed the nature of psychoanalysis from a rigorous scientific perspective based on logic and classification of facts. However, when he wrote about the listening process itself, he likened it to the meditations of contemplative mystics. He held that unconscious phenomena, akin to mystical experience, are beyond comprehension by memory, desire, and understanding. The depths of the mind are "nonsensuous" and are known by means other than sensation, recall, and reason. He used the symbolic notation "O" to represent the otherness of the unconscious and held that it was "known" by its transformations, just as mystics know God through the profound changes that occur in their character and states of consciousness. (See Chapter Twelve for further discussion.)

Since then, a number of mainstream psychoanalysts, primarily with an object relations orientation, have ventured into the realm of mystical and spiritual understanding (Schermer, 2003). Michael Eigen's *The Psychoanalytic Mystic* (1998) used the insights of Bion and Winnicott to explore the unspoken, ineffable dimensions of communication, development, and self-transformation in psychoanalytic psychotherapy, drawing connections to Kabbalistic teachings, which he more recently took up in much greater detail in *Kabbalah and Psychoanalysis* (2012).

Berke and Schneider (2008) drew a comparison between Melanie Klein's "depressive position" and the principle of reparation in Kabbalistic teachings. Nina Coltart (2000) and Mark Epstein (1996) offered crossovers and comparisons between Buddhist teachings and psychoanalysis. Grotstein (1997, 2000) discussed the role of psychic presences in mental development, and put forth the notion of the unconscious as "infinite geometer," a generator of combinations and permutations of thoughts and paradoxes with an implicit order to them, reminiscent of astronomer James Jeans's speculation that "God is a mathematician." Thus, a growing corpus of work on psychospiritual features of psychoanalysis is evolving within the American and British mainstream.

As Vattimo implies, in a postmodern world, mysticism and empiricism, holistic and reductionistic perspectives can exist side by side and work well together despite their differences. This is because their absolute authority has been "weakened." Vattimo allows for a resilient hermeneutics that oscillates between the poles of religion and mysticism on the one hand and scientific explanations on the other.

> Thus, for example, a patient, Calvin, devoted many therapy hours to exploring the impact of his troubled adolescence, during which he was caught between two identities: 1) that of an intellectual with high academic achievement and 2) membership in a violent and criminal street gang in an urban ghetto. The origin of these two polar opposite social selves could be traced back to his early childhood, when Calvin received soft and tender mirroring and stroking from his adoring mother that gave him a sense of self-importance and pleasure, in contrast with overly strict discipline by his father, which left him feeling angry, misunderstood, and marginalized. The untimely illness and death of his mother during Calvin's puberty left both father and son acutely lonely and abandoned. Calvin mourned and honored his mother's memory through intellectual achievement and proved his manhood to his father through participation in street violence. In treatment, as Calvin worked through his unresolved grief and formed a new, safer attachment to the analyst, he was able to reconcile the two conflicting sides of himself and acknowledge the vulnerability and neediness for which he compensated by gang participation and obsessive immersion in his studies.

In the middle of his treatment, appreciating the relief of anxiety brought about by therapy and experiencing a new spurt of sexual prowess and affection in his previously impotent love life, Calvin brought the therapist a gift of a small, framed collage of a mythic warrior bird with broad wings and weapons around its waist. The analyst was taken by the fact that the gift was from a foreign culture, so he asked him about the source of his interest in such things. Calvin said he had a fascination with Japanese culture, which he had studied extensively in college.

Following this occurrence, the analysis took on a new turn as Calvin quietly manifested a state of mind that embodied despair and emptiness, a kind of soul sickness. Calvin began to speak of the lack that he had felt ever since his mother died. There were long periods of silence in the session. During that time, the therapist noticed that his own state of consciousness had trance-like features as if he had left his body for moments. At the same time, he experienced an uncanny feeling that he was in contact with "emanations" from the patient of sub-personalities that seemed to be hallucinatory, haunting presences. He speculated to himself that he was experiencing the projectively identified split-off portions of the patient's personality. But he did not make interpretations to the patient. This pattern recurred intermittently for several weeks. At the end of that time, during which very little analytic "work" was accomplished, the patient said he had a new sense of wholeness and, with some humor said that it was as if the therapist was his Buddhist teacher. In some Japanese myths, the warrior bird evolved as a benign protector from a dog, called Tengu, which represented demonic forces. Was the therapist somehow protecting Calvin from the demoniacal within himself?

In the first stages of Calvin's therapy, the interpretive process was verbal, rational, and reconstructive, and the understanding provided was about the history and etiology of the patient's conflicts and symptoms. After the symbolic gift, however, the "interpretations" consisted of little other than silence, "beyond memory, desire, and understanding," and the only evidence that anything took place between therapist and patient consisted of the therapist's altered states and the patient's subsequent report of self-transformation.

It could be argued that psychoanalytic treatment consists of both components: rational discourse seeking naturalistic biosocial explanations and tacit psychospiritual experiences of "transformations in O" that can lead towards greater integration and wholeness.

Unfolding the dimensions: from "architecture" to "music"

To sum up, some concepts from philosophical hermeneutics can be schematized in terms of hermeneutical dimensions or polarities that show up in psychoanalytic treatment. This viewpoint hopefully allows the therapist to think about theory and practice from the perspective of hermeneutics. It is important to realize, however, that these polarities are not classifications of stasis, of stable unchanging categories or essences, but rather dialogical elements of flux, change, and disequilibrium within a therapeutic process that evolves over time. The hermeneutics of psychoanalytic treatment, or for that matter any other authentic discourse, evolves with continuities, jumps, and starts within the developing relationship. In the next chapter, we look at how these dualities can prove useful in interpretive work during key encounters as the process unfolds.

CHAPTER SEVEN

Hermeneutics in the unfolding process

The interpretive polarities just discussed are phenomenological and dialogical features of discourse. The ways in which they manifest in treatment can be compared with music and the arts. They are analogous to the characters in a play, the themes of a symphony, or the color palette of an artist. Thus, they can appear "on stage" together or appear in different scenes. Like the theme and variations of music, they can occur just once and have a large impact, or be repeated throughout treatment. They can be pure primary colors or mixed together to form a rich variety of shades. Like the notes of a musical scale, hermeneutical dimensions can manifest simultaneously (harmony) or they can shift over time (melody and counterpoint). Like musical notes, they are "already there" as elements of meaning-making and are called into play at any point in time by the exigencies of human experience, expression, and understanding. Hermeneutical dimensions and dualities appear at different junctures within the phenomenological fields of therapist and/or patient, and then recede. They manifest as care structure when they become available for understanding.

Synchronic and diachronic manifestations
of hermeneutics

When such building blocks occur at one and the same time, we can borrow the term "synchronic," that is, simultaneous, from anthropologist Claude Lévi-Strauss's studies of "mythemes," the elements of stories, rituals, and artifacts of a given culture (1972). For Lévi-Strauss, particular mythemes appear throughout the various productions and artifacts of a culture. Psychoanalysis itself can be thought of as an interpretive culture with its own stories, myths, rituals, and artifacts, such as the couch, the analytic attitude, metapsychology, theories, Freudian lore, and so on. Lévi-Strauss classified mythemes in terms of binary oppositions that resemble in some respects the hermeneutical polarities that have been proposed here. However, the psychoanalytic interpretive dimensions that I have proposed derive not from cultures as such, but instead from hermeneutics and philosophy. They represent aspects of being-in-the-world. They schematize the interpretive dialogue that occurs throughout the treatment process.

Like mythemes, hermeneutical dimensions can be viewed in their unfolding over time, which Lévi-Strauss called the "diachronic" temporal movement of the process. The synchronic (simultaneous) and the diachronic (unfolding in time) can be compared to music, where harmony appears vertically on the score and the notes occur all at once; and melody and rhythm, and counterpoint, which move left to right on the staff and develop over time. The previous chapter viewed the polarities as synchronic, while the current chapter regards them in their temporal unfolding during the evolution of the psychoanalytic process. They are the same polarities, the same sets of meanings, but this chapter focuses on their manifestation in specific events and dynamical interchanges.

The temporal development of psychoanalytic psychotherapy

Time and history are fundamental to both psychoanalysis and modern philosophy. Most therapists and patients experience treatment as an evolving sequence of events. History and development are essential components of the life cycle, hermeneutics, and psychoanalysis.

In hermeneutics, time itself is comprehended in diverse ways. Heidegger's time (*Zeit*) is an aspect of being-in-the-world that is related to what Heidegger calls "thrownness," falling, dying, and the existential abyss and is not measurable by a clock or calendar. The philosopher Henri Bergson (1999) defined time as the flow of an experience.

Therapists are aware of how some sessions seem endless, while others are over in the twinkling of an eye. In what follows, I am thinking of time as an amalgam of all three meanings, starting with clock and calendar time marking sequential events, but also aware of subjective time, as well as the existential "press" of time that impinges through mortality, change, and loss.

Stages or phases of treatment

There are several ways to demarcate the unfolding of the psychoanalytic process. Most commonly, treatment is divided into stages or phases. Usually, they follow an orderly sequence but allow for regression to earlier stages and early manifestations of later ones. Each phase is identified by a particular set of themes. Actions possible during one phase are less likely during another, as a handshake is more likely when people meet, but might occur later, as when they make an agreement. Therapeutic strategies are "phase dependent." Freud (Jones, 1953, vol. 2, p. 235) compared psychoanalytic process to a game of chess, with its beginning, middle, and end games. The beginning highlights the contract and rules (the frame), the therapeutic alliance, and the emergence of transference and resistance. The middle game is an extended period of deeper explorations and working through. The end game involves integration and termination of treatment.

The stages of a treatment may be related to a particular disorder, as in Volkan's (1988) *Six Steps in the Treatment of Borderline Personality Organization*. Or the stages may recapitulate those of human development using schemas such as Erikson's (1950) psychosocial stages, Mahler's (Mahler, Pine, & Bergman, 1975) stages of symbiosis, separation, and individuation, or Neumann's (1954) stages of human consciousness. From the standpoint of interpretation, each of Volkan's, Erikson's, Mahler's, and Neumann's stages has its own interpretive matrix, including vocabulary, focal themes, and conflicts. They suggest interpretations of the patient's dynamics, all contextualized and conditioned by the "at hand" needs and expressions of the patient during each stage of treatment or life history.

A contrasting view: the "feeling of what happens"

An alternative to stages as a way to view the movement of psychoanalytic therapy over time is by "the feeling of what happens," to use the apt phrase of neuroscientist Anthony Damasio (1999) with respect to the embodied emotional experience that accompanies cognition and consciousness. "The feeling of what happens" captures the phenomenology of events rather than prematurely classifying them into categories. Especially since the neuroscience of psychotherapy is receiving increasing attention (Cozolino, 2002), I prefer in the present context to use such an experience-based model of "what happens" because it emphasizes the intuitively grasped, implicitly acquired, preconscious, and "already there" aspects of therapy activity, while the stage model uses abstractions not necessarily inherent in the therapy experience itself.

Damasio invokes the concept of neural "maps" to suggest how the brain records, interprets, and "feels" what events mean. Similarly, therapists' interpretations are based upon their acquired internal schema or maps of experience, expression, and understanding. The psychoanalytic process can be understood as a sequence of interpretive maps that emerge in the dyad as the therapy evolves.

Five unfolding psychotherapy events

Each therapist will have his or her own maps for the process and progress of therapy. I have identified five therapeutic unfoldings or event structures which I think may be universally experienced by therapists and patients as part of "the feeling of what happens" in the development of meaningful transformative experience. The five temporal events are 1) the formation of an attachment bond, 2) the extended "working through" process of deepening understanding, 3) the crises of existentially acute situations, 4) the process of self-transformation and change, and 5) termination of treatment. I believe that these experiences are felt and understood organically.

To provide a capsule summary of these events, the most important event in early treatment is the *formation of an attachment bond*. Attachment might be variously conceptualized analytically as transference-countertransference, therapeutic alliance, object relationships, and/or interpersonal relations. Without attachment, therapy becomes didactic: all meaningful emotional growth is the result of attachment. It is the "glue" that holds the therapy together and the "force" that drives it forward. Attachment is like the aerodynamic "lift" of the air flow over the wings that allows an aircraft to ascend. It is also a critical dynamic within most patients' historical narratives, since their lives have often been punctuated by disrupted or traumatized bonds that interfere with healthy development. The quality of the attachment bond is what patients value and remember most about their treatment experience.

As consistent themes emerge in the course of treatment, a "middle game" of *deepening understanding and working through* takes place. For the therapist, "working through" includes "feeling one's way into" the patient's transference and helping him or her to metabolize and apply insight. Importantly, non-understanding and the recognition of radical difference and alterity play just as significant a role in working through as the understanding of dynamics conveyed to the patient. Emotional growth consists partly in an ego-deflating acceptance of the limits of knowing self and other, since neither analyst nor patient are omnipotent or omniscient and life itself is frustrating, ambiguous, and uncertain.

In the course of treatment, difficulties, impasses, and *existentially acute situations* arise, such as impinging life events, treatment destructive resistances, endangerment of the therapeutic relationship, and life-threatening events. These crises are laden with tension and anxiety for both analyst and patient. The therapist is faced with a choice of whether to continue the interpretive work or to step back and supportively attend to the difficulty or crisis, perhaps creating parameters such as a support system to manage grief or suicidality. Sometimes, such acute events call for authentic disclosure of the analyst's feelings, so that the patient is in touch with the therapist's involvement, sees his impact on others, and experiences an encounter that calls his attention to the real life consequences of the situation.

Psychoanalysis emphasizes not only symptom alleviation but deeper levels of *self-transformation*, a process of internalization which commences with the first downbeat of treatment and comes into sharper focus as the analysis begins to have an impact on the patient's symptoms, defenses, and character. There are several related psychoanalytic formulations of the goals of therapeutic transformation such as Freud's dictum "Where id was, there ego shall be," elaborated by Anna Freud (1946) as ego strength; Melanie Klein's depressive position, her resolution of splitting and the acceptance of the caregiver as a separate Other; Jung's individuation, meeting a series of challenges to the self; and Kohut's (1977, pp. 30–32) "transmuting internalizations" that promote self-cohesion.

From the standpoint of hermeneutics, these transformative objectives are encompassed within the wider notion that *self-transformation involves a change in the patient's interpretive matrix, world of meanings, and the way in which life experience is understood.* Importantly, these shifts in internalized meanings transcend rational thought to include phenomenology, the somatic core, and the patient's lifeworld, as well as movement towards a more authentic mode of being-in-the-world. Since self-transformation is the end and aim of psychoanalytic treatment, it merits a fuller discussion in the next chapter.

Fifth, and finally, psychoanalysis allows whenever possible for an extended process of *termination.* Termination really begins with the first session: both patient and analyst are aware that there is an end point, no matter how distant it may seem. The Talmudic saying applies: "As soon as a man is born, he begins to die." However, as the treatment nears completion, there is also a negotiated formal termination process, which often brings issues of separation, loss, and the future into sharp focus.

These five events are summarized, along with a sampling of the meanings they entail, in Figure 3.

Figure 3. Five unfolding events of psychoanalytic psychotherapy.

Unfolding events	Examples of implicit and explicit meanings
Formation of an attachment bond	Relationship, safety, trust
Deepening understanding and "working through"	Meaningful life experience, empathy, "feeling one's way into," emotional growth
Existentially acute situations	Surviving the abyss, holding and containing, traumatic enactments and re-traumatization
Self-transformation	Expanding and integrating the self
Termination	Time, life passages, and mortality; mourning, autonomy, and anticipation of the future.

In order to illustrate in greater detail the events as they unfold, I shall now specifically discuss each of these event structures as they are grasped by "the feeling of what happens" and are manifest in the "maps" or schema that analyst and patient use to understand and come to grips with them. My intention is not to provide a comprehensive picture of the psychoanalytic process, but to suggest how hermeneutics offers useful ways to think about hermeneutical and theoretical dimensions of key events as treatment progresses.

The attachment bond

The patient's attachment to the therapist is what makes therapy more than an intellectual exercise. Indeed, it is a criterion of suitability for psychoanalytic treatment. It was thought by Freud that schizophrenics, withdrawn into their own internal world, do not form attachments and hence are not treatable analytically (Alanen, 2009, p. 33). However, clinical experience has shown that schizophrenics, while seemingly isolated by their hallucinations and delusions, nevertheless develop strong feelings and transference towards their analysts. Similarly, characterological disturbances and rigid defense mechanisms may interfere with attachments, yet the defenses themselves often turn out to be driven by the very attachments they try to ward off. To be human is to attach.

The attachment bond is the basis of the therapeutic alliance and co-transference. Attachment is complex and its dynamics are difficult to tease apart. Indeed, the frustrations and difficulties of analysis itself may disrupt the bond, making it an even more pressing matter to understand and interpret it.

Although "attachment theory" as such has only come into vogue in the past two decades, psychoanalytic discourse has tried from the very start to explain, understand, and modify the bonds formed in infancy and childhood by utilizing the therapeutic relationship to greatest advantage. Freud's disagreements with Ferenczi over the latter's idea that the analyst ought to provide active reparatory nurturing to the traumatized or abandoned patient highlighted the early differences about the causes of transference and what should be done about it (cf. Rudnytsky, 2000). In more recent times, Guntrip (1975), comparing his own analyses by Fairbairn and Winnicott, emphasized how he formed very different attachments to each of them which in turn affected the insight and therapeutic results he achieved with each.

The approach to the patient's attachment is influenced by the analyst's theoretical orientation, with, for example, a Kleinian likely to maintain a greater "neutrality" and social distance (a clear boundary to facilitate accurate interpretation) than, say, a Winnicottian or self psychological analyst. However, beyond theory and technique, there is a deeply personal and relational component to the therapeutic attachment. Youcha (2013, p. 53), for example, reflected that, despite the wealth of interpretations and insights that his analyst, Helen Durkin offered him, what remained in his memory of the analysis decades later was her remarkable warmth and friendliness, which he felt made the treatment a success. Many patients have similar stories of how the attachment to their analyst was the most important ingredient of their treatment. The poet, H.D., Hilda Doolittle (1956), although drawn into analysis with Freud by virtue of his great discoveries, bonded with him affectionately. She sent him a gift of flowers, exchanged correspondence with him, and visited him in London when he was dying. Curiously, Freud completely missed or denied the signs of her attachment, exclaiming to her with frustration, "The trouble is—I am an old man—*you do not think it worth your while to love me*" (p. 21, italics in the original). There is an intangible aspect of the therapeutic bond that emanates from within the deepest selves of the analyst and patient. It is beyond theory and beyond words, but it is not without meaning and understanding. It fuels the transference, but is greater than and different from it. It is rooted in *Dasein*, existence, or the heart if you prefer.

Bowlby's attachment theory and psychotherapy

Not always in common usage, the word attachment itself came into regular psychoanalytic parlance through John Bowlby (1969). Although a psychoanalyst, he viewed attachment through the lens of ethology, the study of animal behavior. He held that attachment and loss are common to many species and are innate responses, not derivatives of other drives like sex and hunger.

Bowlby's initial presentations of attachment theory were greeted with sharp criticism in the British Psychoanalytical Society, most notably by Anna Freud (Vicedo, 2013, pp. 128–135). He unintentionally generated such an angry response because he substituted an ethological behavioral view for that of the dynamic unconscious. Bowlby "couched" his ideas in the language, theoretical frame, and research base of ethology (what Dilthey called "explanation") rather than in terms of the dynamic "understanding" of the unconscious.

To some extent the criticism was justified. Although there are important similarities between animal attachments and human ones, non-human animals do not internalize attachment and loss through phase developmental language-mediated attribution of meaning. To link Bowlby's theory to psychoanalysis, one would need to understand how attachment plays out in thought, fantasy, defense, and intentionality in a human context, that is, how it is assimilated and understood by the developing individual. The task which Bowlby did not deny but largely postponed was to develop a hermeneutics of attachment, a study of its phenomenology, its meanings, and its existential ground. Bowlby's initial writings, based on animal research, encountered the problem of science and humanism discussed in Chapter One.

Although Bowlby eventually became a leading figure in the fields of child development and bereavement, Anna Freud's criticisms in particular put the brakes on Bowlby's influence in psychoanalysis. It took forty years before psychoanalysts felt safe enough to consider the dynamics of attachment using Bowlby's ideas. In the new millennium, Fonagy (2001), Wallin (2007), and others began to link attachment theory to psychoanalytic theory and practice. In addition, they have begun to explore the psychoanalytic treatment of attachment disorders as such, bridging the gap between animal and child observations with psychodynamics, largely from object relations, self-psychological, and intersubjective-relational perspectives. In this way, the study and treatment of attachment disorders has begun to cross the divide between science and humanism, explanation and understanding, existential and empirical paradigms. Contemporary work on attachment and loss is an excellent example of Wilson's notion of "consilience" in the sciences which this book advances. Interpretive work is not the same as empirical science, but it can utilize and in turn inform the sciences. In this case, the study of animal behavior can suggest a conceptual model for understanding attachment—but, importantly, the dynamic interpretation of human attachment is more complex and nuanced than empirical observation and research would suggest.

The following is an example of how Bowlby's and others' understanding of attachment and attachment disorders proved consilient for understanding the patient's dynamics and was enriched by depth interpretation. It can also serve as an illustration of working through and deepening understanding in the "middle game" of therapy to be discussed in the next section.

A patient, Marlene, manifested an "anxious-preoccupied attachment disorder" (Mikulincer & Shaver, 2010, pp. 405–432). In most of her life, as well as in her psychoanalytic therapy, she experienced episodes of severe anxiety invariably related to ambivalent attachments. She expressed a profound need to be close and intimate, often feeling thwarted by acquaintances, friends, and lovers. She tried to overcome her anxiety by further immersing herself in those anxious attachments, in the manner of the repetition compulsion, becoming involved with others to the extent of obsessive and highly charged emotional reactions that overwhelmed both herself and her lovers. Her interpersonal relations became fraught with conflict. Each of her lovers eventually proved inadequate for her. Fearing loneliness and abandonment, she would quickly find a new partner, where the same pattern repeated itself. Similar intense involvement alternating with fears of rejection occurred with friends and co-workers.

Bowlby's understanding of attachment disorders and their application by Wallin to psychotherapy proved useful throughout Marlene's treatment. The therapist, sensing the patient's underlying vulnerability, paid special attention to containing Marlene's affects, helping her to self-regulate her emotional states. This working through process also led to increased trust in the therapist, and her preoccupation with her relationships gradually led to insight. Her tendency to become over-involved with emotionally charged issues and situations transmuted into a valuable "search for the self," seeking to integrate split off and dissociated aspects of her psyche. Her positive transference to the therapist enabled her to mourn her abortive and conflict laden early attachments, especially her mother's lack of attention to her emotional needs, treating her as a latchkey child who was left to take care of herself at a young age, as her mother worked to support the family. As Marlene grieved for her history of misunderstandings and abandonments, she developed more sustained, reliable attachments to her friends and her lovers which included a greater ability to establish boundaries.

Thus, Bowlby's attachment disorder model was helpful in treating Marlene by providing an empirically based explanation of her development and her therapy. It suggested that the patient's anxiety stemmed from overwhelming affect related to alternating feelings of closeness, distance, separation, and safety, all of which are measured in Mary

Ainsworth's "strange situation" in which a child is carefully observed during separation from the parent, encountering a stranger, and reuniting with the parent (Ainsworth, Blehar, Waters, & Wall, 1978). The therapist attended to Marlene's pattern of relationships, including the transference, and contained and interpreted her anxiety with respect to distance, separation, and safety, focusing especially on how she assimilated others' reactions to her in terms of her neediness and fears of abandonment. This schematic approach to the case was meaningful and effective for the treatment.

It is striking how findings from such a straightforward experimental model can be so useful in the complex dynamic setting of psychotherapy, an outstanding example of the consilience between science and humanistic/existential thought. At the same time, it highlights the importance of going beyond the science to the interpretive nuances and dynamics, the inner life, of each patient.

The application of attachment theory brought Marlene to a sustained engagement in the therapeutic process. Yet, on another level, deep and complex interpretive work was essential to resolve Marlene's conflicts. It was important to explore with her how she internalized and played out her experiences and memories of abandonment and how her troubles with her mother affected her self-perceptions and identifications as a woman. A full exploration of these dynamics and their therapeutic implications—which could be done, for example, from object relations and self psychological perspectives—was vital. In addition to awareness of her attachment patterns, it was essential for Marlene to see how her inner sense of self and her interpretations of her experience were altered by the disruption of bonding that occurred with her mother.

Attachment: case illustration of hermeneutical dimensions in the unfolding therapy process

The formation of an attachment bond and other developments of the treatment process includes but goes beyond scientific explanations (such as attachment theory) and more deeply involves the ways both patient and therapist interpret, understand, and internalize "the feeling of what happens." To illustrate how the "feeling of what happens" is accessed, using the "architecture" of hermeneutic dimensions discussed in Chapter Six, I will now discuss Marlene's attachment difficulties in greater detail, taking each of the six hermeneutic polarities and describing how each of them manifested in Marlene's treatment.

1. *Meanings "at hand"* vs. *meanings discerned*

In the course of Marlene's treatment, it became clear that her "at hand" implicit way of relating, of being-in-the-world was to be a protector and caregiver. Her strategy of surviving and existing was to take exceptional care of someone or something other than herself. She tended to plants, pets, children, strangers on the street, and, of course her lovers and her therapist. She bonded with others and indeed her world by helping and rescuing them. Her caring activity was always accompanied by a feeling of dying. The anticipation of death pervaded her existence.

Paradoxically, Marlene's own understanding (meanings discerned) was not about death but about play. She sought dramatic "play" with all beings, especially her lovers, in a way that gave her a sense of a nurturing family environment. She understood her attachments as a way of providing herself with a sense of belonging and closeness through engagement in pleasurable activities ranging from tending a garden to sexual encounters. When the "play" failed, she felt thrown back into the abyss of abandonment. The dialectic of play and death in this patient's life was a re-enactment of her childhood relationship to her mother, in which brief periods of fun together were punctuated by long absences and neglect. Marlene's escape into play can also be seen as a manifestation of Heidegger's flight from the abyss into things, of care for beings in the face of mortality. In that way, while defensive, it was also a form of adaptive ego functioning.

2. *Intra-text understanding* vs. *contextual understanding*

Intra-text understanding takes note of contradictions and gaps in the patient's narrative, and tries to resolve them within the story itself. The contradiction in Marlene's narrative was between her search for intimacy and her repeated choice of persons and situations where the intimacy predictably failed to jell. So she never consummated her desires and interests in a marriage or career, for example.

The interpretive key to understanding Marlene's aborted desires was to be found in the Bergsonian moments when she left her lovers. In this moment, a part of her would "die" or be "killed," but it was not a "death wish" as much as giving life to a relationship by ending it before a feared catastrophe. Marlene's motive was to survive, to find that she could go on being beyond the endings. The repeated enactment of survival under duress was the story of this patient's life that had to be resolved so that she could begin to derive ongoing satisfaction and pleasure in her life.

As we often find in an analysis, context is important. Marlene's autobiographical narrative provided that context. The contextual understanding that helped Marlene work out this dilemma derived from her family background. Both her parents achieved a measure of satisfaction in their work and life outside the family. But their marriage and childrearing eventually foundered. This pattern of family fragmentation could be traced back at least two generations before her parents. As Marlene reflected with the therapist on her family history and her disrupted interactions with her parents, she developed a way of experiencing, expressing, and understanding her own life trajectory on a familial plane. She was then able to "rewrite" her autobiographical narrative as a phoenix rising out of the ashes rather than as a helpless victim.

3. *Objective* vs. *personal and intersubjective experience, expression, and understanding*

Marlene often complained that "People don't understand my emotional needs." She lived her life in profound, distressing contact with her emotions, dreams, and even occasional flashbacks, and when others were objective and detached or analytical with her, she felt misunderstood, ashamed, and abandoned. Of course, the analyst could be such an individual, and this complexity of treatment needed to be made explicit and worked through.

What helped the patient to integrate her perceptions of self and other with her intense emotional life was to facilitate her self-expression, putting words and meanings around feelings, a process which was truncated in a family in which emotions were either "objectified" or else suppressed and never spoken. The therapist, by contrast with Marlene's parents, encouraged her to share details of her phenomenological world with him, opening up experience, expression, and understanding not previously available to her. Her therapy became enriched with dreams, stories, and lively interactions with the analyst. Marlene gradually learned that there is a "middle way" between detached objectivity and emotional flooding. Intersubjective inquiry and interpretation provided "centering" experiences that led to growth and inner security.

4. *Empathy and attunement* vs. *radical difference and alterity*

Marlene had an unrealistic neediness, a wish for totalistic empathy and attunement from others as a compensation for the severe deprivation she suffered in childhood. She experienced herself as an outsider and constantly feared rejection, repeatedly feeling hurt and angry when others, including the therapist, did not immediately respond empathically to her emotions. The therapist, in addition to striving for an empathic mutuality, serving at times as a "real" maternal figure, gradually tried to show Marlene that difference and alterity—being other—was not necessarily cold or dehumanizing. He suggested to her that some of the seemingly alienating traits she identified in herself were also gifts and potentials of her personality that might be misunderstood but could also connect her to others. For example, she initially felt that her obsessive attention to plants was strange and eccentric, but in time she became involved in a horticultural society where she bonded with others with similar interests.

5. *Construction, structure, and presence* vs. *deconstruction, ambiguity, and absence*

    Marlene often "deconstructed" her own narrative by brutal self-analysis. She dissected her beliefs, personality traits, life history, and life skills with Derridian derision. She experienced her life as a postmodern pastiche of disconnected parts (traumatic dissociation). This fragmentation could be seen to be a consequence of her broken attachments. She compartmentalized her life and relationships. She lacked identifications and self-organizing "coping skills" which could bring together diverse aspects of herself into a cohesive self system.

    Much of the interpretive work in Marlene's therapy consisted in making connections between fragments of herself and her attachments, not so much with the idea of reconstructing repressed wishes and memories as to create a woven fabric from the differently colored threads of her daily experience. In many cases of parental neglect like hers, structure is not therapeutically "uncovered" so much as it is created for the first time by a process of "sewing" diverse self-experiences into a unified structural whole. However, in keeping with the nature of psychoanalysis, the therapist does not serve directly as the weaver. Rather, he builds a transitional space, a "play" space where the patient can locate the "pieces" and put them together herself. In Marlene's case, she used photographs, items she carried in her purse, and her hand-held internet device to display to the therapist objects that represented diverse parts of herself. Through the mirroring responses of the therapist, these elements gradually became woven into feelings of wholeness and autonomy, a secure sense of self.

6. *Mystical or organic wholeness* vs. *rational reductionism*

Despite her emotional lability, Marlene, had she been a philosopher, would have been a pure rationalist and reductionist! She rejected religious faith and illusion in a vigorous way that would have pleased Freud or Nietzsche. She was so focused on maintaining her metaphysical version of "the real world" that she rarely watched a movie or read a novel because their imaginative quality disrupted her sense of what is real. Rebelling against her religious upbringing, she was a confirmed "non-believer." Yet when she became depressed, she rivaled Kierkegaard in her "sickness unto death" with despairing thoughts that questioned existence itself. Unlike Kierkegaard, however, Marlene could not find faith at the bottom of the pit. Instead, her life-saving grace was her commitment to helping others. She ruled out suicide on the grounds that those around her would suffer. Since her mother was devoutly religious, the patient's rejection of faith and ritual could be seen to be an expression of their damaged attachment.

Healthy attachments nurture the imagination and the faith of the child in a resilient way that allows the child to access the numinous inner spiritual world of imaginary figures, perhaps but not necessarily including a God, or at least a fairy godmother, an inner being that helps the child to self-soothe and develop a sense of going-on-being, which Eigen (1985) sees as a precursor of faith that develops in the well-nourished infant at the breast. Since Marlene had a deficit in such self-soothing inner objects, and in fact destroyed them *in statu nascendi* by relentless self-probing, the interpretive work of therapy served in part to open her up to a sense of mystery and myth.

In Marlene's case, to offer the patient a spiritual practice or belief system, or to point to the shortcomings of her own rationality, would have further alienated her and led to more feelings of abandonment and neglect. Rather, the analyst capitalized on the patient's own occasional feelings of the uncanny, interpreting their self-soothing and caregiving functions. For example, Marlene sometimes reported feelings of ghostly presences, which occurred when she walked through a wooded area and at night before bedtime. She was not terrified of these presences, but comforted by them. The therapist suggested they might be understood as manifestations of some goodness in the universe. He did not judge their reality or lack thereof, but rather implied that it was "as if" they had these characteristics. The patient could assimilate this idea, and it gave her more room in her psyche for imagination and faith in the way her inner life could nurture her.

Deepening understanding and working through

Marlene's case illustrates the gradual, elaborate, and repetitive interpretive process that is unique to psychoanalysis among the therapies. Indeed, many hours of an analysis have a feeling of Nietzsche's eternal recurrence, what Greenson (1965) called "working through," where the implications of insights attained are reapplied in a variety of contexts and nuances, facilitating adaptive processes in daily life and absorption of new understanding into the personality. For the therapist, this can be tedious, but at other times hardly seems like work at all, more of a process of sitting and waiting.

The patient fills in aspects of personal history, current conflicts, dreams, a film seen, a book read, or an incident. For Heidegger, daily existence consists primarily in such care for the beings (objects, ideas,) of the lifeworld. The patient discloses feelings about the analyst or about the way the therapy is going. The analyst provides interpretations and explanations, and thinks of how the material can be related to the transference and countertransference. If the analysis is going well, both parties are sustained and encouraged by the feeling that they are "getting somewhere," that the experience is becoming richer and more meaningful, that a mutual understanding of and by the patient is unfolding.

Much of the working through process feels like being in a sanctuary or library (of the mind) rather than the bustle of the marketplace. For the analyst, working through resembles maternal reverie, as the mother-analyst holds and contains her infant-patient. There is a great deal of waiting, musing, dreaming. These are the hours that health insurance companies do not want to pay for! There is no "evidence base" that anything "medically necessary" is happening or that the analyst is a "change agent." Yet so much of human development occurs in this gradual, apparently uneventful way. Countless heartbeats, biological, social, and emotional events take place unnoticed. Growth is happening.

This process of sitting, waiting, and deepening runs counter to the emphasis on speed, power plays, and fast-paced technology that characterizes modern culture. The "slowness" of psychoanalysis is anachronistic and countercultural, like small harvesting in an age of mass production mega-farming. This is hermeneutical agriculture, the sowing and reaping of meanings as the weather changes and the seasons pass. One could speculate that Freud's childhood in Freiberg, a small town in Moravia, as well as the pastoral and agrarian themes of German romanticism and *Naturphilosophie*, indirectly led him to provide more time to each patient than virtually any physician who preceded him. Heidegger, who like Freud grew up in a small rural province (Messkirch, Germany) and was influenced by *Naturphiloso-phie*, also emphasized the role of nature as the ground of our being-in-the-world. He wrote about the "fourfold" worlds in which we dwell in meaningful ways, Earth, Sky, Mortals, and Divinities (Heidegger, 1929, pp. 343–364). His aphorism, "Let Beings be" conveys the importance of allowing time for beings and events to evolve and disclose themselves. Although no psychotherapy should be interminable or conducted in the face of continual unresolved impasse, there is much to be said for the gradual evolution of understanding that respects the patient's autonomy and nature's own time clock for development.

Existentially acute situations

While most of the psychoanalytic process unfolds in a gradually evolving manner, it is sometimes punctuated by situations that put patient, therapist, and/or treatment in danger of failing, and in some cases can be life-threatening. Traumatic life events, erotized transference-countertransference, therapeutic regressions, emotional dysregulation, and other factors can lead to situations of real or anticipated acute crisis. In Marlene's case, her therapy was periodically disrupted by suicidal risk, her feeling that she was "breaking down," mistrusting the therapist, and traumatic loss of significant others during the years of treatment. There were also times when the therapist himself felt emotionally vulnerable in his caregiving endeavors, experiencing feelings of inadequacy and fragmentation when Marlene became depressed or felt abandoned by him, as if he were betraying a sacred trust.

The *au courant* name for response to acute therapeutic crisis is "risk management," the use of technical interventions to prevent catastrophe. In the face of possible disaster, the psychoanalytic therapist is faced with a decision whether to continue with depth interpretation, or to provide concrete support, guidance, or direct intervention. Psychologically, crises are experienced by both patients and therapists as disruptions, abandonments, or intrusions that shake the boundaries that preserve the treatment alliance.

Hermeneutics illuminates an additional layer of acute critical events, namely the threat to the "assumptive world" (Kauffman, 2012), the meanings that sustain the inner coherence of the self. One patient summarized this point well when, during periods when she was feeling disconnected or abandoned, often getting drunk or having suicidal thoughts, she said, "I don't exist." In her case, this statement connoted depersonalization and derealization, as if her self and world were dissolving. When the coherence of the self is at risk, the therapist is faced with whether to take the patient through the depths of the experience, the dark night of the soul as it were, in search of understanding, or whether to close off the wound, placing survival over insight and growth. It can be difficult to assess whether the patient "can handle" further inquiry and uncertainty, or needs something "to hold onto." One is reminded of Heidegger's use of the phrase "at hand" with respect to *Dasein*, the being-in-the-world that sustains thought and meaning. In acute crisis, the patient's world and existence are threatened by the abyss, being "thrown," the loosening of his or her moorings of meaning and purpose. Yet it is sometimes by undergoing such a risk to meaning and existence that a more authentic existence becomes possible.

In psychoanalysis, authenticity means opening to the unconscious, to the hidden meanings and moods contained in the "things" of the world and the mind. As mentioned earlier, the patient has to experience mortality, to "die a little" in order to go the level of the unconscious. Depending on the underlying structure of the personality, whether neurotic, borderline, or psychotic, to "die a little" into the unconscious can mean anything from tolerable discomfort, to worsening of the patient's condition, to life-threatening behavior. To properly help the patient resolve such harrowing conditions, the therapist sometimes requires great calm and patience, and at other times quickness of intuition akin to that of an emergency room physician in a triage situation.

The importance of the patient's way of understanding and meaning-making in resolving acute crises

What can hermeneutics add to the rich lore of studies, stories, legalities, and clinical discussions that surround crisis management? Hermeneutics tells us that the interpretive understanding arrived at during the longer non-acute periods of analysis can give the therapist an important tool for bringing a patient through and out of the acute crisis stage. The therapist's ongoing immersion in the patient's phenomenological world and what constitutes meaningful discourse for that individual may be the most useful resource for assessing and intervening in acute crisis. How does the patient himself explain and understand his existence? Grasping the patient's own interpretive matrix provides the strongest basis for crisis intervention.

Consider a patient's interpretive tendency towards one side or other of the hermeneutical duality of objective *vs.* intersubjective experience. One individual might feel understood and supported by a scientific explanation of his dilemma, while another might feel better held and contained by a relational understanding of the predicament. For example, a patient with bipolar disorder was at risk of becoming violent with his spouse. He found it helpful for the therapist to explain the problem in terms of the nature of his disease, that the manic phase caused a difficulty controlling impulses and aggression. That explanation helped him realize that he could prevent violence by staying on his medication, giving internal commands to himself, and when necessary, leaving the volatile situation. Another patient with the same disorder and problem found it therapeutic to explore the difficulty with his spouse in terms of his toxic shame and his needs for power and manhood. These two patients had the same diagnosis, but their personality structures and modes of understanding their worlds were different. One relied on explanations about external causes and actions; the other needed empathy and understanding.

A hermeneutical duality of particular importance and interest for the management of acute crises is that of empathy *vs.* radical difference, attunement *vs.* alterity. A patient who is experiencing a crisis may want and need empathy, to feel understood by the therapist and perceive the similarity between them. Another might require the dignity of Levinas's alterity, the recognition by the therapist that understanding of his plight is impossible since each person's suffering is unique. Thus, in impasses or crises, the therapist must sometimes decide between these alternatives. For example, two patients, each confined to a wheelchair, experienced critical moments with their therapist in which they threatened to break off treatment. Their reasons for "firing him" at the very time when they began to get in touch with their grief and sense of loss about their conditions, were the same: "Someone like you who doesn't have a similar handicap cannot possibly understand what I have gone through, what my life is like. How can I possibly benefit from therapy with someone who takes it for granted that he can walk and have sex and play with his children normally? He just doesn't get it!" In one case, the patient responded to the therapist's empathic understanding of immobility: "It must be devastating to try to move your limbs and find that they don't respond. And it must feel hurtful to you when you see others who don't even have to think about it and who seem to have little compassion for you." In the other, the patient was relieved when the therapist admitted his inability to grasp the patient's experience and said that he hoped he could learn more about it from the patient: "I know that I cannot begin to grasp how difficult this must be for you. But I would appreciate it if you would tell me more, so that I can better understand your pain."

Self-transformation

Psychoanalysis holds out the promise not only of symptom alleviation but also of changes in the patient's personality at deeper levels which enhance the quality of life and reduce the likelihood of future illness. A change in the balance of forces of the id, ego, and superego enhances the patient's resilience and adaptability in life. In some instances, the changes may alter the patient's perspective on the meaning of life and lead to higher levels of awareness, what Grotstein (1993b, pp. 121–134) calls the "transcendent position."

Psychoanalytic self-transformation begins at the first session, with the act of seeking help, admission of symptoms and vulnerability, and bonding with the analyst. The patient may acknowledge his suffering and feel hope and trust that something can be done to help him. As the analysis proceeds, self-awareness deepens, and intrapsychic structures realign themselves. Throughout treatment, the analyst looks for transformations in the patient's defenses, sense of self, object relations, and assessment of reality. Sometimes, in the latter stages of therapy, the patient may manifest a genuinely renewed sense of self and/or brightness of feeling, optimism, spontaneity, acceptance of life's vicissitudes, assertiveness, and creativity. It is as if he or she has been released from possession by demons, or in the language of psychoanalysis, the stranglehold of unconscious guilt, shame, and conflict.

Hermeneutics elucidates several aspects of psychoanalytic interpretation which promote self-transformation. It shows us that depth interpretation introduces paradoxes into the discourse between patient and analyst. Interpretations are metaphorical and polysemous, that is, they evoke more than the words convey and contain multiple connotations and implications. Interpretations awaken "worlds" of the unconscious, a process that is both pleasurable and painful, a merger of the life and death instincts. Such an evocation of complex meanings that had previously been hidden from view enriches the inner life. Moreover, interpretation elucidates the patient's phenomenology, the experience of self, intentionality, and intersubjectivity, altering self perception and motivation.

At the existential level, interpretations are assimilated into the patient's "at hand" being-in-the-world and become part of a dialogue that develops into new forms of attachment. Interpretations bring worlds of understanding onto the horizon and change attitudes. Interpretation as speech is embodied thought and can transform the patient's self and somatic core. Interpretation is an expression of alterity, of the patient's ultimate unknowability to himself, the analyst, and others. Finally, in existential encounter, interpretation binds the patient to an ethic of respect for self and other, an essential dignity.

In these and other ways, interpretations not only alter psychological defenses, object relations, and the balance of desire and guilt (id and superego). At a deeper level, they have the power to change the patient's lifeworld and existence. This enrichment of meaning and purpose may be the most valuable curative factor of psychoanalytic therapy. It receives special attention in the next chapter.

Termination

Termination of treatment is an event, phase, and process that has received relatively little attention in the psychoanalytic literature (Firestein, 2001). The ending of treatment carries negative connotations: death, incompleteness, abandonment, financial loss for the analyst, and in some cases clinical failure, implications which may make it unpalatable as a topic of serious study. Yet termination has its own dynamics, and some treatments succeed or fail depending on the mental realignments that occur during those last sessions. We have few in-depth studies of what happens to patients after treatment, but we can guess that the final sessions "lock in" much of the good and bad that the patient takes with him into his life thereafter. Termination may influence outcomes more than its relatively short duration implies.

Termination is inherent in human relationships, all of which in one way or another end. Yet all attachments are rooted in the fantasy of permanence and perfection that was part of the symbiotic oneness of the mother–infant dyad. In an analysis, such an idealized relationship at first motivates treatment, enhances trust, and fuels the therapeutic alliance. For a good part of the analysis, the idealized "forever" attachment is encouraged (positive transference) while its ending, like death, waits in the wings.

The actual death and dying of the analyst can of course be devastating. One patient was in the middle phase of her treatment, idealizing her analyst and "in love" with him in the transference, when he developed a terminal illness. Even though she had several months with him to say goodbye after he was diagnosed and informed her, upon his death she became severely depressed and psychotic. She was fortunate enough to have a strong support system and a new therapist to nurse her through this difficult time. Of course, her analyst's death, although it occurred in his old age, was tragic in itself. Yet all analysts are mortal, and we know that even mere brief separations due to ordinary events like vacations can be anxiety-provoking. Such eventualities suggest that termination should be in the therapist's mind from the very start, and that, for the sake of the patient's well-being, the depth and breadth of the interpretive work should allow for the ultimate ending of treatment.

Modern hermeneutics has much to say that is relevant to understanding and managing the termination of therapy, and for that matter, separation and loss in general. The first half of the twentieth century was a time of moral, religious, and intellectual disillusionment provoked by social upheaval, two world wars, the Holocaust, and atomic bombs that destroyed two cities in Japan. The philosophy that emerged is punctuated with aspects of death, temporal exigency, suspicion, endings, otherness, disarray, disruption, and nothingness, all of which represent aspects of sociocultural and historical trauma. In modern thought, meaning and interpretation are impregnated with loss, otherness, and alterity. From this perspective, every interpretation made by the analyst is a termination, a disruption of the patient's flow of associations, of a fantasy to which the patient clings, of a childhood object relationship, of desire. Modern hermeneutics discloses the deeper emotional meanings of these "little deaths" that enter into all discourse.

From Derrida's point of view, every understanding, every action, is merely a trace that is disseminated, so that the attachment to the therapist constantly dies and is reawakened somewhere else in the patient's narrative, in the *text*-ure of his life, in a dream. Thoughts, meanings, and interpretations are traces that fade into the unconscious and reappear elsewhere in the discourse. The entirety of treatment also fades upon its termination, and attention needs to be paid to the way it will reside in the patient's unconscious and affect his life thereafter.

Problematic results of termination are "closest to home" for us in those patients who themselves become therapists. They are among the few patients (ours or others') with whom we may be in regular contact (as friends and colleagues) for years after treatment. Some of them seem interminably submissive to their analysts, some appear to have been victims of indoctrination, and some go into a second analysis to undo the negative effects of the first one! In effect, their analyses were never properly terminated. There are doubtless many other patients who fade into our memories who also experienced problematic outcomes.

Termination should release the patient from the analyst's authority. It should facilitate separation and individuation. In hermeneutical terms, this means giving the interpretive matrix back to the patient in a way that he can use it without the need for the therapist to provide the necessary ingredients. Human interdependence, mutual support, and meaning-making are necessary throughout life. Termination should transfer the power back to the patient and help him to utilize his own internal resources and engage in new dialogues with significant others in ways that sustain and enhance the gains made in treatment. In this respect, termination, in addition to being a "closing off" of treatment and an acceptance of loss, is also an opening to new "texts" and relationships that neither therapist nor patient can fully anticipate. In the study of psychological trauma, this capacity for self-renewal is called "resilience" (Bonnano, 2004). Termination should enhance the patient's resilience and ability both to endure necessary suffering and to engage creatively in subsequent stages of the life cycle.

Metamorphosis

In hermeneutics, "resilience" is a function and outcome of experience, expression, and understanding facilitated by personal and social imagination, openness to dialogue, authenticity, and a capacity for self-actualizing emotional experiences that touch the core of one's being-in-the-world. Each of the hermeneutical dimensions of interpretation and the unfolding events of the psychoanalytic process provides its own opportunities for understanding and self-transformation.

At various times in treatment, the therapist witnesses profound transformations in the patient, metamorphoses, radical changes in the self. These alterations can be in the nature of psychoses, what Bion (1966, pp. 7–11) called catastrophic transformations, or at the opposite pole, sea changes in the personality that lead to improved functioning, attitudes, spontaneity, and outlook. We have touched upon self-transformation as one of the key unfolding events of psychoanalytic therapy. In the next chapter, we explore self-transformation in greater depth and detail as the primary aim and objective of psychoanalytic treatment.

CHAPTER EIGHT

Interpretation and self-transformation

Transformation of the self is the promise of psychoanalytic treatment, the ultimate therapeutic objective and justification for the time and financial and emotional investment involved. It strives to produce deep personality changes above and beyond relief from symptoms and psychological suffering.

Yet psychoanalysts are modest about the extent of the changes they produce. They typically do not promise the total realignments that sometimes result from religious conversion or enlightenment, or from life-transforming events and relationships. Rather, psychoanalysts maintain that a successful treatment alters the dynamics of the personality in small quantities that lead to improved functioning in life, love, and work. Whether even these claims are justified has, of course, been disputed by some, but there are sufficient research studies (e.g., Freedman, Hoffenberg, Vorus, & Frosch, 1999) and testimonies from both patients and analysts to support the idea that the rigors of psychoanalytic therapy are well worth it because of the transformational changes that occur, changes that not only relieve symptoms but improve overall functioning and reduce the likelihood of future symptomatology.

A conundrum about psychoanalysis, sometimes posed as a serious criticism of its effectiveness, is how a therapy that relies on talk

159

and ideally minimizes direct suggestion—that is, a dialogical therapy which affirms the patient's freedom—can lead to any changes at all, much less transformation of the personality. Some would argue that psychoanalysts do in fact apply pressure and suggestion, but that does not account for the difference between so-called "transference cures" where the patient recovers in order to assuage the analyst, as against changes that genuinely and spontaneously emerge from self-exploration and insight. There are enough of the latter cases to make us ask what it is about sustained interpretive work that produces changes in the sense of self and the constitution of personhood. How can self-transformation result from understanding alone? The cause-effect relationship can be so elusive that sometimes it is cast in spiritual terms, as in Buber's (1970) depiction of "I-Thou" relationships and Grotstein's (1993b, pp. 121–134) "transcendent position." Even the more reserved accounts of transformation in development such as Freud's dictum "Where id was, there ego shall be," Fairbairn's mature dependence (Simanowitz & Pearce, 2003, p. 18), Mahler's separation-individuation, and Kohut's (1977, p. 123) transmuting internalizations contain many ambiguities about the nature and source of the changes that take place. Winnicott's (1958b) idiosyncratic notion of "ego orgasm" of course defies description! Deep personality change is hard to describe, much less explain. Often, the realization that a metamorophosis has taken place occurs after the fact, and the memory for what happened is obscured by time. We are sorely missing a descriptive psychology of self-transformation.

Like psychoanalysis, philosophical hermeneutics has faced dilemmas and criticisms concerning its understanding of change. Positivist thinkers have accused hermeneutics of linguistic ambiguity and tautological reasoning. Marxists and postmodernists have doubted the utility of thought and discourse in general, pointing to the necessity for action and social change. But, despite such challenges, modern hermeneutics has been sufficiently preoccupied with personal growth that it can offer some additional perspectives on self-transformation in psychoanalysis. As would be expected, hermeneutics sees the "standard" metapsychological and dynamic formulations of personality change as faulted and limited, and it probes the question from many other angles, providing a fuller picture. But before we explore the hermeneutics of self-transformation, it is important to state the "standard" psychoanalytic position and note its value and limitations.

How psychoanalysts view self-transformation

Freud viewed the changes in the personality that occur in analysis to be the result of "making the unconscious conscious" (the topographical model) and ego mastery, "Where id was, there ego shall be" (the structural model.) Within the ego and superego, there are changes in defense mechanisms as well as in self- and object-representations that allow for a greater degree of self-tolerance and acceptance of reality. As these representations reorganize, psychological development moves forward, and a mature identity is formed. Identity governs the whole of the personality, its motivations, its interests, and its values, so that identity formation is indeed a transformation at a profound level.

These deeper changes occur in therapy largely through analysis of the transference, which also suggests the importance of the therapeutic relationship in promoting change. Interpretations and understanding are enabled through the process of care within the therapeutic alliance. After Freud, psychoanalysts have increasingly emphasized the importance of the care structure in the form of holding, containing, attunement, "mirroring and idealization," and so on. The emphasis on care implies a shift towards hermeneutics because the interpretive process becomes a matter of shared human meanings in an interpersonal context rather than a detached depiction of the psyche as a thing or object.

Freud's initial formulations, however, were rooted in the metapsychology of internal drives and objects. Freud mentioned the real relationship and the life narrative (*Erlebnis*) of the patient and analyst only secondarily. The psyche was portrayed by him as a structure taken out of its living context. He viewed interpretations as influences and agents, cognitive interventions influencing a mind that operated according to a set of rules or laws of nature. Freud did emphasize that in order to stimulate change, interpretations required an emotional impact, abreaction, which gave the insight power. He regarded insight as an agent of self-transformation, today conceptualized as self-regulation (Siegel, 2012, pp. 267–306). The psyche reorganizes itself around the combination of self-knowledge, affect, and the patient's transference. There is no consideration of meaning and understanding here, because an abstract structure does not have meaning, only components that are linked in a causal way.

Freud's theoretical stance, which emphasized mental representations, has contributed to an impression that psychoanalytic interpretation takes place as if in a museum or library, a process akin to taking the dust off statues, paintings, and books. In fact, Freud's office was furnished with his statues, library, and some framed pictures. It created an impression of study, not theater, play, family life, or encounter. Freud avidly pursued all these activities in his life, and used them in his thinking, but he did not phrase the analytic process and interpretive work in such ways. He configured them rather as a study of the underlying substance of what was conscious, the noumena underlying the phenomena, the secrets to be exposed by the analyst as curator and detective. Coincidentally, this deportment was a safe position for Freud, who was freed from being an accomplice and a co-participant. In this manner, interpretation took on an abstruse, distant, even dusty quality. Only after quiet deliberation did the analyst interpret the unconscious motives and conflicts. This depiction sounds like a stereotype rather than what analysts actually do, but the stereotype comes from the way many traditional analysts actually operate. They are formal and reserved. They think they are conveying to the patient their logical conclusions derived from fact and reasoning about representations of internal objects and drives.

The basis for regarding thoughts as statements or propositions about representations stems from the Cartesian metaphysics of mind as a separate substance from the body, the lifeworld, and the living history of the person. The "hermeneutical turn" shifts interpretation away from a metaphysical "propositional" view of mind to one that understands lived experience from the standpoints of the interpreter and the subject, psychoanalyst and patient, in authentic involvement and dialogue with one another. This "turn" leads to new perspectives on how and why interpretation can be transformative. If authentic life is by definition meaningful care, then true understanding and insight not only promotes change, it is in itself, in its coming into being at the moment of utterance, transformative.

I wish now to elaborate on how hermeneutical perspectives account for the self-transformative nature of interpretation as authentic dialogue. First, I will suggest that, *far from making true or false statements, in-depth interpretation introduces paradoxes and complexities into the discourse between patient and analyst.* Like poetry and the arts, interpretation is metaphorical, that is, suggestive of something other than itself, and polysemous, containing multiple connotations and implications. Interpretation, like art, discloses, lays bare, unconceals, and awakens "worlds." As Bass (2006; see below; see also Chapter Four) suggests, this process is both pleasurable and painful, a merger of the life and death instincts. Such a process constitutes the opening to the unconscious which gives the psychoanalytic work its special function and quality.

In what follows, we will consider some of the nuances of the interpretive process illuminated by Continental philosophy which elucidate how and why interpretation is transformative. For example, as already noted in previous chapters, these perspectives suggest that interpretation is a phenomenon of experience (Husserl) which includes self, intentionality, and intersubjectivity. Hence to self-consciously introspect about one's experience alters, even if slightly, one's sense of self and intentionality (motivation). Moreover, intepretation is an inherent, at hand part of being-in-the-world (Heidegger). It is part of a dialogue (Gadamer) that develops into an attachment and a relationship. It brings new worlds onto the horizon. Further, interpretation is embodied (Merleau-Ponty): it has flesh. On still another level, interpretation is an expression of alterity, the unknowability of the other to whom one is inextricably bound. Interpretation thus binds us to an ethics of respect (Levinas). In all these ways, interpretation acquires the power to transform, as Nietzsche so strongly emphasized.

Interpretation as metaphorical and polysemous

Interpretation facilitates change by becoming part of an ongoing narrative, dialogue, and understanding that has ramifications for both patient and analyst. As his free-associative narrative and the transference relationship are interpreted to him, the patient negotiates an inner world that incorporates the new understanding. Interpretation of the self is not a logical analysis of propositions about sense data, as the positivists and metaphysicians assert. It is impregnated with language and imagery, and welcomes their paradoxes and inconsistencies as aspects of meanings that may become gradually elucidated in discourse. That is to say, interpretation is metaphorical and polysemous, akin to the conjoining of opposites in the unconscious (Freud, 1910e). Interpretive clarity does not eliminate ambiguity. It uses difference and complexity as pathways to richer understanding. Richer understanding *is* change. It does not have to *cause* other changes. That is a major difference between hermeneutics and metaphysical thinking.

In hermeneutics, understanding is all. Causality is nothing more than a type of understanding based on experience. In fact, the empiricist David Hume said as much in the eighteenth century during the height of the Enlightenment period. He viewed causality as a habit or impression, assigning it no independent existence beyond the understanding (Shanks, 1985). Change is inherent in meaning.

Two language-based means of enriched understanding and self-transformation are *metaphor* and *polysemy*.

Metaphor uses an image or idea to connect or transfer it to something other than itself. Lakoff and Johnson (1980) showed how not only poetic and literary forms, but everyday language is impregnated with metaphors. "*Falling* in love," "that was a *cutting* remark," and "the *foundation* for that idea" are examples of how metaphor (falling in love compared to gravitation; sarcasm to a knife; idea to a building) enriches connotative meaning. Metaphors open up to richer understandings.

A really "good" metaphor goes even further and stirs up worlds within the listener or reader. Consider, for instance, the powerful metaphor of "the tall ashes of loneliness" (Wright, 1990, p. 199), where in that one line of poetry, James Wright captured so much of the human condition: loneliness (ashes) burns us, purifies us, is all that is left of us. Ashes (representing both a tree and the embers of a flame; life and death) are "tall," suggesting pride, a phallus, rising. Loneliness becomes a condition of devastating self-transformation. Wright, a "confessional" poet who was knowledgeable about Freud and psychoanalysis (Graves & Schermer, 1999), depicted his poems as "carefully dreamed" (Wright, 1975). Perhaps the same could be said of the analyst's interpretations. Drawing upon his experience, the analyst seizes upon a patient's narrative as metaphor, and "dreams" it into a larger space and world. A patient says, "It feels cold in here." The analyst replies, "You are talking about my silence in response to your show of affection." He interprets "cold" as a metaphor for lack of responsiveness. The patient then has an opportunity to share his relational experiences. The interpretation gives the patient an opportunity to enlarge his narrative and experience. That is what metaphor does, and much of psychoanalytic discourse is an exchange of metaphors (Cohen & Schermer, 2004, pp. 588–590). Indeed, interpretation has a confessional aspect as well—it always reveals something in the *analyst's* unconscious.

Polysemy refers to the multiple meanings of words, phrases, and images, the richness of an experience or narrative. Much of what we call "depth" and "unconscious" in psychoanalysis refers to the polysemous nature of inner experience. The poet Walt Whitman (2001) wrote, "I contain multitudes." When we go inward, our sense of self grows richer and more meaningful. For example, the analyst takes the "screen memory" not on face value but as polysemous. He invites the patient to go "beneath" or "behind" it, which is itself a metaphor for polysemous experience. Psychological depth and polysemy (breadth, complexity) are closely related to one another.

The hermeneutical view of interpretation is that it enriches experiences and narratives rather than foreclosing on them. That is what gives psychoanalytic interpretation its transformative power. It penetrates into and discloses meaningful networks of ideas, images, and stories that open the person to a richer experience of self as complex, multifaceted, and connected to mood and emotion.

Although psychoanalysis has special features of psychodynamic understanding, the general enrichment of the patient's inner world in itself has therapeutic benefits. It facilitates psychological development by injecting an element of freedom, play, imagination, and improvisation into it. It connects analyst and patient together within a relational intersubjective matrix. It encourages greater tolerance of the mental life and the difficulties of the self. It adds new dimensions to the experience of relatedness.

However, there is an aspect of psychoanalytic interpretation that is more specific and focused than psychological enrichment alone. That element is dynamic understanding, a systematic disclosure of hidden meanings and defense mechanisms specific to the individual in treatment. Interpretation introduces the patient to his own personal unconscious. Nevertheless, in what follows, as throughout this book, we are not concerned so much with specific dynamic contents as with the characteristics of psychoanalytic interpretations that allow them to penetrate to the core of the patient and have an impact.

The interpretive opening to the unconscious

Bass (2006) has captured the special mixture of pleasure and pain, gratification and frustration that is stirred up by the psychoanalytic interpretive process. There is great depth, breadth, and detail to Bass's thinking. Here, I only wish to extract a few key points he makes with respect to interpretation. Again, I can only offer my reading of Bass. I hope it does justice to him.

Bass says that the fundamental nature of interpretation derives from Nietzsche's ideas of the pleasure-pain of "eternal recurrence," the temporal rhythmic return of all phenomena. Bass believes that Freud had a lapse in not realizing that the unconscious begins with pleasure-pain as intertwined from the outset and that, in addition, there is a primitive temporality in the unconscious. (Freud made the pleasure principle central, and held that the unconscious is "timeless.") Like the unconscious, a good psychoanalytic interpretation is both pleasurable and painful, conveying a temporality which is echoed in the death instinct and the repetition compulsion (eternal recurrence). Following Derrida, Bass adds the emphasis on *différance* (Derrida's neologism for combined difference and deferment) as a feature of the unconscious.

Putting these ideas together, Bass sees that the patient's experience of the analyst's interpretation includes measures of both pleasure and pain, the life and death instincts, and a primitive experience of time as mortality and eternal recurrence. That is, interpretation is a homeopathic medicine for the pleasure-pain "disease" and the regressive, repetitive, masochistic quality of the transference. The interpretive quality that stimulates this complex is *différance*: difference and deferment between the analyst's interpretation and the patient's original understanding; deferment as a postponement of gratification and tolerance of frustration. For Bass, interpretation is "strange" care in that it is both a gratification of a wish (for a response, for attachment, for understanding) and a painful frustration of the wish. It is precisely this combination which unlocks the repressed unconscious fantasy life. The pleasure-pain experience of *différance* resonates powerfully with the unconscious world of repressed and infantile experience. It does so because it has a locution familiar to that world.

Expressed more plainly, a depth interpretation discloses the patient's vain and wish-fulfilling attempt to make his fantasies "real" in the here-and-now. This implicitly points to *différance*: a difference between wish and reality and a necessity to delay gratification. The patient will resist this awareness. But the possibility of a deferred gratification through learning and love of the analyst may move him to accept the interpretation and make use of it.

> Thus, consider the patient, Jeri, who reported the dream that she was a newborn baby in a maternity ward, and her parents were watching her through an observation window (see Chapter Two).

Jeri had no trouble accepting her own interpretation that the dream was about emotional deprivation. This awareness of the dream as a metaphor for a severed umbilical cord served to expand her inner world and deepen her connection to the therapist. Working through the details moved the therapy forward and led to an enhanced ability to receive nurturing from significant others. In that respect, it provided genuine insight and catharsis.

However, what remained repressed in Jeri was a web of sexual and aggressive motives as well as narcissistic wishes for mirroring of her grandiose self. As the therapist pressed forward with interpretations of Jeri's use of her love objects for sexual and narcissistic gratification as well as her disdain for significant others, she rebelled against such understanding. She began to question the therapist's credibility, came late for sessions, and got intoxicated after some sessions. The interpretations of unconscious content were difficult for her to assimilate, since they highlighted the differences between her real self and her ego ideal, suggested she might need to defer her sexual impulses, and implied that her image of herself as innocent, flawless, and victimized might have to "die." The therapist, attuned to Jeri's self-sustaining needs and defenses, helped her gradually assimilate the return of the repressed material, reinforce her lovability, and develop a new and more resilient sense of self. Following an interpretation, there is a great deal of assimilation and working through to be done. The patient needs to be held and contained during this pleasurable and painful concatenation of emotional states induced by interpretation.

Thus, the singular nature of psychoanalytic interpretation is the way in which it provides a pleasure-pain opening to the repressed unconscious. Bass's work provides a sophisticated perspective on how interpretation operates to "unlock" the phantasy life, not without conflict, loss, and ambivalence.

Bass captures important essences of modern hermeneutical thought in their dynamic relevance to psychoanalysis. Interpretation is a journey and a life experience, not merely an intervention, and within modern Continental philosophy, there are important nuances which elucidate how and why interpretation is transformative. I will now take up some selected understandings of that transformative experience of both analyst and patient.

Hermeneutical philosophy and self-transformation

The following perspectives on interpretation and self-transformation are especially illuminating, each adding its own particular depth and dimensionality regarding emotional growth and change: 1) Husserl's phenomenology; 2) Heidegger's being-in-the-world; 3) Gadamer's hermeneutical dialogics; 4) Merleau Ponty's embodiment; and 5) Levinas's alterity of the other. I will now take up each of these in turn.

Phenomenology and self-transformation

Husserl tells us that naïve perception can be deceptive. Governed by outwardly directed attention, it attends to a world already constructed (so-called reality) and selects practical elements that help to negotiate that world, such as the location of a coffee cup, a traffic light, a lover's facial expression, etc. Husserl pointed to the deceptive tendency of everyday experience to take those constructions and regard them as perceived "reality." Psychoanalysis, as much as Husserl's phenomenology, instigated the deconstruction of the mundane perceptual world. Psychoanalysis did so by noticing how the inner world of fantasy and defense projects itself into what is seen and thought to be real. However, while Husserl held that perception could be clarified to yield understanding, Freud believed that perception (an ego function) obscured the unconscious forces beneath appearances. Psychoanalysis and phenomenology thus split into separate developments in modern psychology.

Husserl recognized that perception emerges as a self intending towards its object. When perception is observed freshly and as a whole, free of presuppositions (*epoché*), it provides rich new data for understanding human experience. Prominent American psychologists, among them Henry Murray (2007) and Robert White (1966), and psychiatrist Robert Coles (2003), recognized the rich potential of phenomenology for understanding the personality. Asking a person to express in detail how he experiences his life on an everyday plane, what he sees, hears, and feels, is revealing and useful. Giving an individual an opportunity to engage with a researcher or therapist in this process of self-perception and self-expression can in itself be transformative, especially when the co-participant observer does not respond by judging or shaming but with open-mindedness. Moreover, because, as Husserl asserted, the self and its intention are always present in the experience, accessing the richness of the experiential world discloses a great deal about the self and about motivation. (It is important to note, however, that phenomenological interviewing in psychology and psychotherapy rarely conforms to Husserl's method of transcendental reduction. Instead, the interviewer's intent is to capture the lifeworld of the person in all its complexity, not to achieve the "*epoché*," that is, to describe the pure phenomenon. A rare exception, Giorgi (2009) has attempted to follow Husserl's guidelines more closely, and has developed a specialized interview protocol for that purpose.)

Within psychoanalysis, Stolorow, who was Murray's student at Harvard, recognized the importance of phenomenology by advancing the notion of "sustained empathic inquiry" (Stolorow, 1994, p. 45) as opposed to (prematurely) imposing a theory upon the intersubjective experience of patient and analyst. Similarly, Kohut (1977, pp. 302–310) advocated empathic listening and immersion in the patient's experience. But how can such an empathic exchange of experience between analyst and patient be transformative of the latter?

The interplay of phenomenological lifeworlds that occurs between patient and analyst derives much of its transformational impact from enriching and modifying the patient's inner experience at multiple levels. There is much poetic nuance and detail contained in empathic introspection when the analyst fully immerses himself in the listening process for an extended time period and does not superimpose concepts and beliefs too quickly. It is not just a matter of inferring defenses or "self states." The patient's experiential lifeworld is both sensuous and sensual, rich in sensory depth and detail and full of narcissism and desire (and we might add anxiety, shame, and death). Hopefully, an interpretation to the patient would capture some of the richness of such experience, especially when it penetrates to deeper and developmentally formative images, fantasies, and memories.

The question of how phenomenological description can unveil the repressed unconscious (or whether phenomenology even acknowledges unconscious processes) is much more difficult to address. Husserl developed a concept he called the "horizon" to denote aspects of perceived phenomena that surround the objects of experience like a halo of understanding. For example, a person's perception of a table would of course be influenced by the observer's understanding or definition of a table and its use. In other words, perception is always surrounded by a "horizon" of meanings which are not yet articulated. (Heidegger and Gadamer subsequently used Husserl's notion of horizons in a very different way, as we shall see shortly.) The notion of horizons bears some resemblance to "unconscious derivatives" in psychoanalysis. The latter are part of the patient's conscious experience that includes horizons of unconscious processes known only by inference.

Taking the patient to and beyond the horizon of experience

It could be said regarding psychoanalytic interpretation that empathic introspection takes the patient to the horizon of the unconscious by sustained empathic inquiry about the patient's lifeworld. Consciousness of the horizons of one's experience in itself is valuable in self-transformation. The patient becomes aware of aspects of himself which were only on the edge of awareness and can begin to think about their implicit meanings. However, psychoanalytic interpretation would go one major step further in providing further inferences based on the analyst's clinical experience and knowledge of the unconscious. Bion described this process as "shooting beams of darkness" (Grotstein, 1993b) into the patient's mind, bringing out what the conscious mind obscures by its mundane appearances. In other words, the analyst brings the patient to the limits of the latter's own awareness, and then ushers him beyond the horizon to what had previously been inaccessible. It is as if Freud, like Columbus, discovered another "country" beyond the visible horizon, except that Freud explored the realm of thought, previously believed to be encompassed entirely within the horizon of the ego, and discovered a "new world" of the mental life.

The ultimate value of Columbus's discovery is obvious. What we can say about the discovery and penetration of the unconscious is more modest but perhaps equally significant: that it enlarges the scope of our individual and collective selfhood and identity. Grotstein (1978a) developed the notions of "inner space" and its "dimensions and coordinates," holding that psychopathology results from a constriction of that space. The polysemous richness of interpretation transforms the self by enlarging the mental space available to think thoughts and resolve inner turmoil and conflict. For example, a symptom can be considered the result of a constricted space for resolving the situation that originally provoked it and that has become a repressed memory. The interpretive process as empathic phenomenological inquiry takes the patient beyond the horizon of this limited space, introducing a richer self-understanding that can assimilate the memory and make sense of the symptom. In that respect, interpretation does not just extinguish the symptomatic behavior; it dimensionalizes the self in such a way that, in the expanded mental space, the symptom is no longer necessary to resolve the conflict. Perspectives are available that no longer include the symptom, as when, for example, a depressed patient absolves himself of self-punishing guilt by "making a space for" the memories of persons and situations that provoked it in the first place.

Interpretation as unconcealment (alatheia)

Heidegger made use of Husserl's concept of horizon in a way that shattered even Husserl's revolutionary ideas. Instead of the horizon of perception, for Heidegger, the horizon became the place where beings encounter their being-in-the-world, their *Dasein*. Like Freud, Heidegger was critiquing the concepts of consciousness and ego, seeing their role as very limited, but unlike both Freud and Husserl, he felt that at the horizon of thought was the fabric of temporal existence, of worldly, historical life and context. For Heidegger, interpretation and hermeneutics consisted in the authentic unconcealment of our "thrownness" into life and death, the ultimate source of our anxiety.

Heidegger thus cast a new light on the interpretive process. An interpretation, for Heidegger, does not function so much as a specific thought or statement, but more like a rock thrown into a lake. For a moment, one can see in the swirl around the rock that the surface smoothness (consciousness) has been disrupted, and maybe too one can see something in the water that was concealed by the light reflecting on the unperturbed surface. There is no "insight;" indeed, all insight ("reflection") is disrupted by the perturbation. But what is seen beneath the disrupted surface is authentic existence and unconcealment, beyond the deceptive surface smoothness of subjectivity and thought. We all have such an experience when a sudden shock or crisis in our lives makes us aware of an existential imperative we have denied. An interpretation is a psychological disturbance of that kind.

Truth as unconcealment, for which Heidegger used the term *alatheia*, is transformative in that, rather than analyzing subjectivity and thought, *alatheia* allows the perturbing temporality of events to unfold and be understood in their own terms. Heidegger said, "Let beings be." In this sense, the analyst does not "figure out" the interpretation. It comes to him when he lets himself and the patient be. It has a certain "glow" (Heiegger called it "presence") and "swirl" (disturbance), neither of which can be described clearly, and it seems to have no special use—it just has to unfold in its own terms. At the same time, the glow and swirl of an interpretation may be very meaningful, as we all know from personal experiences of confronting the truth about ourselves.

> For example, a patient, Jodie, suffered from severe depression which led her to take long naps just when responsibilities and activities beckoned. She said she overslept because she dreaded facing her day. As an adolescent, already confused and troubled, she was subject to severe criticism and shaming by her parents. Her devastation was so great that she became suicidal and self-mutilating, requiring several hospitalizations. She managed to struggle through to a difficult adulthood on her own, married, and had children. But well into midlife she continued to experience constant dread and a sense of futility about her life, with periods of suicidal despair when fortunately she saved herself by reaching out for help.
>
> In therapy, cognitive insights combined with empathic inquiry about the details of her sense of shame and self-hate helped her to curtail her suicidal impulses, avoid hospitalization, and become engaged in creative activities. But Jodie continued to feel "paralyzed" and go to sleep during crucial parts of her day. At that time, the therapist felt compassion for her, but stymied and helpless to be of assistance. Then, just when he felt he was of no use to her, he "heard" an inner command to be quiet and listen. He stopped trying to help and support her, and just let his thoughts flow. Then he had the unexpected fantasy that Jodie was still in the womb and that he needed to be a "midwife" and help her to be born. He felt a strong sense that he should facilitate this "birth" process. He told himself that he should not yet share this thought with her, but just wait. Interestingly, Jodie did not seem to notice what occurred, but the next session, her mood markedly improved, and she reported having more productive days. This pattern of sustained quiet listening followed by improvement recurred periodically for many months thereafter.

In this instance, the "interpretation" was given by means of silence and patience. It was tacit and unobtrusive, but "at hand," unconcealed in a "clearing," to use Heidegger's terms. To the therapist, it felt like the caesura of a birth process.

Heidegger's existential hermeneutics opens up a realm of self-transformation not covered in the psychoanalytic technical manual, in which the analyst and patient find a clearing for *alatheia*, truth as unconcealment. Bion approached such an idea with his notion of "transformations in O" (see Chapter Twelve), an experience of change "in the absence of memory, desire, and understanding." We are approaching here a hermeneutics of *non*-understanding, a transformation of being rather than thinking.

Interpretation as transformation through dialogue: Gadamer's dialogical hermeneutics

Hans Georg Gadamer (1960) (see Chapter Four) developed Heidegger's turn in philosophy into a broad understanding of interpretation as a process. Gadamer elaborated a philosophical position on interpretation as a dialogical process. He held that interpretation is an effort to arrive at "practical wisdom," what Aristotle called *phronesis*. Gadamer's is therefore not an absolute definition of "truth," but rather an understanding that occurs in dialogue where there is difference and hence something to be learned from one another. For Gadamer, understanding does not result so much from a method of interpretation but from a coming together, a "fusion of horizons" of the languages, idioms, and historical contexts of the partners in a mutual relationship. That one "partner" in interpretation could be a work of art rather than a person showed that Gadamer, like Heidegger, considered relationships not in terms of "subjects" or persons as such, but an interpenetration of *Daseins*, of lifeworlds, language, history, and context; of beings rather than thinkers.

Gadamer asserted that interpretive truth does not result from a method of truth seeking, but from beings encountering other beings at their mutual horizons. On one level, Gadamer's critique of method could be taken as the basis of a radical critique of psychoanalysis. His work calls into question not only objectivity about the psyche (for Gadamer, all we can arrive at is practical wisdom) but, more fundamentally, the notion that any method can yield truth. But what is a psychoanalyst without his method, arrived at through difficult training? That the analyst can have any authority and expertise to begin with is called into question by Gadamer when it comes to interpretation and understanding. For Gadamer, the partners in a dialogue are inherently "prejudiced" by their particular time and place, and never transcendent or objective as such. The only resources the analyst has to offer the patient are his own point of view and the fact that he may have struggled with his own difficulties. After reading Gadamer, we are left to wonder whether there is anything definitive and specific about psychoanalysis at all. The criterion of "practical wisdom" implies only that the dialogue is open and receptive, a meeting of horizons, and a way to better living, human understanding, and relationships. For Gadamer, these goals are indeed difficult to achieve, but, for him, no method can resolve problems of human existence.

Indeed, some analysts would admit to Gadamer's depiction of their humble position. They know that, with all their training and expertise, their patients' difficulties call upon them to be themselves and tap inner resources that are deeply personal and provide little solace or expertise. They know that in many ways, the psychoanalytic dialogue is between equals trying to grasp one another's intentions and struggles. Relational psychoanalysts like Lewis Aron (1996) have made explicit their mutuality and reciprocity with their patients. In the trenches, you have to find some meaningful exchange that connects and that "works" (*phronesis*, practical wisdom). Maybe that is all there is to psychoanalysis.

Our present concern, however, is with self-transformation. How can a conversation and "fusion of horizons" change a person? Gadamer himself sidestepped the issue of how understanding is transformative. For the most part, he stayed out of the therapeutic, political, and social arenas about which other existential thinkers of his time were passionately concerned. The only useful outcome he ascribed to practical wisdom was openness, a receptivity to the other. So, from that point of view, how can practical wisdom cure a troubled soul or a symptom?

As a tentative answer to that question, and on Gadamer's behalf, one could say that, in a world characterized by the hermeneutics of suspicion, where everyday transactions are so often deceptive and mundane, we do not give enough credit to humble but genuine dialogue as a curative, transformational agent. The process of bringing together the interpreter's context, history, and language (which includes how he comports as well as what he says) with those of his subject (patient, work of art, or historical time period), in other words, a fusion of horizons, can certainly change values (superego) and desires (id) in "at hand," implicit ways (unconscious levels).

The following is an unusual example of a dialogue between a therapist and a patient that was largely unspoken yet highly productive. The fusion of horizons developed in the context of a board game:

> A psychoanalytic therapist was called upon to treat an adolescent boy, Rob, who became depressed and oppositional when his divorced mother acquired a boyfriend and wanted to make him part of the family and acceptable to Rob. Rob liked the new man and found him supportive, but he still wanted him "out of the way." He became oppositional, and his schoolwork suffered. His mother tried unsuccessfully to dissuade Rob from his recalcitrance and finally brought him to the therapist to be "fixed." Rob objected to treatment, regarding it as just another attempt on his mother's part to set him straight.
>
> The therapist felt that "talk therapy" would only exacerbate Rob's fear of further pressure. Uncovering therapy might also overstimulate Rob's sexual and aggressive impulses. Moreover, since the mother was planning to marry her boyfriend in a short while, the therapy needed to be brief and effective rather than exploratory.
>
> The therapist decided to treat Rob through an activity rather than talk. Rob said he loved chess, and so did the therapist, so they agreed to play chess in the sessions. The therapist abandoned his neutrality, responding spontaneously and competitively to the frustration, triumph, and defeat engendered in the game of chess, but always remaining cordial and supportive with Rob. Over time, despite the intense competition between them, a feeling of warmth and mutual understanding developed. After several sessions, Rob's mother told the therapist that she was astonished at the improvements in Rob. He was no longer oppositional, there were no signs of depression, his schoolwork improved, and he was getting along well with her boyfriend, now her fiancé.

In this example, the non-verbal "dialogue" consisted in the therapist's and patient's comportment or position vis-à-vis each other: competitors who could also befriend one another. The "horizon" emerged in their chess moves and counter-moves. Nevertheless, the interaction was transformative: it helped Rob resolve his Oedipal dynamics. It is thus possible to understand psychoanalytic process as a meeting of horizons that takes place through culturally mediated rituals and interactions at the level of being-in-the-world. Gadamer's hermeneutical dialogics includes both the explicit and implicit, verbal and non-verbal dimensions of communication. The key ingredient for Gadamer is the emergence of an opening or clearing at the meeting of the horizons of experience of the parties involved. With Rob, it occurred on the playing field of chess.

Interpretation and speech as embodied understanding

While psychoanalysis, especially through its perspectives on hysteria, drew profound attention to the human body as a psychological phenomenon (the somatic core, the drives, physical symptoms), Freud's particular understanding retained the Cartesian mind–body split, so that interpretation was separated from the body and was formulated as a detached verbal statement of ideas (secondary process). Even though patients' symptoms had everything to do with the body, Freud's hope through what might be called a "literary" approach (as distinct from the use, for example, of psychodrama or interpretive dance) was to elevate the patient's thought above the physical plane in order to free it from the infant's state of body-enacted ideas, which in the adult were regarded as fixations and regressions.

Melanie Klein said, "The child is an intensely embodied person" (Guntrip, 1969, pp. 60–62). She could have included any age in that statement. Throughout the life cycle, our sense of self, our language, our concepts, our beliefs are "intensely embodied." The mind "wears" its body as both a thing of beauty and wonder as well as a source of pain and temptation. Then too, some religious teachings regard the body as the cause of evil and misery and encourage us to dissociate from "the flesh." When we learn to fear and hate our bodies, we try to find ways to get out of them.

Psychoanalytic interpretation has suffered from this artificial division between body and mind. Interpretations are too often offered as abstractions to be assimilated by the patient's "mind." But nothing can change the fact that it is always the analyst's body that is "speaking," and the patient "hears" it with his body, which means that both his body and mind are responding to it, "taking it in," "digesting" it, and sometimes "moved" by it.

The French philosopher Maurice Merleau-Ponty (1908–1961) sought to restore the connections between the body, mind, relationships, and interpretation. Among his searching contributions to philosophy, psychology, and the arts, (1963, 1968, 1976, 2002), he advanced the idea that all experience, knowledge, and perception are embodied: they have flesh. Drawing from Husserl's phenomenology, he configured thinking itself as a phenomenon within immediate experience. Thus, for Merleau-Ponty, thinking and interpretation cannot be separated from the experience of "being-in-my-body."

Three quotes from Merleau-Ponty assert in different ways how thought is embodied. The first has to do with relationships. It suggests that we experience and address the other as a body as well as a mind, and that the other's body is intimately an extension of our own. We humans are intertwined through our bodies:

> "… now it is precisely my body which perceives the body of another person, and discovers in that other body a miraculous prolongation of my own intention, a familiar way of dealing with the world". (1976, p. 354)

The second quote suggests that we automatically "get inside" the other, in what is a form of direct empathy:

> "When my gaze meets another gaze, I re-enact the alien existence in a sort of reflection. There is nothing here resembling 'reasoning by analogy'… Between my consciousness and my body as I experience it, between this phenomenal body of mine and that of another as I see it from outside there exists an internal relation which causes the other to appear as the completion of the system". (ibid., p. 332)

The third quote is more subtle. He uses the example of a person, perhaps shopping for an article of clothing, running his hand along the cloth to see what it feels like. There is no separation between the hand and the cloth; one has a simultaneous awareness of the hand and the feel of the cloth. Subject and object are two sides of one coin:

> "Like the cloth, my hand is a part of the tangible world; between it and the rest of the tangible world there exists a 'relationship by principle'. My hand which touches the things is itself subject to being touched. Through this crisscrossing within it of the touching

and the tangible, its own movements incorporate themselves in the universe that they interrogate, are recorded on the same map as it". (1968, p. 133)

So, Merleau-Ponty is saying that our experience of the world is always embodied, "in the flesh." Moreover, the self and the other always occur together in one pattern or gestalt. All understanding, knowledge, and meaning emerge from this living context and return to it.

That knowledge and experience of self and other as embodied and intimate (subject and object are folded onto one another in their embodied existence) has important implications for psychoanalytic interpretation and transformation of the self. The analyst is not merely exchanging ideas with the patient as an objective commentary on the mind. *The analyst's body is speaking to the patient's body.* Speech emanates from the body. Tone, pitch, and rate of speech convey bodily states: excitability, hunger, fear, quiescence (pauses). The body itself "speaks," evoking attention, lust, fear, interest in the other. Hearing is a bodily function. The message as heard is inseparable from the voice that utters it and the ears that hear it. (Think of a baby's cry, the talk between lovers, or the rantings of a demagogue). A dialogical exchange of ideas and meanings is a totality that includes the bodily relationship.

Psychoanalytic interpretation is thus as much a conversation of bodies as between minds. This palpable quality of exchange, ordinarily felt subliminally, becomes highlighted when the body intrudes itself into the dialogue.

> For example, a patient, Barbara (who was seriously devoted to obtaining insight about herself, having seen two psychoanalysts for lengthy treatments, recorded her dreams, and had many intellectualized insights about herself) came to treatment concerned about being a compulsive eater and chronically overweight. She appeared to understand the therapist's interpretations well, paraphrasing them skillfully and pursuing their implications. Nevertheless, the insights failed to get "inside her" in a way that she could use them to good purpose in her life. Her armor of flesh, which seemed to fill the space around her, appeared to keep the interpretations outside her body-mind. Moreover, Barbara's body intruded on the therapist's hovering attention. He was often distracted by her obese physical appearance, which contrasted disturbingly with

her seductive voice. In these circumstances, the therapist became conscious of Barbara's body as an ongoing part of the transference-countertransference relationship.

Another patient, Josephine, a dancer, was obsessed with her body, suffering from anxiety, hypochondriacal preoccupations, and psychosomatic disorders. It was as if her body and mind were absorbed in each other. Sexually abused in adolescence, she subsequently related to significant others as if their bodies were her own and that they in turn controlled her body. She felt invaded and attacked by people. The therapist was impressed with the compensatory marvel of Josephine's special grace and agility as a dancer housed in a body that seemed to be paralyzed by anxiety and assault from inner and outer sources.

A third patient, Linda, became pregnant while in treatment. There was indeed a third body in the room, the fetus. As Linda's abdomen grew in size, the therapist felt "weighed down" just like Linda did. The dialogue became slower and more "labored", heavy in tone. Linda had difficulty fantasizing joyfully about her child-to-be, experiencing the fetus as a cumbersome physical weight. The heavy physical experience of her body-with-a-fetus became prominent in the phenomenology and discourse of both Linda and her therapist, and all explorations and interpretive work felt wrapped in a fetal caul. After Linda gave birth, her mood was cheerful as she showed the therapist photographs of her baby. The "weight," which could easily have been mistaken for depression, was lifted.

While the body is usually not as intrusive and explicit an aspect of the dialogue as in these instances, there is always a "dialogue between bodies." Freud used it in his early cases, where he would press the patient's forehead or touch the patient gently in other ways (Bartole, 2011, p. 378). Embodied dialogue was forgotten in psychoanalysis, relegated to other therapy modalities like dance and movement therapy. But the "dance of bodies" plays a role in every human discourse and is a crucial aspect of psychoanalytic treatment.

For Merleau-Ponty, the dialogue between bodies relates to the fact that bodies are experienced as extensions of one another. They are experienced simultaneously as both the inside and outside of one another. For example, when someone speaks, one hears it as coming from "outside" oneself (but emanating from "inside" the speaker) and almost instantaneously as one's own thought (inside oneself). When patients "internalize" an interpretation, their bodies are "taking it in." Bodies relax or else become tense, eyes go inward or outward, arms and feet move, stomachs gurgle, headaches appear and vanish, and so on. Unfortunately, analysts usually report even less on their own physical reactions than those of the patient. If we were a fly on the wall in the consulting rooms, we might see analysts' bodies become erect, slink back into the chair, gaze out of the window, or lean towards or away from the patient. The conversation of bodies is reciprocal and undeniable, and the patient's body takes it all in as part of the interpretive process.

There are extreme instances that highlight this process. Balint (1968, p. 129) cites an example of a woman who did a somersault in his office. (We do not know how Balint physically reacted to this, although he does tell us that it was a turning point—pun intended—in the therapy.) There are many moments, mostly not so dramatic, when patients' bodies spontaneously express emotional states that evoke bodily reactions in the therapist. The abstinence rule (not to act but put into words) and the couch, while valuable in many other ways, unfortunately mask such physical responses. Balint does consider the importance of the abstinence rule as it applied to this patient's unusual behavior and concludes that it was an allowable exception.

Discourse changes the person deeply only when it is meaningfully experienced within bodily intimacy, that is, as sensuous and somatic. The therapist's language and expressiveness must reach the body of the patient, "move" him. Emotions are embodied thoughts. Words and thoughts have bodily connotations: "penetrating," "hard," etc. The analyst's interpretations are emanations of his body that enter the body of the patient. All this harks back to infantile fantasy and defense as they emerge in physical and facial expressive interactions with the mother. Infant researcher Daniel Stern visualized the mother–infant interaction as a dance, and he studied dance movements to enhance his understanding of attunement. When one thinks of the "dance" of mothers and infants relating to one another, it changes the understanding of the psychoanalytic dialogue. Indeed Stern, in his later work, tried to conceptualize the therapeutic relationship in such terms (Stern, 2007, pp. 42, 66, 142). (See Chapter Eleven for further discussion.)

Interpretation as an expression of alterity

Unknowability, the absolute limit to understanding, is an important preoccupation of both philosophy and psychoanalysis. The metaphysical tradition regards the unknowable as hidden substance or ideal form. Freud (1915e) held that portions of the unconscious, the "primary repressed" are unknowable, inaccessible to consciousness. Bion (1970, p. 4) posited a realm of the psyche, "O," which eluded understanding and is known only by virtue of the transformations it produces.

Heidegger's critique of metaphysics reconceptualized the unknown unthinkable not as a substance or form, but as nothingness, otherness, or as Lawlor (2012, p. 16) puts it, the "outside." Derrida considered unknowability to characterize all knowledge as the deconstructed absence of representational "presence." These perspectives suggest that the limits of interpretation itself may be a crucial factor in how interpretation leads to self-transformation—by virtue of approaching the limits of understanding.

Levinas (1970) held more radically that any person who comes before us is fundamentally unknowable. His term "alterity" means that we are responsible for the other despite the fact that he is unknown to us. When people meet "face-to-face," an ethical encounter takes place, akin to but somewhat different from Buber's "I-Thou meeting." To "face" another means to accept responsibility for him. Face-to-face, we encounter our ultimate subjugation to the other, who remains hidden behind the mask, and who demands that we respect him no matter "who" he may be. (I am somewhat troubled by Levinas's universal portrayal of "face" as subjugation, knowing as we do of patients who masochistically subjugate themselves to others' sadism. But I am sure this is not what Levinas meant; rather he must have meant standing before our fellows with awe, although he does imply "giving oneself over" to the other.) Levinas says that the human face "orders and ordains" us. It calls the subject into "giving and serving" the other. Levinas brilliantly viewed the face-to-face encounter as the phenomenological basis of ethics. For him, ethics is the foundation of ontology and epistemology. The face-to-face encounter is the foundation of being and knowing. Our existence and our world emerge from the imperative of our relatedness to one another.

Certainly, service to the patient in distress is the calling of the psychoanalyst, and such care provides the motive for understanding the patient. But there are differences. Levinas holds that responsibility comes from "face," not from the anonymity of either the couch or the confessional, and certainly not from what we can know and elucidate for the patient, but from our admission of alterity, that there is nothing we can legitimately know about him if we are to give him the respect he deserves. (The reader may see the parallel to the religious idea that submitting one's will to God includes respect for His mystery. Levinas was a Talmudic scholar.)

Levinas thus used the term "alterity" to refer to the wholly other unknowable aspect of the person. Alterity is radically more inaccessible and unknowable than anything implied in Freud's unconscious or even Bion's "O." It is truly "outside" anything we can ever know, and it defines our being and our relation to one another. Freud and Bion held that we can access the unknowable indirectly and inferentially. Alterity, on the other hand, refers to an imperative that certain aspects of the self remain untouched. Winnicott's (1965a, p. 187) "incommunicado core" has connotations that are similar to alterity.

Levinas's alterity poses an enormous challenge to psychoanalysis, which could thereby be understood as the violation of ethical responsibiity and a violent intrusion upon an individual's self or soul. By that account, psychoanalysis is a devilish form of knowledge that violates man's being and wholeness. But there is perhaps a way to rescue psychoanalysis from this serious charge. Psychoanalysis can be understood as a "two-faced" practice. One face is that of the physician ministering to his patient. Here, knowledge of the mental life is medically necessary for treating symptoms and complexes. In my opinion, Levinas would not deny medicine for the mind its useful place.

The second face of psychoanalysis is its extraordinary ethical stance, which may have partly derived from Talmudic influences on Freud. Psychoanalysis is exceptional among human encounters in granting full freedom of choice and respect for the patient's ultimate right to disclose or *withold* experiences. That is what distinguishes psychoanalysis from hypnosis, behavior modification, and other forms of therapy. In this way, alterity is fully respected by the psychoanalytic contract. Indeed, its ultimate efficacy depends on the patient's awareness that he is engaged in a dialogue with a practitioner who accepts his autonomy. The analyst is ultimately bound to the patient's alterity, even if it means the failure or termination of the therapy. I believe that Levinas and Freud would have found much in common between them despite their differences. Even though they publicly distanced themselves from Judaic sources, both were indebted to their ancestral forbear, Moses (Guenther, 2006).

From a vantage point like that of Levinas, self-transformation in psychoanalysis is as much an outcome of alterity as it is of insight into dynamics. Imagine that someone treats you day after day, some-times year after year, with respect for your freedom and otherness. (Alterity is implied even in the analyst's opaqueness and neutral-ity!) The situation will at first seem incomprehensible and unreal. You will undergo the sorts of adjustments and maneuvers that occur in the transference. But maybe if you keep encountering the analyst's non-judging neutrality and persistence at his task, you will eventually arrive at a sense of self conditioned by mutual respect. A mental life seasoned and fructified by such an ethical stance could be freed of at least some symptoms and defenses, and perhaps develop an attitude of care towards self and world.

In such a way, it may be that the very limits of hermeneutics and interpretation contain that which is transformative in them. For Levinas, the unknowability of the other to whom one is inextricably bound is what paradoxically constitutes our freedom. Similarly, it may be a significant source of transformation in psychoanalysis.

Summary: what changes and how?

Such perspectives of philosophical hermeneutics broaden and deepen our perspectives on psychoanalytic interpretation and self-transformation. They expand the impact of interpretive understanding from the mind and its dynamic contents to include richness of meaning, phenomenology, being-in-the-world, dialogue, the body, oth-erness, and alterity. Instead of a reified concept of personality, we begin to think of psychoanalytic psychotherapy as a dialogical process that can transform the life experience of the patient, not so much as an out-side intervention or influence, as by becoming an integral part of that experience.

The common element in the diverse ideas we have discussed here is the living context of what happens when two people (or more, if group or family therapy) engage in meaningful discourse. That context includes the analytic frame and contract, the relationship (transference and non-transference), language, metaphor, phenomenology, authentic being, horizons of understanding, the body, ethics, and what is "outside" the limits of consciousness and mind. A comparison to neural networks can be made. We are looking at rich and intertwined complexes of meanings that are "disseminated" like nerve impulses into the fabric of life, and finding the junctions (neurons, synapses = meaningful exchanges) which promote a shift towards greater openness and resilience. (See Chapter Thirteen for a fuller discussion of hermeneutics and neuroscience.) We do not presume to know these places of change in advance, and sometimes we know them only after the fact, by the changes that occur within the dialogue. An interpretation is more than a statement about the patient's mental processes. It is an encounter on many levels with oneself, the patient, and the lifeworlds of both participants in the therapy.

However, that expansiveness does not mean that we do not rely on trusted and valuable psychoanalytic theories and explanations. These are products of clinical experience and, in some degree, scientific research that capture important clinical wisdom (*phronesis*), leading the therapist to places where the potential for healing and self-transformation is concealed within the patient. (As medical wisdom tells us, the cure lies within the patient.) Again, I am not diminishing the significance of theory and science in our work. Some experiences and their meanings appear to occur repeatedly in psychotherapy, and some theoreticians are very good at understanding and conceptualizing them.

What is important, and helpful, I think, is that we go back to the theories themselves and examine their hermeneutic and philosophical underpinnings, explicit and implicit, placing them properly in the broader context of human experience and meaning-making. This process should allow us to use the theories better in our practice, and also show how they connect with and/or contradict one another. Thus, Part III takes up several theoretical orientations that have evolved in Anglo-American psychoanalysis and that are currently used in training and practice. Parts I and II have provided the broad brushstrokes of psychoanalytic interpretation from the standpoint of hermeneutical philosophy. Part III focuses upon some major theoretical formulations of importance and controversy, exploring the nature of the understandings they offer as well as some of their pitfalls.

PART III

PARADIGMS OF CONTEMPORARY
PSYCHOANALYTIC UNDERSTANDING

CHAPTER NINE

Melanie Klein: the phenomenology of the unconscious

Part I presented a historical and conceptual background for understanding psychoanalysis from the standpoints of hermeneutics and philosophy. I put forth and elaborated the idea that psychoanalysis is fundamentally an interpretive discipline and traced the development of philosophical hermeneutics leading up to Freud and modern Continental thought. Part II organized hermeneutics in a schematic way and took up the relationship between the interpretive process, the unfolding treatment process, and the self-transformative changes that occur in the patient.

Part III will now explore several psychoanalytic approaches and schools of thought from those perspectives. The theory and practice of any particular "brand" of psychoanalysis reflect the ways in which interpretation itself is understood. Arguments will be made in each case to illustrate how philosophy and hermeneutics can illuminate the complex array of ideas within Anglo-American psychoanalysis.

In addition, by looking at specific analysts' contributions and schools of thought, Part III questions the assumption that differing or opposing theories necessarily share the same epistemological and ontological assumptions and so can be readily compared, contrasted, and integrated with one another. Psychoanalytic theories exhibit a slippage of underlying premises that makes it hard to discern their similarities and differences, much less subject them to rigorous test. These variations in epistemology and ontology pose special difficulties in psychoanalytic discourse when explanations and theories are contrasted with and opposed to one another. The proponents sometimes erroneously assume that different theories address the same problems and phenomena. Since such controversies are common, this book constitutes a wake-up call to those who advance a particular theory above others. The call is to think seriously about the full context in which the theories are embedded before drawing conclusions.

My claim is that, whether articulated or not, conscious or not, each "school" embodies its own particular interpretive and philosophical understandings that may differ considerably from one another. They can be compared and contrasted, but to fairly do so, one must discern the underlying philosophical and interpretive matrix of each and then negotiate between them using hermeneutical understanding. The hermeneutical and philosophical differences within psychoanalysis are as fundamental and complex as cultural variations are for anthropologists. One must try to understand each theory from its own world view before comparing them.

In so doing, one encounters surprises, twists, and turns along the road. What appears to be one set of working principles may obscure other premises within the same system or school. Reaching for the thinking underneath the not-so-little philosophical book covered up by the big books of theories is not too different from analyzing patients, except that the "patients" are ideas and their "analysts" are philosophers examining the latent content of theories and theorists.

The first schools of thought to be examined here evolved on British soil: Klein's and Winnicott's object relations theories. They began as a concatenation of ideas under a single umbrella, or as Grotstein (1978b) has said, "divergencies within a continuum," propagated at the British Psychoanalytical Society, at first under the aegis of Freud's ardent disciple, Ernest Jones, who was mindful of their continuity with Freud's work. The mix of ideas became organized into distinct "schools" in the wake of the so-called Controvertial Discussions (King & Steiner, 1991) which took place between October 1942 and February 1944 in which Anna Freud and Melanie Klein and their followers formally debated the value of their theories, forming two "camps." Soon after this great divide was established, those who chose to be flexible and ideology-free formed a third group, the Independent School, and for years thereafter the three "schools," Kleinian, Independent, and Freudian, co-existed together in an uneasy peace. The Independent School, heavily influenced by Ronald Fairbairn and Donald Winnicott, was united by the principle that interpersonal relations are crucial to development, emphasizing the impact of real caregivers on the internal world of the infant and child.

Several fine attempts have been made, such as those of Guntrip (1969), Greenberg and Mitchell (1983), and Bacal and Newman (1990), to describe and compare the diverse object relations theories. They identify differences that center upon a) the interpretation and understanding of preverbal and pre-Oedipal infantile development; b) the significance of real maternal care vis-à-vis internal biologically based dynamics (object *vs.* instinct); and c) the role of the analyst as an interpreter of transference versus that of a real person providing the holding, containment, and attachment necessary to promote the patient's development.

In this chapter and the next, I am going to focus respectively on the ideas of two major figures: Melanie Klein and Donald Winnicott. This is not because I think that others such as Anna Freud, Fairbairn, Guntrip, and Bowlby, as well as successors like Herbert Rosenfeld, Clifford Scott, Christopher Bollas, and Betty Joseph—to name but a few—are unimportant. Rather, I want to suggest that Klein and Winnicott in particular have been profoundly misunderstood, that in fact, they may have misunderstood themselves! The truth is that many of the greatest thinkers have required clarification and reinterpretation of their fundamental ideas—think of Marx, Nietzsche, and—not the least—Freud. And it is usually those of much lesser brilliance who have undertaken those tasks. So I humbly apologize for what some will misperceive as "revisionist" points of view about Klein and Winnicott with the disclosure that I have always viewed both of them with awe and reverence. If my views suggest a revision and "deconstruction" of their theories, that is not my intention. I only want to look at them in a different light.

Melanie Klein: phenomenologist?

When I began my psychoanalytic training at a Freudian and ego-psychological training institute in the 1970s (see Preface and Acknowledgements), I encountered Melanie Klein's ideas in a secondary applied source, the highly respected work of Otto Kernberg (1975) on *Borderline Conditions and Pathological Narcissism*. Then, perhaps driven by what Melanie Klein would call my epistemophilic instinct, I sought out the original writings by Klein, began to read them, and came to class brimming with excitement. When I expressed her ideas about the infant's relationship to the breast, my instructor, a Freudian, glared at me and said that Klein was "all wrong" and that I was a "renegade." Fortunately, he was otherwise a tolerant man with a wry sense of humor and did not have me ejected from the institute, the sorry fate of other renegades in the psychoanalytic community. I soon found another instructor there who had been supervised by Klein when he lived in England. With him, I found true belonging. He loved Melanie Klein's work. Soon, I found other American comrades, some of whom were distinguished analysts like Vamik Volkan and Kernberg himself, who utilized her ideas, especially those about splitting and projective identification. But they always seemed to keep Klein under the radar, like a stealth bomber. Klein herself remained a shadow figure, until I found a fellow rebel of far greater authority than myself, James Grotstein, who brought Klein's work firmly into the American fold. Around that time I also had the honor to meet Hannah Segal who was Klein's most forceful and intelligent exponent. Segal and Grotstein made me feel in good company.

Unlike Segal and Grotstein, many Anglo-American analysts believe that Melanie Klein was dead wrong in attributing complex mental processes to infants and claiming to know what went on in their presumably non-existent minds. Looking back, especially with the hindsight of hermeneutics and philosophy, I believe that Melanie Klein's work was deeply misunderstood by many of her critics because their way of thinking about the psyche was so different from hers and because she herself, despite the novelty of her theories, insisted they were logical extensions of Freud. While she was insistent on the correctness of her theories, she herself did not realize the uniqueness of her understanding. She thought she was just doing what Freud did, only more so.

My contention is that from the very beginning of her career, Melanie Klein manifested an approach and perceptual acuity very different from Freud's, but she presented it throughout her life as if she were a devout believer who took Freud's central theories of the drives and the Oedipus complex as gospel. Repeatedly, she wrote of the power of the life and death instincts, and she regarded her theories of the paranoid-schizoid and depressive positions as extending

Freud's theory of the Oedipal complex back into the first two years of life. She always maintained that she applied Freudian metapsychology to the earliest developmental stages. My belief is that she in fact opened up a whole new world of experience beyond Freud's ability to grasp: the complex phenomenological world of the infant with the mother. Her observational equipment—her microscope as it were—was very different from and keener than Freud's. Her "eye" = "I" for the unconscious was unique, both inwardly in terms of her perceptions and externally in terms of the patient populations she treated. Let us first look at the latter.

Different hermeneutics for different disorders

The majority of Freud's patients were neurotic not psychotic. They all had the ability to verbalize their thoughts, feelings, and associations in a reasonably coherent manner. In theoretical terms, Freud's patients were able to represent (re-present) their experiences (images, memories, thoughts) in coherent language. Freud generalized from these patients to those rare psychotic individuals like Schreber (Freud, 1911c), whom he never met but analyzed on the basis of his memoirs and other information he had about him. Moreover, Freud had only one child patient, Little Hans (1909b), whom he analyzed through communication with Hans's father. Freud's model of the psyche, even applied to children and psychotics, was based on the analytic "microscope" applied to adult neurotic patients possessing the ability to verbalize in a representational and metaphorical manner. His metapsychology, firmly rooted in the Aristotelian notion of representation, was based on his work with patients who could use words as metaphors rather than things. The representation of the mind in language was Freud's remarkable gift, his métier. He rarely gazed directly into the psychotic core.

By sharp contrast, Melanie Klein had the ability to look directly into the eye of the psychoses. Most of her patients, with the exception of training analyses, were children and borderline psychotic or frankly schizophrenic adolescents and adults. Children and psychotics equate words and things. Klein used play therapy with children from the beginning, perhaps she and Anna Freud being the first to do so. Children use toys to concretely express their states of mind projected into things rather than language. Later, she took the most regressed adolescents and adults into analysis, patients who expressed themselves mostly by direct concrete communication of phantasy.

To "analyze" such individuals, whether children or psychotic adults, required a "microscope" very different from the one used by Freud. Freud took manifest content and "translated" it into latent content by a set of interpretive rules. Klein, in effect, got the latent content directly from patients. Her interpretations consisted of restating what the patient said to her—or what children expressed in play—in a language that she intuitively felt highlighted the dynamic elements. She did not have to "decode" their communications, but rather re-express them in a coherent language. This is itself a difficult task, but one in which she, and other noted analysts of her time, like Segal, Frieda Fromm-Reichmann, Harry Stack Sullivan, Hans Loewald, Herbert Rosenfeld, and Harold Searles appear to have had exceptional abilities. Moreover, Klein developed her own theory of the paranoid-schizoid and depressive positions quite differently from Freud, although she always incorporated the theory of psychosexual development within it. Klein's paranoid-schizoid and depressive positions were defined by her not in terms of instincts, but in terms of the infant's (and child's) relation to self and other. In the former, the child is preoccupied with survival of the self and experiences the mother as an extension of himself. In this way, she anticipated Kohut's notion of the selfobject in some respects, although within a drive theoretical framework.

The depressive position is characterized by concern for the well-being of the mother (the infant fears destroying the caregiver, who is now experienced as outside the self) and learns how mother can be both nurturing and frustrating rather than "all good" or "all bad," as in the paranoid-schizoid position. The predominant fear is the loss of mother. Thus, in her depiction of the depressive position, Klein anticipated ideas about grief and loss taken up by Bowlby (1969). Again, Klein articulated her new ideas within the drive theory, and some of her insights were lost as a result. In other words, she overutilized Freud's Cartesian concept of an isolated mind, which unfortunately obscured her nascent understanding of how the unconscious is formed intersubjectively. There is not a thing she says about the infant that does not involve the mother, but she could not get herself to say that the mother is "real!"

The phenomenology of the unconscious

Freud recognized that in psychosis the unconscious becomes visible and apparent, part of the phenomenology of consciousness. In hallucinosis, delusion, dreams, and highly imaginative creative experiences, the unconscious "breaks through" the veil of repression. Primary process dominates the perceptual field, and everyday "outer reality," which the senses are intended to register and interpret, is diminished. Bion, who was a student and analysand of Melanie Klein, understood these "breaking-through" perceptions as unmetabolized "things-in-themselves" (Bion, 1962b), elements of raw exprience prior to "digestion" and representation in language and cognition. Lacan called them aspects of the "real," as distinct from the "imaginary" and "symbolic" orders (Julien, 1994, p. 73). By real, he did not mean the external world, but rather experience that presents itself directly without mediation and symbolization. The unconscious can break through the stimulus barrier and present itself as a phenomenological lifeworld. It is therefore a very different clinical and personal experience to work with a psychotic's lifeworld presented as "real" as opposed to a neurotic's grappling with impulses and desires seeking to find expression and representation in language and in the transference relationship to the analyst.

Partly because she worked with children and psychosis-prone patients who manifested the unconscious directly in raw experience, Klein used the spelling "phantasy" (as distinct from conscious fantasies) for such preverbal non-representational experiences. Moreover, she understood primitive defenses as components of such phantasies, not as "mechanisms" as Freud did. In projective identification, for example, the infant has a phantasy of depositing a part of himself (initially body parts) into the mother's breast. The unwanted "part-objects" (perhaps for example a sensation of hunger or of something being stuck in the belly or mouth) are then contained by and identified with the breast, a much safer situation for the infant. For Klein, this is all part of the infant's raw experience, neither a mental representation nor a theoretical construct. Another way of saying this is that the unconscious impinges directly on the infant; it does not introduce itself gently by means of ideas, words, and stories. The mother is the only buffer against such impingement.

Thus, Melanie Klein was in fact a phenomenologist of the unconscious, which she tried to demonstrate was the infant's and psychotic's experience. Since she expressed herself in Freudian metapsychological (= metaphysical) terms, she created lasting confusion between her own unique understanding of primal experience and Freud's idea of representation, which requires language and thought—which the infant has yet to acquire. As stated previously, Klein (Guntrip, 1969, pp. 60–62) regarded the infant as "an intensely embodied person," a view of children akin to phenomenologist Merleau-Ponty's statement about adults: "… it is precisely my body which perceives the body of another person, and discovers in that other body a miraculous prolongation of my own intention, a familiar way of dealing with the world" (1976, p. 354). For both Klein and Merleau-Ponty, the body and the self originate in the same moment of perception, and that is also how, for Klein, the infant perceives and interacts with the mother, as an embodied self in the moment of need.

Difficulties comparing Klein with other theorists

In my opinion Klein's "microscope" and interpretive mode consisted of descriptive embodied phenomenology, which she herself erroneously confounded with metapsychology and decoding of higher level associations. She "saw" what her patients saw, and in this way was empathically attuned to them much like a self psychologist, except in terms of a primitive, or fragmented, level of experience. Unlike Klein, self psychologists do not describe the details of fragmentation so much as they attend to the developmental "selfobject" deficiencies that foster them. Self psychology thus has a very different sensibility from Kleinian psychoanalysis.

This confusion in the psychoanalytic literature between Husserl's phenomenological description and Aristotelian inference from representations is a prime example of the unstated hermeneutical dilemmas which lead to divisiveness among psychoanalytic schools of thought and which this book is trying to alter. Because of her use of metapsychological language, Klein made it all too easy to assume that she was attributing mature representational processes and cognitive/linguistic capacities to infants. But her concept of unconscious phantasy is not about cognition as such, but rather about unedited infantile and psychotic experience.

It is unfortunate that Klein's own language contributed to the blanket rejection of her ideas by other schools of thought. For example, she attributed a primitive superego and Oedipus complex to the infant. But, in my opinion, and I believe most Kleinians would agree, she was referring to their precursors, features that might later develop into structural aspects of the psyche. Over the years since Klein's death, her followers have accumulated some wisdom in this respect, and there is much less of a sense among Kleinians of an adult "homunculus" sitting in the brain of the infant. Indeed, Freud faced a similar problem when he first attributed sexual feelings and desires to the child. His psychiatric colleagues and the general public thought he was suggesting that the child's world was a pornographic sex manual, when in fact he meant that the wishes and desires of children had sexualized features. He well knew that the phenomenology of Eros in childhood is different from that of adults.

Such unfortunate confusions have led to ideological conflicts among clinicians who could otherwise benefit from each others' knowledge and experience. For example, self psychology and the intersubjective perspective are overlapping approaches both of which are based in phenomenological understanding, emphasizing empathic attunement and inquiry into the patient's world as distinct from interpretations of underlying motives and impulses that are "experience-distant" from that world. Both of these schools have distanced themselves from all varieties of object relations theories because they want to stay close to the patient's phenomenology rather than prematurely superimposing theoretical abstractions upon it. Yet object relations clinical findings, Kleinian or otherwise, include rich phenomenological descriptions of patients' experience. Why throw out the baby (the experience) with the bath water (the abstractions)?

This brings us to an important point about phenomenology that has been lost by psychoanalysts and many philosophers as well. Husserl, a philosopher seeking the basis of all knowledge, sought to discern elements of the phenomenological field that were universal and common to all subjects/observers. However, he also acknowledged in his understanding of individual "lifeworlds" that importantly, and fundamentally, phenomenological experience is not the same for all persons. Psychoanalysts, for example, differ in personality and culture from one another, and therefore attune to different features in the phenomenology of their patients. Some Kleinians, for example, are highly attuned to the hallucinated and fragmented lifeworlds of borderline and psychotic individuals, while some Kohutians might be more attuned to patients with narcissistic types of disorders who are preoccupied with their psychic wounds and "narcissistic injuries." If such diversity of perception among analysts were acknowledged and valued, there would be less contentiousness among analysts and more of an attempt to utilize and integrate clinical experiences of different varieties.

"Projective Identification Begone!" An illustration of hermeneutical misunderstanding

Not too long ago, a dispute within the journal *Psychoanalytic Dialogues* led innovators of the intersubjective perspective to a damning rejection of one of Klein's key concepts. "Projective Identification Begone!" exclaimed the title of their reply to a commentary by a self psychologist, Susan Sands, who identified herself as a friend and ally of both self psychology and intersubjectivity and tried to show that projective identification is a useful construct for such perspectives. Stolorow and cohorts responded as if she had violated a tribal taboo (Stolorow, Orange, & Atwood, 1998; the full exchange also includes Crastnopol, 1997; Sands, 1997; & Sands, 1998).

Sands's argument was that projective identification is a mode of intersubjective relatedness where the patient takes up residence within the analyst's mind (countertransference) as a means of managing primitive experience. She invoked the interpersonal view of projective identification in which the analyst contains the primitive affects and ideation, returning it to the patient in a way that either promotes or damages the development of the self (Langs, 1976, pp. 113–155). She quite reasonably held that *because it is a way of managing the self, projective identification can be a form of selfobject relatedness that Kohut and his followers had neglected.* By placing aspects of self in the analyst, the patient is able to retrieve and experience them in a more organized form. Sands took the position which emerged after Klein, that projective identification is an interaction of two subjects, hence intersubjective, linking it in that way to Stolorow's perspective.

Stolorow and colleagues responded with useful clarifications of differences between self psychology, object relations theory, and their own intersubjective perspective. They then escalated their disagreement into a thorough dismissal of projective identification. In particular, they held that projective identification does not qualify as intersubjective but implies an isolated individual (originally the infant) seeking contact with another (the mother), while intersubjectivity means that all experience is inherently an intertwining of subjective worlds. They argued against the implication of projective identification that the analyst's experience of the patient results from projections the patient "deposits" into the analyst; rather, they said, the analyst and patient each possesses his own subjectivity. They contended that projective identification "pathologizes" the patient and is a one-way process rather than a mutual exchange. On this basis, they held that projective identification is "bad theory."

In so doing, they disregarded fifty years of psychoanalytic work on projective identification. Between the time Melanie Klein had proposed that concept in 1946 and half a century later, it had undergone a definitive change of meaning from encapsulated internal phantasies to phantasy-laden mutual interactions. That shift summarized countless clinical encounters by analysts having diverse experiences in the consulting room and trying to make sense out of them. During that time interval, psychoanalysis itself had undergone a paradigm change from intrapsychic and drive-based understanding to a systems concept of mutual interaction. Analysts rooted in intersubjective and relational views had come to make good use of the concept of projective identification to depict mutual interactions between analyst and patient that included one particular feature: attribution (and export) of self states to another person who reorganizes them, a common aspect of intersubjective experience that serves both adaptive and defensive purposes and is not always pathological. Consistent with intersubjectivity, projective identification had evolved over time from a phantasy-defense configuration to a mutual subjectivity, what Bion (1962b) called a "thinking couple."

Projective identification as dramatic empathy

What makes projective identification unique and useful as an intersubjective construct is that it points to the evocative power with which mothers and infants, analysts and patients, can, almost as a form of possession, create whole states of mind in one another. This makes it different, but related to, Stolorow's notion of "empathic inquiry" in which mutual understanding is acquired piecemeal over an extended period of time. Projective identification can under certain circumstances provide a highly dramatic form of empathic inquiry and dialogue, a type of mimesis, in the Aristotelean sense (see Chapter Two). However, it is possible that some analysts do not go to live theater very much any more, where they might experience the sorts of immediate intersubjective transformations that occur across the proscenium through the veil of the aesthetic illusion, the way that the playwright, the cast, and the audience communicate profound truths deeply with one another by—none other than—projective identification.

I am emphasizing the dismissive response of Stolorow et al. here because it illustrates how psychoanalysts can become contentious and hostile to alternative theories when they construe theories as objective explanations rather than hermeneutics, that is, interpretations of experiences and meanings. Stolorow et al. criticized projective identification as over-objectification and concretization of intersubjective states, which are fluid and self-organizing phenomenological experiences. However, it was they who in fact reified the concept of projective identification after their object relations colleagues had spent years shaping it into intersubjective understanding! Sands was right. Nowadays, projective identification can provide a resilient interpretive tool as part of the intersubjective matrix developing between the patient and analyst in mutual relationship.

An example of scoptophilic projective identification as empathic inquiry

A patient, Irvin, in psychoanalytic therapy was a fine arts painter with exceptional visual interest and acuity. His perceptual giftedness was revealed to the therapist when Irvin came to a session on a rainy day and showed him a small historical artifact he had found wet on the street. (It must have fallen out of the briefcase of a curator or historian, as the office was not far from several museums). It was a remarkable example of scoptophilic selective attention that Irvin noticed the significance of a small piece of paper on the pavement.

A tall, gangly, rather affable man, he would enter the office and seem to take in every detail with his eyes. As treatment progressed, the therapist noticed that Irvin's gaze seemed to take possession of him, experiencing odd sensations of being lifted off his chair. He speculated to himself that Irvin was projectively identifying disavowed parts of himself into the therapist for containment. Over time, he surmised that the patient, an almost saintly type, was depositing his split-off aggression into him. There was historical evidence to suggest that this aggression stemmed from unresolved hostility towards his father, whom he had experienced in childhood as cold and unavailable.

The analyst, however, knew enough about projective identification to realize that he himself was to some extent imposing and projecting his own subjectivity into the patient as well. He realized that he envied the patient, who was, for him, in Kohut's terms, an idealized and mirroring selfobject, an expression of his own suppressed and frustrated desire to be a creative, artistic force. And he also sensed that his appreciation of Irvin's capacities seemed to help the latter feel admired and valued, providing a degree of selfobject nurturing for a man who often felt lonely and isolated in his creative endeavors. So, in addition to analyzing the patient's projections, he sought a way to capitalize and expand upon their budding mutuality. He thought that one way to do this would be to invite the patient to bring some of his art work to a session, so they could have a shared experience that might also disclose elements of the patient's inner reality.

The patient brought in a canvas so large that it took up much of the space in the consulting room. The analyst, again feeling controlled, indeed suffocated, by the largeness and aesthetic power of the painting, nevertheless marveled at its artistic quality and its complex expression of many motifs in a contemporary combination of abstraction and expressionism. He also noted to himself that some of the objects of the painting resembled Kleinian "part objects" like penises and breasts. Again, he refrained from making an interpretation, realizing that he might be projecting his own thoughts in this regard. He was startled, however, when the patient himself pointed to objects in the painting and said they symbolized penises and breasts. "Have you read Melanie Klein's work?" he asked.

The analyst, surprised by the patient's erudition, was again wise enough to realize that this did not prove Klein's theory, and thought about it more in Kohut's terms as an aspect of a mirror or twinship transference. To provide a mirroring response, he emphasized how moved he was by Irvin's art and his willingness to share his work as a part of himself with him. The conjoint experience with the painting seemed to strengthen the mirroring relationship as much as it provided clinical material as such.

The point is that Stolorow et al. were right in emphasizing the intersubjective context of mutual experience as the basis of psychoanalytic psychotherapy, indeed providing its phenomenological underpinnings. However, an aspect of this mutuality that can be of great import is projective identification, the placing of parts of self and inner reality in one another for containment and understanding. In this case, the patient deposited parts of himself into the therapist just as he put those part-objects into his paintings. Projective identification is one instance of attribution of thoughts to the "other," in turn contained and metabolized by the other, an everyday human occurrence in the theater of the mind. And, as Sands held, there is nothing magical or extrasensory about it. It occurs through body language, gesture, and voice—which Freud called unconscious communication and Aristotle called mimesis. Stolorow et al. notwithstanding, intersubjectivity, empathy, and projective identification are varieties of embodied processes that begin at birth.

Hermeneutics as a basis for cooperation and dialogue among divergent schools of thought

The numerous appreciations and critiques of Melanie Klein's work amply illustrate the hermeneutical nature of psychoanalysis. Interpretations are not statements of logic and fact derived from reasoning. They are multilayered creative problem-solving attempts resembling the work of artists and philosophers. Psychoanalytic theories contain complex meanings and implications that can only be ferreted out over time as new experiences and ideas come into conjunction with them. Klein's formulations were "couched" in the individualistic and Cartesian metapsychology of Freud. But her clinical experience was of the phenomenological sort that makes darkness visible, the unconscious prior to repression manifest in the play of children and the hallucinations and delusions of psychotic experience. She confused and condensed three levels of discourse: the concrete, the metaphorical, and the abstract; the real, the imaginary, and the symbolic, and this led to misunderstandings that make it harder for analysts of other persuasions to assimilate her unique and valuable insights. In my opinion, if her critical colleagues had grasped her special phenomenological mode of accessing the primitive raw material of early experience of self and other, they might have taken from her ideas what was useful to them. Rather than over-objectifying and reifying subjectivity, the work of the Kleinians can serve to enlarge the scope of subjective and intersubjective phenomena as they disclose themselves in the consulting room and in human development; and the intersubjective perspective could help place the pioneering work of Klein in its proper phenomenological and relational contexts. A useful dialogue at the "horizons" of different approaches could reinvigorate psychoanalytic discourse.

CHAPTER TEN

Donald Winnicott: the infant's being-in-the-world

In contrast to Klein, who adhered to Freudian doctrine, and while he valued her theories, which served as inspiration for him as a young analyst, Donald Winnicott avoided dogma, seeking his own individualistic vocabulary and ideas. Fittingly, during the Controversial Discussions and afterwards, he never sought to establish a following, although many have borrowed liberally from his ideas.

Winnicott was the rare thinker who did not pose his ideas as definitive truths, but seemed to value diverse human understanding, offering his own observations and ideas as a contribution to an ecumenical mix. By no means a student of hermeneutics (we know little of his knowledge of Continental philosophy or lack thereof), Winnicott nevertheless expressed a view of interpretation akin to that that of Gadamer, as co-created dialogical meaning. Indeed, he sometimes viewed interpretation as a form of spontaneous play, comparable to the "squiggle game" in which he and a child patient together produced a drawing which connected their two horizons (Winnicott, 1971, 1976). Concomitantly, placing great value on spontaneity and individuality, his criteria for mental health were aliveness, authenticity, and openness, rather than adjustment to social norms.

Always a humanist, Winnicott nevertheless displayed a strong grasp of modern science. His was a biosocial psychology with an emphasis on how the child uses objects in his environment. For example, the infant takes from his environment a comforting blanket or piece of cloth for his first "not-me" possession, which has psychological survival value, alleviating anxiety in the absence of mother. Maturation then leads to the choice of a "transitional object," a doll or teddy bear for play and symbolization, finally establishing the "place where we live," a cultural matrix for symbolization, maturation, and growth in a community of significant others. The child thus adapts to wider sectors of his environment (Jacobs, 1995).

Winnicott intuitively utilized scientific theories for his own purposes in his own way. He anticipated interpersonal systems theory when he said, as early as 1942, that "There is no such thing as a baby ... one sees a nursing couple" (Abraham, 1996, p. 165). Well before their emergence in science, Winnicott was aware of chaos and complexity as important aspects of development, considering even destructiveness to be a force for transformation and growth (1969). Further, his notion of the transitional space, emphasizing the "space between" self and other as a region of emotional development (1953), bears a resemblance to the quantum physics notion of continuous waves also consisting of discrete quanta. The transitional space and object connect the infant to the mother (like a continuous wave) and form a boundary between them (like quanta). Transitional phenomena, such as play, culture, and human understanding embodied for Winnicott the paradoxes of continuity and discontinuity, causality and randomness, so crucial to modern physics.

Winnicott was well-schooled in science. Having attended college at Cambridge and then received one of the best medical educations at St. Bartholomew's Hospital Medical School in London, his developing mind was exposed to rigorous science, and as a pediatrician, he was an astute observer of infants' and children's behavior, noticing, for example, subtleties in the way that babies toyed with a spatula (tongue depressor) (Jacobs, 1995, p. 68). So, although he was imaginative, inventive, and humanly sensitive, it would be wrong to attribute to Winnicott a lack of serious discipline and cross-checking of ideas, or an alienation from science and technology. He was equally at home in what C. P. Snow (1998) called the "two cultures" of the sciences and the humanities, Snow's famous lecture and book seeking reconciliation between them. (Snow's lecture was delivered at Winnicott's *alma mater*, Cambridge, in 1959, as Winnicott was coming into his own as a psychoanalyst with unique views. Whether or not he was familiar with Snow's perspective, he exemplified the ideal of a thinker who could live equally in both intellectual worlds.)

I emphasize Winnicott's scientific bent, because the thesis I am going to develop is about his kinship with Heidegger's view of being, and Heidegger was decidedly skeptical of the potential of science and technology to advance human understanding. Winnicott was not. Yet there are some uncanny parallels between Heidegger's thought and Winnicott's notion of human development (cf. Loparic, 1999). It is uncanny, because rarely if ever does Winnicott refer to Heidegger. Indeed, Winnicott in most places is a Socratic and Aristotelian thinker, a combination of one who questions basic beliefs and seeks through observation to demonstrate his ideas. Yet, as I will try to show, his interpretive mode, his type of understanding, like Heidegger's, is centered on "being-in-the-world" rather than the "mind."

First, I will draw parallels between Winnicott and Heidegger. Then, I will suggest how they are different.

Winnicott's "going on being" and Heidegger's "being-in-the-world"

Unlike Freud and Klein, whose primary interests were the infant's drives, unconscious fantasies, and internal objects, Winnicott focused upon the infant's capacity to survive in the world, as he put it, "going on being" (1958a, p. 303). This shift in emphasis from the mind to existence parallels Heidegger's shift from metaphysics and the Cartesian cogito ("I think; therefore I am") to *Dasein*, being there. Moreover, Winnicott, like Heidegger, held that the emotional consequence of encountering one's being is *Angst*, anxiety of the abyss, or what Winnicott called "annihilation anxiety." As in Heidegger's *Dasein*, the Winnicottian infant takes hold of that which is "at hand" and uses it to tolerate the anxiety of going on being. The infant has not yet an identity or language to contain his being, but the mother provides a "holding environment," and during mother's absence, the infant establishes a memory trace and anticipation of her presence that enables him to go on being. He does not "know" that the mother is "out there," but relies on her arrival, on being held by her. The fact that the infant does not yet have language or a concept of the "other" raises philosophical questions which I will take up momentarily.

Care as the basis of existence and development

For Heidegger, that which defines human being-in-the-world is *Sorge*, the German word for care. Similarly, Winnicott's emphasis is on maternal care. Humans are from birth preoccupied with self-care, with managing their world as part of their own being. When the infant begins to perceive the world and his resources as outside himself, he develops what Winnicott (1963) called "the capacity for concern," where the infant begins to shift his interest from self to the welfare of significant others who provide for his continued existence. For Winnicott, this capacity is not inborn but emerges later in development, although as early as the first year of life. So far as I know, Heidegger never asked the question as to when or how presence and aliveness becomes *Dasein*, human being with care for its world. (This is a question related to the concerns of abortion rights proponents and opponents—as to when biological life becomes a human existence.) Maternal care is a central aspect of all of Winnicott's thinking, as *Sorge* is for Heidegger. Winnicott said that initially the care factor resides with the mother and her "primary preoccupation" with the infant. But it could be argued that the infant's attempt to manage his own annihilation anxiety is a precursor of care in Heidegger's sense.

A developmental view of Dasein

Winnicott may have filled a gap in Heidegger's thought by offering a developmental account of how *Dasein* emerges. The newborn, while concerned about survival, does not yet have a coherent "world" to care for. Here, Winnicott offered a developmental picture of how *Dasein* (human being-in-the-world) emerges in infancy and childhood. For Winnicott, or anyone who observes infants, such being-in-the-world is not innate but evolves during the first weeks and months of life. Through the mother's holding (which also includes a tolerable degree of frustration and absence), the abyss (emptiness) of annihilation anxiety transforms into a "potential space" for experience in the world. (Eigen (1985) calls this space "an area of faith" that allows the infant to survive the absence of the mother). It is curious that at this point in his theorizing, Winnicott moves from existential language (annihilation, holding, preoccupation) to abstract geometrical language (space and object). Perhaps he thinks the infant is also moving from chaos to form at this stage. In any event, the infant acquires the ability to make something of himself and his world. That is his *Dasein*.

Ownership and destruction of the object

Here, again, after a divergence into Cartesian coordinates, a similarity to Heidegger recurs. Winnicott depicts an event which he repeatedly observed as a pediatrician. The infant is presented with an object, typically a soothing cloth or blanket, and makes it his own, his "first not-me possession." Both the parents and the infant acknowledge this possession as belonging to the infant and not to be tampered with. It belongs to the self for its use. Such dynamics of "ownership" are rarely alluded to in Freud or Klein. One does not see discourse about ownership in many philosophers either, Heidegger and Karl Marx being notable exceptions. It was a unique observation of Winnicott that ownership is essential for child development.

Heidegger refers to "owning" in a radically different manner from Winnicott, yet a comparison can be made. He holds that making death "ownmost" is what gives *Dasein* the potential for authentic existence (1927, p. 294). That is, by owning our mortality as definitional of our being, we encounter the truth about ourselves. Now, it is far from obvious that the transitional object makes death ownmost for the infant! In fact, it preserves the child's security. But, says Winnicott, the child tears and wears out the transitional object, which eventually outlives its usefulness and is discarded by the child; it "dies." The child works out some aspects of death and loss through the transitional object.

Winnicott observes that the child eventually wears out and sometimes destroys the transitional object, tearing it apart, forgetting about it, or denying its significance. Moreover, he maintains that what assures children of their continued existence is to mentally destroy their caregivers in fantasy (Winnicott, 1969). He believed that mastery of destruction and death (aggression) is a developmental imperative. Winnicott's emphasis on destructive fantasy and the ultimate abandonment of the transitional object parallels Heidegger's idea that making death "ownmost" gives us the possibility for authentic existence. For Winnicott, the child is beginning to own life and death, as choices and possibilities within his own evolving identity and existence. And by life and death, he, like Heidegger, does not mean biological instincts but existential aspects of being and becoming.

True self and authentic being

Heidegger's work is largely about authentic and inauthentic ways of being. We evade awareness of mortality by wearing a social persona that masks our terror and allows us to be like everyone else, what Heidegger termed "the 'they'." Social conformity compromises our authenticity. Of course, a host of other thinkers, from Freud to Nietzsche to Kierkegaard to Durkheim to Tillich to Fromm have developed similar ideas.

Winnicott (1965b) makes a similar distinction: the true and false self. Winnicott's true self is conceptualized differently from Heidegger's authenticity. The true self, in Winnicott's sense, is the self that is connected to and fully experiences its body, its vulnerability, its anxiety, and at the same time, its aliveness, spontaneity, individuality, and creativity. The false self—and here he is with Heidegger—is the image we present to the world. We use it as a defensive maneuver, mask, to protect our true selves from being destroyed by social pressure and conformity. Often, however, the false self becomes equated with our being, and we become inauthentic and lifeless, schizoid and depressed. Winnicott and Heidegger agree that our true selves are related to our authentic existence, while false and inauthentic selves are defined by others' expectations. However, Winnicott's true self is connected to the "inside:" spontaneity, the body, and the incommunicado core; while for Heidegger authentic being has more to do with the "outside," our time-bound existence in the world. For Heidegger, self-consciousness is an obstacle to authenticity, which is an opening to non-self. However, Winnicott and Heidegger may be highlighting two sides of the same experience. For example, when we are in love or deeply immersed in an artistic or religious experience, we feel more alive and in touch with our inner depths, and at the same time, we lose ourselves in the otherness of the object which comes into being for us.

Restoration of the true self through "regression to dependence"

How is the true self strengthened in treatment? Here, Winnicott emphasized the therapeutic holding of the patient during regression to dependence, echoing the infant's state of near-total dependence on the mother. He felt it was necessary to take the patient back to this primal level in order to restructure and heal the traumatic collapse and encapsulation of being that happens to some infants due to the mother's inability to provide a stable and secure holding environment. The adult manifestations of such a catastrophic abandonment in infancy are severe and lasting depression, psychosis, and/or lack of fulfillment in life. Psychoanalyst Margaret I. Little (1990) sought analysis from Winnicott, coming to him with feelings of emptiness and melancholia that persisted despite two previous therapy experiences and a successful professional life. Winnicott, not without difficulty for both of them, helped her regress to dependence and heal the earliest traumatic wounds to the self. She felt, in retrospect, that Winnicott's "holding" helped her regress to relive her infantile experience and heal the underlying abandonment depression.

"Holding" the patient usually means attentive listening and emotional availability on the therapist's part. However, in Little's case, the holding was real. As she experienced overwhelming anxiety in her sessions, Winnicott leaned over the couch and clasped his hands around hers for session after session. He empathized with existential dread as few do, and he knew that sometimes words do not suffice to manage it. Little also required a period of hospitalization during the depths of her regression. According to her own narrative, the psychic fragmentation and reorganization that took place rendered her helpless for a period of time. But she emerged on the other side with a renewed vigor and enthusiasm for life.

There are many patients like Little whose sense of "going on being" is not well-established, and they reach out to significant others (and sometimes to drugs and alcohol) to restore their sense of being-in-the-world. When they cannot restore equilibrium, they can become suicidal. Winnicott (1974) said that suicidality may be a way of paradoxically preserving the true self against excessive social and familial pressure to maintain a false self. Through suicidal ideation, the patient escapes the painful despair that occurs when the true self is intruded upon and violated. Although I do not believe that it is taken up in Heidegger's writings, suicide is a recurrent theme in other existentialist works.

Dread of loss of the true self: "I don't exist"

One such despairing patient, Alana, came to treatment experiencing severe panic episodes with depersonalization which led her to feel, unbearably, "... as if I don't exist." This distressing experience of non-being recurred whenever she was rejected by a lover upon whom she felt totally dependent, or when she failed to achieve a life or career goal. While in therapy, until she learned to reach out to the therapist for support, she responded to her disappointments with either a suicidal gesture such as superficial self-cutting or drinking alcohol to a point of oblivion.

It seemed clear from her history that Alana's mother, who was often detached and cold, had not "held" her sufficiently to facilitate a sense of "going on being" in Alana. The therapist, who appropriately did not want to risk the level of regression which Winnicott allowed with Little, used empathic understanding and telephone contact as supports. He often pointed out to Alana how her failed interpersonal relations led her to isolate from others, and he helped her to communicate her despair rather than withdraw in such situations. Over time, Alana became able to tolerate her relational and existential difficulties without becoming suicidal or intoxicated, and she resumed a disrupted career path. Alana's symptoms abated, but she did not experience a self-transformative restructuring of her personality as did Little. Treating annihilation anxiety and despair of the true self requires good clinical judgment and risk management. Self-transformation may not always be accomplished in such cases.

Heidegger and Winnicott: similar but different

Thus, Winnicott was keenly aware of existential dread as a source of symptoms. He was able to understand and conceptualize the profound consequences of deprivation and abandonment for "going on being." He articulated these insights in a way that is akin to Heidegger's understanding of being-in-the-world, enduring time, nothingness, and mortality sufficiently to establish an authentic existence. Loparic (1999) has gone as far as to suggest that Winnicott's work provides a basis for an existential analysis (*Dasein* analysis) consistent with Heidegger. I do not agree with this proposition. For me, Winnicott was perhaps an intellectual relative of Heidegger, but not an intellectual "brother." I think it is important to see that *psycho*-analysis, while it may have existential aspects, is not the same as *Dasein* analysis nor is it a form of existential therapy. Winnicott's developmental understanding of infancy and childhood is different from *Dasein* analysis. I will now say why I think this hermeneutical difference is important in grasping Winnicott's work.

Heidegger encounters the teddy bear

It is difficult to codify the hermeneutics of Winnicott's approach because it encompasses two divergent philosophies: empiricist/rationalist and existential. On one level he generalizes from facts and observations, and on another level he immerses himself in "at hand" being-in-the-world, and goes even further to impute such experience to preverbal infants. When making interpretations to patients, Winnicott did not shy away from the traditional method of interpreting their repressed memories. However, unlike Melanie Klein, he fully acknowledged the objective reality of maternal care and recognized that the actual traits and actions of the mother, such as intrusiveness versus unavailability, had a real and lasting impact. At the same time, he considered biology of fundamental importance: development is an adaptive, selective process. He never rejected drive or instinct theory, but viewed them from his own perspective on being as signs of life rather than determinants of mind. He always returned in his own way to the fundamental Heideggerian problem of being-in-the-world. It was the condition of human existence that interested him the most. But he also took fully into account the infant's adaptation to the object world (beings as opposed to being) and gave the world of "things" far more significance than did Heidegger.

At the same time, Winnicott believed, in a way that was almost more Heideggerian than Heidegger, that the infant experienced real and vital existential dilemmas. Such a depiction of infancy would pose a serious problem for Heidegger, and I am at a loss about how he would solve it. For Heidegger, being-in-the-world (*Dasein*) is embedded in language. It is language which gives meaning and care to our lives. (Several places in this book, I take exception to this view, suggesting that meaning and interpretation can be pre-linguistic.) Moreover, Winnicott would say that being-in-the-world is a developmental process that can be facilitated or damaged by caregivers, while Heidegger contended it is "already there" by virtue of being human. This is the difference not only between Heidegger and Winnicott, but between philosophy and developmental psychology that haunts all psychoanalytic discourse. Heidegger, despite his emphasis on time, sought universals that are outside of time. Indeed some postmodernists such as Derrida have faulted him for this inconsistency. Winnicott would agree that we do not come into the world ready to "be" in it, but that the infant struggles to survive without words or world, totally dependent on caregivers, until a "world" appears on his radar screen in the potential space and he acquires a beginning vocabulary to describe it. For Winnicott, as for other psychologists, as opposed to philosophers like Heidegger, meaning and existence are not ontological categories (definitional of being); rather they are experiences that evolve in the course of human development. Yet, Heidegger and Winnicott would agree with Hamlet that "to be or not to be" is indeed central to the human condition. The patient, Alana, who felt sometimes as if she didn't exist, would perhaps also concur with the Prince of Denmark in this respect.

The source of hope

Winnicott's hope for human beings was quite different from Heidegger's. Heidegger's hopefulness was almost nostalgic. He sometimes reflected upon and perhaps longed for a return to a state of being prior to science and metaphysics, when man dwelled among mortals and demons, earth and sky, before these fourfold worlds were reduced to the status of mythology (Heidegger, 1946). Unlike other existentialists, Heidegger had an almost utopian vision rooted in the ancients and based on philosophical devotion. Winnicott, by contrast, was a pragmatist and optimist. For him, hope was kindled anew in each person he encountered, in his or her potential aliveness, spontaneity, creativity, and growth, whereby each individual could reach for something new and make it his own. Heidegger believed in history; Winnicott believed in "aliveness" in the present and the future.

Yet there was a common element in Heidegger's and Winnicott's hopefulness. Heidegger said, "Let Beings be," by which he meant life should disclose itself to us on its own terms, rather than be categorized and dissected. Similarly, Winnicott was more about helping patients grow at their own pace in their own way, than about giving them the (metaphysical) "truth" of their dynamics and unconscious motivations. Moreover, he respected Levinas's alterity, recognizing that we can never know another in his entirety, but only through a glass darkly, through the transitional space of work, play, language, and culture which allows us to make attributions and hypotheses. Winnicott's concept of the "incommunicado core" fully acknowledges alterity. He believed there was a part of each individual which was strictly private, never to be revealed, yet life-preserving. This sets a definite limit on what we can know about each other. Heidegger felt that being was hidden and reluctantly disclosed itself. For Heidegger, being only disclosed itself on the horizons of experience. For Winnicott, that horizon consisted in the mother's holding and the transitional space.

The teddy bear as metaphysician

Perhaps the most important difference between Winnicott and Heidegger is embodied in the teddy bear, the transitional object. The teddy bear, among its diverse uses, facilitates the development of a representational world of objects, somewhere between reality and phantasy as Winnicott said, that can be imagined, played with, and become a world of story, autobiographical narrative, and dialogue with others. It evolves into the Aristotelian world of culture, science, and the humanities. Bringing together the existential and objective components of experience, the teddy bear promotes the child's capacity for illusion and representation, which for Winnicott is a developmental milestone, but which for Heidegger is metaphysics, and which he sought to overturn. The teddy bear is truly metaphysical, a material reality or "substance" that is simultaneously a creation of human thought. The teddy bear allowed Winnicott to straddle the existentially vulnerable heart and the playful, resilient, and sometimes penetrating world of the mind and the many objects, memories, and visions that inhabit our lives. For Heidegger, the "mind" and its objects obscured our being-in-the-world. He made it his task as a philosopher to "tear apart" the teddy bear of Western metaphysics.

Crossing the pond

Winnicott was well-received internationally and in particular in the United States. He gave presentations at the William Alanson White Institute and the New York Psychoanalytic Society (Rodman, 2003, pp. 323, 328), and his ideas made sense to American analysts who utilized perspectives which, like Winnicott, emphasized adaptation and the impact of real caregivers. Melanie Klein, on the other hand, never came to the States, a matter which was largely circumstantial because she died in 1960, before the "British Invasion". In any case, her writings seemed radical and unbelievable to many American analysts of the time, although her thinking subsequently took hold in southern California, where James Grotstein, Donald Meltzer, Bion, and others advanced her cause, and at the Menninger Clinic in Topeka, where Ramon Ganzarain and Otto Kernberg introduced and incorporated her ideas. In addition, her work found its way into mainstream discussions of borderline personality disorders (Kernberg, 1975; Volkan, 1988).

Object relations theory thus took hold in America in the 1970s–1980s when interest in the psychoanalytic treatment of borderline and narcissistic disorders reached a peak. During that same time, three uniquely American brands of psychoanalysis emerged: Kohut's self psychology, Stolorow's and others' intersubjective perspective, and Mitchell's relational psychoanalysis. Kohut virtually ignored object relations theory, while Mitchell incorporated British views into his own perspective which emphasized the primacy of relationships over the drives. In the meantime Stolorow's group put forth an intersubjective phenomenology of psychoanalysis. America began to evolve its own unique ways of thinking about psychoanalytic process. We now turn our attention to these "American originals."

CHAPTER ELEVEN

Self psychology, intersubjectivity, and relational psychoanalysis: "American originals"

Self psychology, the intersubjective perspective, and relational psychoanalysis are variants of psychoanalysis that originated in the United States during the 1970s–1990s. Each began as a distinct school of thought. Over time, especially in the new millennium, the three have partially merged through dialogues and syntheses in the literature into a broader psychoanalytic paradigm that prioritizes interactions and relationships, a "multi-person psychology." Before discussing their hermeneutics, I would like to say why I call them "American Originals."

The influence of American culture on psychoanalysis

Although these three approaches have European roots, they emerged and flourished on American soil. The founder of self psychology, Heinz Kohut, came from Vienna to Chicago. The intersubjective perspective was conceived by Robert Stolorow, George Atwood, and Bernard Brandschaft, all at the time at Rutgers University. Relational psychoanalysis was initiated in New York by Stephen Mitchell who was soon joined by Lewis Aron and other American-bred analysts. Mitchell drew heavily on British object relations theory, but identified a new paradigm in the making, and was strongly influenced by interpersonal psychiatry. All three viewpoints have features rooted in American psychology going back more than a century to William James, a heritage which allowed these approaches to find considerable support in the United States.

From its origins as an academic discipline in the late nineteenth century, American psychology emphasized the self that became the center of Kohut's thinking. William James, a co-founder of the first American psychology department at Harvard University, explored the self in depth and detail (1890, pp. 291–350). Subsequently, the sociologist George Herbert Mead (1934) placed great emphasis on the self as a social process, influencing the progressive education movement founded by John Dewey. Modern psychologist Carl Rogers (1951) stressed the value of empathic reflection and nurturing of the patient's self in psychotherapy. Both Mead, and later, Rogers, were at the University of Chicago for extensive time periods before Kohut lived in that city. Lines of intellectual development can be drawn from James definitely to Mead, probably to Rogers, and possibly to Kohut. Unfortunately, Kohut rarely mentioned the sources of his ideas. We are left to speculate how much he knew of American psychology and sociology. However, his focus on empathy and the self parallels Rogers, although Kohut added rich developmental and psychodynamic considerations to which Rogers, an experiential and existential therapist, gave only peripheral importance.

The difference between self and ego

The American "self" is strikingly different in nature and structure from Freud's "ego." Although both self and ego are identified with "I" (perceiver; doer) and "me" (identity), the self is subjective and holistic, an "agent" that takes the world as its own and transforms it, while the Freudian ego is a passively conditioned structure challenged by the forces of instinct, social taboo, and external reality. With the possible exceptions of Winnicott and Guntrip, British psychoanalysis de-emphasized the subjective, holistic self. For continental Europeans, Freud had successfully deconstructed the conscious, unified self-as-agent, rendering it a chimera, a myth, an epiphenomenon. Kohut found a much better cultural and intellectual climate for his emphasis on self in America than he would have in Europe. At the same time, he encountered strong resistances from the psychoanalytic Establishment, heavily influenced by Freudians who had emigrated from Europe, when he first put forth his formulations about the self, but he quickly found many younger colleagues who were entranced by him and his ideas (Strozier, 2001).

Democratic values in social science and psychotherapy

In addition to the emphasis on the self, twentieth-century American psychology was influenced by pragmatist and populist strains of thought that highlighted dialogue and social equality in human relationships. Kohut's interpretive approach based upon empathic understanding reduced the social distance between the patient and analyst, with the latter "walking in the shoes" of the patient when formulating interpretations. Relational psychoanalysis is essentially dialogical, the patient and analyst seeking mutual understanding. One of the forerunners of the relational approach, Harry Stack Sullivan's (1953) interpersonal psychiatry, emphasized dialogue and considered the analyst to be a "participant observer." The intersubjective perspective placed the analyst on the same plane with the patient with regard to their mutual subjectivity. The analyst uses "empathic inquiry" rather than detached observation. It is worth noting that empathic inquiry was a process used in American social work and anthropology (cf. M. Mead, 1930) well before Stolorow, Atwood, and Brandschaft's (1994) formulation. America provided fertile ground for a transition to self psychological, relational, and intersubjective perspectives.

The American connection is important here, because hermeneutics highlights the social and cultural contexts of interpretation and understanding. These three American-based perspectives insist that we relate and interpret to our patients differently from the European style of authority. Their language, attitude, and clinical approach have a different flavor from the European tradition. It will take time for British and Continental analysts to catch up, if they are so inclined.

Each of the three perspectives—self psychological, intersubjective, and relational—has evolved its own interpretive premises. However, up to now, only intersubjectivity has brought philosophical hermeneutics into the fold. It is to the credit of the intersubjectivists that they have steadfastly examined their philosophical underpinnings. One of their major proponents, Donna Orange, has written an excellent book about how hermeneutics and philosophy can enrich clinical understanding (Orange, 2010.) Intersubjectivists are well aware that some of their ideas were rooted in Husserl's phenomenology (Atwood & Stolorow, 1993). More recently, Stolorow (2011) has expressed an interest in Heidegger. Indeed, Stolorow, Atwood, and Orange (2002) have sought to integrate philosophical and clinical dimensions of psychoanalysis.

My purpose is to consider some key philosophical and hermeneutical issues and controversies which the three schools of thought bring to light. First, I will consider the problematic nature of empathy, subjectivity, and the self, a triumvirate of related concepts which both self psychologists and intersubjectivists have regarded as foundations of psychoanalytic understanding. I will contrast them with the European deconstruction of the self and subjectivity, guided by the "hermeneutics of suspicion." Then, I will look at an entirely different issue, namely, what happens in relational psychoanalysis when it makes a paradigm shift from individual psychology to one in which interactions are the primary phenomena, and individual "minds" emerge in the relational process.

Empathy, subjectivity, and the self vs. the "hermenutics of suspicion"

Stolorow recognized similarities between the intersubjective perspective and Kohut's self psychology, and the two corresponded and met with one another (Stolorow, 2010). Self psychology and intersubjectivity have two features in common: 1) a positive valuation of subjective experience—phenomenology—and as a corollary, 2) less emphasis on drive theory and metapsychology as interpretive tools. Such predispositions brought the two schools of thought into dialogue, although considerable differences still exist between them.

Subjectivity and the self became important to Kohut when, in his clinical work, he found that some patients suffered from deficits in the self and hence needed therapeutically to have their fragile selves mirrored and validated in the transference rather than treated as a regressive defense. For him, the self has its own set of primary needs independent of the drives, and he found that many patients suffered from functional deficits due to early parental failures to nurture the narcissistic (self) sector of the personality (Kohut, 1971, 1977).

Subjectivity became central to the intersubjective perspective in a different way, when Stolorow and others held that seemingly objective scientific theories are largely personal and autobiographical in origin

(Stolorow & Atwood, 1979)—hence the analyst operates subjectively (influenced by his own personality and history), and his relation to the patient is therefore (inter) subjective. Experiencing subjects "know" one another primarily through empathy, intuition, and by comparing the other to their own inner worlds and history. In this respect, theory is but a limited component of mutual understanding. The distinction made by Dilthey, between explanations of causes in nature versus human understanding through immersion in each other's experience and context, is important here. Intersubjectivists echo Dilthey's view that understanding results from lived experience.

The challenge of the "hermeneutics of suspicion"

Self psychology and intersubjectivity, each in its own way, rescued subjectivity and the self from what Ricoeur (1970) famously called the hermeneutics of suspicion inculcated by Freud and other modern thinkers. American pragmatic and democratic traditions trust mutual understanding, while modern European philosophical thought is a product and manifestation of radical disillusionment. From the latter standpoint, subjective awareness, in its naïve perception of self and world, denies the harsh realities of existence and cannot be trusted. For Freud, subjectivity was a defense and a self-protective illusion, a blip on the vast landscape of the unconscious. The Freudian analyst is therefore "suspicious" of the patient's sense of self, and listens for inconsistencies in self-reports, believing that accumulated clinical knowledge is more reliable than the patient's subjectivity, typically regarded as transference.

The hermeneutics of suspicion casts similar doubt on the value of empathy in understanding another person. Empathy may reveal similarities between individuals, but it may mask what is different. One could say that "If I put myself in your shoes, it will still be my feet that are wearing the shoes." Herder emphasized the "radical difference" that makes understanding a serious challenge. In terms of Schleiermacher's hermeneutic circle, the whole of what we know about another person may need to be revised based on a single new detail. A rigorous study of another's autobiographical narrative requires the sustained use of disciplined stages of "feeling one's way into" put forth by Herder. The European sensibility is largely skeptical of empathy as more than a rough beginning to real comprehension of the other.

Therefore, to withstand the hermeneutics of suspicion, self psychologists and intersubjectivists must justify their use of subjective experience and empathy and take into account misperception and the fallibility of intuitive understanding. Both Kohut and Stolorow were well aware of this problem. Kohut realized that the narcissist's grandiosity and idealization were illusory features of the self that ultimately needed to be modified through "transmuting internalizations," structural changes in the patient that lead to a more realistic perception of self (Kohut, 1977, p. 4). But beyond these cautionary notes, he might well have regarded "suspicion" itself as a symptom of the prevalence of narcissistic injury and rage in our times characterized by the disintegration of traditional beliefs and values. For Kohut, repair and coherence of the self is thwarted when the patient's subjectivity and sense of self are doubted by the analyst's mistrust of the patient's motives and perceptions. He held that mirroring, an empathic form of relatedness, promotes self cohesion and maturation.

Intersubectivists addressed certain concerns about the limitations of empathy by carefully framing their process of "sustained empathic inquiry." Here, they followed Husserl, Herder, Schleiermacher, and Dilthey, all of whom were profoundly aware of the difficulties inherent in assessing the life experience of another person. The intersubjectivists thus advocated a measured consideration of a patient's experience until a consistent picture of the structure of the latter's inner world, for example, his operating assumptions and beliefs, emerged from the intersubjective field. Empathic inquiry could be thought of on a par with Herder's "feeling one's way into," an ongoing "comparing of notes" between analyst and patient for the purpose of revealing and transforming the latter's enduring maladaptive patterns of experiencing and relating.

Nevertheless, empathy for another's self will always arouse suspicion in some. It must be balanced with questioning and doubt. Grotstein (1986) proposed a dual track of neurobehavioral processing which suggests that therapists "listen" with both cerebral hemispheres, one of which "hears" in a logical manner, while the other "hears" images and non-verbal expressions. It is likely that "suspicion" emerges from the former, and empathy from the latter modes of experience. Both may be necessary for optimal understanding of the patient.

Forms and variants of empathy

The dual nature of empathy

To repeat, empathy is the main feature of the listening process for self psychologists and intersubjectivists. For them, empathy is the only way to know another mind, self, or person. However, much of the difficulty comparing psychoanalytic and other psychotherapeutic schools of thought stems from the varied meanings and implications given to the word empathy. The word "empathy" itself carries a dual connotation. Em-pathy derives from the prefix "em" which means to "go into or on" or to "surround or cover with" and the suffix "pathos," meaning "the capacity to evoke pity or compassion." The empathic one goes into or compares his own experience with another's suffering and has compassion for him. The two components of empathy are thus 1) enveloping, immersed understanding and 2) compassion (fellow-feeling) for suffering. But when the term empathy is used in self psychology and intersubjectivity, it refers to understanding as such, not the analyst's concern for the patient. For them, empathy is a way of mirroring and understanding. An attitude of compassion for the patient's suffering is implied but not stated.

By contrast, in other therapeutic approaches, such as Carl Rogers's (1951) client-centered therapy, additional qualities are attached to empathy, such as acceptance, responsiveness, and fellow-feeling. And when self psychologists themselves use the term empathy, they imply these qualities, without overtly acknowledging them. This lacuna leads to hermeneutical confusion. As self psychologists Livingston and Livingston (2006) pointed out, empathy requires a "focus" on a particular emotional feature of the patient. The focus is partly influenced by the degree of fellow-feeling and compassion the therapist bears towards the patient. Knowledge and compassion are related but differently nuanced aspects of empathy.

An additional distinction is between empathy as a resonance of emotion, as when we mirror another's humor or sadness, and empathy as a cognitive questioning, as when a mother tries to reason out why her child is upset (she is often *not* resonating, in those cases), or when an analyst tries to grasp something of the patient's character structure. (Indeed, processes of empathic inference are even utilized by military intelligence to try to decipher how enemies or dictators might react in certain circumstances—there is very little compassion involved; it is a cognitive construction, and its purpose is not to heal but to control or even kill.)

Empathy may further connote joining in an enactment with the other person, as when the therapist enjoys a patient's joke or grieves with one who has experienced a loss. Patients often subjectively feel most "understood" by such joining, even if little cognitive insight results.

Overall, intersubjectivity and self psychology have contributed to a shift in psychoanalytic interpretation from a position where the "neutral" analyst constructs a working model of the patient's mind for the explicit purpose of insight; and to empathic attunement, including a significant degree of affective resonance and joining, so that the analytic relationship includes a degree of both care and playfulness. Understanding alone, without a degree of resonance and joining, is probably ineffective in making up for the deficits and empathic failures inherent in narcissistic disorders. Mirroring, whether by mother or analyst, provides a necessary dose of engagement and dialogue.

> For example, a patient, Phil, an actor by profession, professed that he could charismatically work up an audience to a trance-like state with his magical control over how they reacted to his performance. He boasted that when he performed his act, he brilliantly manipulated the emotions of his audience. He loved to have his grandiosity mirrored by them, and also by his girlfriend, whom he glowingly depicted as attractive, suave, and seductive. Yet Phil was haunted by feelings of failure, frequently complained that he was "falling apart," and abused drugs and alcohol, the latter a symptom of a narcissistic behavior disorder as defined by Kohut (1977, p. 193).
>
> Early in treatment, the therapist spontaneously appreciated and enjoyed Phil's grandiosity. The hermeneutics of suspicion would say that he was manipulated by Phil's smooth façade, but the therapist's benign attitude appeared to move the treatment forward. He basked in Phil's proud posturing, agreed that, judging from a photograph, his girlfriend was stunning, and was pleasantly flattered that Phil was sure he had chosen the best therapist in the city. In effect, the therapist became Phil's mirroring and idealizing "selfobject" (Kohut, 1977), someone who is joined with the patient's need for validation and nurturance and whom the patient experiences as part of or an extension of his self. (Kohut used the hyphenated "self-object" in 1977, and later dropped the hyphen, a minor

detail that actually betokened a major change in his hermeneutics, from one in which the object is "outside" the self to one in which the object is an integral part of the self, from metaphysics to phenomenology.)

The therapist found that only after many months in which he joined with Phil in this way (becoming an un-hyphenated selfobject) could the latter begin to tolerate interpretations of the underlying hurt and vulnerability of which the therapist was aware on another level from the very start. Until Phil had developed a substantial degree of self cohesion, the therapist's differentiating interpretations only produced slights that led him to become deflated and withdrawn, and he would often miss or come late to the next session. Phil seemed to need a liberal infusion of unconditional warmth, acceptance, and mirroring before he was ready to receive understanding of his vulnerability. Both the mirroring/idealizing and the empathic reflection of vulnerability, however, were differing manifestations of compassion towards Phil, expressed in the first case by joining and in the second by verbal communication.

Existential empathy

Whenever empathy and interpretation involve compassion and care in the form of responsiveness, mirroring, holding, containing, and other functions beyond understanding as such, then *the act of interpretation itself becomes a living, dynamic interpersonal, dialogical process.* Interpretation becomes not only a matter of "saying," but also of being and doing. The therapist in the above example was highly bonded with the patient, and the understanding he offered the patient became part of a broader range of mutual self-expression that included non-verbal elements. When we view empathy as a living process of engagement, we are moving from the phenomenological-descriptive level to the existential level. This shift mirrors the course Heidegger took with his critique of Husserl's phenomenology. Heidegger argued against Husserl that pure "transcendental" description is impossible. Experience, expression, and understanding occur within a historical context of being-in-the-world. For Heidegger, human existence is not detached but engaged in its concern for its being.

Self psychology and the intersubjective perspective are now manifesting a similar existential shift which may in fact be occurring across the whole world of psychoanalysis. Empathy and interpretation have moved from a process of description and inference to a mutual dialogical engagement with the patient. One strong influence on this movement came when engagement, in the form of attunement, became the cornerstone of Daniel Stern's thinking about the mother–infant dyad in his efforts to interpret video recordings of caregiving relations in the first days, months, and years of the child's life.

Daniel Stern's attunement and the development of the self

The transition within American psychoanalysis that brought empathy into conjunction with existential relatedness was reinforced by psychoanalyst and mother–infant researcher Daniel Stern, whose concept of maternal "attunement" is closely related to empathy but includes the high degree of responsiveness that a mother brings to her baby, and which he observed and documented in his pioneering research. (As I write this, I have just learned of Dr Stern's passing. I did not know him personally, but I feel a shock, as if I have lost a loved one. I think the reason my emotion is so strong is because of Stern's enormous presence in the field as well as the care he manifested in both the subject and method of his research. His death also evoked in me incomplete mourning for two close friends and mentors whose thinking echoed Stern's: Drs John Sonne at Thomas Jefferson University and Bertram Cohen at Rutgers.)

Stern reinforced the ideas of self psychologists, intersubjectivists, and relationalists with the crucial data of direct observation of mother–infant interactions. Through examination of videotapes, Stern and others (for example, Brazelton, 1980) found that the infant initiated many of the interactions with mother, shattering the long-held belief that the infant was a passive recipient of maternal care. This finding had a bearing on Aron's (1996) contention that the therapeutic interaction is also a mutual, reciprocal process rather than a patient being "worked on" by a doctor. Stern himself later developed an interpersonal approach to psychotherapy emphasizing affectively attuned "moments" that are analogous to the resonance between mother and infant during times that they are most engaged with each other (2007, pp. 135–208).

The "attunement envelope" of meaning and understanding

Stern's work can be said to depict the "envelope" of mutuality that surrounds the efforts of mother and child, patient and therapist, to understand one another empathically and interpretively. Interpretation does not take place in a vacuum. The unspoken "envelope of attunement" (my term) provides the existential ground for the spoken word. Attunement and attachment inform, facilitate, and influence meaning and understanding.

The attunement envelope that provides the ground and context for understanding, explanation, and interpretation is important for both psychoanalysis and hermeneutics. For every idea, understanding, insight that is developed and communicated, there are multiple envelopes of implicit unstated activity, experience, and expression that surround it, make it possible, and influence its use. The mother's attunement to the infant establishes the post-natal envelope (a psychological extension of the womb?) within which human interaction and mutual understanding unfold. Stern, like Winnicott, suggested that this maternal envelope (Winnicott called it a holding environment) expands over days, weeks, months, and years to include the family unit, language, and culture.

Attunement as reparation

Coincidentally, with regard to the mother's relationship to the infant, the resemblance between the words "attunement" and "atonement" is worth noting. Both terms imply music. "At-tune-ment" alerts us to the melody, rhythm, and harmony of human interaction. "A-tone-ment" suggests that, like religious atonement with God, the mother–infant relationship strives for reparation and restitution of harmony between mother, infant, and world. Thus, mother attunes to discomforts and disruptions in the infant's experience, restoring equilibrium, calmness, pleasure, and other positive affect states. This is the earliest form of affect regulation (Siegel, 2012), suggesting that, through their relationship, mother and infant complete one another, make each other whole, and repair the rifts in their respective worlds.

The same is true of the therapeutic relationship. Berke and Schneider (2008, pp. 217–240) have suggested that reparation, as understood both by Kabbalah and in a different way by Melanie Klein, constitutes the curative factor and unconscious motivation of psychoanalytic psychotherapy. In this respect, there is a connection between attunement and Buber's "I-Thou" relatedness. Understanding is reparative, restoring an intimate, committed level of connectedness. Stern's attunement is more than empathic inquiry; it is an existential act of care.

In psychotherapy sessions, listening and understanding emerge within the attunement envelope of the therapeutic alliance. The therapist responds empathically to the patient's suffering, providing understandings that mitigate the patient's distress and registering the therapist's presence and involvement. Gradually, as in the example of Phil, above, increasing depth and difference (frustration, disagreement, challenge to defenses) in the interpretive process reflects and promotes emotional growth. The alert therapist listens not only to the content of the patient's discourse, but also to its "music," aware of the attunement envelope in which the interpretation of the present moment serves as punctuation. Psychoanalytic therapy develops like the movements of a symphony, from a simple set of themes or motifs to a complex array of conflict, turbulence, and emotional intensity, with a series of variations, followed by resolution. The therapist is aware of the music and movement that is beyond words.

> For example, a patient, Maxine, and her therapist were arriving at a historical understanding of her disrupted relationship with an intrusive and harshly critical mother. (Stern would say that the mother–infant relationship had been "derailed" repeatedly by her mother's misattunement to Maxine's need for mirroring and self-validation. Mother repeatedly responded to Maxine as if her daughter required frequent warnings about a dangerous world, which could be further understood a la Klein as the mother's projective identification of a bad internal object into her child.) Maxine was pleased with the therapist and his insights, and in turn, the therapist experienced mutual rapport with Maxine and felt that she was making progress in treatment. They were well-attuned, and Maxine came to sessions bright and happy.
>
> As the treatment progressed, however, there occurred a series of sessions in which Maxine's mood changed. She became dismayed and hopeless, with none of her previous pleasurable responses to the therapist. At the same time, the therapist found himself mildly agitated, squirming in his seat and feeling annoyed that Maxine was not providing more historical and illustrative material. There was a distinct possibility that the therapeutic relationship could become derailed, just as had Maxine's relationship with her mother.

The therapist thought about Maxine's resistance and transference, that she was avoiding insight through non-communication, repeating with him her relationship with her mother. However, concerned about the potential for derailment, he decided to refrain from commenting and instead chose to listen silently, attuning to his own and Maxine's moods. He remained highly alert and attentive, but silent, seeking to provide a holding environment for her distress.

Maxine continued to be depressed. But in the holding atmosphere of the analyst's quiet presence (what Bion (1962b) called "reverie," a heightened state of the mother's or analyst's awareness), she began for the first time to openly and emotionally express her long-suppressed sadness and sorrow. The therapist empathically reflected to the patient the grief she must be feeling. This restored Maxine's contact with him, and he in turn felt more engaged with her. The attunement envelope was restored and affectively enriched, and Maxine was now able to fully experience and work through complex and conflicted aspects of her relationship with the therapist, her mother, and other family members.

The technical point here is that attunement as relational engagement and active listening must always provide the ground for verbal interpretation, which is enfolded within attunement and other relational and contextual factors that constitute the unspoken existential ground for meaning and understanding. Such enveloping features are discussed by Stern in terms of what he frequently refers to as the "dance" between mother and infant (2007, pp. 42, 66, 142). In psychoanalysis of adults, we listen for the movement of the patient-as-dancer's words (words can dance) and gestures until the tribal/familial ghosts of the past dance in the consulting room. We move from empathy and attunement to an awareness of the existential conditions, "choreography," and contextual envelopes of the past and present, further attuning our interpretations to those conditions and contexts. This is much like the way in which mother and infant develop a common emotional language and culture. They learn to understand one another by virtue of a recurrent process of engagement, attunement, and we would add, mistakes that are transformed into new dance steps. And at the same time, the lifeworld, as context, history, and culture impinges upon them and conditions the interaction.

Stern's "sense of self"

Stern utilized the phrase "sense of self" to describe how the infant internalized the relational experiences he observed during the first days, months, and years of life. (As in Kohut's "selfobject," Stern's "sense of self" emphasizes phenomenology over structure.) He hypothesized four stages of the sense of self: "emergent self" (birth to two months of age); core self (two months); subjective self (seven months); and verbal self (fifteen months; the ages of course are all approximate). He showed how, over time, the child's self becomes more coherent, conscious, symbolized, and aware of others' selfhood (1985, p. 11).

This is not the place to explore these stages and their influence on subsequent personality development in detail. I only want to emphasize that Stern's choice of the "sense of self" as his central concept of internalization of interactions was an ideological and uniquely American hermeneutical choice, one that is consistent with Kohut's self psychology and Stolorow's and cohorts' emphasis on intersubjectivity. Stern never aligned himself with either school of thought. He could well have utilized ego psychology or object relations theory as his conceptual model. However, he chose the vocabulary of the self much as it was used by William James and others in American psychology. He thus distanced himself from Freudian theory in many respects, writing only peripherally about drives, inhibitions, and defense mechanisms as such. He was trying to articulate the development of the child's active co-participation from an interpersonal perspective.

Stern's and others' concept of self bears a direct relationship to hermeneutics because the self is seen as an active, co-participatory vehicle for organizing experience into coherent meanings and narratives. However, as previously mentioned, the hermeneutics of suspicion has challenged the self as an element of understanding human existence in meaningful ways. I wish now to explore the place of the self in hermeneutics and the interpretive process.

The fate of the self in hermeneutics and psychoanalysis

As mentioned, Freud was suspicious about the self in its relation to the unconscious and the forces of nature and society. For him, the self rarely advances beyond the mundane status of an image, an internalized object representation, a component of the ego. (Like Nietzsche, however, Freud did allow for heroic exceptions of genuine assertive selfhood, most notably himself!) Image and representation comprise most of what Freud understood as "self." He did not give much consideration to the apprehending, experiencing, subjective self, the assertive "I" as distinct from the objective "me." The self as subject is closely related to consciousness and will, which it requires in order to "go on being." Symptoms and other unconscious phenomena exhibit an uncanny sense of dissociation. They are not felt to be initiated or decided by the subjective self and appear to occur independently of the will. They have no "author." (For Freud, the "author" became a "force," the unconscious.) Psychoanalysis as a deterministic causal science does not want to deal with consciousness and will.

By contrast with Freud and much of object relations theory, Kohut and Stern, in somewhat different ways, introduced the subjective, conscious, will-ing self into psychoanalytic discourse. For Kohut, the self is "supraordinate" to the ego. It is a cohesive agent with a unique "trajectory." For Stern (1985), the self is, to begin with, a set of "representations that have been generalized" (RIGs), a collection of memories of interpersonal experiences that become templates for new situations. RIGs are consistent with Freud's notion of "self-representations." However, Stern posited the subsequent development of intersubjectivity where there is a conscious "I" that is aware of the "I" in others. And even the neonate must have some subjectivity that allows him to initiate interactions and not just respond passively to external interventions and stimuli. Stern eventually came up with the idea of a "proto-narrative envelope" (2002, pp. 6–7) to describe the implicit "story" in the earliest interactions. "Story" implies at least a rudimentary degree of subjectivity. At the very least, the newborn is a "sentient being" in the Buddhist sense. He feels and suffers and acts. Even without a concept of "I," the newborn functions with an existential "I-ness," a primal concern for being. It already has that basic level of meaningfulness. The newborn goes on being without a linguistic lifeworld to enfold it (see Chapter Ten). By her holding, attunement, and playful engagement with the baby, the mother brings that lifeworld to the infant through a language of utterances that is at first private between them, and gradually incorporates the public language of the culture.

By introducing the conscious, will-ing self into psychoanalysis as the dynamic foundation of human growth and development, both Kohut and Stern entered the arena of modern hermeneutical debate and controversy. This shift has important ramifications for psychoanalysis. Let me try to say why this is so.

The lack of selfhood in Descartes's cogito

The subjective self became problematic in Western thought in part by way of Descartes's cogito: "I think; therefore I am." For Descartes, the subjective "I" is a given. It exists beyond doubt, but it has no shape, form, or substance. For Descartes, the "I," the cogito, is the unembodied perceiver and knower, and as such has no descriptive features of its own. Descartes effectively erased the subjective "I" (self) from scientific scrutiny. "I" is axiomatic, the basis of all knowledge but not a part of it. The psychological self-as-agent, by contrast, has many different qualities, form, and substance, and it interacts with the world. It is "self-conscious," engaged with itself, embodied, a living, organic reality.

The self as thinker, form, agent, and persona

Romantic hermeneutics (fostered by Herder and Dilthey, in particular) veered away from Cartesian metaphysics and allowed the subjective self to become part of human understanding. (So too did William James in America.) The concrete form that the self takes is embedded in language, myth, and culture. We can consider how the self appears in diverse languages, narratives, and individual lives. We can examine how it shows up in consciousness, for example, how people locate their "I" selves physically at the level of the eyes and ears (except when they have "out of body" experiences, which is a phenomenon some neuroscientists use to study self and ego (Metzinger, 2009)). We can study the self anthropologically in terms of its variations in different cultures. We can study individual lives in depth to see how the self develops over time. And of course, we can study the "I" self as it appears in the free associations of patients in analysis, and specifically how it is affected by different forms of psychopathology and symptoms.

However, the problematic status of self in philosophical hermeneutics suggests that we proceed with a critical eye. After the Romantic era, and especially with Heidegger, self and consciousness, which are conceptual Siamese twins, connected but distinct, were for the most part shunned by Continental philosophical discourse. Such an exile of self signaled a shift in human understanding that impacts on all aspects of life, ranging from Durkheim's *Anomie*, the loss of individuality in bureaucracies and technological societies, to behavioristic psychology and pharmacological treatment of psychiatric disorders, to computers, crowd mentalities, and mindless conformity. Gergen (1991) held that today, in an information-driven world, the coherent inner self is replaced by a postmodern pastiche of images and options. In hermeneutics, the demise of the self-as-agent has a particular significance which I will now, barely touching the tip of the iceberg, briefly attempt to explain as it pertains to psychoanalytic interpretation.

The self as disguise and fall from grace

Heidegger hastened the critique of the self with his consideration that being-in-the-world was "at hand" and unstated, as distinct from specific "beings" which are objectified. The self, in this respect, is a disguise, a "fall from grace," an inauthentic avoidance of an encounter with temporality and mortality. Being and self are not the same. Being is not "thought about" by a self—rather, it is defined by its context and its historical moment. This emphasis on context regards the self as a construct or mask rather than an agency and a substance. The centrality of meaning as context and ground as opposed to meaning as conceived by self pervades Continental philosophy and postmodern thought. Such a notion of meaning as context reappears after Heidegger in Gadamer's notion of dialogue as a meeting of "horizons" rather than of persons, in Derrida's emphasis on writing and "text" rather than the spoken word, and in Levinas's moral encounter of "faces," to cite but a few among many instances of the vanishing of self in Continental thought.

Similarly, positivist and pragmatist philosophers have questioned the significance of self as a structure. Wittgenstein (1953) viewed self as an element in a language game. Rorty, the American pragmatist, took a "European" turn in regarding the self as a social convention that is made for a specific purpose and discourse (1979). These thinkers deconstruct the self as a stable entity and structure within the person. Kohut's restoration of the self and Stern's "sense of self" do not mesh well with such intellectual skepticism.

Self vs. non-self in psychoanalysis

The question of whether to reinstate or exile the self is crucial to contemporary psychoanalytic theory, practice, and care. Grotstein (2000), for example, recognized that the patient-in-the-room is not necessarily the same as the dreamer. When we analyze a dream, should we be addressing the patient's conscious, present self or the dreamer, who is in closer contact with the unconscious. Should we think of interpretation as a function of selves in an interpersonal relationship? Or is interpretation a way of getting outside of and beyond "self" to another realm of experience that is non-conscious, non-sensory, and contextual? There are merits to both sides of this argument.

> For example, a patient, Rob, presented a dream in which he went into the woods and encountered a deer. They stared at each other for a moment. Rob said he awoke from the dream feeling anxiety and awe about the encounter. He was at the time going through a difficult transition with a lover. If we regard the patient's self as the "author" of the dream, we can see that it expresses some anxiety about his real-life love relationship. We are thus interested in how the dream fits into his self-narrative as it has evolved in treatment. This is the shared perspective of both self psychology and the inter-subjective perspective. However, we could also consider the dream as an emanation from outside the self, from the primal unconscious. Our interest would then shift to the phenomenology of the dream: the woods, the mutual stare, the presence of a deer. The dream in this respect represents a meeting of the human and non-human. The simultaneous presence and absence of the object world and the mutual gaze between man and animal betoken the uncanny. The patient and analyst might then value the dream as an experience of *non*-self. They might find more experiences of the patient in which the boundaries of the self dissolve, allowing the patient indirectly to restructure his love relationships to include less rigidified, more self-transcendent and numinous experience.

Autonomy vs. self-transcendence

We know that analysts use both approaches—self and "beyond self"—in their work. Kohut, Stolorow, and Roy Schafer (1994) are among those interested in self-narratives. Jung, Bion, and to some extent Grotstein, Epstein, and Bollas are seekers of the unauthored text of the uncon-scious, the archetypes (Jung), "O" or things-in-themselves (Bion), the "infinite geometer" (Grotstein), the "thoughts without a thinker" (Epstein), the "unthought known" (Bollas). Both self and non-self approaches are valued by patients, and the attuned analyst can offer relevant interpretations that are meaningful from either vantage point. But one approach delves into the self, while the other omits (in Husserl's terms, "brackets") self in order to go beyond the persona—the mask—to access the unconscious core. Patients grow and learn under both conditions of interpretation, so long as the analyst is holding and attuning to them.

The ultimate purpose of psychoanalysis as a transformational healing process revolves around this same self/non-self dichotomy. Should the analyst nurture the autonomy, cohesion, assertiveness, and agency of the patient's selfhood? Or should he foster a sense of immersion and surrender to a larger awareness, such as a communal purpose and/or being fully absorbed by the process of living? Is optimal mental health a matter of maturation of an introspective individuated self, or is it self-forgetting, living in the moment?

This dichotomy was highlighted for this author during intensive work with substance dependent persons and their families. Patients with addictive disorders have character structures that are over-individuated, narcissistic, isolated, and focused on self to the neglect of moral imperatives and awareness of inner and outer worlds beyond the self, whether spiritual or communal. (The Alcoholics Anonymous program appears to offer them a return to spiritual and moral principles and to communal living.) By contrast, the non-addicted family members appear as self-sacrificial martyrs, having lost much of their individuality and sense of self, becoming so absorbed in the addict's crises that they lack agency, assertiveness, and individuation. Thus, in psychotherapy with substance dependent patients, it proved imperative to help them access a non-self or larger-than-self fabric for their lives. With family members, an emphasis on building stronger "true self" structures with individual autonomy seemed essential.

These are particular populations, and even within each category, there is complexity and variability. It is likely that, for the wider range of psychiatric patients, a blend and variation of the two interpretive styles I have discussed is necessary for optimal outcomes. Autonomy and self-transcendence are paradoxical but not mutually exclusive possibilities. Achieving the right proportion of self and non-self for each patient is an important and hitherto neglected aspect of psychoanalytic interpretation and care.

Thus far, I have focused upon self psychology and the intersubjective perspective, approaches that are based upon phenomenology and, more recently, existential concerns. As we have seen, they are "American originals" that highlight empathy and the self in contrast with the European deconstruction of the self and the hermeneutics of suspicion.

Similar issues of self and non-self arise within the third of the American originals, relational psychoanalysis. I have reserved this point of view for last, because it brings into sharper focus the still broader question of the locus and nature of mind and the mental life. Paradoxically, psychoanalysis, the most in-depth study of the "mind," has begun to deconstruct "mind." Relational psychoanalysis has taken part in that deconstruction. In it, mind moves from the status of a functional and structural entity, as Freud conceived it, to a metaphor for aspects of a social process.

Relational psychoanalysis and the concept of mind

Relational psychoanalysis overlaps with a variety of other formulations, including those of self psychology, intersubjectivity, Sullivan's interpersonal psychiatry, and object relations theory. Stephen Mitchell, its founder, defined relational principles in his pioneering reflections on the need for a radical change in psychoanalytic theory (1988). For him, relational psychoanalysis incorporated a variety of perspectives that met the following two criteria, previously separated by an intrapsychic and metaphysical gap: 1) an emphasis on relationships in human development, and 2) full recognition of primitive unconscious and early developmental determinants. The latter criterion was very important because the so-called neo-Freudians such as Sullivan and Fromm emphasized social processes more than infantile development, and Mitchell was eager to retain the dynamic and developmental features of the Freudian and object relations corpus.

In his early efforts to develop a relational paradigm, Mitchell (Greenberg & Mitchell, 1983; Mitchell, 1988) explored the multi-person features inherent in the work of diverse psychoanalysts and schools of thought. Even today, most analysts who identify themselves as "relational" are happy to borrow concepts from other perspectives that have a similar interactional focus. Mitchell was a taxonomist of psychoanalytic theories, respecting each of them independently while seeking integration. Thus, his formulation of a relational paradigm also highlighted the theories he sought to bring together under a common flag. Relational psychoanalysis is thus eclectic in its use of theory. Is it fair then to ask, what have Mitchell and his cohorts added to the mix? What is distinct and unifying about "relational theory" as such?

A drawing by M. C. Escher adorns the cover of Mitchell's (1988) pioneering book. The intriguing cover reproduction shows two hands paradoxically sketching one another (!) on a sheet of paper. Like this drawing, Mitchell configured relational psychoanalysis as a mutual "writing" of "I" and "we," a vision of the individual personality inextricably intertwined with interpersonal and social systems. Mitchell's synthesis of individual and interpersonal dynamics is central to his relational understanding. Importantly for the current context, this integration resulted in a shift in the psychoanalytic concept of "mind" itself.

The concept of mind used by Freud was prevalent in Western culture: a coherent structure of perception, cognition, and memory housed in an individual person. It is also the way we Westerners think of mind in everyday life, as located in someone's head. In that respect, the mind (Descartes's "thinking thing") is an "organ" that senses, feels, thinks, and initiates action. It is housed in the brain. By this reckoning, the mind is contained in the person's body. It has contact with reality through perception, intuition, and thought. In this view, mind has substance and location. It is part of an individual person. Psychologists study individual minds and generalize from them. In this understanding, the "collective mind" or "group mind" is only a shorthand way of referring to individual minds taken together or in relation to one another. This viewpoint was clearly expressed in Freud's (1921c) *Group Psychology and the Analysis of the Ego*, where he explicitly accounted for group behavior as a function of individual psychology.

Mitchell's relational psychoanalysis, however, unequivocally takes the mind out of the body and houses it in the fabric of social interaction. It begins with the premise that the primary phenomena of human development, emotion, and cognition are social and interpersonal.

Mind as a social construct

In brief, the argument for mind as social is as follows. Except for physical embodiment and anatomy, no human being exists apart from interactions with others. By the same token, *it is impossible to conceive of a "mind" without a social context*. We could in principle think of an instinct or drive as a wired-in component of an organism, but cognition and language emerge in a relational matrix and social context. Thought and language have innate biological components, but they develop and acquire significance through social interactions. Thus, there is no "mind" independent of relationships. According to Mitchell (1988, p. 3), "Mind is composed of relational configurations," intending this relational reformulation to be a major divergence from Freud's metapsychology, in which all the layers and structures of mind are intrapsychic, housed in the individual.

The idea of mind as social has been articulated in modern philosophy and social science. Marx's "dialectal materialism" held, for example, that "mind" is a capitalist social construct, a convenient illusion that is utilized to attribute ownership to thoughts. Mind becomes material property and a means of exchange. Dilthey considered the fundamental basis of personhood to be intersubjective and relational. Heidegger viewed *Dasein* independently of the subject. That we so often mistakenly attribute our own thoughts to others or vice-versa shows how difficult it is to assign a thought to a location in an individual person or ego. "Ideas" exist in a collective space and are gradually, in a process of social interaction, assigned to individuals. For Derrida, for example, minds are disseminated and "archived" in texts, which are present everywhere. Authorship is assigned in order to privilege and protect particular ideas. As in all these perspectives, *relational psychoanalysis wants to understand mind and the unconscious as social constructs.*

Psychoanalytic developmental psychology has increasingly advanced the view of mind as social. Winnicott held that the mother–infant pair is the primary unit. Bion (1962b) referred to mother and infant as a "thinking couple," well before the infant as an individual has the capacity to think. Fonagy et al. (Fonagy, Gergely, Jurist, & Target, 2002) have considered "mentalization"—the developmental process in which the child comes to understand minds and subjectivities—as an interactive field that fosters individual awareness. For them, *the mind does not pre-exist as a metaphysical entity; rather it arises as a concept of understanding among people and in community.* Mind in this view is an interpersonal construct, an acquired metaphor for a place where thinking resides. It is a manifestation of Vico's *verum ipsum factum* principle, "The criterion and rule of the true is to have *made* it" (italics added.) We literally "make up our minds."

"Unconscious" as a location or structure vs. *"unconsciousness"*
as a quality of existence

If mind is not a coherent individual structure, neither a machine nor a *deus ex machina*, not localized in an individual, then neither is the unconscious, which is a part of the mind. In this way, the relational paradigm of psychoanalysis implies a radical new paradigm of the unconscious, a reconstruction that is already implied in Continental hermeneutics. There, *unconscious* does not refer to a structure or a location. Rather, it is a quality or process attributable not only to a person's thoughts and feelings as such but to meanings, texts, and social interactions as well.

For that, we really need a new term, a qualitative descriptor rather than a noun. For lack of a better word, we can use "unconsciousness" as a pervasive quality that might be described as unknowing, negating, or even perhaps anti-thought. Such a quality is depicted, for example, in T. S. Eliot's (1964) play, *The Cocktail Party*, where the characters find themselves in a milieu where nobody knows himself and no one is sincere or authentic. There is an absence of those thoughts, feelings, dispositions, and actions that are necessary for authentic "going on being." The whole milieu is blind to itself, unconscious.

Unconsciousness can reside anywhere. It is like a Derridean text whose traces, differences, and deferments are disseminated throughout society and history. From this perspective, the course of an analytic treatment could be described as the dissemination and deconstructive exposure of an unconscious textuality that pervades the entire process. The previously mentioned Spielrein affair in which Jung and then Freud treated a young woman who later herself became a psychiatrist, affords a good example. In that "text," story, and "affair" (which has the double meaning of a love affair and an unseemly business), all the key figures as well as the psychoanalytic movement itself manifested an unconsciousness of civilized relationships, so that all concerned were at one time or another victim and/or victimizer instead of providing each other with suitable care. Contextually, this dynamic was suffused with a pre-World War I European culture of alienation and aggression. In a way, Spielrein was not the patient; she was a symptom. The "analysis" of Sabrina Spielrein was ultimately not just of herself as a patient, but of all the parties that surrrounded her, including her two analysts, and of the changing times in which they lived.

The relational paradigm as envisioned by Mitchell is grounded in such an understanding of the unconscious as disseminated quality and process rather than location and archive. Like the mind, the unconscious comes into being—"is made"—in human interaction and communication. One could think of this fabrication and its dissemination as a complex interactive systems version of the unconscious. In this vein, the singular impact of the relational paradigm on clinical work has been a diminution of the tendency to attribute the "causes" of the patient's behavior and symptoms exclusively to the patient, his history, his fantasy life, defenses, and psychopathology. Beginning with Hoffman's (1983) groundbreaking article on the patient's veridical perceptions of the analyst's countertransference, relational analysts have tended to regard all transference as mutual interaction or "co-transference" rather than an emanation from the patient.

Classical training utilizing the principle of psychic determinism insisted that the analyst trace all the patient's free associations to the patient's history and unconscious mind. The analyst's countertransference, the contemporary reality of the patient's life, and the sociocultural milieu were regarded largely as obscuring factors that had to be filtered out of the interpretive equation. While this approach had the heuristic value of uncovering elements obscured and distorted by everyday existence and the self-protective needs of the patient, it also had the authoritarian effect of tautologically proving the analyst's theory correct by default, and absolving the analyst of complicity in the patient's illness. Like self psychology and intersubjectivity, relational psychoanalysis reflects the American democratic traditions. Therefore, Mitchell needed a concept of mind consistent with egalitarianism. Mind, like "equal opportunity" is distributed evenly among the participants.

Hazardous mixtures

The self psychological, intersubjective, and relational perspectives that arose on American soil have thus far shown the potential to expand psychoanalytic awareness of the unconscious to include a broad swath of social phenomena. Conversely, there is a danger that they might attenuate their revolutionary impact by promoting a pragmatic mix of social psychology and subjective self-consciousness which lacks the psychoanalytic attunement to the hidden depths. The idea of psychological depth emerged in conjunction with the emphasis on individual character structure in Romantic philosophy. It is difficult and hazardous to separate the two. A careful attention to the interpretive work itself and the underlying hermeneutical and philosophical principles that drive these "American originals" is imperative to maintaining and enhancing a psychoanalytical enterprise that wins new insights for individual patients and for the panoply of human knowledge.

Such issues invariably resurface around any efforts to alter the Freudian legacy. Freud himself was vigilant about any revisions that could diminish the exploration of deep, repressed unconscious dynamics. He viewed his methodology, the structural theory, and the Oedipus complex as guardians against that possibility. Certainly, the perspectives discussed above have some risk of becoming a psychology of subjectivity and/or social psychology rather than an analysis of the repressed unconscious. Of all analysts, Wilfred R. Bion was perhaps the most keenly aware of this problem and devoted considerable thought to it, utilizing philosophical, mystical, and literary perspectives to try to capture the essence of the unconscious. In the next chapter, we explore Bion's ideas as they are related to psychoanalytic interpretation.

CHAPTER TWELVE

Bion's psychoanalytic work: from positivism and Kant to psychospirituality and beyond

Wilfred Bion (1897–1979) was one of the most original minds ever to grace the halls of psychoanalysis. Often, however, that originality meant "disturbing the universe" of his fellow psychoanalysts, leaving some of them confused and alienated. Much of what he said and wrote was in the form of puzzles and conundrums. At times he wrote like a scientist, at times like a philosopher, at times like a storyteller, and at times in a stream of consciousness. Bion was an honored psychiatrist and psychoanalyst but rarely wrote or spoke like either. It was as if he were trying to learn what psychoanalysis really was about and had to strip it of its verbal trappings in order to discover its essential qualities. One of Bion's earliest childhood memories (1982, pp. 9, 13–14) was when he and his sister mistakenly heard the "Our Father" as "arf arfer," which became for them the voice of authority. When you read him, he sometimes reduces you to that child who cannot understand what the learned stranger is saying. But that is precisely where his wisdom—his hermeneutics of the "absence of memory, desire, and understanding"—is to be found. For Bion, understanding does not supply the answers to the questions he is trying to address.

Bion is best known for his book *Experiences in Groups* (1959), a pioneering work on group dynamics that helped initiate the field of group dynamics and is still highly influential. In it, he applied Melanie Klein's theory of projective identification to groups, adding his own concept of group life as governed by unconscious "basic assumptions," climates and shared beliefs such as dependency, pairing, and fight-flight. He soon shifted his interest, however, to psychoanalysis itself, and in a series of papers, essays, and books spanning two decades, he looked at psychoanalysis from every angle and questioned everything, as if, like Descartes, he were seeking the irreducible "I am" of psychoanalysis. And when he thought he found it, he cryptically used the symbol "O," the Other, the cipher, the infinite, the unfathomable.

Like Descartes, Bion (in his case during a period of writing about psychosis and schizophrenia as clinical phenomena), began by pursuing "a theory of thinking" (1962b). He eventually, however, came to the non-Cartesian conclusion that you *can't* think, that thinking was about not being able to think. In the process he developed many ideas that other psychoanalysts have found useful in their work (cf. Symington & Symington, 1996). But ultimately, for him, all his thinking ended up "on the cutting room floor," as it were, and the final version is a free-wheeling three part novella, *A Memoir of the Future* (1975, 1977, 1979), where he declares his indebtedness to Plato and Kant, but, calling himself Captain Bion, takes the reader on a space travel journey through everything from fetal life to split-off alter egos to science fiction fantasies, rendering the postmodern impression that there is no single position from which to think; rather a concatenation of noumena and phenomena that has no center or ordering principle. In effect, Bion migrated from an Enlightenment thinker of fact, logic, and essences to a postmodern view of a fragmented self and world. In the process, he also touched upon themes that others subsequently explored, such as the mother and infant as a thinking couple, the infinite nature of the unconscious, catastrophic transformation, psychoanalysis as mysticism, and others. His work spawned many reflections and expansions, and there are Bion Institutes in Sao Paulo, Brazil and Bangalore, India. He was the type of thinker who makes others think, and in that respect he deserves to be called a philosopher.

It is difficult to "typecast" Bion when discussing matters of interpretation and hermeneutics. He was seeking the ineffable, non-sensuous experience that evades language and thought. In the ancient Buddhist text, the *Prajnaparamita*, the student Subhuit asks Buddha why absolute knowledge is beyond reach and unattainable. The Buddha replies, "And why is perfect wisdom beyond thinking? It is because all its points of reference cannot be thought about but can be apprehended. ... None of these points can sustain ordinary thought because they are not objects or subjects. They can't be imagined or touched or approached in any way by any ordinary mode of consciousness, therefore they are beyond thinking" (Conze, 2003). Bion ultimately insisted that the unconscious was unknowable in itself, but that one could encounter the depths in a transformative way.

Although he borrowed liberally from Melanie Klein, who was his training analyst, Bion's thought process diverged from hers. He did not so much "see into" the psyche like a Kleinian phenomenologist as he could "see through" the glaze of phenomena, ideas, images, objects, and language to the essence of how things happened or failed to happen. His main interest was Kantian, to learn how "things in themselves" that existed outside consciousness could be transformed into coherent images and ideas. The patients who fascinated him most were psychotic individuals who had notable failures and catastrophes in attempting to bring awareness, sense, and order out of what impinged upon them.

Bion might have found the whole of hermeneutics irrelevant. He felt that the important experiences happen in "the absence of memory, desire, and understanding," echoing the swamis of India where he was born. He seemed to mock understanding, as when he asked in a colloquium whether the superego was "north of id," as if to say that the notion of thoughts "located" in specific structures of the mind was ludicrous (J. S. Grotstein, personal communication, 1985). It is rumored that he delivered a lecture to a psychoanalytic society by maintaining total silence—which would certainly have turned the tables on his audience!

In his skepticism, Bion brought into play an issue that also arises in hermeneutics. Hermeneutics holds that meanings are ambiguous and complex. If meanings are so uncertain, Bion might have asked, why bother with them? Meanings can't be proven. The analyst as interpreter will ultimately be forced to say "I don't know" or "It's my view" or "It works for me." Ultimately, hermeneutics deconstructs itself by demonstrating its own circularity and ambiguity. Bion turned away from this impossible dilemma. He was interested in what was irreducibly true. His approach was the opposite of the German romanticism of Herder and Dilthey and their search for human meaning through language and culture. He wanted clarity, even if what was clear was darkness and silence. Unlike Jung, who was immersed in the analysis of myth and culture, Bion's predeliction was more akin to Wittgenstein, who questioned language and culture as avenues to truth and saw them as conventions that we invent and inhabit in order to live. Bion wanted to get outside of common language. There is a schizoid quality in this desire to avoid the intimacies of language as it is embedded in human existence. When sublimated into a preference for elegance, the same denial of ambiguity and subjectivity leads people to pursue mathematics and science.

So at first it would seem irrelevant and immaterial to include Bion's work in a book about meanings and interpretation. But often what clarifies ideas the most are the exceptions. Considering how Bion looked at psychoanalytic "knowing" as the absence of meaning, we may establish the limitations and the farther reaches of hermeneutics as it applies to psychoanalysis and the unconscious. Bion probably would not have put a word down on paper if he did not think people would try to understand what he meant! As Derrida was forced to admit, writing itself implies a type of meaning, even if that meaning can be deconstructed.

Bion took four broad approaches in his attempt to grasp the mind, the unconscious, and events in the consulting room. The first was that of empirical science: operational, positivistic, and mathematical. The second was the metaphysical search for fundamental categories, Kant's noumena that underlie perception and experience. The third was what could be called quasi-mystical and harks back to Enlightenment turncoats Milton and Blake: if you go sufficiently into darkness, emptiness, and silence, something transformational will happen. Towards the end of his life, Bion veered into a fourth course: the postmodern admission that there is no truth, only diverse versions and stories of truth. Indeed, he was contemplating all four frameworks throughout his career (and maybe his life), and although it is tempting to delineate phases in the evolution of his thought, they all fold around one another at any point in time. For example, he often embraces Plato, Kant, and philosophical idealism. Yet, in one of his major works, *Attention and Interpretation* (1970), he develops a logical empirical approach to psychoanalytic interpretation. At the same time that he explores empirical and idealist foundations of psychoanalysis, he compares the listening process to the mystical experiences of Isaac Luria and Meister Eckhart and discusses "messiah thoughts." Overall, he seemed to evolve from "Let's get out the ruler and compass" to "Let's see what the images on the cave wall are reflecting" to the Zen-like "Let's see what happens if we stop all thought."

My discussion will focus on these four philosophical roots and contexts in Bion. First, I will consider his utilization of logical positivism, which is in many ways an extension of Enlightenment science. Then I will examine his application of Kant. After that, I will look at his turn towards mysticism. And, finally, I will discuss some postmodern features in Bion's exploration of the mind. To some extent, I must leave it to the reader to determine whether each of these positions constitutes a hermeneutics or an anti-hermeneutical stance. For example, does an algebraic form of notation constitute meaning? Is a "thing-in-itself" or a hallucination meaningful? Does ultimate darkness carry meaning? Is the detritus of psychosis and fragmentation meaningful? These are the sorts of difficult questions that Bion's work poses.

The logic and logistics of thinking

We know that Bion was influenced by both logical positivist and neo-Kantian philosophy. In a note made in 1959 and published posthumously (1992, pp. 58–59), he reflected privately on the ideas of Alfred North Whitehead, Bertrand Russell, and Willard Quine regarding symbolic logic and scientific method. Educated at Oxford, he had met the neo-Kantian scholar, H. J. Paton and owned several of his books (Francesca Bion, personal communication, June 21, 2000). Bion repeatedly emphasized Kant's metaphysical concept of the "thing-in-itself" which exists beyond and informs experience. For Bion, the unconscious is the thing-in-itself or noumenon that informs conscious mentation, an idea that influenced Freud (Tauber, 2010, pp. 93–98). Yet, apparently oblivious to the attacks on Kant's metaphysics by Russell and other positivists, he often appeared to be influenced by them as well, as I shall now try to show.

Mathematics and logical notation

Bion's theory of thinking represents his attempt to transform the ideas of Freud and Klein into a rigorous scientific language and notation. For example, instead of mental "associations," he uses the term "links," a non-psychological binary concept that is consistent with Whitehead and Russell's (1910, 1912–1913) *Principia Mathematica* and the development of symbolic logic. A link between thoughts simply is or is not present, while "associations" carry connotations of intensity, intimacy, and so on. He brings in emotions when he says that links can be "attacked." He regards "attacks on linking" as occurring in schizophrenia, sociopathy, deception, and defense. But instead of using psychologically saturated terms like drive and instinct, he utilizes "algebraic notation," the letters "L," "H," and "K." (Note, however, that letters of the alphabet are used as symbols both in refined mathematics and in the Kabbalah, where they have mysterious and magical properties!) L, H, and K presumably stand for love, hate, and knowledge, although he never explicitly says so. When these links are attacked, distorted, or perverted, they manifest with a negative sign as –H, –L, and –K. Further, he uses the notation PS and D, related to Klein's paranoid-schizoid and depressive positions, but he means by them a general oscillation between disorganization/tension and coherence/rest (cf. Bion, 1962b, 1970).

Whether or not they are consistent with a positivist or mathematical agenda, Bion's use of such notation is a brilliant move, because it empties out a host of language-embedded assumptions about the "mind" that have no basis in fact and encourages psychoanalysts to take a fresh look at the phenomena themselves. Love is old, but "L" is new.

In general, this early phase of theorizing is an attempt by Bion to build a symbolic notation for psychoanalysis, to see if it could be a rigorous science. This effort mirrors logical positivism in two respects. First, it reflects a striving, consistent with positivism, to rid psychoanalytic discourse of what might be called the three M's: metaphysics, mysticism, and muddle. For positivism, rigorous thinking consists of the laws of logic applied to sense data. Science is straightforwardly applied logic or mathematics. Everything else is noise. So Bion tries to operationalize his theory in such terms as can be logically or mathematically manipulated. He is concerned that one cannot do that with the Freudian and Kleinian vocabulary because it is complex, connotative, sensuous, and ambiguous.

For instance, the words "love" or "libido" each mean many things on many levels. But the use of the letter "L" is prior to meaning. It is simply algebraic: "There is a variable, L, and we can deal what is constant about it and then fill in the blanks with particular instances." We can then study "L" without prejudice. "L" represents connections, "H" is disruption, and "K" is information. We can then look at the connections, disruptions, and information contained in specific mental phenomena. Here,

Bion is trying to establish a rigorous scientific-mathematical system for psychoanalytic thought, which was Russell and Whitehead's aim for all thought. In his writing, Bion frequently uses mathematical, geometrical, and mechanistic "language" such as "point and line," "constant conjunction," "vertex," "rigid motion transformation," "binocular vision," and so on. He is eager to establish a scientific, operational basis for psychoanalysis, but the reader sometimes wonders, "Isn't he really just making new metaphors?" Physical "real world" events can be operationalized and subject to mathematics because scientists can agree on key observations. Mental events are private and change in character when they are communicated. Bion was applying positivist principles to mental events, a philosophically questionable endeavor.

Second, Bion, like Wittgenstein, was interested in language. For Wittgenstein (1953), language is a "game" that is useful for society but does not carry meaning in the sense of describing knowledge of the world. Words are defined by their connections to other words, not to objects of reality. Certainly, the vocabulary of psychoanalysis is largely a Wittgensteinian "language game," whose meaning is specified within an overall psychological context. Bion expressed a similar idea but from a different angle, namely, the shifting and ambiguous meaning of words and sensations. Memories and desires, Bion (1970, p. 41) said, are "saturated." That is, they absorb sensory elements and images very quickly, making it difficult to think clearly about them. He therefore wanted to minimize the saturated preconceptions (memory, desire, and understanding) the analyst might bring to theory, and the only way to do this was to use algebraic symbols whose meaning could be filled in later in a manner consistent with empirical findings.

The "Grid"

Proceeding with his positivist agenda, Bion went a step further with his "Grid" (see Figure 4), a two dimensional schema for classifying the events in a psychoanalytic session. In principle, the Grid could be used as a way of classifying what the analyst observed and did during a session. It has the quality of a board game, in which pieces (thought process) could move around the board and take up new positions in the matrix. Thus, in principle, a computer analysis of a session could be done by noting the location of the thought process at any point in time.

Figure 4. The Grid.

Bion's Grid

		Definatory hypotheses	Psi	Notation	Attention	Inquiry	Action	...n,
A	Beta elements	A1	A2				A6	
B	Alpha elements	B1	B2	B3	B4	B5	B6	...Bn
C	Dream thoughts	C1	C2	C3	C4	C5	C6	...Cn
D	Pre concep- tion	D1	D2	D3	D4	D5	D6	...Dn
E	Conception	E1	E2	E3	E4	E5	E6	...En
F	Concept	F1	F2	F3	F4	F5	F6	...Fn
G	Scientific deductive system		G2					
H	Algebraic calculus							

Source: Bion, 1977, frontispiece.

The Grid is a matrix of thought. From top to bottom, the vertical axis, it extends from the most primitive thought process (the primal unconscious) to increasingly organized and abstract forms of thought.

At the top of the Grid (but the "bottom" of the psyche!) are "beta elements," raw, unmetabolized "thoughts without a thinker" such as hallucinations, somatic symptoms, and impulsive acting out. One *perceives* (*hears, sees, feels*) hallucinations and somatic symptoms; they are pure sensations. One *acts out* an impulse. No active cogitation is involved, hence thoughts without a thinker. Beta elements manifest the unconscious directly and concretely.

Below the beta elements are alpha elements. These are the most rudimentary coherent images that are capable of being contemplated and thought about, such as those which become woven into dreams and fantasies, the next level. Bion was especially interested in how beta elements are transformed by the mind into alpha elements and called the process "alphabetization." This is a reformulation of "making the unconscious conscious." At the "high end" of cognition, towards the bottom of the Grid, are abstract ideas such as formulated concepts and aspects of science and philosophy, and finally, "algebraic calculus" (formal logic and mathematics), which harks back to Whitehead and Russell.

A significant achievement of the vertical axis is that it breaks down primary and secondary process thinking into a more nuanced set of thought processes, so that alpha, beta, and dreams are subdivisions of primary process, while everything from preconception to algebraic calculus is what Freud called "secondary process." It makes clear that primary and secondary process are too general, formulated by Freud in his early days, well before the emergence of perceptual and cognitive psychology. We now know that there are many forms of thought.

The horizontal axis consists of responses of the analyst to the "vertical" content. For example, the analyst "forms a hypothesis" about a patient's dream (Grid cell 1, C). Proceeding horizontally, he then might either make a note, inquire about a detail in the dream, or, for example, if the dream, along with other data, strongly implies that the patient is going to act out destructively, the analyst might take action by, say, hospitalizing the patient. Along the horizontal axis of actions, the psi function (column 2) is the most interesting. It is the "lie" function, the function of defense. For example, the analyst's countertransference might lead him to ignore, repress, or dissociate from something the patient says, and then he could not proceed to the other columns, or do so in an inappropriate way. In this way, the psi function is a barrier to further investigation.

The axes and elements of the Grid therefore could be considered a methodical way of processing the data of a psychoanalytic session consistent with both logical positivism and cognitive science. It offers psychoanalysis a scientific classification system. Or does it?

The philosophical dilemma posed by beta elements

One notable obstacle in the Grid to fulfilling the positivist agenda of reducing all statements to sense impressions and logic, is the first row, beta elements, which, as just noted, consists of unmetabolized, raw, undigested material of the unconscious. Bion alternately referred to beta elements as "thoughts without a thinker" or "things-in-themselves." Hallucinations and impulsive actions are prime examples of beta elements. They evade sense and reason. They emerge directly from the unconscious, hence are "thoughts" that are not thought about but remain "things." However, Bion's way of considering beta elements as Kant's "things-in-themselves" is inconsistent and troubling, a reflection of the difficult philosophical problem of "knowing the unknowable." For Kant, things in themselves are (metaphysical) elements of reality which are forever unknown. Similarly, Bion viewed beta elements as things-in-themselves, prior to thought. (To a logical positivist, "things in themselves" are metaphysical nonsense.)

The problem is that beta elements, for example hallucinations, though they may be closely related to the unconscious, are phenomena of perception and experience. For Kant, all experience (phenomena) comes to us through a perceptual and cognitive filter. We never experience the thing-in-itself. Thus, for example, when Hamlet sees and hears his deceased father, Bion would characterize the apparition as a beta element. After all, it is convincingly "real," a "thing." But is it a thought without a thinker? (Hamlet was, after all, the quintessential thinker!)

Beta elements are not things-in-themselves but unprocessed sensations (hallucinations), actions, and beliefs (delusions). They are conscious but not readily available for rational thought and decision making. Hamlet's hallucination is not a manifestation of the "thing-in-itself." Hamlet does not "see" his father emerging from either death or the unconscious; rather, he sees what he wants his father to be for him in the moment, one who justifies his resentment against the new king of Denmark. Beta elements are not things in themselves. Like dreams, they are wish-fulfilling constructions, but they delusionally *appear* to be "real" in time/space in the waking state. The specter of their being "real" is an illusion. Bion fell for this illusion. He confused noumena and phenomena. He confounded that which delusionally appears real with the thing-in-itself. Beta elements are "real" in the way that Lacan (Julien, 1994) uses that term, defining "real" in the psychological sense of unmediated, pre-symbolic experience. They "feel" real, but have no real "existence."

Nevertheless, despite that fallacy, Bion's beta elements are a significant contribution to psychoanalytic theory. We could reasonably argue that beta elements are sensory phenomena that arrive "frozen" from the unconscious. They emerge as specters or ghosts or fixed delusional beliefs, and so they make the unconscious *appear* to exist in physical space. Unlike dreams (alpha elements), which the dreamer upon awakening recognizes to be from an intermediate realm and can be reflected upon, hallucinations (beta elements) manifest as frozen relics that are not subject to further thought and consideration. They are in this respect unalterably "bound" to the unconscious. But they are not, as Bion held, "things in themselves." Rather they are sensory phenomena generated by the unconscious, which is never experienced "in itself." This problem haunted Bion's own thought process, possibly leading to his mystical, transformational turn of mind.

From Kant to mysticism: transformations in "O"

In *Attention and Interpretation*, Bion (1970) went beyond the Grid, which appears as the frontispiece to that book, and considered, in depth and detail, the epistemology of psychoanalysis, what it means to "know" about the unconscious. He explored how the analyst listens to the material, and how he formulates his interpretations and theories. Although in that work, he never mentioned Kant by name, at one point (p. 11), he stated: "I am thus positing mental space as a thing-in-itself that is unknowable but that can be represented by thoughts." This is a distinctly Kantian metaphysical statement. He went on to say, "In thought I include all that is primitive ... I exclude, arbitrarily by definition, beta elements." That is, beta elements, as discussed above, are for Bion not representations but things in themselves. But, perhaps on account of the problem of the "real" that I have just delineated, Kant was insufficient for him.

Bion needed another vehicle to depict the much broader realm of the unknowable ultimate reality of the mind, a vehicle that had more dynamic significance and psychological depth than Kant's noumena, which are aspects of logic, mathematics, and physics, not of the unconscious mental life. In a Kabbalistic twist away from both positivism and Kant, he used the symbol "O" (the Other; the zero, cipher) to signify all that is unknowable, making the unconscious a vast realm well beyond noumena, instincts, or anything else we might specify. "O" is a "dark" realm comparable to Milton's "formless infinite." (For Kant, by contrast, things in themselves are ultimate, absolute truths or scientific laws, not dark or formless.) Once he encountered this difference, Bion made it his task to comprehend the dark, formless unconscious, "O."

Up to this point in the evolution of this thinking, Bion borrowed from Kant. He had originally considered "O" to be "the thing in itself" which we know only by implication. Like Kant, he explored rational ways in which we can infer things in themselves (which Plato called essences, and Kant believed was a substrate that underlies all sense perception). Bion agreed with Kant that we can only do so in a partial way through a particular filter, lens, or perspective. In this respect, in the language of geometry, Bion talks about "vertices" of diverse perceptions and theories. He mentions how O (the unknown) can be transformed into K (knowledge). In many of his discussions, he stays well within the tradition of metaphysics from Plato to Kant. In effect, Bion recapitulated the traditional view of psychoanalytic interpretation. The analyst finds words to re-present the patient's experience in ways that "make the unconscious conscious," that clarify the "true" motivations and attitudes of the patient beyond what his ego thinks or feels at the moment.

Then something problematical happened in Bion's discourse. Unlike Platonic essences and Kantian things in themselves, which are constants and absolutes, Bion began to speak of "*transformations* in O." O—the unknowable—can evolve, transform, develop, change. (This is a Kabbalistic notion of reality as a vast ocean of beings that God has created. It also is expressed in the eternal wheel of events in Hinduism.) In effect, Bion switched from Freud's view, consistent with Kant, of the unconscious as the repository of relics, as an inert archeological site, to a view of the unconscious as alive, changeable, quixotic, chaotic, undergoing "catastrophic transformations." Moreover, he asserted that the analyst, rather than merely conveying the dynamics of the patient, must undergo transformations in O with the patient! Examples might be when an analyst falls apart with the patient; or when the analyst becomes the victimizer or "bad object" of the patient's projections. "Something happens" between them, and, ideally, if all goes well, it resolves via the psychoanalytic process (the horizontal axis of the Grid) into a transformation from lies (defenses) into truth (emotional growth).

This highly dynamic view of O, the unconscious, as an alive, developing, ineffable otherness is consistent with Klein's view of the infant's (preverbal, pre-thinking) use of projective-introjective identification to cope with pain and frustration. There are no words. There is no thinker. The mother undergoes changes with the infant that modify the infant's inner condition. (For example, she gets up in the middle of the night when the infant cries, and holds and feeds the baby.) Indeed, Bion formulates the notion of container-contained, the process by which thought develops, in ways that are similar to Klein's notion in which the infant deposits unwanted painful experience into the breast.

But we are here concerned with the hermeneutics and philosophy of psychoanalytic interpretation. In effect, Bion came to believe that the mutual transformations in O that occur in psychoanalysis are not comprehensible by reason and science; rather, they are akin to mystical states. He mentions Meister Eckhart, the thirteenth-/fourteenth-century Christian mystic and Isaac Luria, the sixteenth-century Kabbalistic scholar, especially noting the latter's statement that experiences of God are so awesome they cannot be expressed in books and words (Bion, 1970, pp. 115–116). Like Western and Eastern mystics alike, Bion argues that thinking obscures awareness, hence that the analyst should listen in the absence of memory, desire, and understanding. Here, he is advocating a meditative or contemplative state of mind for the analyst, perhaps an outlying extension of Freud's "listening with evenly hovering attention." Here, Bion has left Kant—who as a quintessential philosopher of the Enlightenment sought to replace mysticism with a scientific and rationalist world view—in the dust.

Indeed, Bion opened the way for psychoanalysts to incorporate religious and mystical teachings into their discourse, teachings that Freud and Klein had shunned. Michael Eigen, in *The Psychoanalytic Mystic* (1998), a sweeping look at mystical states in psychoanalytic theory and practice, discussed Bion throughout. Mark Epstein, in *Thoughts without a Thinker* (1996) and *Going on Being: Buddhism and the Way of Change* (2001), developed a Buddhist perspective on psychoanalysis, citing Bion's work.

It is difficult to assess Bion's own sentiments about religion and spirituality. Although he was exposed to Christian, Buddhist, and Hindu sources, I believe that Bion intended "transformations in O" to refer to altered states of consciousness, not necessarily to a messiah, enlightenment, godhead, or Atman, although he would not have excluded such "transformations" either. (Bion was in California in the 1970s, a time and place of the drug culture, fascination with "altered states," and Eastern thought.)

Was Bion an existentialist?

Bion was at heart a metaphysician and mystic, seeking essences and eternal truths. Yet it appears that, with his notion of transformations in O, he was moving towards an existential perspective but was too attached to positivist and Kantian thought to make the ideological switch to existentialism. For example, "O" has many features of Heidegger's *Dasein*: at hand, always on the horizon of thought, alive but not presenting itself. Heidegger's concept of truth, *alatheia*, as unconcealment, might have had a great appeal to Bion, whose thinking seemed to bring things out of the shadows. Bion speaks of "messiah thoughts," thoughts that disturb the "Establishment," and such thoughts often do not merit proof—they reveal themselves through authenticity. However, Bion's way is very different from Heidegger's. Bion depends so much on "thinking" rather than "being." He would have questioned Heidegger's emphasis on the *Lebenswelt*, our lifeworld. Instead, Bion sought transcendent truth.

The postmodern turn in Bion

Thus, Bion's view of psychoanalysis alternated between the two extremes of 1) reasoning from fact and 2) mystical contemplative thought, with Kant's noumena providing a hub around which they circled. However, at a certain point, Bion's whole system, so carefully worked out, seemed to fall apart for him, and he entered a postmodern phase in which he appeared to surrender to what the postmodernists call "the failure of all metanarratives" (Lyotard, 1974, pp. 18–36), willing to immerse himself fully in the complexity of the unconscious as a fragmented, chaotic pastiche of ideas, images, and fantasies without a privileged position from which to view it all. This postmodern turn is demarcated by the publication in three parts of *A Memoir of the Future* (Bion, 1975, 1977, & 1979), a freely associated narrative, a Joycean novelistic work of stream of consciousness "science fiction," in which psychoanalysis and the unconscious are viewed from a plethora of angles and vertices, and from which nothing permanent or privileged in the way of truth can be concluded. Although it incorporated ideas from his other work, I believe that *A Memoir of the Future* represents Bion's confession that no single theory or point of view can capture the truth about the unconscious, that "O" constitutes itself anew in each moment of the psychoanalytic session, a decidedly deconstructive and postmodern attitude.

A Memoir of the Future is one of the most unusual works in the psychoanalytic literature. It is a free-flowing, creative, and imaginative work rather than an organized treatise. It is comparable to Jung's explorations of his own psychotic processes through drawings, mythology, and meditations (Jung, 2009), except that the *Memoir* is a single narrative with a semblance of a plot. Indeed, some (e.g., Williams, 1985) have regarded it as a self-analysis like Jung's or Freud's. On another level, it comes across as a continuation of Bion's relentless pursuit of the "tiger" of the unconscious, a "summing up" of his thinking, especially since the *Memoir* came to him towards the end of his life. In my opinion, Bion expressed in the *Memoir* his ultimate conclusion that the unconscious was deceptive and inchoate, without discernable form, offering the reader a decidedly postmodern perspective.

In this work, Bion uses a type of free association consisting of alpha elements, dream thoughts, and preconceptions in the Grid. It appears that he is thinking in fantasy about the relationship between the analyst and the unconscious. He is also telling us to "remember in the future" that the unconscious is not comprehensible under a unitary theory or metanarrative. It can only be grasped as a postmodern pastiche of myths, stories, images, ideas—all of which seem to add up to some consistent understanding, but perhaps not. Indeed, Bion here considers it more than plausible that we can only grasp the unconscious by the diverse transformational experiences it calls up for us.

Like in James Joyce's work, the reader can pick up on almost any passage in the book and look for hidden meanings and allusions. For the sake of my argument, I am going to focus on one passage which I take to be a dialogue between the analyst and the unconscious. Bion tellingly calls the analyst "Science Fiction" and the unconscious "the Artist," the creative/destructive force, O. My point is that Bion as a postmodernist is deconstructing all metanarratives—all theorizing—about the unconscious and reveling in its chaos and complexity. The following is a slightly abridged excerpt, with my comments in italics:

> "We are Science Fiction. Who are you?" (*"Science Fiction" is a wry allusion to psychoanalysis itself, as well as the paradoxical futuristic nature of memory implied in the book's title.*)

> "I am the Artist who made the ram caught in a thicket beautiful in gold. I am the hunter who caught the ram in a thicket. I am the thicket in which the ram was caught. Who are you?" (*The hunter and the thicket are the analyst, and the artist is the unconscious dream*

work that transforms the ram (nature; the instincts) into gold (images and objects).)

"I am Science Fiction. I am S.F. I am the Fiction which became Science Fact. I am the tomb robber. I am the drug that stole your senses away. I am the tomb, ugly and frightening. … But who now is this?" (*Bion uses theft, drugs, and robbery of tombs to symbolize the analytic enterprise as a greedy pillaging and blinding. While the ram and thicket are in the natural world, the tomb and drugs are in the human (sociohistorical) world. Psychoanalysis moves between two different modes—biological and social—of understanding life and the mind.*)

"I am what I am. I am God. I am Satan. I am hell fire. I am the burning bush. I am the fire that all men worship. I am Satan. I stole your thicket and refined it in the fire till it burned so brightly that all men worshipped me. I am Mammon. Who is this?" (*In his other writings, Bion never explicitly says that "O" is God. Here, he acknowledges that connection. He also acknowledges that God and the Devil, good and evil, are intertwined, that psychoanalysis, like Hinduism and Kabbalah, goes beyond traditional Western religion in this regard.*)

"I am Strife. I set God against Mammon. I set the vulva against the penis, the contained against its content. I caused the lean to devour the fat. Who are you?" (*All is conflict and duality, whether seen as oppositions of instinct and culture, id and superego, or all good and all bad part-objects.*)

"I am the dreamer. I dream a dream. I am the den in which I was buried. Who are you?" (*The dreamer and the dream are enfolded in one another, as are the tomb and the entombed. For all we know, it might all be a dream.*)

"I am the thought that found a thinker. Who are you?" (*A reference to Kant's "things in themselves."*)

"I am Babel. I am the Tower that all men are made like. Who are you?" (*Babel, the confusion of tongues, is the archetype of postmodern complexity of narratives. If all men are from Babel, how can we ever escape the confusion?*)

(*Bion comes up with more images of knower and known, of knowing the unconscious:*)

"I am the garden into which the serpent found entry."

"I am the beam by which I found a way to enter."

"I am Urania." (*The feminine aspect of science, art, and the spiritual life*) ...

"I am Palinurus by whom the fleet of lesser helmsmen were able to sail." ... (*Palinurus is Freud, or if you prefer, Bion.*)

"I am the disguise robbed from Odysseus who is so wealthy in wiles. I flung reason from his throne. Who are you?" (*Freud exposing the irrationality of man.*) ...

(*Bion turns here to images of the potential dangers and destructive consequences of encountering the unconscious:*)

"'I am the king in whose dream you are but the furniture. If I were to wake you would go out bang!—like a candle. You are?"

"I am a funny story. I am a child's book." ... (*Humor can relieve the fear. The "Memoir" is a humorous child's book.*) ...

"I am the Refiner's fire. The glorious sun who was the revolutionary flame disguised as R.F., the republique franchise, the public thing, the thing that turned the hidden thing to the public thing; who robbed death; who robbed the secret of its cover and exposed it as the monster that it is. Who are you?" (*Making things public and exposing them to civilization, disclosing the unconscious, is not always desirable. We need our secrets, our darkness, our death.*) ...

[The above excerpt is from Bion, 1975, Book I, Chapter Eight.]

It could be said that through the *Memoir*, as illustrated in passages such at this, Bion himself underwent a "transformation in O," a catastrophic change from a man of reason to one who is capable of thinking in dualities and paradoxes and images that go beyond logic to the "tiger" of raw experience. In so doing, he, in his own way, echoed the transformations of Nietzsche and Kierkegaard from logic and religion to a direct confrontation with the core of naked, individual being. In terms of his thought process, Bion ultimately became the quintessential postmodernist, deconstructing his own texts and metanarratives into their disseminations in stories and myths.

Bion, hermeneutics, and psychoanalytic interpretation

To review, Bion's earlier thinking about psychoanalysis pursued a rigorous position emphasizing Kantian things-in-themselves and what he called "invariants," in the attempt to "know" the unconscious by means of reason. He used ideas from philosophy, mathematics, and science to pursue his investigations. In this respect, he applied principles of logical positivism and Kantian philosophy, thus embodying the Enlightenment traditions of empiricism and metaphysics. Bion started out as an intellectual descendant of the Enlightenment.

His views, however, gradually transformed to the direct opposite of rigorous science, acquiring mystical connotations, with "O" coming to represent a dark, incomprehensible realm that could only be apprehended by entering a meditation-like state of openness to experience. His thinking shifted from a rigorous symbol system for representing mental events to a view of the unconscious as a mysterious realm whose nature is ineffable, beyond words.

Thus, Bion alternated between the two outer limits of human understanding: scientific determinism and mystical intuition. As such, it could be argued that his view was decidedly anti-hermeneutical. He was seeking a certainty based alternately on reason and faith that hermeneutical thinkers from Vico to Heidegger, Derrida, Levinas, and Gadamer would seriously question. Reason and faith purport to transcend everyday life and history, while hermeneutics holds that all knowledge is rooted in the latter.

However, an alternative view of Bion compatible with hermeneutics is possible. Science and mysticism are end points of the human exploration of meanings. Science is meaning stripped of ambiguity and contradiction. Mysticism is meaning stripped of the observing subject and sensory experience. Hermeneutics is human-centered and accepts the ambiguity of truth and the influence of the human condition on what is believed and known. Science and mysticism are realms of human experience that lie at either end of a continuum of making sense out of life and its necessities. Bion undertook the difficult "road less traveled" of navigating between them in the vortex of the unconscious.

CHAPTER THIRTEEN

Psychoanalysis and neuroscience: an uneasy marriage

An information explosion is occurring in neuroscience. Thanks to more refined techniques for studying the nervous system much is being learned about the neural correlates of basic psychological functions such as perceptual-motor systems, memory, emotion, and cognition. In addition, due especially to functional brain scans that register brain activity *in vivo*, neuroscientists are looking into subtle and complex dimensions of affect regulation, social interaction, attachment, consciousness, and empathy. It is natural that, even though many of the new studies are exploratory and require further investigation and confirmation, psychoanalysis would like to incorporate such findings from neuroscience. Also expectable would be neuroscientists' turn towards psychoanalysis as a stimulus for their research, whether in agreement or disagreement. Neuroscience and psychoanalysis have always acknowledged a significant if uneasy alliance.

It is easy to understand that, despite the difficulties, a field called neuropsychoanalysis (website: http://www.neuropsa.org.uk/) has emerged, with its own journal and conferences. More surprisingly, however, neuroscientists are engaging with philosophers in a discipline called "neurophilosophy" (Churchland, 1986), attempting to say what insights neuroscience can contribute to the theory of knowledge (epistemology) and being (ontology), and conversely how philosophy could illuminate neuroscience. As a result, there is emerging a new body of research, theorizing, and conversation about the relationship between psychoanalysis, neuroscience, and philosophy. Here, we join some of these discussions, but only from a particular vertex, to address two aspects of the convergence of neuroscience, psychoanalysis, and hermeneutical philosophy: 1) the use of neuroscience-related findings in the consulting room and 2) how the brain and nervous system itself might be understood as an interpretive apparatus. These concerns hark back to the origins of psychoanalysis, which emerged within a neuro-biological context.

Neuroscience and the origins of psychoanalysis

As Sulloway (1979) has thoroughly documented, psychoanalysis was conceived within a biomedical zeitgeist. The biological versus psycho-logical causes of hysteria, as well as a condition known as "railway spine" (pp. 37–39) were heatedly debated by psychiatrists of the time. Freud presented his medical colleagues with his initial psychological work in a context not unlike that of the current "managed care" era, a context that demanded "evidence" and a biological basis of behavior. Freud struggled, sometimes in vain, to make his broader historical and interpretive understanding of the mind acceptable to his peers.

Freud was an accomplished neurologist, and he wanted to link his theories of psychological symptoms and defense to the functioning of the nervous system. For this purpose, he developed concepts which he felt applied to both mind and brain. He considered the largest terri-tory of mind, the "id," to be connected with the biological drives and the somatic core. He derived his principle of "conservation of psychic energy" from the energy conservation equation in physics that had been applied to the nervous system (Amacher, 1965, pp. 63–74.) Although Freud soon diverted his attention away from neurology to psychology, he continued throughout his career to use biological explanations and metaphors for psychological processes. He left a natural science legacy to his followers and subsequent generations of Freudians, Kleinians, and ego psychologists.

By contrast, Jungians and neo-Freudians have given less emphasis to biology and offered alternative perspectives emphasizing the interpersonal, social, and spiritual foundations of the mind. The differences among biological, sociocultural, and mythico-religious vantage points led to divisions among analysts and the formation of diverse schools of thought. In this way, the role of neuroscience has been significant in psychoanalysis from its inception, whether as a fundamental linkage or as a bone of contention.

Two divergent interpretations of Freud's "Project": scientific explanation vs. hermeneutical understanding

In the "A Project for a Scientific Psychology" (Freud, 1950a), an extended essay written in 1895 but never published because he felt it was premature, Freud outlined a theory of neural functioning that he hoped could account for consciousness and other psychological phenomena. He utilized the then new findings about neural synapses to suggest that psychological functioning was established through "traces" of synaptic activity that facilitated diverse neural functions: "breeches" that allowed synaptic transmissions from one neuron to another, "binding" that accounted for stability within flux, "resistances" (electrico-chemical inhibition of nerve conduction) that facilitated the development of higher level mental functions, and other characteristics of neuronal action. Neuroscientist Karl Pribram (1962), in an elegant paper written a few years after the "Project" was discovered and discussed by Ernest Jones (1953, vol. 1, pp. 379–395), suggested how Freud was able to create a reasonable and at times brilliant neurological rationale for psychological constructs such as primary and secondary process, wish fulfillment, ego functioning, reality testing versus hallucination, and other concepts which were soon to become part of a broader psychoanalytic psychology.

Shortly after Pribram, in an entirely different literary-philosophical context, Derrida (1978) also pointed to the profundity of the "Project." Derrida reversed perspective from Pribram, focusing not on its biological importance but, philosophically, in its relation to "writing," Derrida's shorthand for the discourses of literature, history, and philosophy. He used the document to consider the appearance in Freud of two notions: "trace" and "difference" (or "deferral") that supported his own deconstructionism. He argued that, in written texts, nothing is left of an idea other than its trace, its dissemination in other texts, so that assertions and truths dissolved when texts were carefully examined. Thus, Derrida found an ally in Freud, who held that nerve impulses (traces) were "deferred" and impermanent. Derrida used Freud's understanding of trace and difference to question the notions of "presence," representation, and structure in a language and text. For Derrida, the fate of a belief or idea is the same as that of a neural "trace:" it vanishes into the text; it has no substance as such. Derrida was reading the "Project" itself from a hermeneutical rather than neurological vantage point, as "the scene of writing," as a literary text. He used Freud's science-based work paradoxically to deconstruct science and metaphysics as privileged points of view. It was one of the great tours de force in the history of ideas.

The commentaries of Pribram and Derrida amply illustrate two sides of psychoanalysis, scientific and literary. On the one hand, there is the claim, supported by Pribram, that what is valuable in psychoanalysis could ultimately be explained in terms of the neurological basis of behavior, the "reductionist" position that accounts for higher level psychological phenomena in physico-chemical terms. On the other hand, many humanists and hermeneutical thinkers, notably Derrida, have claimed that this reduction cannot be accomplished without sacrificing a full understanding of experience. From the standpoint of Derrida and modern hermeneutics, neuroscience must defer to human understanding, rather than vice versa.

Under that assumption, a chapter on neuroscience should not appear in this book! However, it is possible to argue my position that a degree of "consilience" between neuroscience and psychoanalytic hermeneutics can exist, namely, that these two disciplines, while radically different, overlap in certain key respects, and that it is worth "stretching" our understanding to bring them together, while exercising caution. There are epistemological problems (problems of criteria for "truth") that haunt such a consilience, but there are practical justifications for bringing them together.

Practical application of neuroscience in clinical work

Sometimes, crucially for the patient's well-being and proper care, neuroscience reveals specific organic causes of pathology.

> For example, a patient, Ralph, despite his affable persona, found himself repeatedly scapegoated and rejected by social and therapy groups. He came to treatment hoping to resolve the problem. The therapist treated him from psychodynamic and interpersonal

perspectives, showing the patient how his difficulty stemmed from early experiences of rejection by family members as well as the anxieties and defenses he developed. However, neither such interpretation nor a supportive therapeutic relationship led to a resolution of the problem. When Ralph casually told the therapist that some years ago he had fallen from a high ladder and suffered a head trauma that required surgery, the therapist referred him to a neuropsychologist for testing. The latter's assessment stated that the patient had a lesion in "the part of the brain that reads social signals." This finding probably explained why Ralph was rejected by others, namely that he did not respond to their social communications and thus came across as insensitive and hostile. The neuropsychologist recommended Ralph get a consultation with a neurological rehabilitation specialist, who taught him interpersonal coping skills from which he felt he benefitted considerably.

The difference between interpretation and applied neuroscience

Ralph's case affords a vivid illustration of the use of neuroscience in diagnosis, that is, to detect neurological impairments. But it also points to the paradigm shift that occurs, sometimes much more subtly, when such theories and findings are used in the course of psychoanalytic psychotherapy. The therapist moves from an interpretive stance to one of "applied neuroscience," from an open, receptive listening process and a facilitator of free association to a directive problem-solver. He is no longer doing psychoanalysis as such. However, the analyst is first and foremost a healer, and must do whatever is necessary to help the patient.

The paradigm shift becomes problematical when ideas from neuroscience are utilized to generate psychological interpretations as such rather than to isolate a lesion or impairment. Then we see that neuroscience and interpretive therapy exist in an uneasy marriage.

The use of neuroscience as a basis for psychotherapy

As the scope of neuroscience expands to include complex phenomena like affect regulation and social interaction, the tendency to understand these phenomena from a scientific perspective and utilize these explanations as part of the interpretive work has increased.

A singular example can be found in the important integration of dynamic psychotherapy, mindfulness practice, and neural integration by psychologist Daniel Siegel. Siegel (2012) incorporates neuroscience, psychospirituality, and psychodynamics into a holistic view of psychotherapy as a process of integrating brain functions. He also incorporates knowledge of attachment patterns and psychological trauma into his work, calling upon a wide range of empirical research, from functional MRI and PET scans to attachment research and research on trauma, mentalization, and memory.

Siegel views the dynamic therapy component that facilitates neural integration as the "construction of a coherent narrative." The therapist shifts his attention between his understanding of neural integration and the patient's narrative as he helps the latter to construct and reconstruct a life story that integrates previously disparate elements and incorporates growth-promoting elements of genuine self-esteem and mindful perception of self and world.

I believe that Siegel's work is of great importance for dynamic psychotherapy and of genuine value for patients. The concerns I am going to raise are not meant to dismiss such contemporary applications of neuroscience and cognitive-behavioral research to therapy. It is rather to bear upon them a conceptual rigor based upon philosophical and hermeneutical considerations. It is also perhaps a reminder for us not to prematurely impose concepts and conclusions of research on what the patient brings to the session. Above all, a psychoanalytic psychotherapist needs to maintain an open, receptive listening process. Indeed, Siegel himself suggests that such availability and attention on the part of the therapist may in and of themselves promote neural integration. So it is important to look carefully at how neuroscience "translates" into interpretive interventions in the consulting room.

A "confusion of tongues:" troubling paradigmatic marriages between medical knowledge and psychoanalytic dialogical exchange

Talking with a patient about his brain functions or attachment patterns, or about other biological, medical, or scientific "facts," entails a common illusion. It "feels" as if we are referring to objects in the patient's phenomenological world and memory, like tables, chairs, life events, mothers, bodies, or body parts. After all, the brain is a body part, so the effects of a brain impairment can be readily explained and understood. With instruction and coaching from the therapist, concepts from the sciences seem to weave seamlessly into the patient's narrative, and thus become part of the interpretive process. On that basis we ought to be able to use neuroscience insights, or other research findings to facilitate explanation and understanding for the patient.

This is especially important in treating psychological trauma. It might be useful, for example, for a patient to know that repeated abuse in childhood may have led to traumatic changes in the hippocampus that cause memories to be especially vivid in the form of "flashbacks" (van der Kolk, 1994); or that conversely, dissociation and numbing may have occurred that make it more difficult for the patient to experience the emotions associated with some of the memories. The therapist's understanding of such impairments may help the patient feel less guilty and ashamed about cognitive and interpersonal difficulties for which the patient may have mercilessly blamed himself.

Such use of explanations from neuroscience have utility as metaphors that facilitate improved attitudes and appropriate remediation, analogous to the way a doctor explains to a diabetic how the pancreas regulates blood sugar levels, so that the patient may better understand his symptoms and become motivated to use insulin. Such interventions constitute a counseling modality that applies science to human problems in a helpful way. However, doctor-patient conversations are very different from the psychoanalytic work of "making the unconscious conscious." In some cases, though certainly not all, it may interfere with that work.

Explanations from neuroscience and biology are not aspects of the ready-at-hand phenomenological world of experience that emerges as "manifest content" in psychoanalysis. Far from it—they are the final common path of research and inference that is so abstract and context-specific that only highly trained scientists can fully come to grips with them. That is, they are part of a scientific paradigm rather than everyday discourse. They are inserted into everyday conversation or the consulting room only as shorthand and metaphors. In the lifeworlds of individuals, they have more power than content. Like so much of common discourse, they provide an aura of truth rather than the substance of truth. Psychoanalytic interpretation is hopefully more disciplined than that.

Figure 5. Paradigms of neuroscience and psychoanalytic interpretation compared.

Paradigmatic features	Neuroscience	Psychoanalytic interpretation and dialogue
Universe of discourse	Matter	Mind
Units of investigation	Function and structure	Meaning
	Hypotheses; equations; laws	Narratives and dialogue
Research method	Experiment; fact collection	Internal consistency; hermeneutic circle
Criteria of reliability and validity	Repeatability	Unique experience and change
Theoretical framework	Organizations of neuronal responses	Personality, psychodynamics, and relationships

If we compare the guiding paradigm of neuroscience with that of psychoanalytic interpretation and dialogue, it becomes clear that neuroscientists are working with phenomena quite different from those of the analytic treatment process. Figure 5 summarizes the main characteristics of each paradigm and shows how they differ. We can see how neuroscience and psychoanalysis constitute two different universes of discourse with two distinct modes of investigation. This is patently obvious. But since neuroscience is now having a strong influence on the social sciences and psychoanalysis in particular, a "slippage" can develop where the vocabularies and concepts of the two paradigms merge with little consideration of whether and how they match.

The relationship between brain science and human experience

Classical neuroscience regards the brain as a biological "machine" that creates mind and human behavior as an output (cf. Dennett, 1991). In this view, we just need to wait for all the research to be done, and we will be able to explain all human experience in terms of the nervous system. From this reductionist perspective, psychoanalytic theory would ultimately coincide with the study of neural functioning. Such an objective was anticipated in Freud's "A Project for a Scientific Psychology."

Hermeneutical philosophy, by contrast, argues the opposite, that neuroscience, and for that matter all the natural sciences, are not causes, but rather subtexts of human understanding and meaning. Neuroscience, in this view, has only a limited utility to explain mind, consciousness, and human existence. Hermeneutically speaking, neuroscience is a product of human life, an artifact or tool that requires its own explanation. Simply put, neuroscience is a product of culture. (For example, neuroscience is a male-oriented approach to knowledge. We have no idea how or whether neuroscience might have evolved in a matriarchal society. We do know, however, that mothers perceived phenomena such as interpersonal relatedness in their infants long before they were recognized by neurologists.) Neuroscience derives both its elegance and limitations from the Cartesian mind/body dualism, causal determinism, and predictive probability. By contrast, human life includes considerations like free will, authenticity, and morality that do not fit well with materialistic neuroscience.

Indeed it is possible that the hermeneutics of psychoanalysis, along with philosophy and the history of science, could in time shed light on neuroscience itself. Some neuroscientists such as Francisco Varela (Varela, Thompson, & Rosch, 1992) and Eric Kandel (2012) have begun to think along those lines. Varela brought neuroscience into a threefold dialogue with Buddhist meditation and Husserl's phenomenology, seeking to identify new experiential phenomena for neuroscience to investigate. Kandel, who early trained as a psychoanalyst, has recently combined his own Nobel Prize winning studies of memory and molecular biology with an understanding of the brain as it embodies unconscious processes and creative imagination. Instead of posturing as the ultimate explanation of human mind and behavior, neuroscience could benefit richly from what the social sciences, philosophy, and psychoanalysis have to offer in both the documentation of human phenomena as well as in-depth understanding of complex brain functioning, neural deficits, and even organic lesions.

Consilience of neuroscience and interpretive interventions

Let us return for a moment to the original question: what about the psychoanalyst's use of constructs and findings of neuroscience in the interpretive work of making the unconscious conscious? Is there a place for it? At first approach, as I just asserted, it would seem wiser to avoid such "applied science" in what is essentially a dialogical process of uncovering human meanings and experiences. To begin with, it is preferable for the analyst to clear his mind of judgments and preconceptions when he listens to a patient. Interpretations best carry "truth value," take hold, "unconceal," and transform within a patient when he assimilates them at conscious, preconscious, and unconscious levels in ways that resonate with and amplify his inner world of experience. It does not make sense to complicate such communication with "brain science." It is best to interpret to the patient in language and metaphors that resonate with his inner life rather than constituting abstractions from science. There is also a risk, already manifest to some degree, that overuse of neuroscientific explanations will create a generation of patients who are indoctrinated in the ideology of brain science rather than each finding his own vocabulary and life path. It is thus preferable to center psychoanalytic work in the experience, language, and being of the patient himself.

However, there are justifications for applying neuroscience to psychoanalytic interpretation. As mentioned at various points in this book, I believe there are good grounds for a consilience between psychoanalysis and the natural sciences, that is, for points of reasonable conjunction between disciplines that yet stand apart from one another. In my own practice, I have found that neuroscience and related empirical research such as that on attachment disorders, cognitive-behavioral therapies, mentalization, neural integration, and mindfulness is useful in several ways, which I will now summarize.

First of all, there is an aspect of psychoanalytic psychotherapy which is aimed primarily at ego-building and development of the self rather than disclosing complexes and fantasy-defense configurations. Ego psychologists (Blank & Blank, 1994) and self psychologists have emphasized the importance of promoting developmental processes that have become arrested or severely distorted. Constructing new selves and egos may require more than uncovering the past. It may require educational provisions that enable improved coping skills, mental capacities, interpersonal relations, and self-esteem. Neuropsychological understanding can be useful in this respect in the context of interpretive work.

> For example, a patient, Gustav, had severe social anxiety initiating conversations and relationships with women. He would encounter a woman who attracted him, say a few words of introduction, and then withdraw fearfully from further involvement. A period of

exploratory work with him led not only to awareness of a conflict between motives of sexual conquest versus anxiety about rejection and loss of control of sexual impulses, but also through childhood reconstructions, a lack of play and emotional responsiveness in his parents' response to him. The therapist felt that with Gustav, it was important to facilitate a mirroring process and teach a sense of play. He realized that social learning largely occurs through recognition of self in others and vice versa, which is a possible function of mirror neurons. He also considered that such abilities constituted implicit memory and procedural learning as distinct from explicit verbal learning. He speculated that the patient might have a deficit, generated by early caregiving derailments, in some neural networks of attachment that could be ameliorated by stimulating neuroplasticity. So he geared his interpretations to a process where his comments engaged the patient in a playful responsiveness, for example, by phrasing interpretations in argumentative ways, evoking an active emotional response by the patient rather than passive reflection. Over time, the patient came to sessions increasingly energized and ready to "go at it" with the therapist. This process of dialogical exchange then seemed to take hold for Gustav outside of sessions. Soon he reported spending longer and longer times in conversation with women he met and finding creative and intimate ways to connect with them. In this case, the therapist used his understanding of how development occurs at the level of brain functioning to form a model for relating in dialogue with the patient. His use of neuroscience constituted a consilience between mirror neurons, procedural memory, and neuroplasticity vis-à-vis the psychoanalytic understanding of bonding, the self, and object relations.

A second important value of neuropsychological understanding for interpretive psychotherapy is that it can reduce the pernicious tendency to "analyze" intractable deficits and impairments. With the exception of diagnosed organic brain damage, as in the example discussed above, most therapists treat most patients under the assumption that they have intact, fully functional nervous systems. However, contemporary neuroscience shows that cognitive and relational deficits exist in patients who do not have diagnosed organicity. In addition to the well-documented biochemical deficits now generally acknowledged to accompany schizophrenia, abnormalities and deficits in brain functioning have been associated with conditions such as psychological trauma, attention deficit disorder, severe clinical depression, autistic spectrum disorders, and bipolar disorder (Lake, 2007). Many of these impairments are not easy to detect, and in the interpretive process they may first manifest themselves in what appears to be transference and resistance. For example, a severely depressed patient may have difficulty remembering and fantasizing because his hippocampus and other parts of his brain are deficient in serotonin and neural connections. Instead of persisting with reconstructions of childhood experiences, moving into a more supportive mode with an emphasis on cognitive processing may be very helpful to such patients.

Our state of knowledge regarding neuropsychological deficits is still in its early stages, however, and there is much we do not know. In addition, it has long been recognized that (some but not all) organic damage can result in secondary psychological defenses that are responsive to interpretation (Goldstein, 1939). These complexities make it more difficult to judge how and when to treat secondary consequences of neuropsychological deficits using the psychoanalytic process. The invocation to "do no harm" should make us aware that psychoanalytic modes of free association and interpretation may not always be helpful. Conversely, we should not necessarily exclude patients with neurological impairments from psychoanalytic treatment. Rather, in many cases, an interpretive approach can be very valuable to them, so long as the analyst is sensitively attuned to where the deficits alert him to "tread softly" when pursuing the depths.

A third and related consideration already mentioned is that neuropsychological understanding can usefully inform psychoanalytic interpretation in ways that mitigate excessive shame and guilt resulting from misunderstanding and misperception by the therapist. Shame and guilt can be iatrogenically induced when the therapist imputes motivation and defense to what is in fact the result of a neuropsychological deficit. For example, while we know a great deal about the psychodynamics of manic-depressive illness going back to the insightful work of Karl Abraham (1927) and Melanie Klein (1940), we now know that the biochemical imbalance underlying manic depression plays a crucial role in affect regulation for such patients. It is important for the welfare of the patient that the chemical imbalance is properly addressed with medication. At the same time, psychodynamic psychotherapy can be useful for bipolar patients if the therapist takes into account the interplay of biochemical and psychological causes of behavior.

Psychoanalytic interpretation vs. *narrative reconstruction*

Having pointed to the value of neuropsychological understanding in providing cautionary notes in interpretive exploration of the depths, I want to make a distinction between two ways in which psychoanalytic process is utilized, one of which is sometimes advocated by neuroscience and research-oriented psychologists such as both Siegel and Wallin. It is the subtle difference between interpretive probing of the unconscious and reconstructing the patient's narrative for ameliorative purposes.

Siegel, for example, states that reconstructing the patient's narrative can facilitate self-esteem and neural integration. By this he means that the patient tells his story (autobiographical narrative) and that the therapist's interpretations help construct a new narrative which the patient internalizes to form a healthier self-image and patterns of interpersonal relations. This way of understanding interpretation derives from the philosophy of "social constructivism" (Vygotsky, 1978) which argues that our selves and autobiographical narratives are the result of social interactions. Such a view is also supported by Schafer's (1994) important work on "narratives" as the operative currency of psychoanalysis. The patient "tells his story," and the analyst helps to update and revise it developmentally. Constructivism coincides in some ways with current understanding of neural functioning and neural integration which shows that cognitive functions influence memories and vice versa. Therefore, one could use interpretation as a form of cognitive processing to change memory configurations in a way that produces a new narrative history of self.

Again, I feel that such a constructivist understanding has merit, especially in eclectic therapies that utilize free association in conjunction with cognitive, behavioral, and gestalt therapy interventions. Many patients appreciate and benefit from telling their life stories and examining their past in a free and open style, while at the same time achieving a great deal of new learning in a more structured and directive format. As useful as it is, however, "construction of a new narrative" should be distinguished from psychoanalytic interpretive work as such.

Freud's work was pervaded by disillusionment about the limits of self-awareness, the therapeutic value of psychoanalysis "terminable and interminable," and mankind in general. With the widening scope of psychoanalysis, as well as the work of Winnicott, Kohut, and the relationalists, some of that disillusionment has gradually yielded to greater optimism about human possibilities and the role of creative imagination and emotional nurturance in development and in the treatment process. But there is an element of disillusionment that stems from the interpretive enterprise itself, from hermeneutics. Hermeneutics is the study of the hidden dimension of experience, the implicit meanings of what happens in human life. While modern hermeneutics mostly rejects metaphysics, the substance beneath appearances, it does assert a level of the bare truth that can be arrived at in the search for meaning. For Herder, Schleiermacher, and Dilthey, the truth consisted of accuracy and rigorous thought in the process of reconstructing a life or a text. For Heidegger, it consisted in *"alatheia,"* unconcealing. For Gadamer, it consisted in a responsible, responsive dialogue between interpretive horizons. Even Derrida sought to expose a kind of truth by deconstructing privilege and authority, even though he saw truth as an absence, a "ghost." None of these thinkers could in any way be considered a "constructivist," one who equates truth with story or belief.

The process of interpretation in psychoanalysis is not about constructing a new narrative. It is about an opening up to what is "already there," as Heidegger put it. It is a process of investigation, not the construction of a new story. Surely, one of its favorable outcomes may be a new understanding of the trajectory of one's life, of the events of one's childhood, of one's self and nature. However, that understanding must derive from the rigorous pursuit of truth about oneself and others.

Brains as hermeneutical systems

An alternative way of understanding the nervous system

That the construction of a narrative can produce benefits of improved neural functioning, such as increase of synaptic connections, neural integration, or restructured attachment patterns, is compatible with the Cartesian paradigm of the nervous system as the material underpinning of mind, a machine fulfilling diverse functions and activities. Hermeneutics understands the mind in a very different manner from material reductionism. I now wish to consider the merits of a controversial paradigm, one in which the nervous system is itself not a machine, but rather a complex interpretive system. Such a system uses the properties of the nervous system as a base, but it cannot be reduced to or explained by neural functioning as such. It operates on the basis of meanings rather than functions. In proposing this possibility, I realize that I am differing from prevailing views of both neuroscience and hermeneutics. In taking this stance, I wish in no way to minimize the problems it poses. Neuroscience is neuroscience and philosophy is philosophy. Yet philosophy has always contributed fruitful ideas to the sciences, even though the tasks and methods of the two disciplines are decidedly different. In this respect, philosophy becomes the tempting "mistress" rather than the uneasy "wife" of neuroscience. A true marriage is probably not yet possible. But mistresses do serve a purpose.

I will now try to articulate in barest outline how we might understand the brain as a seat of meanings, a "complex interpretive system." In this schema, I view the nervous system as the hardware, but propose that it operates interpretively, rather than carrying out mechanical cognitive-behavioral functions dictated by neural synaptic transmission and neural networks as such. I am suggesting that, while the individual neuron is an electrochemical mechanism, the brain as a whole is a meaning-making organ.

I am not proposing a mind or soul independent of the body. My theory suggests that some, although not all, of what has evolved in the brain over a few million years is an increasingly adaptive interpretive "understanding" of the "world," far from perfect, but which through evolution and natural selection has led to expanded functional capacity in the evolution of species as well as in individual development.

Traditional neuroscience emphasizes function, localization, and dynamic equilibrium

Three principles have dominated brain science since its inception: function, localization, and equilibrium. The first identifies neural phenomena in terms of their operative functions, such as fight-flight, pleasure-pain, memory, cognition, and other "faculties," and attempts to trace the neural circuitry and activity associated with each. The second, localization, asserts that specific mental functions are situated in particular segments of the brain's anatomy, while acknowledging that some functions are distributed as "mass action" among diverse anatomical regions. Thus, with some recent exceptions, which I will mention later, the tenor of brain science has been primarily functional and anatomical. In addition, much of neuroscience is also mechanistic, regarding the brain as a device (analogies were made in Freud's time to a pump and an electrical circuit; in our time, to a computer). Finally, these functions, locations, and devices serve the overall purpose of maintaining the survival and dynamic equilibrium (tension reduction, homeostasis, adjustment) of the individual organism, and as such are servomechanical in nature, resetting bodily and mental functions to a predetermined state or balance. Freud's theory of the drives and his early neuropsychological speculations in the "Project" are essentially functional and servomechanical.

Recent shifts in neuroscience models and approaches

Recently, several modifications to the mechanistic model of the brain have arisen that go beyond the purely localized, functional, mechanistic, and homeostatic view of the brain. For example, Damasio (1999) presented evidence to suggest that cognitive functions are highly dependent for their proper functioning on the regulation of emotions that occur primarily in the brain stem. That is, emotion and cognition are interdependent functions. Damasio, without stating it as such, invoked a new principle of functional *interdependence*. Emotions facilitate cognition rather than opposing it. Emotions are not irrational but pre-rational or supra-rational! Different brain functions (emotion and intellect) cooperate in achieving higher level goals. That hypothesis is consistent with the psychoanalytic theory of thought disorder (namely that emotional dysregulation disrupts and distorts "secondary process" logic), for it implies that thought is not pure cognition, but involves a holistic organization of attention, affect, and the body, which is expressed in Heinz Hartmann's ego psychology as the synthetic function (Blank & Blank, 1994, pp. 19–31).

Betting on understanding

In the context of accounting for learning of motor skills and adaptation to environmental contingencies, Gerald Edelman (1987) proposed a point of view called "neural Darwinism" in which the brain carries out actions on a probabilistic basis involving an element of chance and risk, and selects its future actions on the basis of "re-entry," that is, the neural replay and probabilistic outcome of a particular action. For example, the child learns to walk by falling repeatedly until his movements result in increasing success staying afoot. Edelman views such learning as not simply "trial and error" but a gradual revision of neural strategies that are recycled and reconfigured at every turn. It is as if the brain is a sophisticated poker player, developing better strategies on the basis of outcomes. Importantly for the present argument, the brain also fills in blanks, "gambling" on its momentary interpretation of events, just as a poker player takes into account the skills and facial expressions of the other players. By seeking strategies that work, the brain is in effect "understanding" its experience, learning how to work with what is "at hand," implicit in the events it encounters.

Edelman's theory is also consistent with Freud's and Jung's idea that psychological development recapitulates the evolution of the species ("ontogeny recapitulates phylogeny"), with Edelman suggesting that the individual brain/mind develops by adapting to the environment in a similar way to Darwin's theory of natural selection. Since human brains have the capacity to generate language and societies, nature must have at some point placed a selection survival value on communal meaning-making (symbol, myth, and ritual). Cozolino (2006) interpreted a range of data from neuroscience, psychology, and psychotherapy to assert that the brain does not function in isolation but is linked to other brains and the social environment. He held that the brain itself functions as a nodal point or synapse in networks of social interactions. The nervous system encounters and interacts with ever-widening systems in the external world, and its proper functioning requires integration with these systems. "No brain is an island."

The brain lives in its own "assumptive world"

Ramachandran (1998) has studied neurological damage resulting in phantom limbs, where the brain thinks and behaves as if the amputated limb is still present. He has held that the brain does not register or represent reality ("the thing in itself") as such, but rather creates a "view" of reality on an inductive basis: it construes and often misconstrues inner and outer reality based upon the limited information it has at its disposal. Its interpretation of its experience depends a great deal on its own inner structure. Thus, a limb amputation does not change the brain's map of that limb, the "story" of which is not in the limb itself but in the brain. Ramachandran has also demonstrated that an experimenter can shake the brain out of its slumber, so to speak, by convincing it to form a new map. Thus, using mirrors, the subject's usable arm, for example, can be made to appear to coincide visually with the missing arm. When he moves the usable arm, the subject develops a sense that the phantom limb is moving, and may experience a reduction in discomfort attributed to the immobility of the phantom limb. There are various interpretations of this experiment, but they all suggest that the brain maintains its own story of the body that is only partially related to the physical state of affairs as such. Neuroscience is moving towards the important idea that the brain's "body" is not so much a representation as it is an interpretation. That is, the brain uses available information to form its own image or metaphor of a world, its lifeworld.

Thomas Metzinger (2003) has proposed that the brain is an interpreter not only of the so-called real world but of itself, thus having a direct bearing on psychoanalysis. His notion of the "ego tunnel" states that only a very narrow amount of information about self and world enters the brain through its sensory and proprioceptive "filters." On the basis of that "tunnel" of information, the brain creates a vision of a phenomenological self involved in its world. For example, we think of our "selves" located at eye level ("I" = eye). But that is only one interpretation of where "I" am located. In out-of-body experiences, the locus of the self is no longer in the head, but outside the body! In this respect, the brain's self is more like a dream image than a realistic representation of where our thoughts are "located." The phenomenological self is housed in a dream (the unconscious) that creates it, not in the real world as such.

Such findings and explanations from recent neuroscience not only challenge mechanistic thinking about the brain. They raise neurophilosophical questions about Cartesian metaphysics and the representational theory that the mind directly apprehends or reproduces reality. The mind does not have representations of reality, but interprets a self and world of its own based upon very limited sensory and bodily input. The brain/mind develops strategic understandings, what neuroscientists call "maps," most of which are non-conscious or pre-conscious, but some of which operate in consciousness (Damasio, 2003). In these and other ways, the new brain science is in many ways consistent with modern hermeneutics, as I shall now try to illustrate.

The interpretive nature of the nervous system

These diverse newer understandings of brain action suggest that the nervous system carries out much of its activity in the manner of a "dialogue" with the environment (internal biochemical and anatomical environment included) and "interprets" that dialogue to have a "meaning" from which it creates an understanding (or "map") of experience that it presents to consciousness. Before going further, however, I want to qualify this statement by recognizing that only in certain cases is the brain operating as a conscious, thinking, feeling self with a past, present, and future. In Daniel Stern's terminology, the brain mostly constructs "protonarratives," which lend implicit meaning to events, although not necessarily conscious of that meaning. Developmentally, however, through language and complex thought processes, the child acquires "self narratives" which he can manipulate consciously at higher levels of awareness. In Heidegger's existential frame of reference, human being-in-the-world, *Dasein*, implies a care structure involving historicity, language, and understanding that characterizes a truly human life. The brain had to evolve language, social awareness, and a sense of time to operate at such a complex level. Nevertheless, even before the development of cognition, subjectivity, and language, the brain generates what I referred to earlier as "meaning without understanding."

It thus can be said that even at primitive levels of evolution and the nervous system, brains may be organized to integrate bits of information into quasi-meanings. Even the "conditioned reflex," Pavlov's stimulus-response arc, implies "interpretation." Conditioned reflexes are context-dependent and allow the response to be modified and attached to new stimuli via learning. A conditioned reflex is the most basic biological form of a "sign," of an expectation that a certain outcome will occur. What makes this process "interpretive" is that it construes a series of external events to have a signification in terms of an inner need. Food, for example, has no "meaning" until the nervous system gives it one in terms of hunger. The reflex arc, while in no way manifesting thought or consciousness, has already interpreted the world in terms of the needs of the organism. That is why it acquired survival value in evolution. It fulfills a need.

Still more relevant to hermeneutics is the way nervous systems organize along these same interpretive lines as they move up the ladder of evolution. For example, parts of the visual cortex are structured to recognize specific features of the environment. Hubel and Wiesel (2005), in Nobel Prize winning research, showed that specific neurons in a cat's brain are structured in a way which allows them to detect the angle of a line presented to the retina from the vast array of nerve impulses from the whole retina. Considerable "analysis" is necessary to discriminate any pattern in the visual field. Particular nerve cells fire in response to "lines" at different angles. (Presumably, this is useful to a cat in determining when and how to leap at a mouse.) Moreover, Hubel and Wiesel showed that these neural responses are shaped, and neural networks established, from the early experiences in the cat's life. The nervous system organizes itself in development to interpret configurations of sensory input in ways useful to adaptation.

With respect to the evolution of social, relational interactions, a primate research team (Gallese, Fadigia, Fogassi, & Rizzolati, 1996) showed that certain neurons in the motor cortex of chimpanzees are specialized to respond to a particular action (such as the lifting of a hand) regardless of whether that hand is the chimp's own or that of the experimenter! These are the so-called "mirror neurons" that respond to an identity between self and other. Some later studies on humans (Iacobini, 2008) using functional brain imaging to identify mirror neuron activity, suggest that mirror neurons are activated by others' expressions of emotions and intentions. Thus, these nerve centers may play a role in empathy. Here the nervous system is configured to compare its own responses to those of another individual. Nature has evolved specialized neurons that register and respond as if they have a primitive identity or relationship to particular actors and actions in the external world. They are interpreting limited sensory input in a sophisticated way that presages social relations.

My point in bringing up these diverse studies—and there are many others that could be invoked—is that brains do not operate as Cartesian minds in bodies. They do not have a direct perceptual or cognitive line to reality or to the workings of the physical body. Rather, in large part, they function hermeneutically like poets and interpreters of poems, dreamers and interpreters of dreams. They take pieces of experience and form self-organized stories, maps, and images which ascribe meaning, consequences, intent, purpose, and action to experience. In other words, nervous systems are not analogous to cameras that form representations of entities presented to them. Rather they are more like weavers who make garments of meanings that the organism wears and uses and which learning and evolution discard when they do not promote survival.

Nervous systems also appear to arrange their maps of meaning in hierarchies in which lower levels serve as "poems" for the higher levels to interpret. The retina "selects" only those light waves that fall within a particular spectrum and within the visual field, and organizes them into a field of primary colors (there are no primary colors in nature!). The visual cortex interprets the input from the eye in terms of aspects of shape, form, color, and distance of objects that it construes as existing "out there." Another system interprets whether there is food, prey, or predator "out there." Still another system establishes the level of threat, pleasure, or security involved. And still another system develops an intent or action based upon the particular value placed on the entire situation.

It is like Gadamer's meeting of horizons of the artist and the critic, the work of art and the observer. One set of neural networks "dialogues" with other sets and interprets the latter in terms that are inherent in its own "world" of meanings. In a manner similar to Gadamer's understanding of dialogue, the interpretive link is not a predetermined "truth" but emerges from the meeting of an array of meanings each of which has its own time, its own history, its own being. The criterion of interpretive truth for Gadamer is "*phronesis*," practical wisdom. By analogy, each nervous system has its own practical wisdom, its own way of being, which allows it to survive, develop, and in some instances learn from experience.

Neural "meaning without understanding" is not the same as human understanding

Now, I must again immediately qualify these ideas by saying that hermeneutical philosophers such as Gadamer are exploring human understanding, while nervous systems for the most part operate without such understanding, without a sense of self, without concern, without, in Heidegger's terms, a care structure. Evolution has housed such care structure somewhere at the edge of the human brain, perhaps at the cortical level, like the rind of an orange, a covering, a concealment underneath which are the juices and fibers of millions of years of evolution. My point is that even less developed nervous systems, such as those of a neonate or a primate, have many networks and components that are similar in structure and function to the fully human level of experience of being-in-the-world. But they lack the awareness and care structure characteristic of human life in history and culture.

My contention is that, in many respects, the nervous system operates by way of meaning without understanding, like the latent content of a dream, like a world before it is born, like a work of art without a creator or audience. In large measure, nervous systems may not "think" or "care" but they have meaningful structures and potentials so well-formed that they can get an organism to see, walk, talk, play the piano, undergo moods, and when slightly mad, like Woyzeck, speculate on the meaning of existence.

A considerable amount of learning and memory, perhaps most of it, is acquired outside of consciousness and language, never articulated but nevertheless encoded in neural networks. Neuropsychologists call such learning and recall, procedural learning. We know and learn a great deal without words. We acquire skills and feeling states implicitly without thinking about them. Riding a bicycle, reading a facial expression, using our hand to grasp an object, are all learned with a minimum of cognition. There is a striking similarity between the neuropsychologist's idea of procedural learning and Heidegger's view that most of what we know is not through thinking but present "at hand," a part of our being-in-the-world. As Polanyi (1966) said, "We know more than we can tell." This is the "unthought known" about which psychoanalyst Bollas (1987) has written. It is non-conscious meaning without understanding. For Heidegger, it is *Dasein*, being-in-the-world, concealed, but always at hand.

It is thus possible to make the case that *non-conscious, implicit meanings without understanding constitute the neural matrix of the unconscious*. Certain aspects of implicit learning become conscious as images, perceptions, words, ideas. Those which are unpleasant, undesirable, or socially unacceptable become detached from them, and return to the matrix of implicit meanings. They are un-conscious. Everything emerges from meaning without understanding, and some of it goes back to that state. Transference is the emergence of implicit meanings from childhood relationships expressed as "procedure," action, without consciousness and words to identify it as such. The analyst's interpretations add the words and images that promote the patient's insight.

An apt metaphor for the exchange of meanings between conscious and unconscious systems is Freud's (1925a) "mystic writing pad." He compared the unconscious to a plaything where the child writes a note on translucent wax paper that sticks to a blackened base wherever the script occurs. The child erases the note by lifting the paper from the base, but a trace of the note is forever etched in the base. The mystic writing pad analogy to the unconscious is relevant to hermeneutics in that, unlike Freud's other metaphors, there is no mention of physical "forces" that "push" conscious experience back into the unconscious. Meanings are unconscious simply as a "trace." As mentioned earlier, the notion of the "trace" is utilized in neuroscience as well as hermeneutics.

Psychoanalysis and the future of neuroscience

The prominent neurologist Oliver Sacks advocated for a consilience of philosophy and neuroscience. According to Sacks (1984, pp. 177–179), "Neuropsychology is admirable, but it excludes the *psyche*—it excludes the subject, it excludes the active, living 'I' ... What we need now, and need for the future, is a neurology of self, of identity ... a 'clinical ontology' or 'existential neurology.'"

If, in addition to its functional, anatomical, and homeostatic structure, the nervous system evolved on the basis of implicit interpretations, meanings without understanding, then it is possible that psychoanalysis may, in the future, be able to contribute a good deal more to neuroscience than it has in the past. Through its lens that projects "beams of intense darkness" (Grotstein, 1993b) into the depths of the mind, psychoanalysis should be able to identify phenomena of non-conscious meanings whose neural correlates could be investigated by neuroscientists. To some extent, this process has already begun. Empathy and attunement have been linked to mirror neurons. The repetition compulsion has been tentatively linked to neurophysiological events (van der Kolk, 1989). The work of Damasio on emotions and that of Kandel (2007) on memory are informed by knowledge first discovered through psychoanalysis. Such work has taken phenomena which are observed in the consulting room and linked them to events in the nervous system. In this way, a bridge is being formed between psychoanalytic interpretation and the brain.

The expanding use of brain imaging may provide one way of furthering the building of such a bridge. Some clinical phenomena can be produced under laboratory conditions and brain activity studied using functional imaging. Which areas of the brain are activated by the child's use of a transitional object? Researchers could give child subjects a teddy bear and other toys and see what brain regions become active. What brain centers become active when an analyst makes an interpretation that resonates meaningfully in the patient? What happens in the brain when a facial expression evinces shame? What is the difference between the brain in the paranoid-schizoid position versus the depressive position? And so on. Through the analysis of brain activity, psychoanalysts and neuroscientists working together can begin to grasp how non-conscious meanings play out in the nervous system, recognizing it as the beginning of an expanded partnership between the two disciplines.

The use of introspective psychology to describe unconscious meanings which neuroscientists can investigate has been advocated by Varela (Varela, Thompson, & Rosch, 1992). Before his untimely death, he introduced the concept of neurophenomenology, based on the writings of Husserl and Merleau-Ponty. In order to discover phenomena for neuroscientists to investigate, he advocated rigorous introspection of subjective experience, for example, to learn more precisely how the perception of an apple or of a person is formed by the nervous system. Varela advocated an embodied phenomenology in which human cognition and consciousness can be understood in terms of the enactive structures in which they arise, namely the body and the experienced lifeworld. Psychoanalysts can add phenomena of memory, fantasy, dreams, and other manifestations at the horizon of the unconscious to enrich such descriptions worthy of study by neuroscientists.

Oliver Sacks's dream of a "clinical ontology" or "existential neurology" is thus within the realm of possibility, and psychoanalysts would be among the best data gatherers for such a new science. For example, self psychologists and relational psychoanalysts could contribute descriptions of existential features of transference, narcissism, authentic engagement, maternal care, or the Oedipal complex which can be investigated in terms of brain activity. Implicit, non-conscious learning is closely related to "being-in-the-world," to ontology, and psychoanalysts are, among other things, researchers of non-conscious learning.

Towards a unification of natural science and human understanding

Up to now, neuroscience has consisted of the study of the apparently passive "blind forces" of nature, and psychoanalysis is based on the study of meanings that involve agency, imagination, motivation, and will. Freud wanted to bring these two worlds together, and made a strong start. But the conceptual tools for such integration have proved elusive in all aspects of human endeavor. For psychoanalysis and neuroscience to work in tandem, the difference between scientific explanation of natural events and hermeneutical understanding of meaningful human experience must ultimately be negotiated.

This reconciliation is a long way from full realization, but it appears that the natural sciences as such are increasingly crossing the divide between cause and effect relationships and meaningful configurations of experience. The quantum inseparability of observer and observed is bringing the two valences into conjunction at the subatomic level. At least one neuroscientist (Lowenstein, 2013) has proposed that some aspects of the nervous system involve quantum phenomena. In particular, he reasons that the interaction between observer and observed, so central to quantum theory, are partly the result of neural molecular phenomena at the subatomic level. DNA is capable of constructing a human mind, suggesting that the genes contain templates for consciousness and cognition. After all, macromolecules interacting with the environment contain the information necessary to produce a psychoanalyst! Although a long way off, the possibility of grasping how meaning and understanding emerge from molecular structure is today a believable if distant vision.

In general, science is relying increasingly on models based on information theory as a supplement to those based on force and momentum (Gleick, 2011, pp. 355–372). Indeed, more than forty years ago, Peterfreund and Schwartz (1971) proposed an information theoretical model of psychoanalysis. And now, information theory is just beginning to address hermeneutics (Gleick, 2011, p. 417). When—a long way into the future—information theory can define the architecture of complex meaningful structures, the gap between science and hermeneutics will be significantly reduced. At that point, psychoanalysis may come closer to neuroscience than Freud could have anticipated. And Sacks's "clinical ontology" or "existential neurology" may fully emerge in neurophilosophy. Although the "marriage" between psychoanalysis and neuroscience has been uneasy, it is possible that if they remain in active dialogue with one another, and incorporate into their relationship what the mistress, philosophical hermeneutics, has to offer, reconciliation may occur.

REFERENCES

Abraham, J. (1996). *The Language of Winnicott: A Dictionary of Winnicott's Use of Words*. London: Karnac.

Abraham, K. (1927). The process of introjection in melancholia: two stages of the oral phase of the libido. In: D. Bryan & A. Strachey (Trans.), *Selected Papers of Karl Abraham, M. D.* (pp. 442–452). London: Hogarth.

Ainsworth, M. D. S., Blehar, M. C., Waters, E., & Wall, S. (1978). *Patterns of Attachment: A Psychological Study of the Strange Situation*. Hillsdale, NJ: Lawrence Erlbaum Associates.

Alanen, Y. O. (2009). The Schreber case and Freud's double-edged influence on the psychoanalytic approach to psychosis. In: Y. O. Alanen, M. González de Chávez, A. S. Silver, & B. Martindale (Eds.), *Psychotherapeutic Approaches to Schizophrenic Psychoses: Past, Present and Future* (pp. 23–27). London: Routledge.

Amacher, P. (1965). *Freud's Neurological Education and Its Influence on Psychoanalytic Theory. Psychological Issues* 4(4), Monograph 16. New York: International Universities Press.

Apprey, M. (1999). Reinventing the self in the face of received transgenerational hatred in the African American community. *Journal of Applied Psychoanalytic Studies, 1*(2): 131–143.

Aristotle. *The Rhetoric and Poetics of Aristotle*. (W. R. Roberts, I., Bywater, & E. Corbett (Trans.). New York: Modern Library, 1984.

282

Aron, L. (1996). *A Meeting of Minds: Mutuality in Psychoanalysis*. Hillsdale, NJ: Analytic Press.

Aron, L., & Mitchell, S. (Eds.) (1999). *Relational Psychoanalysis, Volume 1: The Emergence of a Tradition*. London: Routledge.

Atwood, G. E., & Stolorow, R. D. (1993). *Structures of Subjectivity: Explorations in Psychoanalytic Phenomenology*. New York: Routledge.

Atwood, G. E., Orange, D. M., & Stolorow, R. D. (2002). Shattered worlds/psychotic states: A post-Cartesian view of the experience of personal annihilation. *Psychoanalytic Psychology, 19*(2): 281–306.

Bacal, H. A., & Newman, K. M. (1990). *Theories of Object Relations: Bridges to Self Psychology*. New York: Columbia University Press.

Bakan, D. (1958). *Sigmund Freud and the Jewish Mystical Tradition*. Princeton, NJ: D. van Nostrand.

Balint, M. (1968). *The Basic Fault: Therapeutic Aspects of Regression*. London: Tavistock.

Baranger, M., & Baranger, W. (1961–1962). La situation analitico como campo dinamico. In: *Problemas del Campo Psiconalitico* (pp. 124–164). Buenos Aires, Argentina: Kargieman, 1969.

Bartnes, C. (2010). Freud's The "Uncanny" and deconstructive criticism: Intellectual uncertainty and delicacy of perception. *Psychoanalysis and History, 12*(1): 29–53.

Bartole, T. (2011). Freud on touch: Thinking sexuality in anthropology. *Esercizi Filosofici, 6*: 376–387.

Bass, A. (2006). *Interpretation and Difference: The Strangeness of Care*. Stanford, CA: Stanford University Press.

Basso, E. (1982). The Finnegan Talmud. *Chicago Review, 33*(2): 69–75.

Bergson, H. (1999). *Duration and Simultaneity* (R. Durie, Ed.). Manchester, UK: Clinamen Press.

Berke, J. H., & Schneider, S. (2008). *Centers of Power: The Convergence of Psychoanalysis and Kabbalah*. Lanham, MD: Jason Aronson.

Berlin, I. (1976). *Vico and Herder: Two Studies of the History of Ideas*. New York: Vintage.

Billow, R. M. (2010). *Resistance, Rebellion, and Refusal in Groups: The 3 Rs*. London: Karnac.

Bion, W. R. (1959). *Experiences in Groups*. London: Tavistock.

Bion, W. R. (1961). *Experiences in Groups*. London: Tavistock.

Bion, W. R. (1962a). *Learning from Experience*. London: William Heinemann Medical.

Bion, W. R. (1962b). A theory of thinking. *International Journal of Psychoanalysis, 43*: 306–310.

Bion, W. R. (1963). *Elements of Psychoanalysis*. New York: Basic Books.

Bion, W. R. (1966). *Transformations*. London: Karnac Classics.

Bion, W. R. (1967). *Second Thoughts*. London: Heinemann.

Bion, W. R. (1970). *Attention and Interpretation*. London: Tavistock.

Bion, W. R. (1975, 1977, 1979). *A Memoir of the Future*. London: Karnac, 1990.

Bion, W. R. (1977). *Two Papers: The Grid and Caesura*. Rio de Janiero, Argentina: Imago Editora.

Bion, W. R. (1982). *The Long Weekend: 1897–1919*. Abingdon, UK: Fleetwood Press.

Bion, W. R. (1992). *Cogitations* (F. Bion, Ed.). London: Karnac.

Blank, G., & Blank, R. (1994). *Ego Psychology (second edition)*. New York: Columbia University Press.

Blass, R. (2011). Introduction to "On the value of 'late Bion' to analytic theory and practice." *International Journal of Psychoanalysis, 92*: 1081–1088.

Bleger, J. (1967). Psycho-analysis of the psycho-analytic frame. *International Journal of Psychoanalysis, 48*(4): 511–519.

Bohm, D. (1980). *Wholeness and the Implicate Order*. London: Routledge.

Bohm, D. (1996). *On Dialogue* (L. Nichol, Ed.). London: Routledge.

Bollas, C. (1987). *The Shadow of the Object: Psychoanalysis of the Unthought Known*. New York: Columbia University Press.

Bonnano, G. A. (2004). Loss, trauma, and human resilience: Have we underestimated the human capacity to thrive after extremely aversive events? *American Psychologist, 29*(1): 20–28.

Bowie, A. (2010). Friedrich Wilhelm Joseph von Schelling. *Stanford Encyclopedia of Philosophy*. Web page: http://plato.stanford.edu/entries/schelling/ (last accessed June 4, 2013).

Bowlby, J. (1969). *Attachment and Loss*. New York: Basic Books.

Brazelton, T. B. (1980). Behavioral competence of the newborn infant. In: P. Taylor (Ed.), *Parent–Infant Relationships* (pp. 69–86). New York: Grune & Stratton.

Breuer, J., & Freud, S. (1895d). *Studies on Hysteria. S. E., 2*. London: Hogarth.

Brown, L. (2011). *Intersubjective Processes and the Unconscious*. London: Routledge.

Buber, M. (1970). *I and Thou* (W. Kauffman, Ed.). New York: Charles Scribner's Sons.

Buchner, G. (1963). *Complete Plays and Prose* (C. R. Mueller, Trans.). New York: Hill & Wang.

Churchland, P. S. (1096). *Neurophilosophy: Toward A Unified Science of the Brain*. Cambridge, MA: The MIT Press.

Cixous, H. (1972). Fiction and its phantoms: A reading of Freud's Das Unheimliche [The "Uncanny"], (R. Denommé, Trans.). *New Literary History, 7*(3) (1976): 525548.

Cohen, B. D., & Schermer, V. L. (2004). Self-transformation and the unconscious in contemporary psychoanalytic therapy: The problem of "depth" within a relational and intersubjective perspective. *Psychoanalytic Psychology, 21*(4): 580–600.

Coles, R. (2003). *Children of Crisis.* New York: Back Bay.

Coltart, N. (2000). *Slouching Towards Bethlehem.* New York: Other Press.

Conze, E. (Trans.) (2003). *Perfect Wisdom: The Short Prajnaparamita Texts.* Totnes, UK: Buddhist Publishing Group.

Costelloe, T. (2012). Giambattista Vico. *Stanford Encyclopedia of Philosophy.* Web page: http://plato.stanford.edu/entries/vico/ (last accessed June 6, 2013).

Cozolino, L. (2002). *The Neuroscience of Psychotherapy: Building and Rebuilding the Human Brain.* New York: W. W. Norton.

Cozolino, L. (2006). *The Neuroscience of Human Relationships: Attachment and the Developing Social Brain.* New York: W. W. Norton.

Crastnopol, M. (1997). When does a theory stop being itself?: Commentary on Susan H. Sands's paper. *Psychoanalytic Dialogues, 7:* 683–690.

Cronenberg, D. (Dir.) (2011). *A Dangerous Method.* Los Angeles: Sony Pictures Classics.

Damasio, A. (1999). *The Feeling of What Happens: Body and Emotion in the Making of Consciousness.* New York: Harcourt Brace.

Damasio, A. (2003). *Looking for Spinoza: Joy, Sorrow, and the Feeling Brain.* New York: Mariner.

Darwin, C. (1871). *The Descent of Man and Selection in Relation to Sex. Vols. 1 & 2.* London: John Murray.

Dennett, D. C. (1991). *Consciousness Explained.* Boston: Little, Brown.

Derrida, J. (1978). *Writing and Difference* (A. Bass, Trans.). Chicago: University of Chicago Press.

Derrida, J. (1981). *Positions* (A. Bass, Trans.). Chicago: University of Chicago Press.

Derrida, J. (1998). *Resistances of Psychoanalysis* (P. Kamuf, P. -A. Brault, & M. Naas, Trans.). Stanford, CA: Stanford University Press.

Deutsch, F. (1957). A footnote to Freud's "Fragment of an Analysis of a Case of Hysteria". *Psychoanalytic Quarterly, 26*(2): 159–167.

Doolittle, H. (H. D.) (1956). *Tribute to Freud: With Unpublished Letters by Freud to the Author.* New York: Pantheon.

Edelman, G. (1987). *Neural Darwinism: The Theory of Neuronal Group Selection.* New York: Basic Books.

Eigen, M. (1985). Toward Bion's starting point: Between catastrophe and faith. *International Journal of Psychoanalysis, 66:* 321–330.

Eigen, M. (1998). *The Psychoanalytic Mystic.* London: Free Association.

Eigen, M. (2012). *Kabbalah and Psychoanalysis.* London: Karnac.

Einstein, A., & Infeld, L. (1938). *The Evolution of Physics: From Early Concept to Relativity and Quanta.* Cambridge: Cambridge University Press.

Eissler, K. (1953). The effect of the structure of the ego on psychoanalytic technique. *Journal of the American Psychoanalytic Association,* 1: 104–143.

Eliade, M. (1981). *A History of Religious Ideas, Vol. 1: From the Stone Age to the Eleusinian Mysteries.* Chicago: University of Chicago Press.

Eliot, T. S. (1964). *The Cocktail Party.* New York: Mariner (Harvest).

Ellenberger, H. E. (1979). *The Discovery of the Unconscious: The History and Evolution of Dynamic Psychiatry.* New York: Basic Books.

Epstein, M. (1996). *Thoughts Without a Thinker: Psychotherapy from a Buddhist Perspective.* New York: Basic Books.

Epstein, M. (2001). *Going on Being: Buddhism and the Way of Change.* New York: Harmony.

Erikson, E. H. (1950). *Childhood and Society.* New York: W. W. Norton.

Erikson, E. H. (1958). *Young Man Luther: A Study in Psychoanalysis and History.* New York: W. W. Norton.

Erikson, E. H. (1993). *Gandhi's Truth: On the Origins of Militant Nonviolence.* New York: W. W. Norton.

Feldman, H. (1974). A psychoanalytic addition to human nature. *Psychoanalytic Review, 61*(1): 133–139.

Fenichel, O. (1945). *The Psychoanalytic Theory of the Neuroses.* New York: W. W. Norton.

Ferenczi, S. (1932). The confusion of tongues between adults and children: The language of tenderness and passion. In: M. Balint (Ed.), E. Mosbacher (Trans.), *Final Contributions to the Problems and Methods of Psychoanalysis* (pp. 156–167). London: Karnac, 1980.

Ferro, A., & Basile, R. (2009). *The Analytic Field: A Clinical Concept.* London: Karnac.

Feynman, R. (2005). *The Pleasure of Finding Things Out.* New York: Basic Books.

Firestein, S. K. (2001). *Termination in Psychoanalysis and Psychotherapy (revised edition).* Madison, CT: International Universities Press.

Fonagy, P. (2001). *Attachment Theory and Psychoanalysis.* New York: Other Press.

Fonagy, P., Gergely, G., Jurist, E. L., & Target, M. (2002). *Affect Regulation, Mentalization, and the Development of the Self.* New York: Other Press.

Forster, M. (2002). Friedrich Daniel Ernst Schleiermacher. *Stanford Encyclopedia of Philosophy.* Web page: http://plato.stanford.edu/entries/schleiermacher/ (last accessed June 22, 2013).

Forster, M. (2007). Johann Gottfried von Herder. *Stanford Encyclopedia of Philosophy.* Web page: http://plato.stanford.edu/entries/herder/ (last accessed June 6, 2013).

Freedman, N., Hoffenberg, J. D., Vorus, N., & Frosch, A. (1999). The effectiveness of psychoanalytic psychotherapy: The role of treatment duration, frequency of sessions, and the therapeutic relationship. *Journal of the American Psychoanalytic Association, 47*(3): 741–772.

Frei, H. W. (1980). *The Eclipse of the Biblical Narrative: A Study in Eighteenth and Nineteenth Century Hermeneutics.* New Haven, CT: Yale University Press.

Freud, A. (1946). *The Ego and the Mechanisms of Defense.* New York: International Universities Press.

Freud, S. (1900a). *The Interpretation of Dreams. S. E., 4 and 5.* London: Hogarth.

Freud, S. (1909b). *Analysis of a phobia in a five-year-old boy. S. E., 10*: 3–152. London: Hogarth.

Freud, S. (1910e). *The antithetical meaning of primal words. S. E., 11*: 153–162. London: Hogarth.

Freud, S. (1911c). *Psycho-analytic notes on an autobiographical account of a case of paranoia (Dementia Paranoides). S. E., 12*: 3–84. London: Hogarth.

Freud, S. (1913j). *The claims of psycho-analysis to scientific interest. S. E., 13*: 165–192. London: Hogarth.

Freud, S. (1915d). *Repression. S. E., 14*: 146–158. London: Hogarth.

Freud, S. (1915e). *The unconscious. S. E., 14.* London: Hogarth.

Freud, S. (1918b). *From the history of an infantile neurosis. S. E., 17*: 3–124. London: Hogarth.

Freud, S. (1919h). *The "uncanny". S. E., 17.* London: Hogarth.

Freud, S. (1920g). *Beyond the Pleasure Principle. S. E., 18.* London: Hogarth.

Freud, S. (1921c). *Group Psychology and the Analysis of the Ego. S. E., 18*: 67–145. London: Hogarth.

Freud, S. (1925a). *A note upon the "mystic writing pad". S. E., 19*: 227–234. London: Hogarth.

Freud, S. (1927c). *The Future of an Illusion. S. E., 21.* London: Hogarth.

Freud, S. (1930a). *Civilization and Its Discontents. S. E., 21.* London: Hogarth.

Freud, S. (1950a). *A project for a scientific psychology. S. E., 1*: 295–390. London: Hogarth.

Fromm, E. (1957). *The Forgotten Language: An Introduction to the Understanding of Dreams, Fairy Tales, and Myths.* New York: Grove Press.

Gadamer, H. G. (1960). *Truth and Method (2nd edition).* (J. Weinsheimer & D. G. Marshall, Trans.). New York: Continuum, 1989.

Gallese, V., Fadigia, L., Fogassi, L., & Rizzolati, G. (1996). Action recognition in the premotor cortex. *Brain, 119*(Pt.2): 592–609.

Gardiner, M. (Ed.) (1971). *The Wolf-Man and Sigmund Freud.* New York: Basic Books.

Gayle, R. (2009). Co-creating meaningful structures within long-term psychotherapy group culture. *International Journal of Group Psychotherapy, 59*: 311–333.

Gergen, J. K. (1991). *The Saturated Self: Dilemmas of Identity in Contemporary Life*. New York: Basic Books.

Gill, M. (1983). *Analysis of Transference: Theory and Technique*. New York: International Universities Press.

Giorgi, A. (2009). *The Descriptive Phenomenological Method in Psychology: A Modified Husserlian Approach*. Pittsburgh, PA: Duquesne University Press.

Gleick, J. (2011). *The Information*. New York: Pantheon.

Glover, E. (1931). The therapeutic effect of inexact interpretation: A contribution to the theory of suggestion. *International Journal of Psychoanalysis, 12*: 397–411.

Goldstein, K. (1939). *The Organism: A Holistic Approach to Biology Derived from Pathological Data in Man*. New York: American Book Company.

Graves, M., & Schermer, V. L. (1999). The wounded male persona and the mysterious feminine in the poetry of James Wright: A study in the transformation of the self. *Psychoanalytic Review, 85*(6): 849–870.

Greenberg, J. R., & Mitchell, S. (1983). *Object Relations in Psychoanalytic Theory*. Cambridge, MA: Harvard University Press.

Greenson, R. R. (1965). The problem of working through. In: *Explorations in Psychoanalysis* (pp. 256–257). New York: International Universitites Press, 1978.

Greenson, R. R. (1967). *The Technique and Practice of Pscyhoanalysis. Vol. 1*. New York: International Universities Press.

Grondin, J. (2012). *Introduction to Metaphysics: From Parmenides to Levinas*. New York: Columbia University Press.

Grotstein, J. S. (1978a). Inner space: Its dimensions and coordinates. *International Journal of Psychoanalysis, 15*: 110–169.

Grotstein, J. S. (1978b). *Freud and Klein: Divergencies within a continuum*. New York: Psychotherapy Tape Library.

Grotstein, J. S. (1986). The dual track: Contribution toward a neurobehavioral model of cerebral processing. *Psychiatric Clinics of North America, 9*(2): 353–365.

Grotstein, J. S. (1993a). Towards the concept of the transcendent position: Reflections on some of "the unborns" in Bion's "Cogitations." *Journal of Melanie Klein and Object Relations, 11*(2): 55–73.

Grotstein, J. S. (1993b). *A Beam of Intense Darkness: Wilfred Bion's Legacy to Psychoanalysis*. London: Karnac, 2007.

Grotstein, J. S. (1997). "Fearful symmetry" and the calipers of the infinite geometer: Matte-Blanco's legacy to our conception of the unconscious. *Journal of Melanie Klein and Object Relations, 15*(4): 631–646.

Grotstein, J. S. (2000). *Who is the Dreamer Who Dreams the Dream? A Study of Psychic Presences.* Hillsdale, NJ: The Analytic Press.

Grunbaum, A. (1984). *The Foundations of Psychoanalysis: A Philosophical Critique.* (Pittsburgh Series in Philosophy and History of Science). Berkeley, CA: University of California Press.

Guenther, L. (2006). "Like a maternal body": Emmanuel Levinas and the motherhood of Moses. *Hypatia, 21*(1): 119–136.

Guntrip, H. (1969). *Object Relations and the Self.* New York: International Universities Press.

Guntrip, H. (1975). My experience of analysis with Fairbairn and Winnicott (How complete a result does psychoanalytic therapy achieve?). *International Review of Psycho-Analysis, 2*: 145–156.

Handelman, S. A. (1982). *The Slayers of Moses: The Emergence of Rabbinic Interpretation in Modern Literary Theory.* Albany, NY: State University of New York Press.

Harshav, B. (Ed.) (2003). *Marc Chagall on Art and Culture.* Stanford, CA: Stanford University Press.

Hartmann, H. (1939). *Ego Psychology and the Problem of Adaptation.* New York: International Universities Press.

Heidegger, M. (1927). *Being and Time.* (J. Macquarrie & E. Robinson, Trans.). San Franscisco: HarperCollins, 1962.

Heidegger, M. (1929). *Basic Writings.* (D. F. Krell, Ed.). London: Harper Perennial Modern Thought, 2008.

Heidegger, M. (1946). *Poetry, Language, Thought.* (A. Hofstadter, Trans.). New York: Harper and Row, 1971.

Heidegger, M. (1959–1969). *The Zollikon Seminars: Protocols, Conversations, Letters* (M. Boss, Ed., R. Askay & F. Mayr, Trans.). Evanston, IL: Northwestern University Press, 2001.

Heidelberger, M. (2004). *Nature from Within: Gustav Theodor Fechner and His Psychophysical Worldview* (C. Klohr, Trans.). Pittsburgh, PA: University of Pittsburgh Press.

Herman, J., & van der Kolk, B. (1987). Traumatic antecedents of borderline personality disorder. In: B. van der Kolk (Ed.), *Psychological Trauma* (pp. 111–126). Washington, DC: American Psychiatric Press.

Hoffman, I. Z. (1983). The patient as interpreter of the analyst's experience. *Contemporary Psychoanalysis, 19*: 389–422.

Hubel, D. H., & Wiesel, T. N. (2005). *Brain and Visual Perception: The Story of a 25-Year Collaboration.* Oxford: Oxford University Press.

Husserl, E. (1936). *The Crisis of European Sciences and Transcendental Phenomenology* (D. Carr, Trans.). Evanston, IL: Northwestern University Press, 1970.

Husserl, E. (1900–1901). *Logical Investigations* (2 vols.) (D. Moran, Ed.). London: Routledge, 2001.

Iacoboni, M. (2008). *Mirroring People: The New Science of How We Connect with Others.* New York: Farrar, Straus and Giroux.

Israels, H., & Schatzman, M. (1993). The seduction theory. *History of Psychiatry, 4:* 23–59.

Jacobs, M. (1995). *D. W. Winnicott.* London: Sage.

James, W. (1890). *The Principles of Psychology, Vol. 1 & 2.* New York: Dover, 1950.

James, W. (1902). *The Varieties of Religious Experience.* New York: Longmans, Green.

Jones, E. (1953). *The Life and Work of Sigmund Freud (3 vols.).* New York: BasicBooks.

Joseph, B. (1985). Transference: The total situation. *International Journal of Psychoanalysis, 66*(4): 447–454.

Julien, P. (1994). *Jacques Lacan's Return to Freud: The Real, the Symbolic, and the Imaginary.* New York: New York University Press.

Jung, C. G. (2009). *The Red Book* (S. Shamdasani, Ed., M. Kyburz, J. Peck, & S. Shamdasani, Eds.). New York: Philemon Series & W. W. Norton.

Kandel, E. R. (2007). *In Search of Memory: The Emergence of a New Science of Mind.* New York: W. W. Norton.

Kandel, E. R. (2012). *The Age of Insight: The Quest to Understand the Unconscious in Art, Mind, and Brain, from Vienna 1900 to the Present.* New York: Random House.

Karen, R. (1994). *Becoming Attached: First Relationships and How They Shape Our Capacity to Love.* Oxford: Oxford University Press.

Kauffman, J. (Ed.) (2012). *Loss of the Assumptive World: A Theory of Traumatic Loss.* London: Routledge.

Kernberg, O. F. (1975). *Borderline Conditions and Pathological Narcissism.* New York: Jason Aronson.

King, P. H. M., & Steiner, R. (1991). *The Freud-Klein Controversies 1941–1945.* London: Tavistock-Routledge, New Library of Psychoanalysis.

Klein, M. (1940). Mourning and its relation to manic-depressive states. *International Journal of Psychoanalysis, 21:* 125–153.

Klein, M. (1946). Notes on some schizoid mechanisms. In: *Envy and Gratitude and Other Works: 1946–1963* (pp. 1–24). New York: Delta, 1977.

Klein, M. (1955). The psychoanalytic play technique: Its history and significance. In: *The Writings of Melanie Klein, Vol. 3: Envy and Gratitude and Other Works 1946–1963* (pp. 122–140). New York: Free Press, 1975.

Kleinberg, E. (2010). Freud and Levinas: Talmud and psychoanalysis before the letter. In: A. D. Richards (Ed.), *The Jewish World of Sigmund Freud: Essays on Cultural Roots and the Problem of Religious Identity* (pp. 112–125). Jefferson, NC: McFarland.

Kohut, H, (1959). Introspection, empathy, and psychoanalysis. *Journal of the American Psychoanalytic Association, 7:* 459–483.

Kohut, H. (1971). *The Analysis of the Self.* New York: International Universities Press.

Kohut, H. (1977). *The Restoration of the Self.* New York: International Universities Press.

Kovacs, M. G. (Trans.) (1998). *The Epic of Gilgamesh.* Web page: http://www.ancienttexts.org/library/mesopotamian/gilgamesh/tab1.htm (last accessed May 9, 2013).

Kuhn, T. (1962). *The Structure of Scientific Revolutions.* Chicago: University of Chicago Press.

Lacan, J. (1977). *Ecrits: A Selection* (A. Sheridan, Trans.). New York: W. W. Norton.

Lacan, J. (1981). *The Language of the Self: The Function of Language in Psychoanalysis.* Baltimore, MD: Johns Hopkins University Press.

Lake, J. (2007). *Textbook of Integrative Mental Health.* New York: Thieme Medical Publishers.

Lakoff, G., & Johnson, M. (1980). *Metaphors We Live By.* Chicago: University of Chicago Press.

Langs, R. (1976). *The Bipersonal Field.* New York: Jason Aronson.

Langs, R. (1992). *Science, Systems, and Psychoanalysis.* London: Karnac.

Laplanche, J. (1976). *Life and Death in Psychoanalysis* (J. Mehlman, Trans.). Baltimore, MD: Johns Hopkins University Press.

Lawlor, L. (2012). *Early Twentieth Century Continental Philosophy.* Bloomington, IN: Indiana University Press.

Lemma, A. (2008). *Introduction to the Practice of Psychoanalytic Psychotherapy.* New York: Wiley.

Levinas, I. (1970). *Alterity and Transcendence* (M. B. Smith, Trans.). New York: Columbia University Press, 1999.

Lévi-Strauss, C. (1958). *Structural Anthropology.* C. Jacobson & B. Grundfest (Trans.). London: Penguin, 1968.

Lévi-Strauss, C. (1972). The structural study of myth. In: R. DeGeorge & F. DeGeorge (Eds.), *The Structuralists from Marx to Lévi-Strauss* (pp. 169–194). New York: Anchor.

Levy, D. (1988). Grünbaum's Freud. *Inquiry: An Interdisciplinary Journal of Philosophy, 31*(2): 193–215.

Little, M. I. (1990). *Psychotic Anxieties and Containment: A Personal Record of an Analysis with Winnicott.* New York: Jason Aronson.

Livingston, M. S., & Livingston, L. R. (2006). Sustained empathic focus and the clinical application of self-psychological theory in group psychotherapy. *International Journal of Group Psychotherapy, 56:* 67–85.

Loparic, Z. (1999). Heidegger and Winnicott. *Natureza Humana*, 1(1): 103–135.

Lowenstein, W. R. (2013). *Physics in Mind: A Quantum View of the Brain.* New York: Basic Books.

Luborsky, L., & Luborsky, E. (2006). *Research & Psychotherapy: The Vital Link.* Lanham, MD: Jason Aronson.

Lyotard, J. (1974). *The Postmodern Condition: A Report on Knowledge.* Minneapolis, MN: University of Minnesota Press.

Mahler, M. S., Pine, F., & Bergman, A. (1975). *The Psychological Birth of the Human Infant.* New York: Basic Books.

Makkreel, R. A. (2011). The continuing relevance and generative nature of Dilthey's thought. In: H. -U. Lessing, R. A. Makkreel, & R. Pozzo (Eds.), *Recent Contributions to Dilthey's Philosophy of the Human Sciences.* Stuttgart, Germany: Frommann-Holzboog.

Matte Blanco, I. (1975). *The Unconscious as Infinite Sets: An Essay in Bi-logic.* London: Duckworth.

McClendon, D. T., & Burlingame, G. M. (2011). Has the magic of psychotherapy disappeared? Integrating evidence-based practice into therapist awareness and development. In: H. Bernard, R. Klein, & V. Schermer (Eds.), *On Becoming a Psychotherapist: The Personal and Professional Journey* (pp. 190–211). New York: Oxford University Press.

Mead, G. H. (1934). *Mind, Self, and Society: From the Perspective of a Social Behaviorist* (C. W. Morris, Ed.). Chicago: University of Chicago Press.

Mead, M. (1930). *Coming of Age in Samoa.* New York: William Morrow.

Merleau-Ponty, M. (1963). *The Structure of Behavior* (A. L. Fisher, Trans.). Boston: Beacon Press.

Merleau-Ponty, M. (1968). *The Visible and the Invisible* (A. Lingis, Trans.). Evanston, IL: Northwestern University Press.

Merleau-Ponty, M. (1976). *Phenomenology of Perception* (C. Smith, Trans.). London: Routledge & Kegan Paul.

Merleau-Ponty, M. (2002). *Husserl at the Limits of Phenomenology* (L. Lawlor & B. Bergo, Eds.). Evanston, IL: Northwestern University Press.

Metzinger, T. (2003). *Being No One. The Self-Model Theory of Subjectivity.* Cambridge, MA: The MIT Press.

Metzinger, T. (2009). *The Ego Tunnel: The Science of the Mind and the Myth of the Self.* New York: Basic Books.

Mikulincer, M., & Shaver, P. R. (2010). *Attachment in Adulthood: Structure, Dynamics, and Change.* New York: Guilford.

Milner, M. (1969). *The Hands of the Living God: An Account of a Psychoanalytic Treatment.* New York: International Universities Press.

Mitchell, S. (1988). *Relational Concepts in Psychoanalysis: An Integration.* Cambridge, MA: Harvard University Press.

Moorhead, J. L. (Ed.) (1998). *Conversations of Goethe with Johann Peter Eckermann* (J. Oxenford, Trans.). Boston: Da Capo Press.

Moran, D. (2000). *Introduction to Phenomenology.* London: Routledge.

Murray, H. A. (2007). *Explorations in Personality. 70th Anniversary Edition.* New York: Oxford University Press.

Neumann, E. (1954). *The Origins and History of Consciousness.* Princeton, NJ: Princeton University Press.

Nietzsche, F. (1882). *The Gay Science, with a Prelude of Rhymes and an Appendix of Songs* (W. Kaufmann, Trans.). New York: Vintage, 1974.

Norris, C. (1988). *Derrida.* Cambridge, MA: Harvard University Press.

Ogden, T. H. (2004). The analytic third: Implications for psychoanalytic theory and technique. *Psychoanalytic Quarterly, 73*(1): 167–195.

Orange, D. M. (2010). *Thinking for Clinicians: Philosophical Resources for Contemporary Psychoanalysis and the Humanistic Psychotherapies.* New York: Routledge.

Orne, M. T. (1962). On the social psychology of the psychological experiment: With particular reference to demand characteristics and their implications. *American Psychologist, 17*(11): 776–783.

Patanjali. *The Yoga-Sutra of Patanjali* (C. Hartranft, Trans.). Boston: Shambhala, 2003.

Peterfreund, E., & Schwartz, J. T. (1971). *Information, Systems, and Psychoanalysis: An Evolutionary Biological Approach to Psychoanalytic Theory.* New York: International Universities Press.

Polanyi, M. (1966). *The Tacit Dimension.* Chicago: University of Chicago Press.

Polanyi, M. (1974). *Personal Knowledge: Towards a Post-Critical Philosophy.* Chicago: University of Chicago Press.

Pope, K. S. (1996). Memory, abuse, and science. Questioning claims about the false memory syndrome epidemic. *American Psychologist, 51*(9): 957–974.

Popper, K. (1959). *The Logic of Scientific Discovery.* London: Hutchinson.

Pribram, K. (1962). The neuropsychology of Sigmund Freud. In: A. J. Bachrach (Ed.), *Experimental Foundations of Clinical Psychology* (pp. 442–468). New York: BasicBooks.

Pyle, R. L. (2003). The good fight: psychoanalysis in the age of managed care. *Journal of the American Psychoanalytic Association, 51S*: 23–41.

Ramachandran, V. S. (1998). The perception of phantom limbs: The D. O. Hebb lecture. *Brain, 9*(121): 1603–1630.

Ramberg, B. (2003). Hermeneutics. *Stanford Encyclopedia of Philosophy.* Web page: http://plato.stanford.edu/entries/hermeneutics/ (last accessed June 3, 2013).

Richards, R. J. (2004). *The Romantic Conception of Life: Science and Philosophy in the Age of Goethe.* Chicago: University of Chicago Press.

Ricoeur, P. (1970). *Freud and Philosophy: An Essay on Interpretation.* New Haven, CT: Yale University Press.

Rodman, F. R. (2003). *Winnicott: Life and Work.* Cambridge, MA: Perseus.

Rogers, C. (1951). *Client-centered Therapy: Its Current Practice, Implications and Theory.* London: Constable.

Rollinger, R. D. (1999). *Husserl's Position in the School of Brentano.* New York: Springer.

Rorty, R. (1979). *Philosophy and the Mirror of Nature.* Princeton, NJ: Princeton University Press.

Rotenberg, M. (1991). *Dia-logo Therapy: Psychonarration and PaRDes.* Westport, CT: Praeger.

Rudnytsky, P. L. (2000). *Ferenczi's Turn in Psychoanalysis.* New York: New York University Press.

Sacks, O. (1984). *A Leg to Stand On.* New York: Touchstone.

Safranski, R. (1999). *Martin Heidegger: Between Good and Evil.* Cambridge, MA: Harvard University Press.

Sands, S. H. (1997). Self psychology and projective identification—whither shall they meet? A reply to the editors (1995). *Psychoanalytic Dialogues, 7*(5): 651–668.

Sands, S. H. (1998). Reply to Commentary. *Psychoanalytic Dialogues, 8*(5): 727–730.

Schafer, R. (1994). *Retelling A Life: Narration and Dialogue in Psychoanalysis.* New York: Basic Books.

Schermer, V. L. (1999). To know a mind: Freud, Oedipus, and epistemology. *Psychoanalytic Studies, 1*(2): 191–210.

Schermer, V. L. (2003). *Spirit and Psyche.* London: Jessica Kingsley.

Schermer, V. L. (2010). The subjectivity/objectivity/hermeneutical triad: The epistemological foundations of psychoanalysis and their relevance to contemporary pluralism. [Unpublished lecture.] York University Conference on Psychology, June 3–6.

Schermer, V. L. (2011). Interpreting psychoanalytic interpretation: A four-fold perspective. *Psychoanalytic Review, 98*(6): 835–858.

Searles, H. (1979). The patient as therapist to his analyst. In: *Countertransference and Related Subjects* (pp. 380–459). New York: International Universities Press.

Sellars, W. (1962). Philosophy and the scientific image of man. In: R. Colodny (Ed.), *Frontiers of Science and Philosophy* (pp. 35–78). Pittsburgh, PA: University of Pittsburgh Press.

Shanks, D. R. (1985). Hume on the perception of causality. *Hume Studies, 11*(1): 94–108.

Siegel, D. J. (2012). *The Developing Mind: How Relationships and the Brain Interact to Shape Who We Are (second edition).* New York: Guilford.

Simanowitz, V., & Pearce, P. (2003). *Personality Development*. Maidenhead, UK: Open University Press.

Snow, C. P. (1998). *The Two Cultures*. Cambridge: Cambridge University Press.

Sonne, J. (1992). Triadic transferences of pathological family images. *Journal of Marital and Family Therapy, 18*: 53–61.

Stern, D. N. (1985). *The Interpersonal World of the Infant*. New York: Basic Books.

Stern, D. N. (2002). *The First Relationship*. Cambridge, MA: Harvard Unversity Press.

Stern, D. N. (2007). The *Present Moment in Psychotherapy and Everyday Life*. New York: W. W. Norton.

Stolorow, R. D. (1994). The nature and therapeutic action of psychoanalytic interpretation. In: R. D. Stolorow, G. E. Atwood, & B. Brandchaft (Eds.), *The Intersubjective Perspective* (pp. 43–56). Northvale, NJ: Jason Aronson.

Stolorow, R. D. (2007). *Trauma and Human Existence: Autobiographical, Psychoanalytic, and Philosophical Reflections*. London: Routledge.

Stolorow, R. D. (2010). My long distance friendship with Heinz Kohut. *International Journal of Psychoanalytic Self Psychology, 5*(2): 177–183.

Stolorow, R. D. (2011). *World, Affectivity, Trauma: Heidegger and Post-Cartesian Psychoanalysis*. New York: Routledge.

Stolorow, R. D., & Atwood, G. E. (1979). *Faces in a Cloud: Subjectivity in Personality Theory*. New York: Jason Aronson.

Stolorow, R. D., Atwood, G. E., & Brandchaft, B. (Eds.) (1994). *The Intersubjective Perspective*. Northvale, NJ: Jason Aronson.

Stolorow, R. D., Atwood, G. E., & Orange, D. M. (2002). *Worlds of Experience: Interweaving Philosophical and Clinical Dimensions in Psychoanalysis*. New York: Basic Books.

Stolorow, R. D., Orange, D. M., & Atwood, G. E. (1998). Projective identification begone! Commentary on paper by Susan H. Sands. *Psychoanalytic Dialogues, 8*(5): 719–725.

Stone, L. (1961). *The Psychoanalytic Situation*. New York: International Universities Press.

Strasser, S. (1985). *Understanding and Explanation*. Pittsburgh, PA: Duquesne University Press.

Strozier, C. (2001). *Heinz Kohut: The Making of a Psychoanalyst*. New York: Farrar, Straus and Giroux.

Sullivan, H. S. (1953). *The Interpersonal Theory of Psychiatry*. New York: W. W. Norton.

Sulloway, F. J. (1979). *Freud, Biologist of the Mind: Beyond the Psychoanalytic Legend*. Cambridge, MA: Harvard University Press.

Symington, J., & Symington, N. (1996). *The Clinical Thinking of Wilfred Bion*. London: Routledge.

Tauber, A. I. (2010). *Freud: The Reluctant Philosopher*. Princeton, NJ: Princeton University Press.

Taylor, C. (1977). *Hegel*. Cambridge: Cambridge University Press.

Trevarthen, C. (1985). Facial expressions of emotion in mother–infant interaction. *Human Neurobiology*, 4(1): 21–32.

Van der Kolk, B. A. (1989). The compulsion to repeat the trauma. Re-enactment, revictimization, and masochism. *Psychiatric Clinics of North America*, 12(2): 389–411.

Van der Kolk, B. A. (1994). The body keeps the score: Memory and the evolving psychobiology of post-traumatic stress. *Harvard Review of Psychiatry*, 1(5): 253–265.

Varela, F. J., Thompson, E. T., & Rosch, E. (1992). *The Embodied Mind: Cognitive Science and Human Experience*. Cambridge, MA: The MIT Press.

Vattimo, G. (2010). *The Responsibility of the Philosopher* (F. D'Agostini, Ed., W. McCuaig, Trans.). New York: Columbia University Press, 2012.

Verene, D. P. (Ed.) (1987). *Vico and Joyce*. Albany, NY: State University of New York Press.

Vicedo, M. (2013). *The Nature and Nurture of Love: From Imprinting to Attachment in Cold War America*. Chicago: University of Chicago Press.

Vico, G. (1710). *De Antiquissima Italorum Aapientia ex Linguae Latinae Originibus Eruenda Libri Tres (On the Most Ancient Wisdom of the Italians Unearthed from the Origins of the Latin Language*, including *The Disputation with "The Giornale de' Letterati d'Italia"*) (L. M. Palmer, Trans.). Ithaca, NY: Cornell University Press, 1988.

Vico, G. (1725). *Scienza Nuova* (*The First New Science*) (L. Pompa, Ed. & Trans.). Cambridge: Cambridge University Press, 2002.

Volkan, V. (1988). *Six Steps in the Treatment of Borderline Personality Organization*. New York: Jason Aronson.

Vygotsky, L. (1978). *Mind in Society*. London: Harvard University Press.

Waldrop, M. M. (1992). *Complexity: The Emerging Science at the Edge of Chaos*. New York: Simon & Schuster.

Wallerstein, R. S. (2005). Will psychoanalytic pluralism be an enduring state of our discipline? *International Journal of Psychoanalysis, 86*: 623–626.

Wallin, D. (2007). *Attachment in Psychotherapy*. New York: Guilford.

Weigelt, S., Koldewyn, K., & Kanwisher, N. (2012). Face identity recognition in autism spectrum disorders: A review of behavioral studies. *Neuroscience and Biobehavioral Reviews, 36*: 1060–1084.

White, R. W. (1966). *Lives in Progress*. New York: Holt, Reinhart & Winston.

Whitehead, A. N., & Russell, B. (1910, 1912, 1913). *Principia Mathematica* (*Vols. 1, 2, and 3*). Cambridge: Cambridge University Press.

Whitman, W. (2001). *Song of Myself*. Mineola, NY: Dover Publications.

Williams, M. H. (1985). The tiger and "O." *Free Associations: Psychoanalysis, Groups, Politics, Culture, 1*: 33–56.

Wilson, E. O. (1999). *Consilience: The Unity of Knowledge.* New York: Vintage.

Winnicott, D. W. (1953). Transitional objects and transitional phenomena: A study of the first not-me possession. *International Journal of Psychoanalysis, 34*: 89–97.

Winnicott, D. W. (1958a). *Collected Papers: Through Paediatrics to Psychoanalysis.* London: Tavistock.

Winnicott, D. W. (1958b). The capacity to be alone. *International Journal of Psychoanalysis, 39*: 416–420.

Winnicott, D. W. (1963). The development of the capacity for concern. *Bulletin of the Menninger Clinic, 27*: 167–176.

Winnicott, D. W. (1965a). Communicating and not communicating leading to a study of certain opposites. In: *The Maturational Processes and the Facilitating Environment* (pp. 179–192). London: Hogarth.

Winnicott, D. W. (1965b). Ego distortion in terms of true and false self. In: *The Maturational Processes and the Facilitating Environment* (pp. 140–152). London: Hogarth.

Winnicott, D. W. (1969). The use of an object and relating through identifications. *International Journal of Psychoanalysis, 50*: 711–716.

Winnicott, D. W. (1971). *Therapeutic Consultations in Child Psychiatry.* New York: Basic Books.

Winnicott, D. W. (1974). Fear of breakdown. In: C. Winnicott, R. Shepherd, & M. Davis (Eds.), *Psychoanalytic Explorations: D. W. Winnicott* (pp. 87–95). Cambridge, MA: Harvard University Press.

Winnicott, D. W. (1976). *The Piggle: An Account of the Psychoanalytic Treatment of a Little Girl.* London: Penguin, 2008.

Wittgenstein, L. (1953). *Philosophical Investigations* (G. E. M. Anscombe, Trans.). Oxford: Blackwell.

Wolf, E. S. (1988). *Treating the Self: Elements of Clinical Self Psychology.* New York: Guilford.

Wright, J. (1975). James Wright: The art of poetry XIX. (Interview with Peter Stitt.) *Paris Review, 16*(62): 34–61.

Wright, J. (1990). *Above the River: The Complete Poems.* Middletown, CT: Wesleyan University Press Edition, Farrar, Straus and Giroux and University Press of New England.

Wurmser, L. (1978). *The Hidden Dimension: Psychodynamics in Compulsive Drug Use.* New York: Jason Aronson.

Youcha, I. (2013). Long term psychological and physiological consequences of trauma in childhood revisited: Implications for the group therapist's use of methods and styles of leadership. *Group, 17*(1): 41–56.

Zee, A. (2007). *Fearful Symmetry: The Search for Beauty in Modern Physics.* Princeton, NJ: Princeton University Press.

INDEX

abortion 204
Abraham, Gunter 115
Abraham, Karl 115, 268
abstinence rule 180
Age of Insight, The (Eric Kandel) 3
Ainsworth, Mary 144–145
alatheia 171–173
    authentic emotion as 128
    Heidegger's truth 90–91, 270
    unconcealment as 93–94, 252
Alcoholics Anonymous 231
alterity 98–99, 153, 181–183, 210
ambiguity 18–19, 23, 109
analysts *see* patients and
    analysts
Andersen, Hans Christian 95
Angst 203
animals 143
Anomie 228
Arendt, Hannah 85
Aristotle 39–43
    Freud's dream interpretation and
    110
    heritage of 36, 54
    importance of art forms to 45–46
    Langs and 105
    literary criticism and 58
    mimesis 197, 200
    phronesis 62, 173
    representation 191, 194
    theory of knowledge and
    methodology 15
    Winnicott and 203, 211
Aron, Lewis 174, 213
attachment 142–149, 156

attachment bonds 138–139, 141–142,
    145
Attention and Interpretation (Wilfred
    Bion) 131, 242, 249
attraction 80
attunement 223–225 *see also* empathy
Atwood, George 82, 213, 215–216
authenticity 91, 93
autonomy 231

Babel xvii, 10, 25, 254
Bakan, David 48–49, 51
Balint, Michael 180
Barangers (Madeleine and Willy) xiii
Bass, Alan 94, 128, 163, 165–167
being 85–87, 92
Being and Time (Martin Heidegger)
    81, 85–86
Bergson, Henri 136, 146
Berke, Joseph H. 132, 223
Berlin Psychoanalytic Institute 115
Beyond the Pleasure Principle
    (Sigmund Freud) 69
Bible 50, 57, 67, 120
binocular vision xii–xiii, xvi
Bion Institutes 240
Bion, Wilfred xii–xvi, 239–256
    Attention and Interpretation 131
    beta elements 246–248
    catastrophic transformations 158
    Eigen and 131
    Grid 245–247
    hermeneutics of 239
    highly original mind of 239
    journey represented by xiii

Kant and 240–243, 248–252, 254, 256
Klein and xii, 193, 212
links 243–244
"O" xv–xvii, 249–255
    alterity and 182
    meaning and unconscious 19
    realm of psyche 181
    "things in themselves" 230
    trance-like state of 47
    transformations in 121, 173
reverie 225
"selected facts" 6
Sod 53–54
sources of various ideas 11
theory of groups xiii
theory of thinking 10
"thinking couples" 197, 234
unconscious, capturing the essence of the 237
vertex xiv
Blake, William 242
Blanco, Matte 19, 96
bodies 176–180, 194
Bohm, David 23
Bollas, Christopher 230, 278
Borderline Conditions and Pathological Narcissism (Otto Kernberg) 190
Boss, Menard 86
Bowlby, John 8, 142–144, 192
brain, the 271–277, 279–280
Brandschaft, Bernard 213, 215
Brentano, Franz 33, 39
British Psychoanalytic Society 142, 188
Buber, Martin 98, 160, 181, 223
Buddhism
    Epstein and 132, 251
    meditation 265
    Prajnaparamita 240–241
    sentient beings 227

Zen Buddhism 127, 243
care 161, 204, 209–210, 275, 277
causality 15, 164
Cerf, Walter xx
Chagall, Marc 24
change 163–164
Chicago, University of 214
children see also infants; mothers
    analysts invoking childhood 84
    child development 22, 24
    destruction in the development of ego 128–129
    Melanie Klein on 176, 190–194
    mother and 64, 123–124
    parental sex and 62–63
    parents and 129
    sexual feelings of 195
    Winnicott and Klein 20
Civilization and Its Discontents (Sigmund Freud) 87
Cixous, Hélène 125
Cocktail Party, The (T. S. Eliot) 235
Cohen, Bertram 222
Coleridge, Samuel Taylor 61
Coles, Robert 168
Coltart, Nina 132
Columbus, Christopher 170
conditioned reflexes 275
consilience 22, 25–26, 143, 260
constructivism 269
Controversial Discussions 188, 201
Conze, Edward xvi
countertransference 105, 236 see also transference
Cozolino, Louis 273

Damasio, Anthony 138, 272, 279
Dangerous Method, A (David Cronenberg) 31
Darwin, Charles xiv, 24, 272–273

Dasein
"at hand" 152
Bion's "O" and 252
bond between analyst and
    patient 142
care structure of 275
constituent elements of 119
embedded in language 209
Erlebnis and 60
experience and "being-in-the-
    world" 85
Gadamer extends concept 89, 92,
    173
Heidegger develops idea of
    87–88
Heidegger's relevance for
    psychoanalysis 94
Heidegger's view of 234
horizons 171
meaning and 88, 116
Winnicott and 203–205, 208
deconstructionism 94–98, 125
De Italorum Sapientia (Giambattista
    Vico) 59
"demand characteristics" 117
DeMare, Patrick 23
depressive position 132, 192
depth psychology 51–52, 72
Derrida, Jacques 94–98
centrality of deconstruction 125,
    270
concept of difference 123
critiques of representation 43
différance 95–96, 166
emphasis on writing and text 229
Freud's "Project" and 259–260
Jewish background of 48
Lacan and 115
mind and text 234
oppositions manifesting together
    115
trace and difference 44–45

traces disseminated 156, 235
unknowability 181
writing as meaning 242
Descartes, René
Bion and 240
Enlightenment and 130
Freud's metapsychology 200
Heidegger and 203
Husserl's critique 81
inner life as self-contained 37
isolated mind, concept of 192
metaphysics of 162
mind and reason 60, 233
mind–body dualism 35–36, 120,
    176
nervous system paradigm 270
subjective self and 228
Vico's critique 59
Winnicott 205
Dewey, John 214
différance 95–96, 166
Dilthey, Wilhelm 71–75
basis of personhood 234
Bion and 241
Bowlby and 142
Erlebnis 60
explanation and understanding 115
German romanticism and 61
Husserl influenced by 83
lived experience 217–218
romantic hermeneutics 228
Schleiermacher's influence on 68
truth 270
disconformability 18–20
DNA 281
Doolittle, Hilda 142
dreams 29–31 *see also Interpretation of
    Dreams, The*
case studies 126–128
Freud and 14, 34–35
interpretation 13–14, 32
self and 229–230

Durkheim, Emile 228
Durkin, Helen 142

Eckhart, Meister 242, 251
Edelman, Gerald 272–273
ego
    changes under psychoanalysis
        161
    concepts of 139
    ego building 266
    "ego orgasm" 160
    Freud's Cartesian concept of 81
    self and 214
    Talmudic studies 53
    theatrical role of 47
    using language to conceal 44
    Winnicott on children 128
Eigen, Michael 53–54, 131, 149, 251
Einfühlung 64–67, 80, 123
Einstein, Albert 17–18, 37
Eissler, Kurt 104
Eleusinian Mysteries 47
Eliot, T. S. 235
emotion 272
empathy 219–222
    Einfühlung as 65
    experiencing on emotional and
        personal level 66
    Kohut proposes 63, 169, 214
    mother and child 123–124
    need for 123
    projective identification and
        197
    "sustained empathic enquiry" 80
    United States 215
"Emperor's New Clothes, The" (Hans
    Christian Andersen) 95
empiricism 76
Enlightenment, the
    Bion and 243
    causality and epistemology 15
    Heidegger's attitude to 94

Husserl's attitude to 78
    importance of science 61
    meaning without understanding
        38
    metaphysics 41
    Plato, Aristotle and Freud 54
    quantum theory and 21
    Vattimo's modernism and 130
    Vico questions 55, 59, 61
Epstein, Mark 132, 230, 251
Erikson, Erik 120, 137
Erlebnis
    concealed and suppressed
        aspects of 74
    Dasein and 60
    Freud and 161
    lived experience 73, 75, 83
Escher, M. C. 233
evolution (of the species) 273, 277
existentialism 33, 36, 77, 85–86
experience 81, 84, 163, 248
Experiences in Groups (Wilfred Bion)
    239
experimental method, the 17–18
experimentum crucis 17–18

facticity 73, 93
Fairbairn, Ronald 141, 160, 189
Fechner, Gustav 17
Fenichel, Otto 105
Ferenczi, Sándor 141
Feynman, Richard 21
First New Science, The (Giambattista
    Vico) 60
Fliess, Wilhelm 69
Freiberg 151
Freud, Anna
    Bowlby and 8, 142–143
    Controversial Discussions 188
    ego strength 139
    Gunther Abraham and 115
    play therapy for children 191

Freud, Sigmund *see also Interpretation*
     of Dreams, The
  accessing the unknowable 182
  analysis of "Dora" 8–9
  Bion and 243
  biosocial emphasis 2
  body contact 179
  change through psychoanalysis
     161
  chess comparison 137
  childhood 151
  children's sexual desires 195
  curative value of psychoanalysis
     25
  Dangerous Method, A 31
  "day residue" xiv
  depth psychology 52
  Derrida's reading of 94
  Descartes and 81, 200
  determinist science, a xix
  dream work 14, 34–35, 110
  ego and self 214
  Ernest Jones and 188
  evolution and 273
  Ferenczi and 141
  free thinker aspects of 77
  God as comforting illusion 130
  Heidegger and 33, 85, 87
  Herder and 67
  hermeneutic circle and 69
  hermeneutics of suspicion 217
  Hilda Doolittle and 142
  id and ego 139, 160
  instinct 74
  interest in antiquity 39
  Jewish roots 48–50
  Jung and 115, 130
  Klein and 190–193, 200
  legacy of 16–17
  Levinas and 183
  medical practice, use of 111
  mind–body split 176
  "mystic writing pad" 278–279

  neural functioning theory 258–260
  Oedipal discovery 53
  pleasure principle 166
  projective identification 200
  psyche, model for 191
  psychoanalysis begins with 120
  reality principle 40
  Romantic age hermeneutics and 58
  schizophrenics, his view of 141
  scientific approach 108
  self 226–227
  self-representations 227
  sources drawn on by 32–33, 36,
     38–39, 46
  Spielrein affair 235
  Stern and 226
  subjectivity 217
  tally argument and 20
  "The Uncanny" essay 125
  traumatic events 121–122
  unconscious
     Aristotle's influence on 105
     Heidegger's being-in-the-
        world and 85
     internal logic of 60–61
     "mystic writing pad", 278–279
     nature of 97
     noumenon, as 243
     portions unknowable 181
     primal nature of 88
     repository of relics 250
     system unconscious, the 37–38
     trace elements in 96
  volition 37
  Wolf Man 20–21
  workplace 162
"Freud and the Scene of Writing"
     (Jacques Derrida) 95
Future of an Illusion, The (Sigmund
     Freud) 40, 68

Gadamer, Hans-Georg 173–176
  Aristotle and 39

dialogue and attachment 163
hermeneutics of 62, 90
horizons 270, 277
interpretation theories of 89–90
Winnicott resembles 201
world of dialogue 92, 229
Galileo Galilei 17
Gandhi, Mahatma 120
Ganzarain, Ramon 212
Gayle, Robin xx
Gergen, Kenneth J. 229
German romanticism
    Bion and 241
    Freud born into 54–55, 71
    interpretative understanding of 58
    pastoral and agrarian themes 151
    Schleiermacher and 67
    Vico and 61
Gilgamesh 34
Giorgi, Amedeo 169
Glover, Edward 105
God
    atonement 223
    Bion on 254
    death of 130–131
    mathematician, as 132
    presence of 127
    Tower of Babel and xvii
Goethe, Johann Wolfgang von
    113–114
Going on Being: Buddhism and the Way
    of Change (Mark Epstein)
    251
Greenacre, Phyllis 58
Grotstein, James S.
    divergences within a continuum
        188
    dreaming patients 229
    "infinite geometer" 230
    inner space 170
    neurobehavioral processing 218
    psychic presences in mental
        development 132

taking Klein's ideas to America
    190, 212
term for unconscious 19
"transcendent position" 154, 160
Group Psychology and the Analysis of
    the Ego (Sigmund Freud) 233
Grunbaum, Adolph 15, 21–22
Guntrip, Harry 141, 189, 214

Hamlet (William Shakespeare) 210,
    248
Hands of the Living God, The: An
    Account of a Psychoanalytic
    Treatment (Marion Milner)
    131
Hartmann, Heinz xiv, 272
Harvard University 169, 214
Hegel, Georg Wilhelm Friedrich 115
Heidegger, Martin 85–92
    alatheia 171–173, 270
    Bass on 94
    Being and Time 81
    Bion's "O" and 252
    care structures 277
    concerns of daily existence 150
    Dasein 60, 116, 152, 275, 278 see
        also Dasein
    debt to Dilthey 72–73
    Derrida and 96–97
    difference, the importance of 123
    flight from the abyss 146
    Freud and 33, 85, 87
    Gadamer and 39, 89–90, 173
    hermeneutics and 68, 71, 94
    Husserl and 79, 83–84, 87, 115,
        221
    interpretation and being-in-the-
        world 163
    old metaphysics challenged by
        36, 76, 90, 181
    relevance to psychoanalysis 94
    rural background 151
    self 228–229

Stolorow's interest in 216
time, attitudes to 37, 136
truth 270
Winnicott and 203–206, 208–211
Herder, Johann Gottfried von 62–67
    Bion and 241
    Dilthey and 72
    Einfühlung 80
    individual's life experience 218
    interpretive principles of 61
    "radical difference" 123, 217
    romantic hermeneutics 228
    Schleiermacher and 68, 72
    textual understanding 115
    truth 270
hermeneutic circle 68–70, 217
hermeneutic spiral 70
hermeneutics *see also* interpretation
    as basis of psychoanalysis 29,
        109–110
    background to 25–26
    Bion's 239, 241
    defining the main ingredient of
        existence 78
    definitions 3, 12, 270
    doubting the patients 42
    enters philosophical discourse 31
    Gadamer 62, 90
    German Romantics' legacy 71
    Heidegger 68, 71, 94
    history and development 59
    interpretation and 12, 25–26, 34
    neuroscience and 265
    of suspicion 41–42, 217–218
    openness and humanity required
        of analyst 4, 104
    personal growth and 160
    philosophical hermeneutics 57
    Plato 39
    radical difference 65
    Romantic era 61–62
    Schleiermacher and Herder 68
    self-transformation and 154

termination of therapy 156
time in 136
understanding in 164
Vattimo's division 130
Winnicott 209
Hinduism 52, 98
history 136
Hoffman, Irwin 42, 236
Holocaust 156
holography xvii
horizons 169–171, 173, 175–176, 270,
    277
Hospers, John xx
Hubel, David 275–276
humanism 14
Hume, David 164
Husserl, Edmund 78–84
    a basis for all knowledge 195
    Brentano, Freud and 33
    challenging old mataphysics 36
    Dilthey and 72–73
    Heidegger and 79, 83–84, 87, 115,
        221
    hermeneutics and meaning 71
    horizons 169–170
    individual's life experience 218
    interpretation and experience 163
    intersubjectivists and 216
    Merleau-Ponty and 177
    perception 168–169
    phenomenological description 194
    Sacks on 280
    Varela and 265
hypertext 49
hysteria 176

id 36, 160, 258
identity 161
"implicate order" 23
Independent School 189
infants *see also* children; mothers
    breast, relationship with 190
    Husserl on 83–84

infantile sexuality 110
inferred and observed 11
mental processes 190
mother and
    empathy between 123–124
    interpretation between 12–13
    separation 121
    Stern 180, 222–227
    Winnicott 203–205, 234
stages of the self 226
Stern on 224
Winnicott on 203–207, 209
information theory 281
insight 91, 178
instinct 74
intention 82
intentionality 33
interpretation 6–9, 11–16, 18–21 *see
    also* hermeneutics; patients
    and analysts
agent of change, as 25
ambiguity in 18, 23
biblical 120
Bohm 23
central limitation of method 69
construction and deconstruction
    128–129
definition of 6
différance and 166
disclosure in 47
dreams and 13–14, 24, 34–35
empathy in 221
experience and 163
Freud and 162
Gadamer's work 90, 173
Heidegger and 88, 171
Herder's principles 61
hermeneutics and 12, 25–26, 34
holistically 68
Husserl on 84
integral part of human nature 99
interpretive horizons 92
leading to the unconscious 165

meaning and 33
Melanie Klein 192
miscellaneous processes of 155,
    163–165
miscellaneous views of 163
nature of 117, 162–163
negotiated transactions 42
neuroscience and 266
of another's mind 31
original framework 45
patient and analyst 90
practical problems 9
psychic pain of 94
psychoanalysis and *see*
    psychoanalysis:
    interpretation and
remit 7
route to the unconscious 165
shared reality 40
"standard edition" view 91
Talmudic 50
testing the truth of 20
theories of 8
unifying factor in psychoanalysis
    11
Winnicott and Klein 19–20
*Interpretation and Difference: The
    Strangeness of Care* (Alan
    Bass) 94
Interpretation of Dreams, The
    (Sigmund Freud)
    hermeneutics and 26, 71
    importance of 29
    subjects covered 12
    summary of 38–39, 54
    synthesis in 3, 32
intersubjective perspective 114, 213,
    215–218, 226

James, William 68, 214, 226, 228
Japan 156
Jeans, James 132
Jones, Ernest 188, 259

Joyce, James 49, 252–253
Judaism 48, 50
Judeo-Christianity 127, 130
Jung, Carl
    A Dangerous Method 31
    archetypes 88, 230
    Bion's Memoir of the Future and
        253
    breaks with Freud 8
    collective unconscious 61
    evolution 273
    Freud and 115, 130
    individuation 139
    myth and culture 242
    Spielrein affair 235
    supernatural realms 22
    understanding of religion 68

Kabbalah
    Bion's "O" 249
    Freud and 48
    Isaac Luria 251
    James Joyce 49
    letters of the alphabet 244
    others influenced by 131–132
    reparation 223
Kabbalah and Psychoanalysis (Michael
        Eigen) 131
Kandel, Eric 3, 265, 279
Kant, Immanuel
    Bion's debt to 240–243, 248–252,
        254, 256
    categories xvi–xvii
    Dilthey's synthesis 72
    Herder and 62
    no lover of metaphysics 76
    noumena 81, 242, 249, 252
Kernberg, Otto 124, 190, 212
Kierkegaard, Søren 149, 255
Klein, Melanie 188–197
    Bion borrows from 240–241,
        243–244, 250–251

breast and womb envy 97
children 20, 176
depressive position 19, 132, 139
Freud and 190–193
infants 190–191, 224
interpretation by 192
Kohut and 199
manic depression and 268
objects relations theory and 10
paranoid-schizoid position 19
projective identification xii
psychotics, work with 191
reparation 223
summary 200
terminology of 83
United States and 211
vertex xiv
Winnicott and 201, 209
Kohut, Heinz 213–216
    empathy stressed by 63, 124, 169
    narcissism and 195
    objects relations theory and 212
    optimism from 269
    "selfobjects" 121, 192, 196, 199,
        220, 226
    self psychology 77, 120, 218, 227,
        229–230
    "transmuting internalizations"
        139, 160
Kuhn, Thomas 21

Lacan, Jacques
    aspects of the real 193
    Derrida and 97, 115
    essay on Poe 97
    linguistics element to 10, 43
Langs, Robert 105
language 42–45
    Bion on 242, 245
    Herder 63, 68
    Tower of Babel xvii
Lawlor, Leonard 99, 181

learning 278
Lebenswelt 82–83, 252
Levinas, Immanuel 181–183
    alterity 153
    difference, concept of 123
    "faces" 229
    Herder and 65
    interpretation and respect 163
    Little, Margaret I. 84
    Merleau-Ponty and 115
    presence and alterity 98–99
    Winnicott respects 210
Lévi-Strauss, Claude xvi, 136
links 243–244
Little, Margaret I. 84, 207–208
logical positivism 243–244
Loparic, Zeljko 208
Luria, Isaac 242, 251
Luther, Martin 120

Mahler, Margaret 121, 137, 160
Mammon 254
manic depression 268
Marx, Karl 130, 189, 205, 234
Mead, George, Herbert 214
meaning
    at hand and discerned 116–117
    Bion on 241
    Dasein and 88–89
    Derrida on 44
    experience and 84
    Gadamer on 89
    interpretation and 11–12, 33
    language and 43
    readers of 111
    unconscious 8, 19
Mediterranean 34, 39
Meister Eckhart 242, 251
Meltzer, Donald 212
Memoir of the Future, A (Wilfred Bion)
    252–253, 255
memory 87

Menninger Clinic, Topeka 212
mentalization 124
Merleau-Ponty, Maurice 177–179
    bodily perception 194
    Levinas and 115
    on interpretation 163
    phenomenology of perception 72
    Varela on 280
Messkirch 151
metaphor 32, 46, 164
metaphysics
    Cartesian 162
    Heidegger challenges 36, 86–87,
        90
    Kant and 76, 243
    modern hermeneutics rejects 270
    Plato's underlying reality 41
metonymy 32, 46
Metzinger, Thomas 274
Milner, Marion 131
Milton, John 242, 249
mind 35–36, 59–60, 120, 176, 232–235
mirroring 220–221
Mitchell, Stephen 212–213, 232–234,
    236
molecular structure 281
mothers see also children; infants
    case studies 92–93, 145–146
    dance of mother and infant 180,
        225
    Daniel Stern 222–225
    depressive position 192
    early separation from 121
    empathy and playfulness 123–124
    Klein on 191
    meanings of 42–43
    recognizing a child's wants 64
    Winnicott on mother and infant
        203–207, 209, 234
Murray, Henry 168–169
mysticism 131–132
mythemes 136

narcissism 124, 195, 216, 218
narratives (of patients) 269
natural selection 24
Naturphilosophie 61, 151
Nazis 85
nervous system 274–281
Neumann, John Von 137
neurons 95, 276, 279
neurophenomenonology 280
neuroscience 257–281
    brain, the 271–277, 279–280
    Derrida 260
    Freud and 258–259
    hermeneutics and 265
    interpretation and 266
    nervous system 274–281
    psychoanalysis and,
        a comparison 264
    psychoanalysis and, Sacks's view
        279–280
    psychoanalysis and neurological
        conditions 268
    Siegel's holistic view 262
New York Psychoanalytical Society
    211
Nietzsche, Friedrich
    assertive selfhood 226
    Bion and 255
    clarification and reinterpretation
        189
    critiques of metaphysics 76
    each man creates his world 41
    eternal recurrence 166
    German romanticism and 61
    hermeneutic circles 70
    repression of desire 87
    transformative power of
        interpretation 163
    Vattimo on 130
noumena 81, 162, 240, 242–243,
    248–249, 252
null hypothesis 18

"O" *see* Bion, Wilfred
object relations theory 124, 188–189,
    195, 212
"objects" 83
Oedipus
    Freud 237
    Freud and Klein on 190–191
    Freud, Aristotle and 39
    Gilgamesh and 34
    infantile development and 189, 194
    other-worldly elements 53–54
    patient objects to interpretation
        129
    Teiresias 47
Ogden, Thomas H. 121
oppositions 114–116
Orange, Donna 215–216
"Origin of the Work of Art, The"
    (Martin Heidegger) 88
Orne, M. T. 117

"Pair of Shoes, A" (Vincent van
    Gogh) 88
PaRDeS, 52–54
patients and analysts *see*
        also interpretation;
        psychoanalysis
    addictions, patients with 231
    adult patients 225
    alterity 98
    analyst emptying mind xv
    analyst's mental processes 107
    analyst's resources 174
    attachment bonds 141–142, 145
    attraction between 80
    awareness increased 170
    Bass on 166
    Bion's Grid 247
    body and mind involvement 176,
        178–80
    coherence of patient's self at risk
        152

connections 13
empathy between 4, 64, 104, 124
free associations traced 236
Freud's patients 191, 217
"holding" the patient 207
important aspect for patient 91
interpretation and 7, 90, 99
Klein's patients 192–194
Lang's bipersonal field 105
mutual feelings of envy xvii
mutual subjectivity 215
neuroscience and 263
patient as player in drama 47
power and authority between 117
psychotic patients 42
relations between 106–107, 110
roles of 150
Sands on 196
Schafer on 269
self and the dreamer, the
    229–230
self-transformation 154–155, 161
Siegel on 262
tension and anxiety 139
termination of treatment 140,
    155–157
traumatized patients 66, 122
unconscious, patient's
    introduction to 165
understanding between 65, 127
Winnicott's interpretations 209
work involved 125
working model of patient's mind
    created 220
Paton, H. J. 243
perception 72, 168, 170
Peterfreund, Emanuel 281
phantasy 193
phantom limbs 273–274
phenomenology 79–85
    Freud and 36
    Husserl and Brentano 33

Merleau-Ponty and Husserl 177
neurophenomenology 280
object relations theory and 195
split with psychoanalysis 168
Stolorow's emphasis on 169
summarizing Melanie Klein 200
unconscious, of the 192–194
philosophy, aims of 75
phronesis 62, 173–174, 184, 277
Pisa, Leaning Tower of 17
Plato 39–41
    being and 87
    Bion's debt to 240, 242
    essences 250
    disembodied ideas and timeless
        forms 37
    heritage of 36, 54
    Ideal Forms xvi–xvii
    skepticism re art 45
plurality 6, 10
Poe, Edgar Allan 97
Polanyi, Michael 21, 278
polarities 115–116, 135–136
polysemy 164–165, 170
Popper, Karl 18–22
postmodernism 240, 252–253
Prajnaparamita 240–241
presence 97–98
Pribram, Karl 259–260
Principia Mathematica (Alfred North
    Whitehead and Bertrand
    Russell) 243
"Project for a Scientific Psychology,
    A" (Sigmund Freud) 17, 36,
    95, 259–260, 264
projective identification xii, 196–200,
    240
psyche 161, 191
psychic determinism 37
psychoanalysis see also patient and
    analyst
    as journey 47

Bion's breakthrough book 131
Bion's overall work 240
changing the history of 8
cutting edge exploration, as 32
determinist science, a xix
different schools of 108, 188–189
different views of 127
Dilthey's position 74
dualistic psychology, a 115
Gadamer's critique 173–174
German Romantic hermeneutics
    and 71
Heidegger's relevance 94
Herder's impact 64
hermeneutics and 29, 109–110
in crisis 9–10
interpretation and: 108–110
    central place of 3, 75
    concealed and inaccessible,
        the 7
fundamental basis of xix
    subject matter of 78
    unifying core of 103
language in 63
Levinas's challenge to 182
musical analogy 224
neuroscience and, see
    neuroscience
new ways of thinking 35
patient and analyst 106–107, 110
presence in 98
relational 232–233
root purpose 4, 6, 25, 122, 231
Schleiermacher and 70
science and 14–18, 22–26
    ambiguity in 19
    Dilthey's work 73
    Heidegger on 90–91
    history and approach 105–106
    observation in 107
    progress in reconciliation 281
self-transformation and 139,
    154–155, 159–163

slow process, a 150
transference, importance of 58
Psychoanalytic Dialogues 196
Psychoanalytic Mystic, The (Michael
    Eigen) 131, 251
Psychoanalytic Situation, The (Leo
    Stone) 104
Psychoanalytic Theory of the Neuroses,
    The (Otto Fenichel) 105
psychophysics 17
psychosis 42, 82, 191
psychotherapy 138, 262
"Purloined Letter, The" (Edgar Allan
    Poe) 97

quantum theory 21–23, 202, 281
Quine, Willard 243

radical difference 64–65, 123, 217
Ramachandran, Vilayanur 273
reality 79, 273
reality principle 40–42
regression 84
relativity 37
reparation 223
representation 42–45
Rhetoric and Poetics (Aristotle) 46
Ricoeur, Paul 41, 217
risk management 151
Rogers, Carl 214, 219
Romantic era 57, 59, 61 see also
    German romanticism
Rorty, Richard 43–44, 229
Rosenfeld, Herbert 42
Russell, Bertrand 243, 245
Rutgers University 213

Sacks, Oliver 279–281
Sands, Susan 196, 198, 200
Sartre, Jean-Paul 60, 85
Satan 254
Saussure, Ferdinand 43
Schafer, Roy 230, 269

schizophrenia 122, 131, 141
Schleiermacher, Friedrich
   contribution to intellectual
      history 67–68
   developments in hermeneutics 71
   Dilthey's attempted synthesis 72
   hermeneutic circle 217
   individual's life experience 218
   interpretive methodology 62, 70
   textual understanding 115
   truth 270
Schneider, Stanley 132, 223
"schools" of psychoanalysis 108,
   188–189
Schwartz, Jacob T. 281
science 14–18, 22–26
   ambiguity in 19
   Dilthey's work 73
   Freud and 110
   Heidegger and 90–91
   objectivity 105–106
   observation in 107
   psychoanalysis and see
      psychoanalysis: science and
   Romantics' view of 61
Searles, Harold 42
Segal, Hannah 190
self 178, 206, 214–222, 226–232
"self-objects" 121, 194, 220–221
self-transformation 159–163, 168–170
   Heidegger opens up 173
   Levinas and alterity 183
   psychoanalysis and 139–140,
      154–155
Siegel, Daniel 11, 161, 223, 262, 269
Six Steps in the Treatment of Borderline
   Personality Organization
   (Vamik D. Volkan) 137
Snow, C. P. 1, 202–203
Socrates xx, 40, 203
Sonne, John 222
Sorge 204
speech 178

Sphinx 34–35, 53
Spielrein, Sabrina 31, 235
St. Bartholomew's Hospital Medical
   School 202
Stanislavski, Constantin 66
Stern, Daniel 180, 222–227, 275
Stolorow, Robert D. 196–200
   hermeneutics of suspicion 218
   integrating work of 216
   intersubjective perspective 114,
      212–213, 226
   phenomenology and 169
   self-narratives 230
Stone, Leo 104
stream of consciousness 49
suicide 207–208
Sullivan, Harry Stack 215, 232
Sulloway, Frank 258
superego 161, 194
surrealism 33

tally arguments 15, 20
Talmud 48–54, 110, 140, 182
teddy bears 211
therapists see patients and analysts
thinking 240
Thoughts Without a Thinker (Mark
   Epstein) 251
time 37, 136–137
Torah 48, 51–52
Tower of Babel xvii, 10, 25, 254
transcendence 81
transference see also
      countertransference
   analysis of 119–120
   emergence of implicit meanings
      278
   Freud, Plato and 41–42
   theatre 47
   unique interpretive principles
      58
transitional space 202
trauma 66, 114, 121–122, 263

treatment 137
truth 59, 270

"Uncanny, The" (Sigmund Freud) 125
unconscious, the
    Bion on xv, 131, 237, 252–253
    collective 61
    depth psychology and 52
    Freud and *see* Freud, Sigmund:
        unconscious
    Freud and Heidegger 85
    Freud and Vico 60–61
    interpretation leads to 165
    many faces of 7–8
    meaning and 19
    mind and 235–236
    phenomenology of 192–194
    psychological reality of 45
    thought in 38
    unconsciousness 235
    unknowability of parts of 181
understanding 65, 127, 164
United States xvii, 211–214, 226, 232
unknowability 181, 241

van Gogh, Vincent 88–89
Varela, Francisco 265, 280
Vattimo, Gianni 130–132
vertex xiv
Vico, Giambattista 55, 59–61, 234
volition 37
Volkan, Vamik 137, 190

White, Robert 168
Whitehead, Alfred North 243, 245
Whitman, Walt 165
Wiesel, Torsten 275–276

William Alanson White Institute 211
Williams, Corbett xx
Wilson, E. O. 22, 143
Winnicott, Donald 201–211
    annihilation anxiety 93
    approach to subject matter 201
    background 202
    development of child's ego
        128–129
    "ego orgasm" 160
    Eigen and 131
    Gunther Abraham and 115
    Guntrip and 141
    Heidegger and 203–206, 208–211
    holding environments 223
    Independent School and 189
    infants and their mothers
        203–207, 209, 234
    interpretation, on 19, 201
    object relations 188
    optimism from 269
    "ownership" 205
    "regression to dependence" 84
    suicide, on 207–208
    teddy bears 211
    transitional space 202
Wittgenstein, Ludwig 43–44, 242, 245
Wolf Man 20–21
women 97
World War I 235
Wright, James 164
Writing and Difference (Jacques
    Derrida) 95

Zen Buddhism 127, 243
Zollicon Seminars 86